Jewish Muslims

Jewish Muslims

*How Christians Imagined Islam
as the Enemy*

David M. Freidenreich

UNIVERSITY OF CALIFORNIA PRESS

University of California Press
Oakland, California

Library of Congress Cataloging-in-Publication Data

Names: Freidenreich, David M., author.
Title: Jewish Muslims : how Christians imagined Islam as
    the enemy / David M. Freidenreich.
Description: [Oakland, California] : [University of
    California Press], [2023] | Includes bibliographical
    references and index.
Identifiers: LCCN 2022017142 (print) | LCCN 2022017143
    (ebook) | ISBN 9780520344716 (hardcover) |
    ISBN 9780520975644 (ebook)
Subjects: LCSH: Christianity and other religions—Islam. |
    Islam—Relations—Christianity. | Christianity and
    antisemitism. | Islamophobia. | BISAC: RELIGION /
    Islam / History | SOCIAL SCIENCE / Jewish Studies
Classification: LCC BP172 .F675 2023 (print) | LCC BP172
    (ebook) | DDC 261.2/7—dc23/eng/20220609
LC record available at https://lccn.loc.gov/2022017142
LC ebook record available at https://lccn.loc
    .gov/2022017143

Manufactured in the United States of America

28 27 26 25 24 23 22
10 9 8 7 6 5 4 3 2 1

*For Sara Shoshana, my rose,
for Ren, our joy,
and for Jacob Meir, our light.*

Contents

Illustrations

Introduction: Jewish Muslims?

Muslims are not Jewish.

This would normally go without saying, but perhaps it needs reinforcement lest someone misinterpret this book's title, *Jewish Muslims*, by reading it literally. Muslims do not self-identify as Jews, and self-identifying Jews do not regard Muslims as Jewish either. Jews and Muslims have interacted in a wide variety of ways across history, but even in the context of close relations it has been obvious to the participants and to outside observers alike that Jews are not Muslim and that Muslims are not Jewish. Although Judaism and Islam are similar in certain respects—both are monotheistic, forbid pork consumption, and revere common figures such as Abraham, to cite only the most familiar examples—these traditions ground their beliefs, practices, and foundational stories in different sets of sacred texts that refer to mutually exclusive conceptions of divine revelation. The Bible makes no reference to Muslims, because Islam postdates biblical texts by many centuries, and the Quran refers to the Jews as a group distinct from its own audience.

Premodern Christians fully understood that Muslims are not Jews. Precisely for this reason, many found it useful to allege that Muslims *are* Jewish—or, if you prefer, "Jew-ish"—as a means of defining Muslims and Islam as the enemies of Christians and Christianity. This intentionally counterfactual assertion of similarity bordering on identity, like the insult, "you're a pig!," is metaphorical: it adds value to rhetoric by

distorting reality. The metaphor "my love is a rose" illustrates this definition in a positive fashion. The person I love has neither petals nor thorns,
but by associating that person with a rose I conjure up images and experiences of beauty, fragility, pain, and care that profoundly enrich my depiction of that person and our relationship. The assertion that Muslims are
Jewish is also an intentional distortion that, many Christians believed,
increases the value of their rhetoric by applying to Muslims familiar negative ideas about Jews.[1]

Polemicists (the term for those who aggressively disparage their rivals)
branded Muslims as Jewish in an effort to accomplish something that
they otherwise would not achieve as readily. Examination of this rhetoric offers valuable insights not only into premodern Christian ideas about
Muslims and Jews but also into the polemicists' goals and techniques.
Although polemicists today are unlikely to allege that Muslims are Jewish, they often employ the same techniques as their predecessors in pursuit of similar goals. For that reason, the study of premodern rhetoric
about Jewish Muslims can help us to better understand contemporary as
well as historical anti-Muslim and anti-Jewish sentiments. (I use the term
"premodern" to encompass late antiquity, the Middle Ages, and the
early modern period. The premodern period of Christian engagement
with Muslims begins with the seventh-century rise of Islam and, for the
purposes of this book, concludes in the early seventeenth century.)

"JUDAISM" AS GRIST FOR POLEMICAL METAPHORS

Muslims were not the only non-Jews to be tarred in derogatory fashion
with the label "Jewish," and that label often bears little resemblance to
the beliefs and practices of actual Jews in any case. Recent historical
scholarship demonstrates that this disconnect is commonplace in premodern Christian rhetoric about Judaism. As Jeremy Cohen explains,
"the Christian idea of Jewish identity crystallized around the theological purpose the Jew served in Christendom; Christians perceived the
Jews to be who they were *supposed* to be, not who they actually *were*."
Sara Lipton demonstrates that this dynamic characterizes artistic no less
than literary sources. Daniel Boyarin takes this point further, emphasizing that, in premodern times, the very term *Judaism* consistently refers
not to the religion that Jews observed but rather to beliefs and practices
that Christians regarded as antithetical to Christianity. David Nirenberg shows that Western intellectuals used Judaism as a negative foil
when thinking not only about matters of theology but also about "top-

ics as diverse as politics and painting, poetry and property rights," even in contexts without any actual Jews. Nirenberg makes a powerful case that *anti-Judaism*, as he calls such thinking, constitutes a rhetorical tool with which Christians, Muslims, and others from antiquity to the present critique the world—and one another.[2]

Anti-Judaism does not merely define Jews as the Other. Rather, it promotes the cultivation of certain characteristics by virtue of their opposition to characteristics it associates with Judaism. In this respect, *anti-Jewish* resembles the current term *antiracist*, which refers not merely to those who oppose racism but more specifically to those who seek to promote racial equity while combatting policies and ideas that foster racial inequity.[3] Unfortunately, many people in the past regarded Judaism (as they defined it) to be as harmful to society as we now know racism to be. Still more unfortunately, some today continue to hold this negative opinion of Judaism, continue to regard racism as beneficial, or both.

The ideas that underpin anti-Judaism often have nothing to do with actual Jews, and the targets of this rhetoric often do not self-identify as Jews either. Premodern polemicists routinely labeled fellow Christians as "Jews" in the course of alleging that these rivals display negative characteristics that the polemicists ascribed to Judaism. Anti-Jewish assertions of this nature, like those that label disliked individuals as "pigs," are inherently metaphorical because they disparage their targets through intentional, derogatory, and even shocking misrepresentation—in this case by calling a Christian a Jew. This distortion of reality enhances the perceived value of the accompanying rhetoric: to call someone a pig, after all, is far more impactful than to state, for example, that this person behaves in an uncivilized manner. Calling someone a pig implies that the target's behavior is inhuman and, in the process, powerfully reinforces certain ideas about what constitutes proper human behavior. Similarly, rhetoric that employs Judaism as a negative foil forcefully disparages its target as un-Christian and, in doing so, promotes contrasting characteristics as authentically Christian.

Anti-Jewish statements, although diverse and occasionally contradictory, collectively constitute an influential discourse, a body of interrelated rhetoric powerful enough to shape popular attitudes and behaviors as well as governmental policies. The discourse of anti-Judaism brands as "Jewish" specific characteristics (beliefs, practices, traits, etc.) that non-Jews also display in order to critique as deviant those characteristics and their bearers, whoever they might be. Christian anti-Judaism reflects deep anxiety over the ease with which Christians themselves can become

Jewish, metaphorically speaking, by straying from normative beliefs and practices.

Anti-Judaism, as defined here, differs in several crucial respects from its more familiar cousin, antisemitism. Most fundamentally, the discourse of antisemitism asserts that Jews are inherently different from non-Jews in negative ways, while the discourse of anti-Judaism urges audiences to *differentiate themselves* from Jews precisely because it recognizes that the characteristics of Jews and non-Jews are often not so different after all. The simplest current definition states that "Antisemitism is discrimination, prejudice, hostility, or violence against Jews as Jews (or Jewish institutions as Jewish)."[4] Anti-Judaism, in contrast, seeks to motivate self-improvement through the cultivation of beliefs and practices opposed to those that the polemicist brands as Jewish. Antisemitic rhetoric specifically targets Jews; anti-Jewish rhetoric instead targets all who bear purportedly Jewish characteristics, especially non-Jews. Although antisemitism and anti-Judaism both seek to minimize the influence of Jewishness within society, antisemitism condemns *what Jews are* while anti-Judaism condemns *what certain people do or think*.

This distinction between antisemitism and anti-Judaism reflects the fundamental difference between the essentialism of racist logic and the presumption of choice that underpins not only moral exhortation but also the very process of asserting one's own identity. As theorist of religion Tim Murphy observes, the differentiation associated with anti-Judaism "*constitutes* identity" in asymmetrical terms: "Religious differentiation does not merely say 'I differ from you,' it says 'I differ from you' so that it may also say 'I am *better* than you.'"[5] The prominence of anti-Judaism within the long history of Christian rhetoric reflects the fact that many Christians defined what it means to be Christian in terms of differentiation from that which they denigrated as Jewish.

Many prior scholars distinguish anti-Judaism from antisemitism on different grounds—for example, by associating anti-Judaism with theological beliefs and antisemitism with racist beliefs or, relatedly, by stating that the former discourse aims to convert Jews to Christianity while the latter seeks to eliminate Jews.[6] David Nirenberg, however, shows that the discourse of anti-Judaism is not always theological and often does not aim to convert Jews. His banner example is Karl Marx's polemical association of capitalism with Judaism.[7] Marx condemns all capitalists, most of whom are not Jews, and his proposed solution (socialism) would likewise affect everyone in society, not just Jews. Why, then, does Marx allege that capitalism is Jewish? Because this derogatory metaphor increases the persuasiveness of his anti-capitalist rhetoric: Marx taps into his audience's existing disdain for Judaism and channels that disdain toward capitalists, regardless of their religious or ethnic identity. If capitalism itself is Jewish, then those who want to differentiate themselves from Jews should embrace the inverse of capitalism—namely, socialism. Marx's anti-Jewish rhetoric differs sharply from that of antisemites, who employ allegations about the malicious activities of Jewish capitalists to promote discriminatory policies that target Jews alone.

The discourses of antisemitism and anti-Judaism often function in tandem as distinct but mutually reinforcing forms of a broader phenomenon that one might call Judeophobia. The contemporary white nationalist rallying cry, "Jews will not replace us!," exemplifies the overlap. This rhetoric does not merely promote discrimination and violence against Jews: more fundamentally, it seeks to motivate fellow whites to oppose policies that foster immigration or promote diversity as a societal value by branding these policies and their proponents as Jewish. Through such opposition, these whites differentiate themselves from all who value diversity and racial equity just as Marx's followers differentiate themselves from all capitalists.[8]

This book devotes hardly any attention to antisemitism: antisemitic rhetoric emphasizes purported differences between Jews and others, but this study focuses on rhetoric that emphasizes purported similarities between Muslims and Jews. Muslims, according to this rhetoric, are Jewish because they bear negative characteristics that Christians associated with Judaism. These allegations, we will see, advance the goal of promoting opposing characteristics: Christians should differentiate themselves from Muslims just as they differentiate themselves from Jews because Muslims, too, are Jewish, metaphorically speaking.

Christians who condemn Muslims for their purported Jewish characteristics employ the discourse of anti-Judaism while contributing to the anti-Muslim discourse commonly known today as Islamophobia.[9] *Jewish Muslims* examines how and why premodern polemicists selectively fused these discourses. In doing so, this study further demonstrates the lesson that literary critic Edward Said derives from the modern discourse of Orientalism: "discourses construct what they purport to describe." Premodern Christian discourse constructed Jewish Muslims that do not exist in the real world.[10]

Most anti-Jewish rhetoric, of course, does not target Muslims. Similarly, most premodern anti-Muslim rhetoric does not draw on anti-Judaism but rather on early Christian discourses about pagans and heretics or ancient Greek discourses about Africans and "Orientals" (that is, people from the region now known as the Middle East).[11] Although relatively uncommon, rhetoric alleging that Muslims are Jewish offers especially valuable insights into the premodern discourse of Islamophobia as a whole precisely because the metaphorical nature of this rhetoric is readily apparent. Many Muslims, after all, were in fact from Africa or the East, and prior generations of scholars assumed that Christians genuinely mistook Muslims for pagans or heretics: these scholars misinterpreted metaphorical assertions, such as "Muslims are pagan," by reading them literally. Because the parallel statement "Muslims are Jewish" is clearly not literal, we can more easily recognize the ways in which this claim and others like it intentionally distort reality, and we can more readily deduce the reasons why those who make these counterfactual claims find value in employing metaphorical language.

Premodern polemicists construct comparisons that emphasize purported similarities between Muslims and Jews (or pagans, or heretics) for three related purposes:

1. to explain Muslims in biblical terms;
2. to justify military and political assaults against Muslims on theological grounds; and, especially,
3. to motivate self-differentiation through the cultivation of proper Christian characteristics.

These purposes build on one another: polemicists explain Muslims in biblical terms in order to justify assaults and motivate self-differentiation, and rhetoric justifying assaults against Muslims defines such discriminatory behavior as proper. Most rhetoric about Jewish Muslims, however, motivates Christians to cultivate behaviors that have no direct impact on either Muslims or Jews: the primary thrust of this rhetoric, like that of anti-Judaism more broadly, is self-differentiation rather than discrimination.

In *The Jew, the Arab: A History of the Enemy*, cultural theorist Gil Anidjar contends that the very identity of Christian Europe, past and present, rests on its self-differentiation from both Jews and Muslims, imagined as distinct but indissociable. Anidjar simultaneously emphasizes the distinct but indissociable roles that religion and politics play in structuring European ideas about self and other. In his reading, however, the enmity ascribed to Jews is theological in nature, rooted in the

Bible and Christian doctrine, while that of the Muslims is entirely political, enacted through warfare and other forms of state-sanctioned violence. (For this reason, Anidjar employs the ethnic term *Arab* instead of
Muslim, which refers to a person's religious identity.) The present book,
in contrast, demonstrates that premodern Europeans regularly ascribed
theological enmity to Muslims, either by branding them as Jews or by
employing other means of reading Muslims into the Bible. Christians, in
other words, defined their enmity toward Muslims not only in political
terms but also in theological terms, thanks in part to rhetoric about
Jewish Muslims. The association of Muslims with Jews renders both
groups alike as anti-Christians: the timeless enemies—even, as Anidjar
demonstrates, the singular enemy—not only of Christendom, the collective body of Christians, but also of Christ and Christianity. In the process, this rhetoric reinforces specific conceptions of Christianity and, by
extension, of Europe (and America, one might add).[12]

Representations of Jewish Muslims, we will see, draw on distinctly
Christian ideas, address exclusively Christian audiences, advance explicitly Christian objectives, and employ specifically Christian forms of
rhetoric. To the extent that this is true more broadly, Islamophobia is
not really about Muslims at all, even as Muslims suffer its consequences:
it is about how to be a proper Christian and, today, a proper European
or American. As such, this discourse functions in the same way as the
discourse of anti-Judaism, which is also not really about Jews or even
directed toward Jews, although it often affects Jews in terrible ways
through the antisemitic acts it inspires. Anti-Judaism and certain forms
of Islamophobia construct foils against which to define Christianity and
with which to promote specific normative beliefs and practices.[13]

Jewish Muslims, in short, is about neither Muslims nor Jews. This is
a book about Christians who intentionally misrepresented Muslims as
Jewish because they believed that such rhetoric would spur their audiences to become better Christians. It shows how these Christians
employed metaphors and other forms of comparison to define Muslims
and Jews alike as hostile to Christ, Christianity, and Christendom. Contemporary polemicists also frequently portray Muslims, Jews, and other
outgroups in derogatory fashion for the purpose of promoting self-
differentiation: these polemicists seek to motivate members of their own
community to adopt specific characteristics by warning that they would
otherwise resemble disfavored outsiders. By explaining premodern rhetoric, I hope to help readers more fully appreciate the goals of moral
exhortation and self-identification that underpin rhetoric we encounter

within our own societies, including Islamophobic and anti-Jewish rhetoric often perceived solely in terms of discrimination.

This book focuses primarily on two sets of premodern polemicists: those who lived in the region now known as the Middle East during the seventh through ninth centuries, primarily under Muslim rule, and those who lived in Christian-dominated Western and Central Europe during the seventh through early seventeenth centuries. (In the process, regrettably, I largely overlook Christians from other regions, as well as Eastern Christians who lived during and after the tenth century.) We will see that Eastern Christians and European Christians alike find value in branding Muslims as Jewish but that these polemicists do so in different ways, often in pursuit of distinct objectives. I use the term *polemicists* broadly, including all who employ aggressively disparaging rhetoric even if they do not produce works whose primary focus is polemical. Unless there is clear evidence otherwise, I do not presume that these polemicists are familiar with one another's rhetoric, just as I do not presume that contemporary polemicists are familiar with these premodern works: the patterns I highlight in their rhetoric reflect similar goals as well as reliance on shared foundational sources and frames of reference. To compile my dataset, I explored an intentionally broad range of literary and artistic genres in search of rhetoric that seems to associate Muslims with Jews; I refer in this study only to sources in which this association is demonstrable. Because Christian allegations regarding Jewish Muslims have very little to do with the beliefs and practices of actual Jews or Muslims, this book devotes minimal attention to Judaism and Islam on their own terms.

HOW TO ANALYZE POLEMICAL COMPARISONS

My love is not really a rose, Muslims are not really Jews, and those who make such associations know that metaphorical claims like these are literally false. The very dissimilarity of a metaphor's elements—a person and a plant, a Muslim and a Jew—underpins its rhetorical effectiveness. As theologian and philosopher Janet Martin Soskice observes, "the good metaphor does not merely compare two antecedently similar entities, but enables one to see similarities in what previously had been regarded as dissimilars."[14] When analyzing metaphors and other forms of comparison, we need to pay careful attention to the objectives of the people who create them and the reasons they regard their comparisons as useful.

Premodern Christians selectively associated Muslims with Jews, pagans, and heretics notwithstanding the real and recognized differences among these groups. These comparisons are inherently polemical, as they disparage Muslims by emphasizing alleged similarities with an already reviled group. Although the creators of premodern Christian polemical comparisons did not represent either the ruling class or the masses, they sought to influence rulers, commoners, and future generations—and, in many cases, they succeeded.[15]

Polemical comparisons contain six elements. Imagine, for example, a candidate for elected office who declares, "My opponent is a pig!" The comparison itself contains not only a *target* (the opponent) and a *reference* (pigs), but also an implicit *criterion of comparison* according to which the target allegedly resembles the reference. The statement's immediate context is also crucial: the *polemicist* (the candidate) addresses an *audience* (voters) in pursuit of an *objective* (winning the election). This book demonstrates that a wide variety of premodern Christians (polemicists) employ biblically grounded truth claims (criteria) to associate Muslims (targets) with Jews (reference) in an effort to motivate coreligionists (audience) to think and act in accordance with specific Christian norms (objective). To fully understand their polemical comparisons, we need to consider all six elements. Part 1 of this book introduces the range of Christian polemicists who branded Muslims as Jewish and examines the criteria of comparison they employ. Part 2 focuses on the audiences and objectives of these polemicists. Part 3 emphasizes the ways in which these polemicists represent their targets and their reference.

Jewish Muslims foregrounds recurring themes and patterns; dynamics of change over time, although quite important, are of secondary significance to the overarching argument. For that reason, I have organized this book thematically, not chronologically. I employ three tools to help readers keep track of when premodern polemicists lived: I include dates when introducing each author and work; I label the primary time period covered by each chapter in its title; and I provide a comprehensive chronology that appears just prior to the endnotes.

Part 1, "Biblical Muslims," demonstrates that the criteria by which Christians compare Muslims with Jews derive from the Bible and the discourse of anti-Judaism that crystallized during the first Christian centuries. Chapters 1–3 examine Christian rhetoric about the spiritual heirs of Hagar, the slave of Abraham's wife Sarah, in three distinct periods: pre-Islamic times, the early years of Muslim domination over Eastern Christians, and the medieval period of European Christian expansionism. Paul, in the New Testament's Letter to the Galatians, establishes a black-and-white contrast between his allegedly Hagar-like rivals and the adherents of his own teachings, whom Paul associates with Sarah. Later interpreters, who appreciated the motivational force of this comparative rhetoric, customarily identified Jews as the spiritual heirs of Hagar from whom Christians should differentiate themselves, but polemicists also applied Paul's allegory to Muslims. Eastern Christians portrayed Muslims as quasi-Jewish heirs of Hagar in order to explain their own subjugation in biblical terms, while Europeans used Paul's allegory to provide theological justifications for campaigns of conquest and expulsion.

Chapter 4, which examines associations of Jerusalem's Dome of the Rock with the Jewish Temple that once stood on the same site, demonstrates additional ways in which authors and artists imagined Muslims in terms of biblical texts and traditional Christian worldviews. The representation of Muslims as biblical enemies of God's true followers enables Christians to derive actionable lessons related to contemporary Muslims from the Bible itself. Because biblical and early Christian sources provide the criteria that shape anti-Muslim rhetoric while information about actual Muslims plays a relatively minor role, one might say that Christian ideas about Muslims predate the seventh-century rise of Islam.

Premodern Christian pedagogy frequently involves Jewish foils who model the opposite of what good Christians should think and do. Part 2, "Judaizing Muslims," demonstrates that rhetoric about Muslims who purportedly behave like Jews also addresses Christian audiences and often advances the same goal: to motivate self-differentiation through the adoption of specific beliefs, behaviors, and understandings of the Bible. By misrepresenting Muslims as Jewish, Christians gain the ability to promote more effectively their conceptions of proper Christianity and their visions of a proper Christian society.

The first three chapters of Part 2 analyze rhetoric about Islam's purported Jewishness from the late seventh through the early seventeenth century. Chapter 5 examines Eastern works that defend Christian truth claims, chapter 6 traces the evolution of stories about Muhammad's Jewish associates from their Eastern origins into medieval Europe, and chapter 7 focuses on medieval and early modern European works that depict Muhammad's teachings and even Muhammad himself as Jewish. The distinction between Eastern and European Christians is of fundamental importance to understanding rhetoric about Jewish Muslims because most Eastern Christians lived under Muslim rule while most European Christians did not. Eastern Christian authors, we will see, craft their anti-Muslim rhetoric in a manner that acknowledges and capitalizes on their audience's familiarity with Islam. These relatively powerless polemicists motivate Christians to differentiate themselves from the dominant members of their own society lest, through assimilation, they become quasi-Jewish themselves. European authors, who did not have such concerns, take advantage of their audience's ignorance of Islam by employing wildly inaccurate rhetoric about judaizing Muslims to reinforce specific notions about what it means for a society to be Christian. In all cases, however, polemicists seek to craft tales that are both plausible and useful: plausible because they reinforce their audience's preconceptions and useful because these polemicists regarded rhetoric about Jewish Muslims as more compelling than rhetoric that focuses on Jews, Muslims, or other targets independently.

Chapter 8 shows how European Christians in positions of dominance over Muslims used the allegation that these Muslims bear Jewish characteristics to justify subjecting them to discriminatory legislation and persecution that originally targeted Jews alone. This chapter examines the process of textual interpretation through which Roman Catholic authorities defined Muslims as legally equivalent to Jews during the twelfth and thirteenth centuries, as well as the consequences of this definition for Spanish Muslims and their baptized descendants during the late fifteenth through early seventeenth centuries. Christians imagined Muslims as Jewish for the benefit of fellow Christians, whom they sought to safeguard from exposure to purportedly Jewish beliefs, practices, and interpretations of the Bible. Anti-Jewish rhetoric like this, however, generated terrible suffering for actual Jews and Muslims. Power, after all, shapes not only the ways in which Christians interpret texts but also their ability to act on those interpretations.

Part 3, "Anti-Christian Muslims," analyzes the ways in which European polemicists apply ideas about Jews as biblical enemies of Christ to contemporary Muslim enemies. By misrepresenting Muslims as Jews, Christians gain the ability to ascribe theological significance to their political conflicts with Muslims. This fusion of theological and political enmity, which rests on the ability to derive actionable lessons about contemporary Muslims from the Bible itself, generates explosive rhetorical energy that powerfully advances the objective of promoting proper Christian beliefs and practices. The chapters in this part affirm and refine Gil Anidjar's assertion that "in Europe, in 'Christian Europe,' they—the Jew, the Arab on the one hand, religion and politics on the other—are distinct, but indissociable."[16]

Chapters 9 and 10 explore themes in European rhetoric about Jewish Muslims that emerge in the eleventh century and persist into late medieval and early modern times. The first of these chapters examines associations of Muslims with Jewish Christ-killers, while the second considers allegations that Muslim rulers collaborate with Jews in their efforts to undermine Christianity and conquer Christian kingdoms. Jewish antipathy toward Christ constitutes the motive behind these alleged assaults on Christendom, while Muslim power provides the means. In both sets of cases, Christians frame the danger they ascribe to Muslims in terms of Judaism rather than Islam—in fact, these polemicists devote no attention at all to Islamic beliefs or practices. We will see in chapter 9 how rhetoric of this nature can inspire violence against Muslims and, in chapter 10, that polemicists can also employ such rhetoric to justify violence against local Jews.

Chapter 11 examines the impact on anti-Muslim rhetoric of an important development in Christian ideas about Judaism. Beginning in the thirteenth century, European polemicists alleged that Jews past and present do not merely misunderstand God as revealed in scripture and in the person of Jesus Christ but rather knowingly and willfully reject God. As a result of this shift, Christians increasingly portrayed Jews and Muslims alike as anti-Christians who worship not God but rather the false deity named Muhammad. Martin Luther, whose polemics are the subject of chapter 12, takes this rhetoric a step further by including Catholics and rival Protestants within the broad category of anti-Christians who fail to worship God. Luther's polemics vividly illustrate the ways in which premodern Christians more broadly employed biblically grounded rhetoric about Jews and Muslims to promote specific ideas about how to be a good Christian.

Luther also introduced an innovation that contributed to the subsequent decline of Christian rhetoric about Jewish Muslims: he alleged that Paul's letters and other biblical texts directly condemn Islam no less than Judaism. In so doing, Luther ascribed theological significance to Islam itself—or, rather, to the set of negative ideas, practices, traits, and so on that Luther associated with Islam. Luther and his predecessors alike found great value in the discourse of anti-Judaism because it motivates Christians to cultivate characteristics that allegedly differentiate them from Jews and, likewise, from Muslims who purportedly bear Jewish characteristics. Luther inaugurated a parallel discourse, equally grounded in the Bible and, more specifically, in Paul's binary rhetoric, that condemns purportedly Islamic characteristics on their own terms.

This discourse, which I call *anti-Islam*, differs from other forms of Islamophobia just as anti-Judaism differs from antisemitism: it serves to motivate self-improvement through the cultivation of characteristics opposed to those that the polemicist brands as Islamic.

Like the hybrid monsters who populate medieval art and literature, Jewish Muslims have become extinct, even as a rhetorical trope. This is not, however, because the conflation of Jews and Muslims is inherently unnatural: as Jonathan Z. Smith observes, "there is nothing 'natural' about the enterprise of comparison."[17] The portrayal of Muslims as Jewish has become less useful because the discourse of anti-Islam renders this metaphorical depiction unnecessary; at the same time, this portrayal has also become less plausible because ideas about Judaism and Islam evolved in very different ways during modern times. Many, however, continue to employ Islamophobic and Judeophobic rhetoric not only to justify assaults on Muslims or Jews but also, and especially, to motivate American and European audiences to cultivate beliefs and behaviors that purportedly differentiate them from rivals who are neither Muslim nor Jewish. Analyses of this rhetoric that focus solely on discrimination overlook crucial dimensions of their subject matter. The afterword offers a few examples to illustrate how contemporary rhetoric about Muslims and Jews seeks to promote specific and hotly contested ideas about what it means to be a good American, just as premodern rhetoric about Jewish Muslims promotes specific conceptions of what it means to be a good Christian. Scholars of other places, time periods, and religious traditions can no doubt provide additional examples of polemical rhetoric whose primary objective is self-differentiation rather than discrimination.

Comparison, we will see, can be a powerfully destructive polemical weapon. The same tool, however, can also yield especially valuable insights when used for the purpose of understanding rather than misrepresenting similarities and differences. For that reason, I not only analyze comparisons constructed by premodern Christians but also employ comparison as a principal method for understanding the ways in which these Christians perceive themselves in relation to their rivals. *Jewish Muslims* examines premodern texts and images produced over the course of sixteen centuries in places as distant as Britain and Baghdad not only in their own historical and regional contexts but also in relation to one another. Existing scholarship refers, at least in passing, to most primary sources that we will examine, but the juxtaposition of these sources is original. These juxtapositions generate new insights not only into specific sources whose features might not otherwise seem significant but also into the general nature and function of anti-Jewish and anti-Muslim discourses. In many cases, the comparisons I construct take the form of taxonomies: by recognizing patterns, common features, and changes over time, we gain a deeper understanding of how Christians used ideas about Jews to think about Muslims and why they found value in doing so. This study also draws on knowledge of one thing to propose ways of better understanding something else in light of the similarities and differences between those two things. Used in this illuminative mode, comparison generates ideas that can be tested directly on the subject matter we seek to understand.[18]

NOTES ON NAMES, PRONOUNS, TRANSLATIONS, AND TRANSLITERATIONS

I wrote this book for the benefit of all who seek to understand past and present rhetoric about Jews and Muslims, specialists and nonspecialists alike, and for that reason made every effort to write in an accessible and inclusive manner. These efforts include the following practices:

I consistently refer to the prophet of Islam as "Muhammad," reflecting the proper and increasingly familiar pronunciation of his name and in keeping with my general practice of referring to premodern individuals by names that will be most recognizable to contemporary readers. This practice departs from that of scholars such as John Tolan, who reserves the name "Muhammad" for the historical person who lived in the early seventh century and for Islamic portrayals of him. Tolan explains that his book, *Faces of Muhammad*, "is not about Muhammad, prophet of Islam, but about 'Mahomet,' the figure imagined and brought to life by European authors." To mark this distinction, Tolan makes a point of reproducing the names that European authors employ: "Machomet, Mathome, Mafometus, Mouamed, Mahoma, and above all Mahomet."[19] There are in fact many more European variations on Muhammad's name than these, and the use of diverse names for the same person can generate confusion. More fundamentally, Christians speak of the same figure as Muslims do even when they imagine Muhammad in fundamentally different—and, oftentimes, historically inaccurate—ways. Premodern Christians likewise misrepresent a wide range of other figures, as well as Muslims and Jews collectively, yet they speak of familiar figures and communities. Some of their ideas, in fact, underpin contemporary stereotypes about Muhammad, Muslims, and Jews. I believe it is important to confront these hostile representations rather than obscure them by means of antiquated or foreign names. There is, however, one partial exception: because the terms that premodern Christians used for Muslims—such as Ishmaelites, Saracens, and Turks—carry distinctive meanings, I explain those terms and employ them as synonyms for "Muslims" when speaking of the targets of premodern Christian rhetoric.

As readers may already have noticed, I use the first-person singular when speaking of myself as the author and the plural "we" in reference to myself and my readers. In this book as in my classroom, I seek not to be a tour guide ("If you look over there, you will see . . .") but rather a co-participant in a process through which we all learn together, albeit with different roles and degrees of expertise. I avoid gendered pronouns for God as well as for people whose gender is irrelevant, such as the imaginary candidate discussed above.

I often employ translations prepared by other scholars, revising them as necessary based on my own understanding of the original text. (I personally consulted the originals of all sources except those written in Armenian, for which I relied on the linguistic expertise of a colleague.) I note the presence of substantive revisions but do not indicate simple emendations, such as "Muhammad" in place of "Mahomet." Unless otherwise indicated, biblical translations in this book follow the New Revised Standard Version, sometimes revised in light of the Hebrew or Greek original. Unattributed translations of postbiblical texts are original. Whenever possible, I limit citations of secondary sources to the most relevant English-language works, trusting that fellow scholars will take advantage of the more comprehensive bibliographies that those works provide.

I do not presume that readers of this book know how to interpret diacritics, the dots and lines that scholars place above or below letters to indicate how foreign words are spelled in their original alphabets. For that reason, I generally avoid the use of diacritics and refer, for example, to the Eastern Christian monastery of *Bet Hale* instead of *Bēt Ḥālē*. (The lines indicate long vowels in Syriac, while the dot under the *H* indicates a guttural sound absent from English but common in Semitic languages as well as in Spanish words like Guadalajara.)

PART ONE

Biblical Muslims

CHAPTER I

Paul's Rivals and the Early Christian Discourse of Anti-Judaism

First through Sixth Centuries

Aside from Jesus himself, no one exercised greater influence on Christianity than Paul of Tarsus. Paul, along with followers writing in his name, authored more than half of the works that make up the New Testament, and Christians ever since have employed Paul's words as a source of guidance. Even though Muslims did not exist during Paul's lifetime, we cannot understand Christian ideas about Muslims without first examining Paul's teachings, both on their own terms and as understood by influential interpreters who also predate the rise of Islam.

Paul, according to his own account (Galatians 1:13–17), initially persecuted fellow Jews who, even after Jesus's death, regarded Jesus as the messiah (Greek: *christos*) foretold in Jewish scriptures. Sometime around the year 34 CE, however, Paul experienced a vision of the risen Christ. He joined the small community of those who believed that the crucified and raised Jesus would soon establish the kingdom of God on earth for the benefit of the righteous. To call this community *Christian*, however, would be anachronistic. That term, invented several decades after Paul's death, implies an identity entirely distinct from Jewishness, but Paul and most other followers of Jesus during the mid-first century proudly self-identified as Jews. For that reason, I instead refer to the members of this first-century community as *Christ-followers*.[1]

Paul believed that God appointed him to spread the gospel (that is, the good news about Jesus Christ) to gentiles (that is, non-Jews): they too can be reckoned among the righteous in the kingdom of God if only they renounce their worship of other gods and place their faith in Christ. Paul preached this message throughout the eastern Mediterranean, establishing far-flung communities of formerly pagan Christ-followers and guiding them by means of public letters he wrote during the 40s and 50s CE. Fellow followers of Christ, however, challenged Paul's conception of what former pagans must do to participate fully in the predominantly Jewish community of Christ-followers and, ultimately, in the kingdom of God. These rivals made their case directly to members of Paul's gentile churches, including those he founded in Galatia, a region within present-day Turkey. Paul, infuriated, offers in his Letter to the Galatians a spirited defense of his position and a stinging rebuke of his rivals.

At a key moment in his argument, Paul associates his own community with Abraham's wife Sarah and his Christ-following enemies with Hagar, Sarah's spurned slave. Paul motivates members of his audience to differentiate themselves from his rivals by establishing a black-and-white contrast between the characteristics of each group. This rhetorically powerful method of comparison crystallized into the discourse of anti-Judaism and also shaped anti-Muslim discourse, although Paul himself could not have anticipated either development.

Before turning our attention to Galatians, let me review the story about Abraham, Sarah, and Hagar to which Paul refers. The biblical book of Genesis recounts that Abram and Sarai, as they were originally named, were childless for many years. At Sarai's urging, Abram impregnates her slave Hagar, but when Hagar looks with contempt on her mistress, Sarai treats her so harshly that Hagar flees. An angel instructs Hagar to return and prophesies that her son Ishmael "shall be a wild ass of a man, with his hand against everyone, and everyone's hand against him; and he shall live at odds with his kin" (Genesis 16:12). Several years later, Abraham and Sarah have a son of their own: Isaac, about whom God declares, "I will establish my covenant with him as an everlasting covenant for his offspring after him" (17:19). When Isaac begins to grow up, Sarah demands of her husband, "Drive out this slave and her son, for the son of this slave will not share in the inheritance with my son, Isaac" (21:10). Abraham, reluctantly, sends Hagar and Ishmael into the wilderness. According to Genesis, Sarah's descendants via Isaac's son Jacob, known as the Children of Israel and later as the Jews, inherited Abraham's unique relationship with God as well as the promises associated with this covenant. Paul and his successors, however, declare that the true heirs to the Abrahamic covenant and its blessings are those who follow Christ properly.

GENTILE CHRIST-FOLLOWERS AND PAUL'S TABLE OF OPPOSITES

In order to understand Paul's remarks about Hagar and Sarah, we first need to review and unpack earlier sections of his tightly interwoven Letter to the Galatians. Paul begins by critiquing his gentile audience: "I am astonished that you are so quickly deserting the one who called you in the grace of Christ [that is, Paul himself] and are turning to a different gospel—not that there is another gospel, but there are some who are confusing you and want to pervert the gospel of Christ" (1:6–7). Do not follow any teachings that contradict mine, Paul demands, because my teachings come from God. Paul insists that the acknowledged leaders of the Christ-following community—fellow Jews, including Jesus's brother James and the apostle Peter—recognized that Paul "had been entrusted with the gospel for the uncircumcised, just as Peter had been entrusted with the gospel for the circumcised" (2:7). Notice the categories of humanity that Paul takes for granted—Jews on the one hand, gentiles on the other—and his decision to label each category with reference to the practice of male circumcision, which Jews performed but gentiles in the Greco-Roman world did not.

Although Paul claimed recognition from the leaders in Jerusalem, he and his Jerusalem-based colleagues disagreed fundamentally over what gentiles must do as full members of the predominantly Jewish community of Christ-followers. Figures associated with James apparently believed that these former pagans must observe all the rules spelled out in the Torah (the first five books of the Bible), the vast majority of which apply solely to Jews. In particular, it seems, Jerusalem-based Christ-followers sought to persuade their male Galatian counterparts to adopt the symbolically significant practice of circumcision as if they, too, were Jews. Paul, in contrast, insisted that it is both unnecessary and counterproductive for gentiles to "judaize"—that is, to behave like Jews—by adhering to norms that the Torah imposes on Jews alone (2:14).[2]

Paul emphatically maintains that gentile followers of Christ should not adopt circumcision or other specifically Jewish customs. Rather, these gentiles should live as "ex-pagan pagans" by adhering only to biblical norms that Paul and other Jews of his era regarded as universally binding—most notably the requirement to worship the one true God alone. Because Paul did not write to Jewish audiences, he never explicitly addresses the question of whether Jewish Christ-followers should continue to observe distinctive practices such as circumcision; he seems, however, to take for granted that they should.[3]

Rhetoric about Abraham plays a major role in Paul's argument to the Galatians, and we may reasonably suspect that Paul's Christ-following rivals appealed to Abraham as well. First-century Jews, after all, regarded Abraham as someone who proclaimed monotheism to pagans and as the honorary father of those who reject idolatry, so he is an obvious reference point for Jews speaking to gentile Christ-followers. Not only that; the Torah presents Abraham as the first practitioner of ritual circumcision, which Genesis 17 defines as a prerequisite for participation in God's covenantal community. Paul's opponents presumably drew heavily on this text in their efforts to persuade male gentile Christ-followers to become circumcised. Paul seeks in part to reclaim Abraham's legacy from his rivals and, indeed, to brand these rivals as proponents of a false set of beliefs grounded in a misinterpretation of scripture. Later Christians would call such rivals *heretics*.[4]

To persuade his Galatian audience to follow his teachings rather than those of his rivals, Paul crafts an elaborate table of opposites, a rhetorical chart whose positive attributes apply to adherents of Paul's teachings and whose negative attributes characterize Paul's rivals and their adherents. To understand this binary table in its original context, we need to recognize that its two sides do not correspond to Paul's two categories of humanity—Jews and gentiles. Rather, Paul contrasts two types of Christ-followers: all who share Paul's beliefs, whether Jewish or gentile, fall on the positive side of this table of opposites, while the negative side encompasses not only the Christ-following Jews who demand circumcision but also the gentile followers of Christ who adopt and endorse this practice. As we will see, later Christian readers of Paul's letter interpret Paul's binary rhetoric differently.[5]

Paul lays out the core claim of the Letter to the Galatians as follows:

> we know that a person is reckoned as righteous not through works of Law but through faith in Jesus Christ. And we have come to trust in Christ Jesus, so that we might be reckoned as righteous through faith in Christ, and not through works of Law, because through works of Law no one will be reckoned as righteous. (2:16)

In other words, "we"—Paul refers here to himself and his rivals alike—agree that faith in Christ is the sole means by which one can be "reckoned as righteous" (or, in other translations, "justified") and therefore eligible to enter the kingdom of God. Paul derives this term from the Torah's description of Abraham: when promised that his still-nonexistent descendants would become as numerous as the stars, Abraham "believed God, and it was reckoned to him as righteousness" (Genesis 15:6). Paul both quotes this passage and associates Abraham's faithfulness with the faith of those who trust in Christ (Galatians 3:6–9). To be reckoned as righteous, to be declared just notwithstanding one's imperfections, one must trust in Christ—this is the message of Paul and his rivals alike.

Note that Paul does not quote a verse from Genesis 17, in which God's covenant with Abraham's offspring depends on male circumcision, but instead draws on an earlier account of the covenant that makes no reference to this practice. In contrast to his Christ-following rivals, Paul regards faith in Christ not only as a necessary prerequisite to being reckoned as righteous but also as a fully sufficient condition for attaining this status. Gentiles need not—and, for that reason, should not—adopt in their entirety the practices enjoined within the Torah, known in Greek as "the Law." Paul insists that biblical practices such as circumcision are irrelevant because "if righteousness comes through the Law, then Christ died for no purpose" (2:21). The Galatians, moreover, should already know from their own experience of accepting Paul's teachings that God bestows the Spirit on those who follow Christ even if they do not observe biblical practices enjoined upon Jews alone. This is why Paul berates his Galatian audience: "Having started with the Spirit, are you now ending with the flesh" by performing "works of Law" (3:3–5)?

As Christ-followers, Paul declares, gentiles qualify as descendants of Abraham and inherit the Abrahamic blessing not on account of works but faith: "Christ redeemed us from the curse of the Law . . . so that we might receive the promise of the Spirit through faith" (3:13–14). Paul emphasizes that the biblical commandments revealed to the Jewish people on Mount Sinai hundreds of years after God established the covenant with Abraham cannot annul or modify the terms of God's covenantal promise to Abraham and his offspring. This promise, Paul asserts, refers to none other than Christ, and all who have faith in Christ, gentiles no less than Jews, are its beneficiaries.

As he offers his interpretation of God's covenant with Abraham, Paul establishes a set of linked opposites that distinguish his teachings from those of his Christ-following rivals (table 1). According to Paul, these rivals and their adherents—both Jewish and gentile—understand the Law revealed at Sinai as the grounds for salvation and regard performing works of the Law, including circumcision, as a necessary prerequisite for

TABLE 1 PAUL'S TABLE OF OPPOSITES (PARTIAL)

	Rivals and their adherents	Paul and his adherents
State of salvation	Cursed	Reckoned as righteous
Grounds of salvation	Law revealed at Sinai	Covenantal promise to Abraham
Prerequisite for salvation	Works of Law, including circumcision	Faith in Christ
Associated with	Flesh	Spirit
Status	Imprisoned	Free
Identity	Slaves	Heirs to God's promise

attaining that state. Paul and his adherents—both Jewish and gentile—instead believe that salvation is grounded in the covenantal promise to Abraham and regard faith in Christ as the sole prerequisite for attaining salvation. Paul associates his rivals with the flesh and his followers with the Spirit; those who observe his rivals' teachings suffer from the "curse of the Law" while his own community is reckoned as righteous. Paul proceeds to add two more pairs of opposites: those who rely on the Law are "imprisoned" (3:23) and "no better than slaves" (4:1), while those who rely on Christ are free and are heirs to the Abrahamic covenant. The formerly pagan Christ-followers of Galatia, Paul declares, were once enslaved to beings other than God on account of their idolatry, but when they accepted Paul's teachings, they became adopted children of God through their faith in Christ. Why, Paul asks, would they wish to become slaves once more by subjecting themselves to the Law revealed at Sinai? "I am afraid that my work for you may have been wasted" (4:11).

After an autobiographical paragraph, Paul proceeds to offer the allegorical interpretation of Abraham's family that resonated across centuries of Christian anti-Jewish and anti-Muslim rhetoric.[6] He does so in the form of a direct speech to gentile Galatians who, under the influence of Paul's rivals, think they need to observe all the requirements of the Torah. Notice that Paul does not address his rivals: Paul's disparaging rhetoric about them aims to persuade his Galatian audience to reject the rivals' teachings and instead to adopt his own.

> Tell me, you who desire to be subject to Law, will you not listen to the Law? For it is written that Abraham had two sons, one by a slave woman and the other by a free woman. One, the child of the slave, was born according to the flesh; the other, the child of the free woman, was born through the promise. (4:21–23)

Paul seeks to demonstrate that his teachings alone derive from the proper interpretation of scripture; "listening to the Law" serves as the test to prove that Paul's message is accurate and that his rivals' teachings are flawed. Paul emphasizes that, in the Torah's account of Abraham's family, only the child of the "free woman," Sarah, was born on account of the covenantal promise of offspring, while the "child of the slave" is merely the result of fleshly sexual intercourse. By identifying Hagar and Sarah as slave and free and by associating their sons with the flesh and the Spirit (4:29), Paul applies to these characters the terms of his carefully constructed table of opposites. This rhetorical move enables Paul to link his adherents with Sarah and his rivals with Hagar.

Paul then unlocks what he presents as the deeper meaning of the Hagar and Sarah story by relating dynamics within Abraham's family to those within the contemporary movement of Christ-followers.

> Now this is an allegory: these women are two covenants. One of these is Hagar, from Mount Sinai, bearing children for slavery. Now Hagar is Mount Sinai in Arabia and corresponds to the present Jerusalem, which is in slavery with her children. The Jerusalem above, in contrast, is free, and she is our mother. (4:24–26)

Hagar the slave woman, Paul explains, represents the covenant of the Law that God established at Mount Sinai. Paul links Hagar with Sinai because she and her son settled in the vicinity of that mountain after Abraham drove them away (Genesis 21:21). Through this linkage, Paul reinforces his association of the Torah revealed at Sinai with slavery itself. Paul also links Hagar with "the present Jerusalem," home to the leaders who insist that gentile Christ-followers must adhere to the Torah in its entirety. These rivals, Paul asserts, misunderstand scripture and, for that reason, erroneously believe that salvation depends on adherence to works of the Law. Because they bind themselves to Sinai's laws, they and their followers are no less enslaved than Hagar and her son.

There is, however, another divine covenant: the one associated with Sarah and the heavenly "Jerusalem above." This, Paul teaches his followers, is *our* covenant, the one that rests solely on faith in Jesus Christ. Paul, who dismisses the relevance of fleshly ancestry when it comes to entering the kingdom of God, contends that Sarah is the figurative mother of all followers of Christ—Jews and gentiles alike—who share her faith in the divine promise. "Our mother," as opposed to the figurative mother of Paul's rivals, represents not the flawed present-day Jerusalem but its ideal celestial counterpart.[7]

Paul brings this portion of his letter to a close by explaining to the Galatians why there is conflict within the community of Christ-followers and what they should do about it.

> Now you, my friends, are children of the promise, like Isaac. Moreover, just as at that time the child who was born according to the flesh persecuted the child who was born according to the Spirit, so it is now also. But what does the scripture say? "Drive out the slave and her child; for the child of the slave will not share the inheritance with the child of the free woman" [Genesis 21:10, adapted]. So then, friends, we are children, not of the slave but of the free woman. For freedom Christ has set us free. Stand firm, therefore, and do not submit again to a yoke of slavery. (Galatians 4:28–5:1)

Just as Hagar and Sarah represent two competing ideas about the prerequisite for entering the kingdom of God (adherence to the Law or faith in Jesus Christ), Ishmael and Isaac represent rival factions within the Christ-following community. Those who adhere to Paul's teachings are freeborn "children of the promise, like Isaac." They too are (re)born through the Spirit and, as adopted sons, are heirs to the kingdom that Christ will inaugurate upon his return to earth.

Abraham's sons not only reflect the nature of the competing factions of first-century Christ-followers but also prefigure the ways in which these factions necessarily interact. Paul believed that Ishmael "persecuted" his younger brother.[8] He alleges that Ishmael's present-day successors, the Jerusalem-based Christ-followers and their supporters, likewise torment the Isaac-like Galatians by insisting that these gentile newcomers adopt Jewish practices such as circumcision rather than rely solely on the promise of salvation through Christ.

Recall that Paul opened his letter by acknowledging that he himself "was violently persecuting the church of God" (1:13) before he saw the light and joined that community himself. As persecutors, Paul's Jerusalem-based rivals are enemies of the true Christ-followers and, implicitly, do not really belong to the community at all. Paul therefore urges his audience to fulfill the instructions of their spiritual mother, Sarah, by figuratively driving out those who want them to observe the Torah in its entirety. Gentiles who enslave themselves to the Law, after all, will not share the inheritance of Abraham's covenantal promise. Paul and his adherents, however, lack the power of expulsion that Abraham wields over Hagar: the most Paul can do is "wish those who unsettle you would castrate themselves!" (5:12).

Through his interpretation of the biblical story of Hagar and Sarah, Paul greatly expands his table of opposites (table 2). The Galatians'

TABLE 2   PAUL'S TABLE OF OPPOSITES (COMPLETE)

	Rivals and their adherents	Paul and his adherents
State of salvation	Cursed	Reckoned as righteous
Grounds of salvation	Law revealed at Sinai	Covenantal promise to Abraham
Prerequisite for salvation	Works of Law, including circumcision	Faith in Christ
Associated with	Flesh	Spirit
Status	Imprisoned	Free
Identity	Slaves	Heirs to God's promise
Interpretation of scripture	Flawed	Accurate
Figurative ancestors	Hagar, Ishmael	Sarah, Isaac
Homeland	Present-day Jerusalem	Heavenly Jerusalem
Behavior	Persecute followers of Christ	Drive out enemies

choice ought to be simple: as adherents of Paul's teachings, they stand on the proper side of each dichotomy and should therefore "stand firm" in their freedom from circumcision and from the corpus of biblical law that it represents. "You who want to be declared righteous by the Law," Paul declares, "have cut yourselves off from Christ" (5:4). To return to the elements of polemical comparison that I defined in the introduction, Paul (polemicist) uses the terms of his table of opposites (criteria) to associate his rivals (target) with Hagar (reference) in order to persuade the Galatians (audience) to follow Paul's teachings (objective). The contrast Paul draws between his adherents and his rivals provides powerful motivation for audience members to differentiate themselves from those who fall on the wrong side of the table and, in so doing, to assert their identity as the true followers of Christ.

Paul does not object to the practice of circumcision when performed by Jewish Christ-followers: "For in Christ Jesus neither circumcision nor uncircumcision counts for anything; the only thing that counts is faith working through love" (5:6; cf. 6:15). Paul, after all, does not seek in this letter to condemn Jews or Judaism. Rather, his objective is to teach former pagans who trust in Christ how their new faith should guide their behavior. Paul grounds his instruction in his table of opposites: "Live by the Spirit, I say, and do not gratify the desires of the flesh" (5:16). Paul proceeds to characterize the former in terms of love, generosity, and self-control; he lists idolatry, jealousy, and forbidden sexual relations among examples of the latter.

The Letter to the Galatians gives voice to one side of a dispute among Jewish Christ-followers regarding the obligations incumbent on gentile Christ-followers. These ex-pagan pagans ultimately resolved the dispute in Paul's favor, as Paul's gentile followers came to dominate the Christian community. Their acceptance of his teachings—and their incorporation of Paul's letters into the Christian Bible—contributed to the formation of Christianity as a religion distinct from Judaism no less than from paganism. Paul himself, however, did not perceive a conflict between Judaism and Christianity: these were not opposing categories during Paul's lifetime, and Paul himself was among many who proudly self-identified simultaneously as a Jew and as a follower of Christ.[9]

Written in response to a specific situation, Paul's allegorical depiction of Sarah and Hagar gained much broader significance through its inclusion in the New Testament. Later Christian readers of Paul's allegory, who believed that Paul spoke not only to first-century Christ-followers but also to them, understood Sarah as the representative of Christians while Hagar represents Jews first and foremost—and also, we will see in later chapters, Muslims. These readers continued to employ the four categories of humanity implicit in Paul's Letter to the Galatians: Christians (those who follow Christ properly), heretics (Christians with improper beliefs), pagans (who worship false gods), and Jews. Premodern Christians often placed Muslims into one or another of these categories, depicting Muslims as heretics, as pagans, or as Jews depending on the rhetorical objective at hand. Paul's successors also frequently employed the rhetorical techniques that Paul uses so effectively in Galatians: they too defined their own community through contrast with a negative foil, and they too polemicized against outsiders as a means of motivating insiders to differentiate themselves through the cultivation of proper beliefs and behaviors.

HAGAR—AND HERESY—AS JUDAISM

Christianity became a predominantly gentile movement, so later readers of Paul's letters interpreted the Letter to the Galatians within a very different context than that of Paul's original audience. Paul used Hagar to represent rival followers of Christ, but later Christians understood Paul's allegory to condemn what they began to call Judaism. These readers also drew on Paul's depiction of Hagar in polemics against their own Christian rivals, whose allegedly heretical beliefs and practices they often branded as "Jewish." Most fundamentally, early Christians followed in

Paul's footsteps by defining the proper characteristics of their own community through binary opposition with its various rivals.[10]

New Testament works composed several decades after Paul's death helped to shape the new understanding of Paul's teaching about Abraham's descendants. According to the Gospel of Matthew, probably written in the 80s CE, John the Baptist issued a stern warning to fellow Jews who came to him for baptism. "Do not presume to say to yourselves, 'We have Abraham as our ancestor'; for I tell you, God is able from these stones to raise up children to Abraham. Even now the ax is lying at the root of the trees; every tree therefore that does not bear good fruit is cut down and thrown into the fire" (Matthew 3:9–10). The mere fact that Jews descend from good stock, John the Baptist teaches, will not save them from divine wrath because what matters is not one's ancestry—God can make anyone a child of Abraham—but rather the quality of one's "fruit."

The Gospel of John, written in the late first or early second century, reports that Jesus goes even further, rejecting rival Jews' very claim to Abrahamic descent.

> I know that you are descendants of Abraham; yet you look for an opportunity to kill me, because there is no place in you for my word. . . . If you were Abraham's children, you would be doing what Abraham did, but now you are trying to kill me, a man who has told you the truth that I heard from God. . . . Why do you not understand what I say? It is because you cannot accept my word. You are from your father the devil, and you choose to do your father's desires. (John 8:37, 39–40, 43–44)

According to this account, Jesus acknowledges that the Jews who challenge his authority are descendants of Abraham in a biological sense. He declares, however, that their thoughts and actions—their "fruit," to use the Gospel of Matthew's language—reveal these Jews to be spiritual children of the devil himself.

The Jesus of John's gospel, like John the Baptist in Matthew's gospel, completely dismisses the relevance of Jewish genealogical claims to the Abrahamic covenant. What matters is one's relationship to Christ, which "Jews"—a term that now excludes Jesus and his followers—categorically lack. Those who read the Letter to the Galatians in light of these texts could easily conclude that Paul similarly condemned Judaism itself. From their perspective, the positive side of Paul's table of opposites represents Christians while the negative side represents Jews, who are nothing less than enemies of Christ acting on behalf of the devil.[11]

Whereas Paul and his original Galatian audience were concerned about ideas advanced by fellow Christ-followers, the late-second-century theologian Tertullian takes for granted that Galatians is Paul's "primary letter against Judaism," which Tertullian regards as a set of beliefs and practices distinct from and antithetical to Christianity. Paul's interpretation of Sarah and Hagar, he asserts, demonstrates that "the noble dignity of Christianity has its allegorical type and figure in the son of Abraham born of the free woman, while the legal bondage of Judaism has its allegorical type in the son of the slave woman." Tertullian, in other words, believed that the Bible itself represents Christianity through the figures of Sarah and Isaac, and Judaism through Hagar and Ishmael. This anti-Jewish reading of Paul's allegory became typical among early Christians: Jerome, writing in the late fourth century, observes that "nearly all the commentators on this passage interpret it to mean that the slave woman Hagar represents the Law and the Jewish people, but that the free woman Sarah symbolizes the Church." Ishmael's persecution of Isaac, Jerome explains, prefigures "the madness of the Jews who killed the Lord, persecuted the prophets and apostles," and purportedly continue to persecute Christians in Jerome's own day. As the spiritual heirs of Hagar and Ishmael, Jews are inherently anti-Christian.[12]

Jerome and John Chrysostom, another influential figure active in the late fourth century, also understand Paul's allegory as a warning to Christians who interpret scripture in a supposedly "Jewish" fashion or who participate in Jewish rites. "I shall choose to risk my life rather than let [a fellow Christian] enter the doors of the synagogue," Chrysostom declares in the first of his so-called *Discourses against Judaizing Christians*. "I shall say to him: What fellowship do you have with the free Jerusalem, with the Jerusalem above? You chose the one below; be a slave with that earthly Jerusalem which, according to the word of the Apostle, is a slave together with her children."[13] Recall that Paul himself berates those who urged gentile Christ-followers to "judaize" (Galatians 2:14), a term that refers to the adoption by non-Jews of Jewish characteristics. Unlike transitive verbs such as *demonize*, which describe an action that one person performs on another—"Chrysostom demonized Jews"—the verb *judaize* (similar to *apologize*) refers back to its subject: "According to Chrysostom, errant Christians judaize." Chrysostom understands Paul's table of opposites to condemn these judaizers alongside the Jews themselves.

Chrysostom brands Christians who enter synagogues as quasi-Jewish heirs of Hagar, and he also contends that Christians who regard Jesus

Christ as less than fully divine are no better than Jews, who reject Jesus's divinity entirely. These judaizing Christians, Chrysostom declares, forfeit the divine promise represented by Sarah and become equivalent to Jews, whom Chrysostom associates not only with Hagar but also with dogs, beasts, and demons. Metaphorical associations of this nature define the Christian community's boundaries and norms by branding specific beliefs or practices as emphatically un-Christian, and they motivate Christian audiences to differentiate themselves from deviant Christians no less than from Jews in order to self-identify as true Christians.[14]

Like Paul, Chrysostom addresses members of his own flock even as he polemicizes against outsiders; in both cases, the targets of their polemical comparisons differ from their audiences. Chrysostom (polemicist) constructs a table of opposites that distinguishes Christianity from Judaism on the basis of how each interprets scripture and understands Christ (criteria of comparison). By the binary logic of his rhetorical framework, nonconforming Christians (targets) become Jewish (reference)—notwithstanding the fact that these Christians in no way self-identify as Jews. Chrysostom both conflates errant Christians with Jews and demonizes Jews themselves for the purpose of promoting specific beliefs and practices (objective) to fellow Christians (audience). In doing so, Chrysostom exemplifies the discourse of anti-Judaism, which seeks to motivate proper Christian behaviors through contrast with behaviors ascribed to Jews. Later polemicists employ anti-Muslim rhetoric, especially allegations that Muslims themselves judaize, in similar fashion.

THE ABSENT ISHMAELITES OF PAUL'S ALLEGORY

Paul said nothing in his Letter to the Galatians about Hagar's biological descendants, the offspring of Ishmael. Jews in Paul's day commonly identified these Ishmaelites with the nomadic Arabs who dwelled in the desert region that stretches from the Sinai Peninsula into present-day Jordan and Saudi Arabia, and this notion evidently underpins Paul's association of Hagar with "Mount Sinai in Arabia" (Galatians 4:25).[15] Paul, however, had no interest in Arabs: the purpose of his allegory is to condemn his Christ-following rivals. For that reason, Ishmaelites themselves—and even the name *Ishmael*—are entirely absent from Paul's allegory. Early Christians drew liberally on Paul's table of opposites and his rhetoric about Hagar's spiritual heirs when disparaging their rivals, both Jews and heretics, but they too devote no attention to Hagar's biological descendants when interpreting Galatians.

Augustine (d. 430), whose ideas profoundly shaped European forms of Christianity, explains this absence well: "In terms of fleshly origins, the Jews—that is, the Israelites—belong to Sarah and the Ishmaelites in fact belong to Hagar. In terms of the mystery of the Spirit, however, the Christians belong to Sarah and the Jews to Hagar."[16] The fact that Ishmaelites are Hagar's literal descendants bears no theological significance, just as Jewish descent from Sarah does not ultimately matter. After all, Paul emphasized that Christians should concern themselves with the Spirit, not the flesh. Jews figure prominently within early Christian interpretations of Galatians because Christians read Paul's table of opposites through the lens of anti-Judaism, but these Christians saw no reason to read Ishmaelites into his allegory.

I am aware of only one pre-Islamic source that applies the rhetoric of Galatians to Arabs, and this sixth-century exception proves the general rule. Euthymius, after instructing Arab converts, "allowed them to depart, no longer Hagarenes and Ishmaelites but descendants of Sarah and heirs to the promises, by baptism transferred from servitude to freedom."[17] These Arabs emulate Paul's ex-pagan community in Galatia by choosing to follow Christ. In so doing, they become the spiritual heirs of Sarah rather than the biological descendants of Hagar and Ishmael. Without baptism, Arabs remain Hagarenes and thus, potentially, "Jews" according to the common interpretation of Paul's table of opposites. It is only with the rise of Islam, however, that Christians seize this potential to portray Muslim Arabs (and Muslims more broadly) as Jewish.

Early Christians did, of course, draw on biblical texts other than Galatians when writing about Ishmaelites. For example, they cited the statement that Ishmael "lived in the wilderness and became an expert with the bow" (Genesis 21:20) to explain the nomadic and violent way of life they ascribed to the Arabs with whom they came in contact. Christian writers also appealed to the Bible to account for various aspects of Arab culture, explaining, for example, that Arabs customarily practice male circumcision because Abraham and Ishmael did so.[18]

Familiarity with the Bible also shaped the ways in which Christians understood the term *Saracens*, which first appears in a second-century CE Greek geography in reference to inhabitants of the Sinai Peninsula but which came to refer to nomadic Arabs in general. Greek and Latin authors of late antiquity often depicted Saracens as uncivilized raiders and marauders, and Christians reinforced that stereotype by declaring that Saracens follow in the path of their ancestor, Ishmael. After the rise of Islam, many Christians applied the term *Saracens* to all Muslim Arabs or even to all Muslims regardless of their ethnicity.[19]

Jerome, who wrote the authoritative Latin translation of the Bible in the late fourth century, interprets the angelic prophecy that Ishmael would be "a wild ass of a man, his hand against all" (Genesis 16:12) as a reference to "the Saracens who wander with no fixed abode and often invade all the nations who border on the desert." Jerome also contends that these Ishmaelites, allegedly ashamed of their descent from Hagar the slave, "now call themselves Saracens, falsely usurping the name of Sarah, thus appearing to be born of a free lady." Whereas Paul asserts that followers of Christ can legitimately claim spiritual ancestry from Sarah on the basis of their faith in the divine promise, Jerome alleges that Saracens falsely claim biological descent from Sarah, demonstrating not only their deceitfulness but also their misguided orientation toward fleshliness. (In fact, Arabs never used this term to refer to themselves; nor did they claim descent from Sarah; nor, in any case, does the term *Saracen* have an etymological relationship with the name Sarah.) Elsewhere, Jerome depicts the Saracens of his day as idolatrous worshippers of the planet Venus, which he calls Lucifer.[20]

European Christians regarded Jerome as an authoritative expert on matters related to scripture and thus, by extension, on matters related to Ishmaelites. As a result, many medieval and early modern authors writing about Muslims continued to allege that the Saracens of their own day are violent idolaters who deceitfully seek to conceal their origins as slaves and their true nature as allies of Lucifer, a term these authors associated with the devil.[21] This utter misrepresentation of Islam, a religion that emerged two centuries after Jerome's death, would be ludicrous if only it were a laughing matter. Misrepresentations like these, however, had serious and lasting consequences for Christian-Muslim relations. While some Christians familiar with the tenets of Islam rejected the allegation that Muslims practice idolatry, others used accurate information to reinforce false claims by alleging, for example, that the Black Stone of the Kaaba, the sacred Islamic shrine in Mecca, is actually an idol that Muslims worship. European polemicists, we will see, used the allegation of idolatry to provoke and justify Christian violence against Muslims.[22]

This example vividly illustrates the degree to which Christian rhetoric about Muslims draws heavily on sources that predate Islam itself—namely, biblical texts read in light of commentaries by Jerome and other authoritative interpreters. In this case and many others, the result is a portrayal of Muslims as pagan. The next two chapters examine ways in which Christians similarly employed traditional understandings of Galatians to define Muslims as Jewish. Paul declared that rival followers of Christ are the heirs of Hagar, early Christian interpreters branded Jews as such, and later interpreters applied Paul's rhetoric to Muslims as well. By placing Muslims on the negative side of Paul's table of opposites, these Christians were able to motivate Christians to differentiate themselves not only from heretics and Jews but also from purportedly Jewish Muslims.

CHAPTER 2

Making Sense of the Muslim Conquests

Seventh through Ninth Centuries

Who are these people, why do they rule over us, and what should we do now?

These questions troubled many Christians after Muslim armies conquered Palestine, Syria, Egypt, and Persia in the mid-seventh century. Romans had dominated the Eastern Mediterranean since before the time of Jesus, and the rival Persian Empire was even older. No one expected that to change, and many Christians even regarded the strength of the Roman Empire as proof of divine favor toward Christianity. Since Arab marauders constituted at most a periodic nuisance, few people paid much attention to developments in the Arab world.

Under the leadership of Muhammad (d. 632) and his successors, called caliphs, disparate Arab tribes submitted not only to the will of the sole God as taught by their prophet but also to a pact of mutual nonaggression with their fellow Muslims. Instead of fighting one another, the Arabian Peninsula's Muslim tribes banded together to attack their neighbors to the north, in Palestine and Syria, and they quickly discovered the weakness of the Roman and Persian empires. These superpowers of late antiquity had recently concluded a devastating war during which the Persians, based in Iran, seized much of that region. Heraclius, the Roman emperor of Byzantium (present-day Turkey), regained full control of Syria and Palestine in 629/30 CE, but his hold was now tenuous. As historian Hugh Kennedy observes, "The coincidence that the first Muslim armies appeared in the area immediately after the traumatic events of the great war between Byzantium and Iran was the essential prerequisite for the success of Muslim arms." Kennedy also notes that the region had been weakened by repeated waves of bubonic plague.[1]

Muslim forces seized wide swaths of Roman territory and proceeded to destroy the Persian Empire entirely. Within a century or so, Muslims ruled over as much as half of the world's Christian population in an empire that stretched from India to Spain.[2] These Christians, however, did not perceive the Muslim conquests in terms of political or military, let alone bacteriological, history. Nor, for that matter, did Christian writers pay much attention to the beliefs that motivated their overlords, especially during the seventh and early eighth centuries. Instead, Christians made sense of their subjugation by drawing primarily on theological concepts rooted in the Bible. Many depicted Muslims as a divine scourge sent to punish Christians for their sinfulness. Others drew solace from biblical accounts of the end of days, portraying the Muslim conquests as a sign of Christ's imminent return. The works we will examine in this chapter employ the long-standing discourse of anti-Judaism to account in various ways for why Muslims persecute Christians.[3]

The authors of these texts—who espoused different Christian theologies, wrote in different languages, and were not familiar with one another—expressed different ideas about Muslims. Sophronius, the Byzantine patriarch of Jerusalem who surrendered that city to its Muslim conquerors in 638, portrays these "Saracens" as generic agents of divine punishment. In his Greek-language sermons, Sophronius defines the sins of faithlessness and disobedience toward God that triggered this punishment as "Jewish," even though self-identifying Christians committed them. The patriarch does not, however, associate the Muslim conquerors themselves with Jews. The anonymous Armenian author of the mid-seventh-century *History of Sebeos*, in contrast, describes Jews and Muslim "Ishmaelites" as brethren and as allies in the conquest of Palestine. Both, he asserts, are heirs of Hagar who lay false claim to the Abrahamic covenant and whose persecution of Christians is foretold by scripture. The author of the *Bet Halé Disputation*, a member of the Syriac-speaking Church of the East writing at the turn of the ninth century, also appeals to Paul's teachings about Hagar's heirs as he makes the case that Christians alone will enjoy the heavenly kingdom, the "Jerusalem above" (Galatians 4:26), notwithstanding the Muslims' present-day power on earth. By reading Muslims into the table of opposites that Christians understood to distinguish themselves from Jews, this author implies that Muslims are quasi-Jewish.

These differences notwithstanding, all three authors rely on the discourse of anti-Judaism to explain who Muslims are and why they rule over Christians; Sophronius and the Bet Halé author also address the ways in which Christians ought to believe and behave in the face of Muslim power. A more fundamental commonality is that these authors disregard information about actual Muslims. The most significant characteristics of the Muslims they describe, including their purported Jewishness, derive entirely from the Bible. This evidence supports a broader claim about Christian responses to the Muslim conquests: to the extent that they describe their conquerors at all, Christian writers render Muslims in biblical terms. Doing so enables these writers to interpret political developments within established theological frameworks.

SOPHRONIUS, SARACENS, AND THE DANGER OF JUDAISM

Sophronius penned what may be the oldest surviving reference to the Muslim conquests in the spring or summer of 634, when he wrote a formal letter to his superior in Constantinople acknowledging his appointment as patriarch of Jerusalem. He concludes this letter with a prayer that God empower the Roman emperors "to break the pride of all the barbarians, and especially of the Saracens who, on account of our sins, have now risen up against us unexpectedly and ravage all with cruel and feral design, with impious and godless audacity." Sophronius's explanation of Saracen violence as the consequence of Christian sinfulness is both traditional and commonplace: the notion that God punishes the sins of God's chosen people through the agency of foreign invaders is prominent in biblical texts and recurs frequently in seventh-century Christian accounts of the short-lived Persian conquest of Palestine. The actual beliefs and motivations of these "barbarians" are irrelevant within this worldview.[4]

Sophronius focuses his Christmas Sermon of 634 on the sins he believes provoked the Saracen invasion, sins he defines as "Jewish" notwithstanding the fact that Christians committed them.[5] At the time of this sermon, the Christian patriarch still governed Jerusalem but Muslim invaders occupied the nearby town of Bethlehem, Jesus's birthplace and the traditional site of Christmas celebrations. "On account of our innumerable sins and grievous failings," explained Sophronius, "because we are unworthy of the contemplation of the divinity, we have been prevented from being there on pilgrimage." Unlike the biblical magi, who fearlessly traveled to greet the newborn Christ, the Jerusalemites are trapped at home, afraid of the invaders: their faith and their deeds are insufficient. If only we followed God's will in true and orthodox faith, the patriarch declares, "we would blunt the Ishmaelite sword, turn back the Saracen dagger, and break the Hagarene bow." Notice that Sophronius does not advocate military engagement with the invaders but rather repentance and faithfulness: the true problem, he teaches, is not the physical might of the Saracens but the spiritual shortcomings of the Christians themselves.

Sophronius proceeds to equate utter faithlessness with Jewishness and to encourage members of his Christian flock to redouble their faith. Unlike the Jews, he declares, "we have accepted the savior Christ and shine with faith in him—indeed, we hate and trample upon the faithlessness of the Jews as something loathsome and, in their total madness, utterly profane." Sophronius does not speak of actual Jews, who had long since been banished from Jerusalem, but instead of the Jews whose rejection of Christ features prominently in several books of the New Testament. Jeremy Cohen, an historian of European Christian ideas about Jews, refers to such figures as "hermeneutical Jews," whose characteristics derive from scholarly engagement with sacred texts, not from familiarity with actual Jews.[6]

Like his early Christian predecessors, Sophronius defines Judaism as the antithesis of Christianity and portrays abhorrence of Jewish characteristics as an essential demonstration of Christian identity: hating the faithlessness of biblical—and, by extension, contemporary—Jews makes manifest one's own faith in Christ as savior. Sophronius does not ascribe similar significance to hatred of present-day Saracens. The proper response to the Saracen invaders, he teaches, is repentance. "If we were to live as is dear and pleasing to God, we would rejoice over the fall of our Saracen adversaries: we would shortly observe their ruin and see their utter destruction. For their bloodthirsty sword will enter into their hearts, their bow will be shattered, and their own arrows stuck in them."

Sophronius envisions not a Roman military victory but the self-destruction of the Saracens in accordance with God's will. Because the patriarch understands the latest incursions into Palestine in terms of Christian sin and divine punishment, he regards repentance and renewed faithfulness as the only essential responses. Seen in this way, the Saracen threat is merely symptomatic of the infection that truly endangers Jerusalem's Christian community: a faithlessness that, if left unchecked, will render Christians metaphorically Jewish. Sophronius, like John Chrysostom and many other Christian rhetoricians, frames this internal danger in terms of Judaism in order to motivate his followers to combat their own sinful characteristics, which Sophronius portrays as alien to their true Christian selves.

Sophronius speaks somewhat differently of the Saracen invaders in his Sermon on Holy Baptism, perhaps delivered in 637; this and the Christmas Sermon are the only surviving sermons in which the patriarch refers to Saracens.[7] Here, Sophronius draws on biblical depictions of the end of days to understand the increasingly successful conquerors. He no longer calls Saracens merely "godless," but rather "God-hating" and "God-fighters"; their leader is the devil himself. Saracens embody "the abomination of desolation clearly foretold to us by the prophets" in their accounts of the terrifying period before Christ's second coming (see Daniel 9:27; Matthew 24:15).

Sophronius's sermon, written in Greek, is the earliest Christian work to read Muslims into apocalyptic prophecies, biblical texts that predict the end of the world as we know it. Similar interpretations appear in a variety of seventh-century Eastern Christian texts, among them the Armenian *History of Sebeos*. Other authors composed new works, most notably the Syriac *Apocalypse of Pseudo-Methodius*, in which postbiblical figures receive divine revelations foretelling the Muslim conquests and the imminent Second Coming of Christ. These works, produced independently in different regions and languages, reflect the widespread Christian practice of using the Bible and biblical frames of reference to explain current events in general and the Muslim conquests in particular. Those who describe Muslims in apocalyptic terms need not—and, for the most part, do not—associate them with Jews.[8]

As in his Christmas Sermon, Sophronius attributes Saracen success entirely to Christ's anger at his own people, this time for their insulting disregard for the gifts of purification and salvation expressed through baptism. Drawing on classic themes of anti-Judaism, the Sermon on Holy Baptism depicts Jews as exemplars of those who reject the true faith, who fail to appreciate the Old Testament as a source of instruction about Christ, and who dismiss the power of baptism by human hands. Sophronius insists that if Christians wish to differentiate themselves from the faithless Jews—and if they want the Saracens to disappear—they must turn to Christ with all their soul in anticipation of the boundless grace promised through the ritual of baptism.

Sophronius repeats John the Baptist's condemnation of Jews who rely solely on their descent from Abraham to save them from divine wrath at the end of days (Matthew 3:7–10). True Christians, the patriarch teaches, emulate Abraham's faith and deeds, whereas Jews allegedly reject both. Sophronius could easily have seized this opportunity to associate Jews and Saracens as the biological yet spurned descendants of Abraham. The patriarch, however, saw no reason to make such an association because he perceived Jews and Muslims to be utterly distinct: Jews constitute the foil for proper Christian belief and practice, while Saracens are agents of the apocalyptic end of history whose beliefs and religious practices are irrelevant. Sophronius does not employ the rhetoric of anti-Judaism to describe Muslims themselves.

Even so, the patriarch's Muslims, no less than his Jews, are "hermeneutical" in Jeremy Cohen's sense of the term. The characteristics of Sophronius's Muslims derive from his interpretation of biblical texts, not from social interaction, familiarity with the conquerors' beliefs and motives, or reports about their unnamed leader. We cannot be certain what the patriarch actually knew about the Muslims to whom he ultimately surrendered Jerusalem because he sees no reason to include such information in his sermons. Sophronius defines both Jews and Muslims on the basis of scripture alone, but he associates these groups with different texts, assigning to each group its own distinctive place within his Christian worldview.

Many later writers, in contrast, perceived value in constructing their hermeneutical Muslims and their hermeneutical Jews out of the same texts and traditions, in effect creating Jewish Muslims. The earliest work to define Muslims themselves by means of anti-Jewish rhetoric is the *History of Sebeos*, composed in the year 655 or shortly thereafter. This chronicle's anonymous Armenian author draws heavily on the end-times prophecies of Daniel to explain later stages of the Muslim conquests, but when recounting the conquest of Palestine he instead references Paul's Letter to the Galatians.[9]

SEBEOS, ISHMAELITES, AND FALSE CLAIMS TO THE ABRAHAMIC COVENANT

"I shall speak of the stock of Abraham, not of the free woman but of that born from the slave woman, concerning which the unerring divine word was fulfilled: 'His hand against everyone, and everyone's hand against him' (Genesis 16:12)."[10] This is how the *History of Sebeos* introduces its lengthy treatment of the Muslim conquests. One might expect the historian to elaborate immediately on the activities of Ishmaelites, the biological descendants of the son to whom the prophecy in Genesis refers. Instead, his account of the Muslim conquest of Palestine begins with and focuses considerable attention on the Jews, whom Christians had long associated with the "slave woman" in Paul's allegory (Galatians 4:22). *Sebeos* makes sense of contemporary Muslims by drawing on the Pauline interpretation of Sarah's heirs as the true church and Hagar's heirs as its Jewish—and now Muslim—rivals.

Right after quoting the Bible's depiction of Ishmael, *Sebeos* reports that "the twelve tribes of the Jews, comprising all their clans, went and gathered at the city of Edessa," a Syrian border town conquered by the Persians but relinquished to the Romans in 629/30 as part of the treaty that ended their war. The reference to the biblical twelve tribes suggests that the Jews who gathered in Edessa represent all the world's Jews. This reference also signals that the historian speaks of hermeneutical, not actual, Jews: as educated Christians knew, most of the twelve tribes disappeared from history during biblical times. The Jews in Edessa sought to prevent Roman forces from entering the city, as befits the biblical enemies of Christ and the persecutors of Christ's followers. The Roman emperor Heraclius besieged Edessa and, when the Jews parlayed for peace, ordered the tribes to return to their areas of habitation. The Jews immediately went to the desert, home of the nomadic Ishmaelites.[11]

The Jews allegedly summoned the Ishmaelites to their aid "and informed them of their blood relationship through the testament of scripture." These Ishmaelites readily acknowledged this Abrahamic kinship, but they could not bring themselves to concerted action on behalf of their Jewish kin until Muhammad, "as if by God's command," unified them in worship of their ancestral deity, the God of Abraham. Muhammad drew on Jewish claims to the Land of Israel in order to rally the Ishmaelites to this faith, saying, "With an oath God promised this land to Abraham and his seed after him forever. And he brought about as he promised during that time while he loved Israel. But now you are the sons of Abraham, and God is accomplishing his promise to Abraham and his seed for you. Love sincerely only the God of Abraham, and go and seize your land which God gave to your father Abraham."[12] The monotheistic Ishmaelites, Muhammad reportedly teaches, are the new heirs of the Bible's Abrahamic covenant. Ghewond, a later Armenian historian familiar with *Sebeos*'s account of the Muslim conquests or, perhaps, the underlying source, reports that the Jews themselves assured Muhammad's followers that God would grant them dominion over Judea on account of their Abrahamic ancestry.[13]

Biblically literate readers would immediately recognize the unfounded nature of these assurances. God promised the land to those who inherit Abraham's covenant, explicitly excluding Ishmael's heirs (Genesis 17:20–21). Not only that; Paul makes clear in Galatians that Christ's followers are the sole heirs of this divine promise, and the Gospels make clear that the Jews have forfeited their genealogical claims to the covenant and its blessings on account of their rejection of Christ (e.g., John 8:37–44). Muslims are like Jews in that both illegitimately lay claim to the covenant and misinterpret the Bible. Although the Ishmaelites' conquest of Palestine succeeded, it cannot possibly constitute the fulfilment of biblical prophecies.

The *History of Sebeos* recounts that the Ishmaelites immediately set off from the region of Havilah and Shur and the wilderness of Paran—the areas in the Sinai Peninsula that the Bible associates with Ishmael and his sons (Genesis 21:21, 25:18)—in a farcical reenactment of the Exodus from Egypt. They divided themselves into twelve tribes, albeit in accordance with the sons of Ishmael (25:13–16) rather than those of Jacob/Israel. Instead of marching straight toward the Promised Land by way of Gaza, the Ishmaelites reportedly retraced the circuitous route of the biblical Israelites. (Other sources report a major battle between Muslims and Romans near Gaza in 634 CE, but inclusion of information about that event would have undermined this chronicler's efforts to depict the Ishmaelites as mimicking the Israelites.) East of the Jordan River, the Ishmaelites defeated Roman forces exactly as the biblical Israelites wreaked vengeance on the Midianites: in both cases, a thousand men from each of the twelve tribes set out from the Plains of Moab to confront their adversaries (Numbers 31:1–12).[14]

The Jews, meanwhile, purportedly formed a large army of their own and issued an ultimatum to the Romans: "God gave that land [i.e., Palestine] to our father Abraham as a hereditary possession and to his seed after them. We are the sons of Abraham. You have occupied our land long enough. Abandon it peacefully and we shall not come into your territory. Otherwise, we shall demand that possession from you with interest."[15] The "we" to whom these Jews refer evidently includes the Ishmaelites; the emperor certainly understood it that way, as he retorted, "Your lot of inheritance is the desert," and proceeded to send troops to Arabia (that is, the region of the present-day country of Jordan). After this disastrously ill-advised attack, perhaps a reference to the decisive Battle of Yarmuk (636 CE) that established Muslim control over the region, "they"—Jews and Ishmaelites alike—crossed the river without resistance and camped at Jericho, just as the Israelites do in the Bible.

By associating Jews with Ishmaelites, by portraying the Ishmaelites as mimicking the behavior of biblical Israelites, and by blurring the line between these Ishmaelites and contemporaneous Jews, *Sebeos* renders the Muslim conquerors as would-be Jews who lay claim to Palestine on account of their association with Abraham and the People of Israel. The anti-Christian behavior of the Jews in this story, however, confirms that Jews are not the true heirs of Isaac either. Ishmaelite efforts to behave like Jews are thus not only ridiculous but also futile: their own actions, like those of the Jews, reinforce their common status as heirs of Hagar the slave. The Armenian historian's introductory allusion to Paul's allegory of Sarah and Hagar primes his well-educated audience to understand this entire narrative in light of Paul's message that Christians alone participate in the divine covenant and that their contemporary rivals persecute the followers of Christ just as Ishmael once persecuted Isaac.

The theme of Jewish enmity toward Christians also animates a later chapter in the *History of Sebeos*, according to which the prince who governed Jerusalem after the Muslim conquest was himself "from among the Jews." Fellow Jews falsely accused Christians of defiling the city's Ishmaelite house of prayer with the blood of pigs, and only the testimony of a pious Muslim witness prevented the prince from using this allegation as a pretext for massacring the Christian population. Jews, in short, seek not only to seize control of Palestine from the Christians but also "to exterminate all the Christians of Jerusalem." Ishmaelites eagerly abet these Jewish efforts and likewise persecute the true beneficiaries of God's promise to Abraham. Unlike Sophronius, who saw no reason to associate Muslims with Jews, this chronicler finds value in portraying Muslims as participants in the timeless enmity between the heirs of Hagar and Sarah.[16]

The *History of Sebeos*'s account of the Muslim conquest of Palestine is so closely patterned on the Hebrew Bible that it has limited value as a record of seventh-century events, let alone of the beliefs that actually motivated Muslim conquerors. The work's rhetorical power, however, rests not on historical accuracy but on the way in which its author situates Muslims within biblical frames of reference and, more specifically, within the table of opposites that Paul constructs in Galatians. The Armenian historian emphasizes the Ishmaelites' descent from Abraham's slave and their persecution of Christians. He highlights their fleshly claims to the Abrahamic covenant and the present-day Jerusalem, claims that he portrays as stemming from a fundamentally flawed reading of scripture. The Ishmaelites who appear in the *History of*

Sebeos are just as hermeneutical as their Jewish counterparts in that both are depicted entirely on the basis of biblical texts; in fact, many of their purported beliefs and practices stem from the same passages. Through this representation, the Armenian historian contends that the Muslim conquests do not represent a new threat but rather the latest version of the timeless conflict between the heirs of Sarah and Hagar, a conflict in which Sarah's heirs ultimately prevail. Audiences familiar with Genesis and Galatians can therefore be confident in the eventual triumph of Christians over their rivals.

THE MONK, THE MUSLIM, AND THE STATUS OF CHRISTIANITY

The *History of Sebeos* associates Muslims and Jews so closely that it is sometimes unclear whether this work attributes particular acts to Jews or to Muslims. The *Disputation between a Muslim and a Monk of Bet Halé*, a Syriac text written in Iraq around the turn of the ninth century, portrays Muslims in an entirely different fashion. Jews appear only once in this work where, as in Sophronius's sermons, they constitute a foil for proper Christian faith unrelated to Muslims. Although the anonymous author of the *Bet Halé Disputation* draws many of his arguments from an earlier anti-Jewish work, he in no way suggests that his Muslim character is Jewish. Like the *History of Sebeos*, however, the *Bet Halé Disputation* nonetheless renders Muslims "Jew-ish" by employing Pauline rhetoric about the true relationship between the free woman and the slave.[17]

The *Bet Halé Disputation* recounts a fictional debate between a powerful Muslim official and a humble monk affiliated with the Church of the East, the predominant Christian community in Iraq. The purpose of Christian disputation literature is to reinforce the self-confidence of Christian audiences, so it comes as no surprise that the Muslim ultimately concedes the truth of Christianity. A central motif of this particular text is the imbalance in power and status between the debate partners. In the opening section of the work, the monk-narrator repeatedly describes himself and his community as "weak" and "of low estate" while the Muslim, a former steward of the emirate, is "very great" and quite overbearing. By the end of the disputation, however, the monk demonstrates that Christians in fact hold a higher status than Muslims despite their powerlessness. The Bet Halé author marks this inversion by changing the way in which he refers to Muslims.

The primary term for the Muslim participant in the *Bet Halé Disputation* is *tayyaya*. This Syriac word, like the originally Greek term *Saracen*, initially referred to a specific Arab tribe but over time came to refer to all Muslims, to the exclusion of Arab Christians; in this work, the term carries neither positive nor negative connotations. The narrator, however, introduces his debate partner as "the son of Ishmael." This is not a mere synonym: throughout this text, the monk refers to Muslims as "children of Ishmael" specifically when he addresses their political dominion.[18] For that reason, we should understand this opening depiction as the first of many references to the Muslim official's this-worldly power, recalling that the Bible describes Ishmael as "a wild ass of a man, with his hand against everyone" (Genesis 16:12). The monk-narrator's rhetoric about contemporary Muslims also calls to mind Paul's words about the ongoing nature of Ishmael's behavior: "Just as at that time the child who was born according to the flesh persecuted the child who was born according to the Spirit, so it is now also" (Galatians 4:29).

The disputation itself begins with the Muslim laying out several arguments for the superiority of Islam over all other religions. His culminating proof of divine favor toward Islam is that God "has given us authority over all faiths and all peoples." The monk rebuts this point first, contending that "you children of Ishmael, you control a small part of the earth, and it is not the case that the whole of creation is subjected to your authority."[19] The power that Muslims possess, therefore, does not signify divine favor. The conversation then shifts to matters of ritual and faith, beginning with several practices that the author explicitly relates to Abraham, Ishmael's father. The monk patiently explains why Christians perform baptism instead of circumcision, why they regard Abraham's near sacrifice of Isaac (Genesis 22) as the foreshadowing of Jesus's crucifixion, and why they celebrate the Eucharist instead of offering animal sacrifices as Abraham did.

The monk proceeds to address queries regarding the three-in-one nature of God as Father, Son, and Holy Spirit; Christian reverence of crosses and other physical objects; and the Christian practice of facing eastward during prayer. The "disputation" has turned into a question and answer session, and the critical modern reader cannot help but suspect that the Bet Halé author places in the mouth of his Muslim character precisely those questions that he thought might trouble members of his Christian audience. More significantly, the author draws both his questions and answers from earlier works that feature Jewish foils. He also draws heavily on scriptural evidence to justify contentious aspects of Christianity, as his fictional Muslim concedes the authority of proofs drawn from the Old Testament. (We will return to this text in chapter 5, which examines Eastern Christian portrayals of Muslims as adherents of the Old Testament.)[20]

It is in this context that Jews make their only explicit appearance in the *Bet Halé Disputation*. When the Muslim challenges the Christian practice of worshipping the cross, the monk explains that the cross deserves such veneration: it was the means by which Jesus saved those who believe in him, it continues to work miracles for the faithful, and it will eventually signal Christ's second coming. Present-day Jews, the monk declares, are ashamed to look on this sign of eternal Christian victory because they crucified their Lord. (Notice the conflation of contemporary and biblical Jews, a telltale sign of rhetoric about hermeneutical Jews.) "Anyone who is a Christian but does not worship the cross and does not gaze upon it as though on Christ, truly he is lost from life." True Christians revere the cross; those who fail to do so judaize and, because they adopt Jewish characteristics, forfeit the eternal life of God's heavenly kingdom.[21]

Like Sophronius and pre-Islamic Christian writers, the monk of Bet Halé uses Jewish disbelief to reinforce his conception of how Christians themselves ought to believe and behave. The practice of venerating physical objects was under pressure in the late eighth and early ninth centuries as some Muslims—and some powerful Christians—actively opposed the use of icons. As we will see in chapter 10, contemporaneous polemicists alleged that Jews inspired this hostility toward the veneration of objects and images. The humble monk, however, defends the practice of cross worship without attacking Muslims for judaizing. Such a slur, after all, would be out of character for a figure who emphasizes the power imbalance between Christians and Muslims and, as we will see, who regards his own powerlessness as a sign of Christianity's favored status.

The Muslim professes himself to be fully convinced by the monk's responses to his queries about Christian beliefs and practices, but he still struggles with the issue of Muslim power: "I acknowledge that your religion is seemly, and also that your way of thinking is better than ours, so for what reason did God deliver you into our hands?" The monk begins his response by recounting a series of biblical instances in which God subjected the Children of Israel to oppression at the hands of foreign rulers.

> And you also, children of Ishmael, God did not give you power over us because of your own righteousness, but because of our sins, and because God loves us and does not wish to deprive us of the heavenly kingdom. For it is said: "Those whom God loves God chastises," and "if you remain with-

out chastisement you will be strangers and not God's children." The good and merciful God desired to chastise us in this passing world of brief and fleeting life so that there [in the heavenly kingdom] God might cause us to inherit eternal life.[22]

Christian powerlessness reflects not a debased status before God but rather divine favor: only legitimate children receive discipline from their loving parents. More importantly, this suffering prepares God's favored people to receive a far greater reward not in this world, but in the eternal afterlife. The monk, like Sophronius and in keeping with biblical precedents, depicts his foreign overlords as God's unwitting agents.

Whereas Sophronius and the author of *Sebeos* perceive the Muslim conquests as a sign of the impending end-times, the *Bet Halé Disputation* offers no suggestion that Christ's second coming is imminent. At the time of its composition, after all, Muslims had ruled for over 150 years with no end in sight. The monk of Bet Halé instead points to the duration of the Muslims' chastisement-free rule to demonstrate that God regards the children of Ishmael as strangers or foreigners whose power in "this passing world of brief and fleeting life" is ultimately meaningless. God does not care about Muslims as such, so Christians need not do so either; instead, they should focus on the eternal prize.

The monk's prioritization of the heavenly kingdom over the present world sets the stage for the Muslim's final question, which he prefaces by reminding the monk to answer truthfully without regard for his social status: "Will the children of Hagar enter the kingdom, or not?" This reference to Hagar, unique within the *Bet Halé Disputation*, calls to mind Paul's allegory, in which Hagar's heirs possess the present-day Jerusalem but only Sarah's heirs can lay claim to its heavenly counterpart. The monk explains that although a Muslim with fine deeds will escape hell and dwell in mansions just outside paradise, "he shall be considered as a hired hand, not as a son." As Christ himself declared, "Anyone who is not born of water and the Spirit shall not see the kingdom of God" (John 3:5).[23] Hagar's heirs cannot attain the same privileged status as Christian children of the Spirit no matter how well they conduct their lives. Readers of Galatians commonly understand Jews to be the spiritual heirs of Hagar, but the *Bet Halé Disputation* reads Muslims into this lineage as well.

The *Bet Halé Disputation* differs from the *History of Sebeos* in that it never directly links Muslims with Jews, but both ascribe to Muslims at least half of the negative characteristics on Paul's table of opposites, which later Christians commonly understood in terms of Judaism

TABLE 3   ELEMENTS OF PAUL'S TABLE OF OPPOSITES APPEARING IN EASTERN
CHRISTIAN DEPICTIONS OF MUSLIMS

	Negative characteristics	History of Sebeos	Bet Halé Disputation
State of salvation	Cursed		x
Grounds of salvation	Law revealed at Sinai		
Prerequisite for salvation	Works of Law, including circumcision		x
Associated with	Flesh	x	
Status	Imprisoned		
Identity	Slaves	x	
Interpretation of scripture	Flawed	x	x
Figurative ancestors	Hagar, Ishmael	x	x
Homeland	Present-day Jerusalem	x	
Behavior	Persecute believers	x	x

(table 3). Muslims, the Bet Halé author teaches, are the descendants of Hagar and Ishmael; they fail to interpret scripture properly; they remain preoccupied with fleshly circumcision; and they violently persecute Christians. Even Muslims with fine deeds cannot enter the heavenly kingdom because they do not participate in God's true covenant. By using Pauline rhetoric to depict these Muslims as quasi-Jewish, this author seeks to bolster the commitment of his Christian audience to the beliefs and practices that Paul associates with the true followers of Christ.

Recall that the Galatian community suffered from what Paul describes as persecution, and its members lacked the ability to take direct action against their rivals. Christians who found themselves in a similar position relative to Muslims may have regarded this community as a role model. The History of Sebeos and the Bet Halé Disputation both employ Pauline rhetoric to reiterate the underlying message of Galatians: Christians should stand firm in their faith and differentiate themselves from their more powerful rivals despite the persecution they experience. By demonstrating that Muslims, like Jews, are nothing more than Hagar's heirs, these works also hold out hope that Christians, like Sarah and Isaac, will have the last laugh. The very act of depicting Muslims in biblical terms reinforces the authority and trustworthiness of the Bible itself, which, as Sophronius and Paul himself also emphasized, not only describes the past but explains and offers guidance for the present as well.

CHAPTER 3

"Drive Out the Slave and Her Son"

Eleventh through Fourteenth Centuries

Paul's allegorical reading of the Sarah and Hagar story is not merely an exercise in biblical interpretation, nor is it solely an attempt to use past events to make sense of present-day dynamics within Paul's community of Christ-followers. Paul demands action: he seeks to persuade the Galatians to embrace his teachings and, in so doing, to forcefully reject those who fall on the wrong side of the binary he constructs. Paul grounds the second portion of this agenda in Genesis 21:10, the only biblical verse regarding Abraham's wives that Paul quotes. "What does the scripture say? 'Drive out the slave and her son; for the son of the slave will not share the inheritance with the son of the free woman'" (Galatians 4:30).

The version of this verse within Genesis itself explicitly addresses a one-time act. Sarah, speaking to Abraham, demands that he expel "*this* slave and her son"—not, as Paul says, "*the* slave"—"for the son of *this* slave will not share in the inheritance with *my son, Isaac*" (emphases added). Paul adds another layer of meaning to this verse by speaking more generally about "the son of the free woman": he teaches that Sarah speaks not only to her husband but also, on the allegorical plane, to contemporary followers of Christ. After all, Paul declares that the members of his community "are children of the promise, like Isaac," and that Paul's circumcision-promoting rivals trouble this community just as Ishmael persecuted his brother (Galatians 4:28–29).[1] Only children of the Spirit will inherit the kingdom of God, and they should not tolerate those who are fleshly in orientation. God instructs Abraham to obey Sarah's order, and Paul similarly instructs his followers, the figurative heirs of Abraham and Sarah, to drive out Hagar's figurative heirs. Paul's allegorical interpretation of Genesis generates new implications from within this ancient, sacred text.

Paul and his Galatian followers lacked the power necessary to carry out this instruction literally. Later generations of Christians, however, understood Paul to speak to them as well, and many of those who could do so reenacted Abraham and Sarah's maltreatment of Hagar and Ishmael by driving out or physically harming their own rivals. So, for example, Augustine appeals to Sarah and Paul to justify violence against a group of fourth- and fifth-century Christians whose beliefs he condemned. "When God wishes to stir up the authorities against heretics, against schismatics, against the wreckers of the Church," he declares, "this is God stirring up Sarah to give Hagar a beating." In Genesis, Sarah beats Hagar so badly that Hagar flees to the wilderness (16:6); Augustine urges Roman forces to do the same to errant Christians of his own day.[2]

We saw in chapter 1 that Augustine and other Christians who lived before the rise of Islam understood Paul to refer not only to heretics but also and primarily to adherents of Judaism, which these readers regarded as the archetypal rival of Christianity. Chapter 2 examined ways in which Christians subject to Muslim domination applied the Pauline depiction of Hagar's spiritual heirs to their conquerors as well. These Eastern Christians, who were in no position to punish or expel their Muslim rivals, drew on Galatians to make sense of the persecution they experienced. The present chapter focuses on a much more powerful group of Christians: those who lived in medieval Western Europe and entertained visions of extending Christian dominion into majority-Muslim lands. These Christians could readily apply the New Testament's command, "drive out the slave and her son," to their own political circumstances precisely because Paul, Augustine, and other authorities taught that this order does not refer solely to a one-time event. European Christians applied Paul's allegory of Hagar and Sarah to Muslims in order to legitimate and motivate anti-Muslim violence in the form of conquests of Muslim-ruled lands and expulsion of Muslims from conquered territories.

Paul's words, however, do not inevitably generate policies of expulsion. Augustine, for example, identified Jews as the heirs of Hagar but nevertheless insisted that Jews ought to live within Christendom. Jews, Augustine taught on the basis of other biblical texts, play essential roles for Christians: they attest to the authenticity of Old Testament prophecies that Christians believe refer to Jesus Christ, and they demonstrate through their subjugation the punishment that befalls those who misinterpret these prophecies. Even Christians who possess the power to expel Jews from their midst should not do so, Augustine maintained, so that Jews can continue to serve as unwitting witnesses to Christian truth claims. Augustine's ideas about Jews shaped European Christian thought for many centuries, but we will see in this chapter and, especially, in chapter 11 that new ideas came to the fore in the late Middle Ages. Because the Bible and its interpretative tradition contain multiple voices and perspectives, Christians possessed a range of authoritative traditions from which to select those best suited to their own circumstances and objectives.[3]

This chapter begins with a work of church art created around the year 1100 whose depiction of Hagar and Ishmael as contemporary Muslims legitimates military action against Spain's Muslim kingdoms by framing such action in terms of the timeless conflict between Christianity and its rivals. The anti-Jewish overtones that Christians commonly perceived in biblical stories about Abraham's wives and sons animate this image and underpin its political message even though the work features Muslim villains rather than Jews. We will then consider ways in which twelfth-century rhetoric associated with the Crusades, holy wars that sought to reclaim Christian territory from Christendom's enemies, could inadvertently motivate violence not only against Muslims but against Jews as well. The application of anti-Jewish rhetoric to Muslims, after all, reinforces long-standing ideas about Jewish enmity toward Christ and Christians. The chapter concludes by examining legal literature regarding the proper treatment of Muslim and Jewish populations subject to Christian rule. We will focus on the work of Oldradus de Ponte, a fourteenth-century lawyer in the papal court who argued that Paul's teachings authorize not only military aggression in Spain but also the expulsion from Christian kingdoms of Jews and Muslims alike. His works illustrate the ways in which Christians could either conflate or distinguish a biblical text's anti-Muslim and anti-Jewish layers of meaning depending on the interpreter's agenda. Oldradus and others chose to brand Muslims as Jewish precisely when their objective was to render Muslims as biblical/theological and not merely political/military enemies of Christendom—in other words, when they sought to portray the contemporary Christian-Muslim conflict as analogous to the timeless conflict between the heirs of Sarah and Hagar.

PAUL AND CHRISTIAN CONQUEST IN
THE KINGDOM OF LEÓN

Twelfth-century pilgrims traveling the popular route to Santiago de Compostela, as well as other members of the general public, often visited the Church of San Isidoro in León, capital city of what was, at the time, the most powerful Christian kingdom in present-day Spain. This church, patronized by the royal family, contained the relics of two saints: Isidore of Seville (d. 636), the most renowned bishop of Spain's Visigothic (pre-Islamic) era, and Pelagius (d. 925), who, according to traditional accounts, was martyred because he refused the sexual advances of a Muslim king. Visitors entered the church through a massive doorway flanked by statues of these saintly embodiments of Visigothic greatness and defiance of Muslims. Atop this doorway, constructed around the year 1100, is a monumental sculpture known as the Lamb Tympanum whose innovative depiction of Abraham, his sons, and his wives generates a powerful set of messages about the efforts of Leonese monarchs to conquer Muslim territory and restore Christian rule over the entire Iberian Peninsula (fig. 1). King Alfonso VI (r. 1072–1109) took a dramatic step toward realizing that vision by seizing the ancient Visigothic capital of Toledo from Muslim control in 1085.[4]

The Lamb Tympanum depicts the climactic episode in Abraham's life: God instructs Abraham to offer his beloved son, Isaac, as a sacrifice, and Abraham dutifully prepares to do so, only to be stopped at the last moment; he sacrifices an animal instead of his son (Genesis 22). The center of the sculpture features Abraham with his knife, Isaac bound for slaughter, and, above them, the Lamb of God, which symbolizes Christ's self-sacrifice on behalf of the Christian faithful. The message of this juxtaposition is clear and conventional: Abraham and Isaac prefigure the ultimate sacrifice made by the divine Father and Son. Isidore of Seville, in his influential remarks on this biblical passage, draws particular attention to the Jews' persecution of Jesus and their inability to understand this sacrifice.[5]

Lamb of God imagery, however, usually appears in artwork surrounding the eucharistic altar, where it reinforces belief in the ritual reenactment of Christ's sacrifice. Art on the exterior of twelfth-century churches in Spain and France tends instead to convey social and political messages. The Lamb Tympanum does just that by illustrating not only the Sacrifice of Isaac but also Paul's allegory of Hagar and Sarah, an exceedingly rare subject in medieval art but especially relevant in the

FIGURE 1. The Lamb Tympanum atop the south portal of the Church of San Isidoro, León (ca. 1100). (Photo: Antonio García Omedes, courtesy of the photographer.)

context of this church. Paul's rhetoric about emulating the behavior of one's ancestors dovetails with the efforts of Leonese royalty to stress their own Visigothic ancestry and gain dominion over territory that the Visigoths once governed. Although Paul himself obviously did not have Muslims in mind, his rhetoric about Hagar and Ishmael resonated with special force in the capital city of a Spanish kingdom bent on driving out Muslim rulers.[6]

Sarah, symbolic mother of the Christian faithful, appears in the bottom right of the tympanum (fig. 2). She stands in a doorway, just as she did when she received the promise that she would bear a son in her old age (Genesis 18:10). Paul teaches that this promise refers to the sacrifice of Jesus Christ on behalf of those who live by faith (Galatians 3:13–14), the very sacrifice depicted in the central portion of the Lamb Tympanum. Sarah, who gazes toward the Sacrifice of Isaac and the Lamb of God above it, represents those who believe in the power of Christ's crucifixion and in the truth of Christ's resurrection—Jesus, like Isaac, survives his ordeal. Isaac himself appears three times on the Lamb Tympanum, in the medieval equivalent of a cartoon strip that progresses from right to left:

FIGURE 2. From right to left: Sarah in doorway, Isaac on donkey, Isaac removing shoes, Abraham about to sacrifice Isaac; detail (lower right) from the Lamb Tympanum. (Photo: Antonio García Omedes, courtesy of the photographer.)

he rides a donkey toward the site of the sacrifice, removes his shoes when he reaches holy ground, and submits to the sacrificial blade.

Hagar and Ishmael, meanwhile, appear on the far left of the tympanum (fig. 3). In contrast to Sarah's chastity and faithfulness, Hagar lifts her skirt in a gesture that demonstrates her licentiousness. Ishmael the archer (Genesis 21:20) aims his trademark bow and arrow toward the Lamb of God. His murderous gesture calls to mind the first-century Jews who sought Jesus's death, but the Lamb Tympanum's Ishmael does not represent the Jews. He wears a turban, a clear marker of Muslim identity in Iberian art of the period, and he rides his horse in the manner of the Muslim warriors against whom Leonese soldiers fought. The Lamb Tympanum associates these warriors with Ishmael and with Paul's rivals, all of whom persecute faithful Christians (Galatians 4:29). Hagar's pose calls to mind not only Christian stereotypes of contemporary Muslims as lustful and dangerously seductive but also Paul's warning that children of the Spirit should not engage in works of the flesh such as fornication and licentiousness (5:16–21). The eleventh-century heirs of Hagar and Ishmael follow the example set by their biblical ancestors, and Leonese Christians, as "children of the promise, like Isaac" (4:28), should likewise emulate their own spiritual ancestors.[7]

The Lamb Tympanum is one of several Iberian works that draws on rhetoric about Ishmael to polemicize against Islam. A contemporary of the tympanum's sculptors cites Muhammad's descent from Hagar and

FIGURE 3. Ishmael on horseback, Hagar lifting skirt; detail (lower left) from the Lamb Tympanum. (Photo: Antonio García Omedes, courtesy of the photographer.)

Ishmael as evidence that he must be inferior to Christ, who descends from Isaac and therefore inherited the divine promise.[8] A later author presents biblical evidence that Ishmael and Hagar are excluded from God's covenant with Abraham as proof that Islam must be false.[9] Paul, of course, uses that same logic to clinch his argument against rivals within the Christ-believing community: they purportedly resemble Hagar in their fleshliness and their slavish fealty to Old Testament law and, for that reason, deserve to be driven out of the church.

The Lamb Tympanum, however, offers an even sharper anti-Muslim message because of the ways in which it reads Muslims into the standard anti-Jewish interpretation of Paul's allegory offered by Isidore of Seville and many others. Muslims are not merely excluded from the Abrahamic covenant and inferior to Christians as Ishmael is inferior to Isaac, they also take the place traditionally assigned to Jews as rivals and persecutors of the true believers. The tympanum's representation of local Muslims as the descendants of Hagar in a scene that typically focuses on the difference between Christianity and Judaism serves to render these Muslims not only as contemporary political rivals but also and more fundamentally as timeless theological enemies condemned by the Bible itself.

By opposing Ishmael not only to Isaac but also to the Lamb of God, the Lamb Tympanum elevates the mundane conflict between Spanish kingdoms to existential proportions: Muslims, like Jews, are the enemies of Christ, whom Christians defend by attacking their Muslim rivals. As such, this work of art suggests that León's military campaigns constitute far more than mere land grabs: they reflect faithful obedience to the divine will expressed by Sarah and reframed by Paul: "drive out the slave and her son." The success of these campaigns constitutes a fulfillment of the blessing that God gave Abraham after his near sacrifice of Isaac: "your offspring shall possess the gates of their enemies" (Genesis 22:17). The Lamb Tympanum, with its accompanying statues of Isidore and Pelagius, proclaims that the king of León is heir not only to the Visigoths and the tradition of Christian resistance to Muslim rulers but also to the Abrahamic promise itself. This work of art reinforces the message that Leonese monarchs play a leading role in the eternal battle between Christianity and its antithesis and, for this reason, deserve to rule over all of Spain. Traditional anti-Jewish rhetoric animates the Lamb Tympanum even though this work depicts not Jews but rather quasi-Jewish Muslims whom it reads into an especially significant biblical scene.

ANTI-MUSLIM—AND ANTI-JEWISH—VIOLENCE IN THE ERA OF CRUSADES

Knights from the region of present-day France played crucial roles in Leonese assaults on nearby Muslim kingdoms. These Franks were motivated not only by the prospect of material rewards but also by a papal offer to release warriors on the Spanish frontier from the torments of hell they would otherwise suffer on account of their previous sins. The knights evidently assaulted not only Muslims but Jews as well, prompting Pope Alexander II to express concern about their overzealousness in a letter he sent to Spain's bishops in 1063. The pope praised bishops for protecting their local Jewish communities and insisted that "there is in fact a difference between the case of the Jews and that of the Saracens. It is just to fight against the latter, who persecute Christians and expel them from their cities and their own residences. The former, however, are everywhere prepared to be subservient." Muslims, in other words, are legitimate targets of Christian violence because they emulate Ishmael, their ancestor; the pope's use of the term "persecute" alludes to Galatians 4:29. Jews, in contrast, have a right to dwell in peace within Christendom because they accept the servile position that befits the spiritual heirs of Hagar and that enables Jews to serve as witnesses to Christian truth claims—the role Augustine ascribed to them.[10]

Paul's injunction to "drive out the slave and her son," Alexander II insists, applies to Muslims but not to Jews. Many Christian warriors, however, saw little reason to distinguish Jews from Muslims. When Frankish knights set off in 1096 to battle Muslims in what historians call the First Crusade, they slaughtered hundreds of European Jews along their route toward Jerusalem. The use of traditional anti-Jewish rhetoric to motivate holy warfare against Muslims presumably contributed to this violence.

Pope Urban II called for a military campaign to liberate Jerusalem, and Eastern Christendom more broadly, from Muslim domination, and he offered participants in this "crusade" the same release from the torments of hell that his predecessors granted to warriors on the Spanish frontier. The original version of Urban's inspirational sermon no longer survives, but its anti-Muslim rhetoric clearly struck a nerve. Historian Jonathan Riley-Smith estimates that well over one hundred thousand Europeans participated in the First Crusade alone, and he notes that many more of their family members must also have agreed to sacrifice their own resources to support this extraordinarily expensive endeavor. Despite long odds, in 1099 crusaders captured what they began to call the "Holy Land," and European rulers maintained control over Jerusalem until 1187.[11]

Crusaders sought to exact vengeance on Muslims, whom they perceived as illegitimate occupiers of the Holy Land, desecrators of churches, and merciless tormenters of Christians. Robert the Monk was one of several early crusade chroniclers who reported that Pope Urban II himself portrayed Muslims in this fashion so as to stir up a desire for revenge. Robert's version of Urban's crusade sermon draws on a familiar anti-Jewish trope to render Muslims especially despicable: Muslims, the pope purportedly declared, forcibly "circumcise Christians and pour the resulting blood either on the altars or into the baptismal vessels." Polemicists had long accused Jews of forcibly circumcising Christians, an allegation that persisted throughout the Middle Ages and that derives its force in part from Paul's charge that his rivals "persecuted" the Galatians by compelling circumcision.[12]

Rhetoric of this nature, however, is liable to stir up vengefulness not only toward Muslims but also toward Jews, and some crusaders regarded Muslims and Jews as distinct yet equally legitimate targets of Christian retribution. Bands of warriors massacred Jewish communities in Europe, "claiming that this was the beginning of their crusade and service against the enemies of Christianity," as Albert of Aachen reports in his chronicle. Neither the pope nor any other Catholic official called for anti-Jewish violence in this context; many, in fact, condemned or sought to prevent these massacres, in keeping with the teachings of Augustine and Alexander II. Riley-Smith observes, however, that "in respect of the desire for vengeance a significant number of crusaders did not distinguish between Muslims and Jews and could not understand why, if they were called upon to take up arms against the former, they should not also persecute the latter." Anti-Muslim rhetoric did not negate anti-Jewish sentiments and could actually intensify them, intentionally or otherwise, because this rhetoric often employed biblical themes long associated with Jews and Judaism, including Paul's allegory of Hagar and Sarah.[13]

William of Tyre, a late twelfth-century historian writing in the Latin Kingdom of Jerusalem, imagined that the First Crusade was inspired not by a desire for vengeance but by the Bible: his version of Pope Urban II's sermon features soaring rhetoric grounded in dozens of scriptural references. Paul's allegory holds pride of place in this sermon, where it introduces Urban's description of the present Jerusalem.

> The cradle of our salvation, the fatherland of our Lord, the mother of religion, is now forcibly held by a godless people, the son of the Egyptian slave woman. Upon the captive sons of the free woman he imposes desperate conditions under which he himself deserves to serve enduringly, the relations being reversed. But what is written? "Drive out the slave and her son."

Paul's version of God's command constitutes an especially direct prooftext to justify the crusading enterprise.[14]

William was one of many Crusade chroniclers who condemned assaults on Jewish communities as outrageous excesses of the undisciplined masses: crusading activity, he believed, should target Muslims alone. Even his rhetoric, however, carries the seeds of anti-Jewish violence. William's identification of Muslims as the heirs of Hagar, after all, does not displace Jews from that traditional role. Even though William adds a new layer of meaning to the interpretive tradition, the older reading remains available to those who wish to use it. In fact, a mid-fourteenth century author used William's depiction of the crusaders' violent conquest of Muslim Jerusalem as a model for his own portrayal of the Romans who massacred the city's Jews in the first century.[15]

The dynamics associated with layering anti-Muslim rhetoric on top of long-standing anti-Jewish interpretations of Paul's allegory are especially apparent in a Psalms commentary composed in the mid-twelfth century. The anonymous commentator, introducing Psalm 5, explains the contemporary significance of Sarah and Hagar as follows: "The free woman signifies the New Law, her son Isaac denotes the Christian people. The slave woman is the Old Law, her son Ishmael is the infidel horde." This commentator, following the traditional line of interpretation, understands Paul's declaration that the two women are two covenants (Galatians 4:24) in reference to the Jewish Old Testament and the Christian New Testament. Now, however, those who oppose Christians are not Jews but rather Ishmaelite "infidels"—that is, the crusaders' Muslim enemies. Anti-Jewish and anti-Muslim interpretations of Paul's allegory literally appear in the same sentence, inviting readers to conflate the two groups.[16]

Anti-Jewish interpretations of Psalm 5 have a distinguished pedigree that goes back to Jerome, the fourth-century author of the standard Latin translation of the Bible. The enormously popular Interlinear Gloss to this psalm, for example, channels Paul in its explanation that the psalm's opening inscription, "Unto the end, for her that obtains the inheritance," refers to "the free woman, that is, Sarah, as opposed to Hagar, that is, the Synagogue." Anti-Muslim interpretations begin to complement this traditional anti-Jewish reading during the era of the Crusades. To cite another example, the prologue to Psalm 5 in the mid-twelfth-century Eadwine Psalter rehearses the standard explanation that Hagar represents the Jews while Sarah represents the gentile Church but then adds that Hagar also represents the "infidels," most likely a reference to Muslims. "Although the Church is now seen by the infidels as contemptuous and dishonorable, in the future the infidels will be driven out by the one who eternally obtains the inheritance." Crusade chroniclers and psalms commentators alike added new layers of meaning to biblical texts and long-standing tropes without challenging or even obscuring earlier interpretations. If anything, anti-Muslim readings of biblical texts served to highlight their anti-Jewish dimensions. To the extent that polemicists used these interpretations to motivate violence, Jews and Muslims alike could suffer the consequences even if polemicists themselves sought to distinguish these groups.[17]

LEGITIMATING THE CONQUEST AND EXPULSION
OF PEACEFUL MUSLIMS AND JEWS

Pope Alexander II's words about Saracens as legitimate targets of violence and Jews as illegitimate targets found their way into the *Decretum Gratiani,* a twelfth-century collection of canon law that, along with the thirteenth-century collection called the *Liber extra,* defined proper and improper behavior within the Roman Catholic Church until the early twentieth century. The pope's distinction, however, proved short-lived because of changing political circumstances. When Leonese and other Christian kings actually conquered Muslim territories, they sought to persuade Muslims to remain in place—otherwise, the local economy and tax base would collapse. Unlike Alexander II, who sought to safeguard docile Jewish populations within Christian Spain, interpreters of his words needed to justify the continued presence of docile Muslim populations. They did so by emphasizing the pope's rationale: if Saracens, like Jews, are willing to be subservient to Christian rulers, then Christians should not drive them out either. Many supported this argument by citing a Roman law from the Code of Justinian that prohibits Christians from disturbing peaceful Jews or pagans. Lawyers regarded this precedent as relevant because they treated Muslims as legally equivalent to pagans; recognizing that Muslims are neither Jews nor Christian heretics, premodern lawyers often placed Muslims in the only remaining category within traditional Christian conceptions of humanity.[18]

Oldradus de Ponte (d. ca. 1337), a lawyer in the papal court of Avignon, confronted a different set of political circumstances. The last remaining Muslim kingdom in the Iberian Peninsula, based in Granada, posed no military threat by the early fourteenth century, but Christian kings sought to conquer it notwithstanding the legal norm that peaceful Muslims should not suffer attack. Meanwhile, to the north, King Edward I expelled all Jews from England in 1290 and King Philip IV of France followed suit in 1306, despite the norm that subservient Jews ought to dwell within Christian domains. As we will see in chapter 10, the debate over retaining or expelling Jews remained lively in France after Philip's son allowed some Jews to return in 1315. Sometime during this period, Oldradus weighed in with a series of carefully argued opinions that justified the conquest and expulsion of peaceful Muslims and Jews despite explicit norms to the contrary. His briefs, called *consilia* (singular: *consilium*), rely heavily on biblical rhetoric about Hagar, whom Oldradus associates with Muslims primarily by way of prooftexts that portray Hagar as the figurative ancestor of contemporary Jews.[19]

Oldradus opens Consilium 72, on "Whether a war against the Saracens of Spain is licit," by suggesting that the answer is no: "It is evident that those wishing to live in peace and quiet ought not to be disturbed . . . so it seems that war can be undertaken only against persecutors." This assertion summarizes the standard interpretation of Pope Alexander II's remarks about violence against Jews and Muslims; in support, Oldradus cites both Alexander's statement and Roman law about peaceful Jews and pagans. To these, he adds a series of legal proofs that Christians may not compel anyone to accept the true Christian faith and that Christians ought to battle spiritual rather than fleshly enemies. These citations refer not only to infidels, pagans, and human beings—obvious categories for thinking about Muslims within medieval canon law—but also Jews and Christian heretics. These latter categories play a crucial role as Oldradus makes his argument in favor of conquering Muslims.[20]

Notwithstanding the weighty arguments to the contrary, Oldradus offers three overlapping justifications for a war of aggression against the Muslims of Spain. His most sweeping claim, grounded in a hotly contested legal theory, is that Christians may justly conquer any non-Christian territory because Christ exercises dominion over the entire earth and charged his apostles and their successors with doing the same.[21] Oldradus also makes a narrower argument that rests on more firmly established legal foundations: Spain was once Christian territory, so Christian rulers have the right to "reconquer" it in what amounts to a belated defensive war against past Muslim aggression. Oldradus's third and most innovative argument focuses specifically on Muslims as the heirs of Hagar.

Even if Saracens do not currently attack Christians, Oldradus asserts, "war ought to be waged against them because it is quite likely that whenever they have the chance they will attack and persecute Christians and the Church, for this seems to be in their nature" as descendants of Ishmael. Oldradus proceeds to cite evidence that present-day Saracens fulfill the violent prophecy regarding Ishmael: "He shall be a wild ass of a man, with his hand against everyone" (Genesis 16:12). Oldradus returns to this verse later in the consilium, citing it to support his assertion that "Saracens are called beasts literally" and for that reason are subject to the pope's authority and disciplinary power.

Oldradus, however, is less interested in defining Saracens as descendants of Ishmael than he is in demonstrating that they are heirs of Hagar, whom Paul established as representative of the Christian community's chief rival. To prove that Saracens descend from Hagar's son Ishmael, Oldradus cites a surprising legal source: "*The slave woman:* this is Hagar, who represents the Synagogue. *The free woman:* this is Sarah, who represents the Church. From Hagar, the slave of Sarah, descend these people who ought to serve those who descend from Sarah, on whom the church is founded." This explanation of Paul's allegory comes from the Ordinary Gloss to *Liber extra* 5.6.13, in which Pope Innocent III forbids Christian women from serving as wet nurses in Jewish households. Neither the pope nor the commentator makes reference to Muslims in this context. Oldradus, however, conflates Muslims and Jews as heirs of Hagar so as to apply Paul's teachings to the Saracens of Spain.[22]

Oldradus returns to Paul's allegory of Sarah and Hagar at the climax of Consilium 72, reading Christian dominion over Muslims into Abraham's words to Sarah: "your slave is in your hand; treat her as you wish" (Genesis 16:6).

> Sarah signifies the Holy Catholic Church; the slave Hagar, the accursed sect of Muhammad which took its origins from her. Therefore, the Holy Church, symbolized by Sarah, may treat that accursed slave as the blessed Sarah had treated her, by beating her. She may treat her as the Lord commands, by driving her out and depriving her children of inheritance and possession, that they not share with the free children.

On the surface, Oldradus simply offers an allegorical reading of Genesis similar to that of Paul but with Muslims playing the role of Hagar's heirs. His supporting prooftexts reveal a more complex picture. To associate the "sect of Muhammad" with Hagar and to justify the "beating" of its adherents, Oldradus appeals not to genealogy but to Augustine's assertion that Roman forces, emulating Sarah, ought to persecute Christian heretics.[23] In the sentence that follows those quoted above, Oldradus draws again on Pope Innocent III's decree about wet nurses in Jewish households: he refers to Muslims as "slaves reproved by the Lord," quoting the pope's description of Jews as the present-day heirs of Hagar. Oldradus, after all, does not claim to offer a new allegorical reading of Genesis but instead seeks to demonstrate that his argument about Muslims derives directly from Paul's teaching as interpreted by the preeminent authorities Augustine and Innocent III. Oldradus does so by equating Muslims with those to whom Paul's words had long been applied—namely, Jews and rival Christians.

Oldradus concludes that because war against Saracens in Spain accomplishes "the expulsion of that accursed slave and her offspring, there can be no doubt that it is licit." He returns to this theme in Consilium 87, on "whether a prince can, without sin, expel Jews and Saracens from his kingdom and confiscate their goods; and whether the pope can order or urge princes to do so."[24] This consilium is striking in that, aside from its opening sentence, it contains no reference to Saracens. Instead, Oldradus makes the case that princes have the right to expel Jews, and he takes for granted that this ruling applies equally to Muslims—notwithstanding the fact that several of his arguments both for and against expulsion depend on precedents that apply to Jews alone. These arguments include Augustine's teaching that Jews should remain within Christendom as witnesses to Christian truth claims.

Oldradus draws once again on Sarah's treatment of Hagar to clinch his case in favor of expulsion: "All this seems clearly prefigured in that slave woman from whom they descend since she was expelled because she conducted herself haughtily and ungratefully to the free woman, who signifies the church." The pronoun "they" in this sentence refers primarily to the Jews, whom Oldradus describes as the descendants of Hagar without further comment. Paul's allegory, Oldradus maintains, justifies the expulsion of Jews from Christian kingdoms notwithstanding Augustine's argument to the contrary. Unlike eleventh- and twelfth-century figures like Pope Alexander II, who sought to protect Jews from the anti-Muslim violence that they themselves encouraged, Oldradus intentionally promotes an assault against docile Jews and Muslims alike. Oldradus makes no effort to prove that Paul's order to "drive out the slave and her son," along with other traditionally anti-Jewish sources, also applies to Muslims, either because he regards this claim as self-evident or because he cannot find authoritative sources to support it.

Oldradus depicts Muslims and Jews alike as the heirs of Hagar when he wishes to legitimate their expulsion. In other contexts, however, he maintains the distinction between these communities. In Consilium 264, evidently written for a client opposed to expelling non-Christian subjects, Oldradus contends that "without a legitimate reason a prince cannot expel peaceful Jews, Saracens, and other pagans from his lands." Jews and Muslims, in other words, have the right to dwell in Christendom "unless they are persecutors" like Paul's rivals and Ishmael before them. Here, unlike in Consilia 72 and 87, Oldradus emphasizes that contemporary Saracens do not necessarily emulate their ancestors: "where the Hagarenes abide humbly and do not deceive simple Christians to follow the cult of their vile Muhammad they are on account of this not to be expelled but to be accepted." More significantly, Oldradus does not associate Muslims with Jews in this brief. He reiterates Augustine's arguments for the place of Jews in Christian society as unwitting witnesses to the truth of Christianity, but he does not grant similar significance to the ongoing presence of Muslims, nor does he associate Jews with Hagar in this context. Consilium 264 portrays Jews and Muslims alike as human beings with certain fundamental rights and as monotheists rather than idolaters, but it does not suggest that these identities are interchangeable. The same may be said regarding Consilium 51, which addresses the question of whether a Jew should be punished for converting to Islam. Oldradus argues that there should be no punishment, both because the Church tolerates Jewish and Muslim communities alike and because it is worse to be a Jew than to be a non-Christian gentile: the convert has chosen "the path of lesser evil."[25]

Interpreters familiar with a canonical text's anti-Jewish and anti-Muslim layers of meaning could draw on either or both of those layers strategically to advance specific objectives. Oldradus only finds it useful to equate Jews and Muslims as fellow Hagarenes when he wishes to place Muslims alongside Jews within Paul's classic table of opposites. Oldradus and fellow Christian polemicists can, after all, readily associate Saracens with Ishmael and Hagar on the strength of Genesis alone, without reading that text through the lens of Galatians; this is precisely what Oldradus does in Consilium 264. By associating Muslims and Jews as the heirs of Hagar, Christians can define Islam, like Judaism, as the binary antithesis of Christianity and can more readily legitimate efforts to drive Muslims and Jews alike out of Christendom. Jewish Muslims—as opposed to Muslims imagined in other ways—are not merely the descendants of Hagar and Ishmael but also and more importantly heirs to the "Jewish" enmity that plays such an important role in premodern Christian self-identification. As such, Muslims deserve to suffer the fate that Paul prescribes for the rivals of his church.

. . .

Christians associated Muslims with Jews as the heirs of Hagar throughout the Middle Ages, using biblical sources about Hagar and Ishmael to account for the behavior of Muslims and to predict their ultimate demise. Muslims, we have seen, purportedly lay claim to the Promised Land on the Jewish grounds of biological descent from Abraham. They occupy the present-day Jerusalem in accordance with Paul's teachings about Hagar and Sarah, which simultaneously affirm that Christians alone possess the heavenly Jerusalem. Muslims persecute Christians just as Ishmael persecuted Isaac, but, like Hagar and Ishmael, they will be driven out by those who implement God's will. The conflict between Christians and Muslims is preordained, and so too is the ultimate Christian victory. Anti-Muslim polemicists use Pauline rhetoric to bolster the confidence of politically weak Christians and to inspire boldness in those who are capable of taking political action against Muslim rivals. If Christians follow in the footsteps of their ancestor Sarah, they can be sure that Muslims will suffer the fate of Hagar.

Rhetoric about Hagar's heirs also serves to place the Christian-Muslim conflict at the core of Christian history. This conflict does not rival the fundamental dichotomy between Christianity and Judaism but rather expresses that very dichotomy precisely because Muslims are figuratively equivalent to Jews. Christians understood that Muslims are not Jews in a literal sense. On the metaphorical plane, however, these Christians could render Muslims and Jews as one and the same, just as Paul employed allegory to associate his contemporary rivals with Sarah's despised and rejected slave.

The variety of Eastern and European Christians who seized this opportunity is striking. In the past two chapters alone, we have encountered rhetoric about Jewish Muslims in the works of patriarchs and royal propagandists, chroniclers and educators, biblical commentators and canon lawyers. The next chapter will introduce even more types of polemicists, among them authors of apocalyptic literature and diverse visual artists; still others appear in subsequent chapters. This variety reflects the wide range of ways in which premodern Christians found value in employing the discourse of anti-Judaism when portraying Muslims.

CHAPTER 4

Imagining the Dome of the Rock as the Biblical Temple

Seventh through Fourteenth Centuries

The Dome of the Rock has dominated Jerusalem's skyline since the end of the seventh century. Premodern Christians, however, often imagined that this iconic building already stood during Jesus's lifetime, or even in the days of King Solomon a thousand years earlier. The dome encloses the rock associated not only with Muhammad's ascent to heaven but also—and not by chance—with the Holy of Holies, the most sacred space within Solomon's Temple. Many premodern Christians believed that the Dome of the Rock not only stands in the location of the biblical Temple but also replaces that sacred structure. For this reason, artists frequently represented the Temple by means of a dome-topped and window-pierced drum that calls to mind the Islamic sanctuary of their own era (figs. 4, 5). European Christians customarily referred to the Dome of the Rock itself as the Temple of Solomon or the Temple of the Lord (that is, Christ), notwithstanding the fact that the Bible repeatedly emphasizes both the Babylonian destruction of Solomon's Temple and the Roman destruction of the Temple that stood in Jesus's day. This curious anachronism illustrates the fundamental dynamic we explored in chapters 2 and 3: premodern Christians regarded not only the Dome of the Rock but also Muslims themselves in biblical terms.[1]

Abd al-Malik, the Muslim caliph (supreme ruler) who inaugurated construction of this magnificent Islamic sanctuary in 691/92 CE, represented himself as a latter-day Solomon and his religion as the true manifestation of the divine revelation purportedly corrupted by Jews and

FIGURE 4. The Dome of the Rock. (Photo: © Andrew Shiva / Wikipedia / CC BY-SA 4.0.)

Christians.[2] Why did medieval Christians also adopt the notion that the Dome of the Rock is, in effect, the biblical Temple? Doing so enabled them to ascribe theological significance to a building whose presence within the sacred city of Jerusalem they simply could not ignore. More fundamentally, rhetoric depicting the Dome of the Rock as the biblical Temple defines contemporary Muslims in terms of biblical frames of reference. Anti-Muslim polemicists, after all, saw no need to limit themselves to sources about Hagar and Ishmael. Nor, we will see, did they limit themselves to associating Muslims with Jews.

This chapter examines in turn three distinct Christian representations of the Dome of the Rock that appear in diverse texts and works of art over many centuries. The Dome of the Rock signifies the impending end of days, constitutes the site of biblical events, and symbolizes the Church's abiding rival, the Synagogue. Although these representations are contradictory, the conceptions of Muslims that they reinforce are complementary. The first representation depicts Muslim caliphs as Antichrist, the second facilitates portrayals of Muslims as quasi-pagan usurpers of Christian sacred space, and the third equates Muslims with

FIGURE 5. *The Passion of Christ in the Panorama of Jerusalem.* The central domed building is labeled *Templum Salomonis*, "the Temple of Solomon." Anonymous (Flemish), ca. 1500. Lisbon, Museu Nacional do Azulejo. (Photo: Manuel Palma, DGPC / Arquivo de Documentação Fotográfica.)

Jews. All three render Muslims, like Jews, as theological enemies of Christendom, embodiments of a conflict foretold in the Bible itself.

THE BUILDING AT THE END OF TIME

Early Christians taught that the Jewish Temple has no place in the era inaugurated by Christ's death and resurrection. For that reason, many seventh- and eighth-century writers concluded that this era must be over: because Muslims have built a shrine on the site of Solomon's Temple, Christ is about to return to earth. Christians pointed to the Dome of the Rock and other Islamic structures on the Temple Mount as evidence that the Muslim conquests marked the final stage before Christ's Second

Coming. Christians inclined to read contemporary events in light of apocalyptic literature—which is to say, texts that foretell the long-awaited end of history—defined the conquerors themselves as Antichrist, "the personification of human resistance to the work and person of Christ" who, Christians believed, will play a crucial role in the end-times.[3]

Jesus, the Gospels report, prophesied about the Jerusalem Temple that "not one stone will be left here upon another; all will be thrown down" (Matthew 24:2 and parallels). According to the book of Revelation, even the New Jerusalem that will descend from heaven in the end of days contains no literal Temple, "for its temple is the Lord God the Almighty and the Lamb," which is to say Christ himself (21:22). Early Christians such as Justin Martyr, Origen, and Eusebius (of the second, third, and fourth centuries, respectively) portray the Temple's destruction as divine punishment for the crucifixion of Christ and as proof that God now favors Christians rather than Jews. The Temple will never stand again, they declare, not only because of the severity of the Jews' unforgivable sin but also because God rejects fleshly sacrifices and literal observance of the Law; its ruins demonstrate that God desires Christian worship and spirituality instead. Eusebius describes the Church of the Holy Sepulchre, built by the Christian emperor Constantine in the early fourth century, as the new Temple and nothing less than the "New Jerusalem proclaimed in prophetic oracles." Its glorious presence opposite the desolate Temple Mount, Eusebius declares, demonstrates the triumph of Christianity.[4]

Julian (r. 361–63), the emperor who sought to restore paganism and its sacrificial rites to the Roman Empire, invited the Jews to rebuild their Temple. Christians delighted in recounting the earthquake and fires that allegedly thwarted this effort, along with other miraculous demonstrations of divine support for Christianity and God's wrath toward the unbelieving Jews. Church historians saw in these events evidence for the ongoing relevance of Christ's prophetic words. Many feared, however, that Jews might once again attempt to reclaim Jerusalem, rebuild their Temple, and seek revenge.[5]

Because of this history, the successful construction of religious buildings on the Temple Mount demanded the attention of seventh-century Christians. Consider, for example, the *Apocalypse of Pseudo-Shenute*, an originally Coptic text composed late in the seventh century, most likely during the years in which the Dome of the Rock was under construction. This text, which presents itself as the prophecy of a fifth-century monk, reports that the descendants of Ishmael will rebuild the Temple that is in Jerusalem. When that happens, know that the end of time has come near. Then, also, the Jews will expect the Deceiver [that is, Antichrist], while they arouse the peoples at his coming. When you will see the abomination of desolation of which the prophet Daniel spoke, it is those who deny my sufferings which I received upon the cross, while they move freely inside my church without being afraid or frightened. Then those who crucified me will fall in with the Antichrist, and they will reject my holy resurrection.[6]

Construction of the Dome of the Rock, this author contends, signals the onset of the end-times, when Jews—and, it seems, Muslims—will align themselves with Antichrist.

The *Apocalypse of Pseudo-Shenute* is not the oldest surviving work to allege that the Muslim "Ishmaelites" were interested in restoring the biblical Temple. That distinction belongs to the *History of Sebeos*, which, as we observed in chapter 2, portrays Jews as the driving force behind the Muslim conquest of Jerusalem. This mid-seventh-century chronicle asserts that these Jews "decided to rebuild the Temple of Solomon. . . . But the Ishmaelites, being envious of them, expelled them from that place and called the same house of prayer their own." *Sebeos* does not refer to the Dome of the Rock, constructed several decades later, but rather to an earlier structure. Arculf, a traveler from present-day France who visited Jerusalem in the 670s, similarly reports that "in that famous place where once stood the magnificently constructed Temple . . . the Saracens now frequent a rectangular house of prayer." Arculf most likely refers to a precursor to the Aqsa Mosque on the southern end of the Temple Mount platform that Muslims call the *haram al-sharif*.[7]

By alleging that Ishmaelites seized the new Temple of Solomon for their own use, the *History of Sebeos* cements their identity as would-be Jews. According to another account, Muslims themselves sought to build a new Temple but it repeatedly collapsed, in keeping with Christ's prophecy that not one stone would stand on another. The Muslim ruler turned to the Jews for advice, and they informed him that he first needed to remove the cross that stood on a church opposite the Temple Mount; after doing so, the new sanctuary stood firm. These tales, which portray Muslims and Jews as allies in an assault on Christianity and Christendom, render Muslims themselves as quasi-Jewish in their efforts to re-establish the biblical Temple.[8]

The *Apocalypse of Pseudo-Shenute* is also not alone in reinterpreting Daniel's prophecies about the end of days in light of the Muslim conquest of Jerusalem and the presence of Islamic shrines on the Temple

Mount. We saw in chapter 2 that Sophronius likewise described the Saracen invaders of Palestine as "the abomination of desolation clearly foretold to us" (in Daniel 9:27). The patriarch of Jerusalem spoke these words in a sermon he delivered several months before surrendering the city to its Muslim conquerors. The early ninth-century chronicler Theophanes, however, associates this statement specifically with an incident that reportedly occurred on the Temple Mount when the Muslim caliph Umar accepted that surrender.

> Umar entered the holy city dressed in filthy garments of camel hair and, showing a devilish pretense, sought out the Temple of the Jews—the one built by Solomon—that he might make it a place of worship for his own blasphemous religion. Seeing this, Sophronius said, "Verily, this is 'the abomination of desolation standing in a holy place, as has been spoken through the prophet Daniel.'"[9]

Sophronius here applies Jesus's prophecy about the onset of the end of days (he quotes Matthew 24:15) to Umar's arrival in Jerusalem. This story captures not only the sense of violation that many Christians experienced when contemplating Muslim rulers and Islamic sanctuaries on the once-sacred Temple Mount, but also the belief that events taking place in seventh-century Jerusalem fulfill the Bible's apocalyptic predictions.

Theophanes and the *Apocalypse of Pseudo-Shenute* draw on a rich Christian tradition that interprets Daniel's prophecy with reference to Antichrist, the Jews, and a rebuilt Temple in Jerusalem. The author of the biblical book of Daniel uses the term "abomination of desolation" to describe something standing within the Temple precincts in his own lifetime, most likely an idol or idolatrous altar erected on orders of the Greek king Antiochus IV in the era of the Maccabees (167 BCE). Hippolytus of Rome, in his influential early third-century commentary on Daniel, interpreted this phrase in reference to the person known as Antichrist, who, Hippolytus believed, would rebuild the Jewish Temple and persecute Christians at the urging of his Jewish followers. Cyril of Jerusalem, preaching in the mid-fourth century, explained that "if [Antichrist] is to come as Christ to the Jews and wants their worship, with a view to deceiving them further, he will manifest the greatest zeal for the Temple; he will create the impression that he is the descendant of David who is to restore the Temple of Solomon."[10]

Cyril imagined that Antichrist would be a future Roman emperor, and later church historians understood his words with reference to Emperor Julian's abortive construction effort. Theophanes and the *Apocalypse of*

Pseudo-Shenute instead identify Umar or an unnamed Muslim caliph as Antichrist. An eighth-century Syriac chronicler similarly reports that the caliph of his own day, al-Mansur, acted "according to what Daniel prophesied about the Antichrist" when rebuilding the Temple Mount's Aqsa Mosque after it suffered damage from an earthquake.[11]

Through their "updates" to Daniel's prophecies about the end of days, these Christian authors preserve hope that the return of Christ is imminent. What happens in the present-day Jerusalem and, especially, on its Temple Mount has cosmic significance precisely because Muslims allegedly play the biblical roles that earlier Christians ascribed to Antichrist and the Jews. Abd al-Malik may well have designed the Dome of the Rock as a monument to the victory of Islam over Christianity, but at least some Christians instead regarded it as a sign that the triumphant return of Christ was at hand. Pre-Islamic traditions about the biblical Temple enabled these Christians to justify their optimism.

THE TEMPLE OF THE LORD

The world as we know it did not come to an end following the construction of the Dome of the Rock.[12] Instead, this structure transformed perceptions of Jerusalem's landscape to the point that Christians could not imagine the city without it. Many believed that, even if the Dome of the Rock postdates Solomon and Jesus, it nonetheless represents, resembles, and effectively replaces the Temples that stood in biblical antiquity. These Christians therefore claimed this building as their own, just as they laid exclusive claim to the Bible's stories, heroes, and promises of covenantal blessing irrespective of competing Jewish and Islamic claims. Portrayals of the Dome of the Rock as the site of events in Christian sacred history render Muslims as false claimants and quasi-pagan usurpers of an essentially Christian sanctuary. Such rhetoric legitimates the massacre and expulsion of Muslims by the crusaders who conquered Jerusalem in 1099.

Ninth-century artists and architects already imagined the biblical Temple in terms of the Dome of the Rock. Charlemagne, who founded the Holy Roman Empire, cultivated images of himself as a latter-day King Solomon and portrayed his capital city, Aachen, as the New Jerusalem. As part of this effort, Charlemagne constructed a house of worship that calls to mind Solomon's Temple by employing design elements found in the Dome of the Rock: both that structure and Charlemagne's Palatine Chapel, constructed between 795 and 803, are octagonal in shape, feature a dome atop a windowed drum, and bear inscriptions on the inner walls identifying its royal donor.[13]

The creators of a richly illuminated manuscript known as the Harley Golden Gospels, who were most likely active in Charlemagne's early-ninth-century Aachen, also regarded the Dome of the Rock as emblematic of the biblical Temple. When depicting the Gospel of Luke's initial scene, in which the angel Gabriel speaks with the priest Zechariah (1:8–20), these artists show that this conversation took place in Jerusalem's Temple by depicting a golden dome atop a windowed drum (fig. 6). This is the medieval equivalent of a cinematographer shooting a scene set in the time of Jesus on location at the Dome of the Rock, as if that building itself was present in the first century.[14]

Later Christian artists often rendered the biblical Temple in similar ways. Consider, for example, a thirteenth-century *Bible moralisée*, a work that draws Christian lessons from the Old Testament by juxtaposing biblical scenes with illustrations of their true meaning. This work presents King Solomon's physical Temple—depicted as vaguely round with a golden dome and windowed drum—as a precursor to Christ's Roman Catholic Church (fig. 7). Solomon's prayer of thanksgiving on completing the Temple (1 Kings 8), the *Bible moralisée* teaches, foreshadows Christ's gratitude to God the Father for bringing the Church to fruition. Even though the biblical text itself describes a rectangular building with a flat roof (1 Kings 6:2), the artist chose to portray Solomon's structure with a dome because the Dome of the Rock had long since become a conventional model for Christian representations of the Temple.[15] The convention of depicting a domed Jewish Temple persisted into early modern times. The presence of this structure, in fact, became the iconic symbol identifying the visual representation of a city as Jerusalem.[16]

The Latin Christian works of art and architecture we have examined thus far make no allusions to Muslims—or, for that matter, to Jews. They depict biblical figures like Solomon and Zechariah as Christian heroes and the domed Temple in Jerusalem as a thoroughly Christian building. Many Christians likewise attempted to erase Muslim connections to the actual Dome of the Rock. The objective of the Holy Land Crusades, after all, was to reclaim Jerusalem in the name of Christ. Crusaders imagined the Dome of the Rock to be the biblical Temple that Jesus himself visited, and they regarded Muslims as usurpers and polluters of this sacred Christian space.[17]

Following the crusader conquest, Christians transformed the Dome of the Rock into a church known simply as the Temple of the Lord (that is,

FIGURE 6. The beginning of the Gospel of Luke in the Harley Golden Gospels. The image in the initial "Q" depicts an angel foretelling the birth of John the Baptist to his father in the Jerusalem Temple. Germany (Aachen?), early ninth century. London, British Library, Harley MS 2788, fol. 109r. (Photo: © British Library Board. All Rights Reserved / Bridgeman Images.)

Christ), and they installed a gilt cross atop its dome. The Temple of the Lord's significance within the Latin Kingdom of Jerusalem rivaled that of the Church of the Holy Sepulchre itself, and visitors portrayed the sanctuary as if this building was the site of events described in the Gospels. Saewulf, among the earliest European pilgrims to Jerusalem (ca. 1102), describes how Solomon built the Temple and recounts numerous events that took place within this building during Jesus's lifetime, among them the angelic revelation to Zechariah. Just as the illuminator of the Harley

FIGURE 7. Solomon's prayer (top) and Christ's counterpart (bottom) in a *Bible moralisée.* The bottom caption reads: "That Solomon gave thanks to God when he had finished the Temple and God gave him His blessing signifies Jesus Christ who gave thanks to the Father of Heaven for finishing the Holy Church and the Father of Heaven descended and gave Him His blessing and His grace." Vienna, Österreichische Nationalbibliothek, Cod. 2554, fol. 50v. Paris, 1220s. (Digitized by the Austrian National Library, http://data.onb.ac.at/dtl/2246547.)

Golden Gospels invites viewers to place that scene at the present-day Dome of the Rock, Saewulf implies that this and other New Testament events occurred in and around the very sanctuary he visited. Saewulf clearly knew the Bible well and refers to a wide range of biblical texts, but he neglects to mention the destruction of the buildings known to Solomon and Jesus. This telling silence enables readers to imagine the Dome of the Rock as a sacred Christian structure to which Muslims have no legitimate claim. Other authors of Jerusalem pilgrimage accounts do the same: of the eighteen texts by Christian authors in John Wilkinson's collection, only one states unequivocally that "the church which is there now was built by a Saracen chieftain."[18]

Chroniclers recount that the crusaders were eager to seize not only the Church of the Holy Sepulchre, the traditional site of Christ's resurrection, but also the Temple of the Lord. Fulcher of Chartres and Raymond D'Aguilers report that the joyous crusaders proceeded directly from the Church of the Holy Sepulchre to the Temple Mount, singing apocalyptic hymns about the New Jerusalem. Two later chroniclers, Baldric of Bourgueil and William of Tyre, even present the Dome of the Rock's liberation as an original objective of the crusading enterprise. In Baldric's version of the fiery sermon that launched the First Crusade, Pope Urban II bemoans the present state of "the Temple of Solomon—or rather, of the Lord—in which the barbarous nations venerate the idols they erected in violation of human and divine law." The Dome of the Rock, in other words, is itself in some sense the Temple known to Solomon and Christ, and Muslims are its wrongful occupiers. William of Tyre reports that the pope compared the current demon-infested state of the Temple to its condition at the time of the biblical Maccabees, when Greeks defiled the Jewish sanctuary with their idolatry. These chroniclers present the crusaders as worthy heirs of the zealous Maccabean warriors. In the process, they cast Muslims not as Jews but rather in the role of the Greek villains who seized and abused God's sanctuary.[19]

This association of crusaders with the Maccabees accounts in no small measure for Christian allegations that the Muslims of Jerusalem, like the Greeks portrayed in biblical literature, worshipped idols: this allegation rests not on observations of Islamic worship but on the logic of the Maccabean analogy. Consider, for example, the image that introduces the First Book of Maccabees in the bible created for King Louis IX of France while he was on crusade in the Holy Land (1250–54; fig. 8). In the top left scene, biblical Greeks slaughter Jews within the domed Jerusalem Temple. The Maccabean hero Mattathias—dressed as

FIGURE 8. Frontispiece of the First Book of Maccabees, illustrating 1 Macc. 2:24–25, in the Arsenal Old Testament. Acre, 1250–54. Paris, Bibliothèque de l'Arsenal, MS 5211, fol. 339r. (Digitized by the Bibliothèque nationale de France.)

a crusader—appears twice in the top right scene: he prepares to behead a Greek just as Greeks beheaded Jews, and he kills a turbaned figure worshipping an idol. This image portrays the Maccabees as exacting perfect retribution against the Greeks and suggests that crusaders do the same when slaughtering Muslims. The image represents Muslims as idolaters simply because they constitute the contemporary equivalents of the Greeks whose idolatry animates the plot of 1 Maccabees. Similarly, Raymond D'Aguilers depicts the massacre that occurred on the Temple Mount after Muslims surrendered in 1099 as "poetic justice that the Temple of Solomon should receive the blood of pagans who blasphemed God there for many years." The metaphorical association of contemporary Muslims with ancient Greeks distorts reality so as to render Muslims as the contemporary equivalents of biblical enemies and, in so doing, justifies acts of violence that transgress the norms of chivalrous warfare.[20]

Another work from the Latin Kingdom of Jerusalem offers an even more manifestly anachronistic rendition of a biblical scene. The psalter created for Queen Melisende sometime between 1131 and 1143 depicts Christ's entry into Jerusalem as if he is visiting the crusaders' Temple of the Lord, complete with a cross on its domed drum (fig. 9). An idol stands atop a building behind Christ, opposite the Temple. That structure seems to represent the worship that took place in Jerusalem before crusaders, following in Christ's footsteps, retook the Lord's city and Temple. Depictions of Islamic worship as the idolatrous inverse of Christian worship also appear in crusade literature and popular works such as the *Song of Roland* (see chapter 11). Judaism and idolatry alike constitute traditional foils for Christian self-definition, and premodern polemicists freely draw on both in their representations of Islam.[21]

The Melisende Psalter suggests that the conflict between Christianity and Islam is as old as the rivalry with Judaism and as central to the construction of Christian self-identity. Both conflicts manifest themselves in control of what Paul calls "the present Jerusalem" (Galatians 4:25): just as Roman emperors barred Jews from the city, so, too, the rulers of the Latin Kingdom expelled Muslims and Jews alike in the process of remaking Jerusalem into an emphatically Christian site. In doing so, crusaders followed not only Roman precedent but also Paul's exhortation to "drive out" Hagar's spiritual heirs (4:30).

THE SYNAGOGUE OF THE SARACENS

While some European Christians regarded the Dome of the Rock as an intrinsically Christian sanctuary, others embraced a fundamentally different rhetorical tradition that represents this structure as emphatically Jewish. This tradition dates at least to the ninth century, when a Frankish visitor described the Dome of the Rock as "a Saracen synagogue."[22] Medieval artists often depicted this building not merely as a synagogue but rather as Synagogue with a capital *S*: the personification of Judaism and the fallen rival of *Ecclesia*, the Church personified. In so doing, they portray Islam no less than Judaism as defeated and outdated, its adherents similarly destined for hell in keeping with Paul's teachings about

FIGURE 9. Christ's entry into Jerusalem in the Melisende Psalter. Jerusalem, 1131–43. London, British Library, Egerton MS 1139, fol. 5v. (Photo: © British Library Board. All Rights Reserved / Bridgeman Images.)

FIGURE 10. Christ crowning the Church and expelling the Synagogue in the *Liber Floridus*. Saint-Omer, ca. 1120. Universiteitsbibliotheek Gent, BHSL.HS.0092, fol. 253r. (Digitized by Ghent University Library, https://liberfloridus.be.)

Hagar's heirs. Allusions to the present Jerusalem and present-day Muslims give crisp, contemporary relevance to traditional theological claims about the disgraced Jews and the triumphant Church.

Figures of Synagogue and of Jews often serve a cautionary function in Christian art: they exemplify beliefs and practices that Christians themselves might, but emphatically should not, adopt. Literary depictions of a conflict between Church and Synagogue, often personified as female figures, predate the rise of Islam, and visual depictions of these figures feature prominently in medieval art. The *Liber Floridus*, an illustrated encyclopedia completed in 1120, offers an instructive example (fig. 10). Church stands victorious on the viewer's left of this image, her flagged standard held high as Christ crowns her with his right hand. With his left hand, Christ rejects Synagogue and pushes her toward the jaws of hell. Synagogue once held God's favor, but she has now forfeited her crown and her standard is broken.[23]

Most medieval portrayals of Church and Synagogue are set in the timeless present. The *Liber Floridus*, in contrast, depicts the apocalyptic end of days. Christ stands on the Mount of Olives, the anticipated site of his Second Coming and his defeat of Antichrist—whom, we have seen, Christians associated with the Jews and their Temple and, subsequently, with Muslims as well. The *Liber Floridus* devotes special

FIGURE 11. The Fall of Synagogue, detail from the south tympanum of the Abbey Church of Saint-Gilles-du-Gard (mid-twelfth century). (Photo: © Mary Ann Sullivan.)

attention to the recent crusader conquest of Jerusalem and describes this event in apocalyptic terms. In this context, Synagogue may represent not only the Jews but also the Muslims of the Holy Land.

Such a representation appears more explicitly on the now-damaged south tympanum of the abbey church of Saint-Gilles-du-Gard, executed in the mid-twelfth century.[24] Saint-Gilles, a Mediterranean port town, served as the point of departure for pilgrims and crusaders bound for the Holy Land; its ruler, Raymond of Toulouse, led the Christian army that conquered Jerusalem in 1099. As was the case in the *Liber Floridus* image, Synagogue stands to the left of the crucified Christ (the viewer's right) on the Saint-Gilles tympanum, with Church on Christ's favored right-hand side. An angel pushes Synagogue with such force that she falls and loses her crown—which is shaped like the Dome of the Rock (fig. 11).

This image celebrates the "fall of Jerusalem" by representing the Christian-Muslim conflict in terms of the timeless contest between Church and Synagogue. As such, it also ascribes theological significance to the ongoing efforts of Jerusalem's military orders, with which the abbey of Saint-Gilles maintained especially close ties during the mid-twelfth

century. Raymond, the crusaders, and members of these orders participate in a divinely sanctioned mission to suppress Islam and, in so doing,
bring glory to the Church. The imagery of Christ's forceful rejection of
Synagogue provided an ideal model for representing this unprecedented
conception of sacred violence and another method for defining Muslims
as Christendom's eternal enemies.

The illuminator of the *Liber Floridus* and the sculptors who created the
Saint-Gilles tympanum imagined, or at least hoped, that crusaders would
maintain everlasting dominion over the sacred sites of Jerusalem just as
Church has eternally triumphed over Synagogue. History, however, did
not conform to theology: Muslims regained control of the city in 1187,
promptly smashing the cross atop the Dome of the Rock. Muslims eventually replaced that symbol of Christianity with a crescent moon. Ironically, one of the earliest surviving attestations of the crescent moon's presence in this context appears in a Christian depiction of the biblical Temple:
Melchior Broederlam's Champmol Altarpiece, completed in 1399.

The Champmol Altarpiece depicts four Gospel scenes arranged from
left to right on two facing panels. On the first panel, an angel announces
to the Virgin Mary her impending birth of Jesus; next, Mary visits Elizabeth, mother of John the Baptist. On the second panel (fig. 12), we see
Mary's presentation of the newborn Jesus in the Temple and then her
flight into Egypt to save her baby from Herod, the murderous Jewish
king. Broederlam portrays the relationship between Christianity and
Judaism not through female personifications of Church and Synagogue
but rather through distinctive architectural features. Mary, who gave
birth to the new, Christian era, appears within Gothic structures that
call to mind the cathedrals of thirteenth- and fourteenth-century Europe.
(In many works, among them fig. 7, a Gothic cathedral represents the
Church itself.) Broederlam renders other parts of the Temple using old-
fashioned architectural elements that represent the old and soon-to-be-
obsolete covenant between God and the Jews. These include round
arches and the now-familiar domed drum, its windows tellingly dark
even as Mary is bathed in light (fig. 13).

Broederlam, however, does not merely follow artistic convention in
depicting the Temple with a dome-topped and windowed drum: according to art historian Pamela Berger, Broederlam is the first Christian artist
to paint an Islamic crescent atop this biblical building. By doing
so, Broederlam links the Muslims of his own era with the Jews who
sought to kill the newborn Christ, forcing Mary to flee Jerusalem just as
Muslims expelled the crusaders. Broederlam also extends the superses-

FIGURE 12. A panel of the Champmol Altarpiece by Melchior Broederlam (1393–99). Dijon, Musée des beaux arts. (Photo: © Erich Lessing / Art Resource, NY.)

FIGURE 13. Crescent atop the biblical Jerusalem Temple, detail from the Champmol Altarpiece. (Photo: © Erich Lessing / Art Resource, NY.)

sionist logic of premodern Christianity to Islam, which he represents as old notwithstanding the chronological relationship between Muhammad and Jesus. By grafting symbols of Islam onto traditional depictions of Synagogue and the Temple, the Saint-Gilles tympanum and the Champmol Altarpiece alike draw on classic anti-Jewish tropes to express ideas about contemporary Muslims and their relationship to the Church.[25]

. . .

In certain respects, Christian representations of the Dome of the Rock are mutually contradictory: the sanctuary cannot simultaneously be the work of Antichrist and the Temple of the Lord, nor can it be both exclusively Christian and emblematic of the Church's perennial rival,

Synagogue. The accompanying representations of Muslims, however, are complementary. Muslims can follow Antichrist, lay illegitimate claim to Christian sacred spaces, and resemble Jews at the same time. After all, Christians accused Jews themselves of following Antichrist and laying illegitimate claim to the divine covenant. By applying the same allegations and their underlying biblical prooftexts to Muslims, Christian thinkers and artists weave Muslims into foundational Christian myths and, simultaneously, emphasize the relevance of ancient tales to contemporary challenges. Rhetoric about the Dome of the Rock as the biblical Temple furthers this broader effort to define Muslims no less than Jews as theological enemies of Christendom.

This dynamic exemplifies a much broader phenomenon: Christian conceptions of Muslims originate before the rise of Islam. That is, premodern thinkers and artists often represent Muslims not on the basis of information about actual Muslims but rather by applying biblical texts that they read through a long-standing anti-Jewish (or anti-pagan, etc.) interpretive lens. To make sense of this rhetoric, we need to understand the ways in which Christians interpreted the Bible as well as the negative characteristics they ascribed to Judaism—characteristics they feared that fellow Christians might adopt. More fundamentally, we need to understand the reasons why they chose to represent Muslims in a distorted fashion that does not correspond to reality. In other words, we need to identify the objectives that motivate their rhetoric.

At the start of this book, I introduced an imaginary candidate for elected office who declares, "My opponent is a pig!" That simple example illustrates the six fundamental elements of polemical comparisons: not only the target (the opponent) and the reference (pigs) but also the polemicist (candidate) and the criterion of comparison (the frame of reference according to which the opponent is a pig) as well as the polemicist's audience (voters) and objective (to win the election). The chapters in part 1 focused on two of these elements: they introduced a wide range of Christian polemicists and demonstrated that premodern criteria for branding Muslims as Jews—and, similarly, as pagans— derive from the Bible and, to a lesser extent, other pre-Islamic sources. The chapters in part 2, to which we now turn, focus on another pair of elements: audience and objective. Premodern polemicists addressed fellow Christians and sought to cultivate proper Christian characteristics through portrayals of Muslim foils who behave in allegedly Jewish fashion. Put simply, Christians brand Muslims as Jews for the benefit of fellow Christians.

PART TWO

Judaizing Muslims

CHAPTER 5

"New Jews": Muslims as Foils for Educating Eastern Christians

Seventh through Ninth Centuries

The Muslim conquests reshaped the political landscape of the region now known as the Middle East. In important respects, however, the challenges that Eastern Christian theologians and educators confronted did not change, as they still needed to instill their own particular doctrines within a diverse marketplace of ideas. The region was home to three forms of Christianity with competing beliefs about the relationship between Jesus Christ's divinity and humanity: the Church of the East, which was dominant within the Persian Empire including present-day Iraq; Miaphysite churches, which became dominant in the region of Syria; and Chalcedonian churches, supported by the Roman Empire. To motivate members of their own communities to differentiate themselves from so-called heretics through the cultivation of normative beliefs and practices, polemicists often alleged that rival Christians "judaize," Paul's term for non-Jews who adopt disdainful characteristics associated with Judaism (Galatians 2:14). Some teachers also began to direct anti-Jewish rhetoric against Muslim figures who allegedly misinterpret the Old Testament, refuse to accept reasoned argumentation, and adopt purportedly Jewish practices. These quasi-Jewish Muslim foils, they believed, render traditional anti-Jewish arguments more relevant and novel claims more persuasive to Christian audiences who possess a healthy respect for their Muslim overlords.[1]

The works we will examine in this chapter, written independently between the late seventh and early ninth centuries, offer *apologies*—from the Greek term *apologia*, "defensive arguments"—on behalf of Christianity. Although they take the literary form of dialogues with Muslims, they are in fact fictional accounts written for Eastern Christians. Muslims, in other words, constitute the rhetorical target but are not part of the intended audience whom the polemicist seeks to impress and persuade. The authors of these works address fellow Christians and seek to reinforce Christian truth claims. The traditional discourse of anti-Judaism provides both the reference and the criteria for their polemical comparisons.

We will begin with arguments on behalf of Christianity ostensibly addressed to Muslims who, like Jews, accept the authority of the Old Testament but nevertheless question core Christian teachings. These fictional Muslim foils, who voice doubts that Christians themselves might harbor, provide opportunities for anonymous authors to reinforce the convictions of their coreligionists by means of traditional anti-Jewish lessons. We will then turn to the work of Timothy I, patriarch of the Church of the East, who develops an innovative defense of Christian faith grounded in philosophical rather than purely scriptural reasoning. Timothy, however, portrays Muslims not as a new kind of rival to Christianity but rather as "new Jews," a familiar foil whose critiques of Christian truth claims Christians can readily dismiss. The chapter's final case study, an explicitly fictional dialogue by the educator Theodore bar Koni, fuses elements of the previous cases: a Christian teacher addresses a Muslim student who accepts the authority of the Old Testament but who is ultimately "like a Jew" in his refusal to accept that Christ is the Son of God. The actual Christian students who studied Theodore's manual of instruction learned from this dialogue how to properly understand the biblical foundations of core Christian beliefs and practices so as to avoid judaizing themselves. Good Christians, these apologetic texts teach, should accept their community's doctrines and methods of biblical interpretation not only because these doctrines and methods are sound but also because failure to do so is inherently Jewish.[2]

NEW FOILS FOR FAMILIAR ARGUMENTS

Patricia Crone and Michael Cook set off an academic firestorm in the 1970s when they made the case that Islam originated as a messianic movement of Arabs who accepted the authority of the Torah, the initial and most important portion of the Jewish Bible. These eminent scholars based their radically revisionist argument about the movement they called "Judeo-Hagarism" on Christian texts purportedly written in the seventh century, reasoning that these works offer more reliable evidence regarding the beliefs of contemporaneous Arabs than do Islamic sources written at a later time.[3] In fact, however, Christian texts are often quite inaccurate in their depictions of Muslims, who even in the seventh century regarded the Torah as a corrupted account of divine revelation with no contemporary authority. Although the Judeo-Hagarism hypothesis no longer holds currency among scholars of early Islam, the observations made by Crone and Cook remain quite relevant for our purposes. How—and, more importantly, why—did Eastern Christians of the first Islamic centuries depict Muslims as adherents of the Old Testament notwithstanding the inaccuracy of this depiction?

One of the texts that inspired the Judeo-Hagarism hypothesis, *John and the Emir*, purports to recount a dialogue between the Miaphysite patriarch of Antioch and an unnamed "emir of the Hagarenes" that allegedly took place shortly after the Muslim conquests of Palestine and Syria in the 630s. Michael Penn makes a compelling case that this work, written in Syriac, does not reflect an actual conversation with a real Muslim governor. Rather, it is a carefully crafted defense of Christian teachings composed in the decades around the year 700, when Muslims began to polemicize against Christianity in inscriptions on coins and on buildings such as the Dome of the Rock. *Hagarenes* (Syriac: *mhaggraye*) was a common term for Muslims during the eighth century; while the word may not relate etymologically to the name Hagar, Eastern Christians probably made the association nonetheless. The anonymous author of *John and the Emir*, however, makes no effort to brand Muslims as Hagar's heirs. Instead, he paints Muslims as all but Jewish on the grounds that they embrace the Old Testament but deny the authority of the New. This portrayal of Muslims enables the author to craft a bracingly relevant narrative within which to reiterate longstanding anti-Jewish arguments on behalf of Christian doctrines.[4]

Over the course of their dialogue, the emir poses four challenges to the patriarch, each in the form of a two-part question. He begins by asking whether Christians of all types revere the same text of the New Testament; the patriarch affirms that they do. Having set up his challenge, the emir tries to land his punch: "Why, when the gospel is one, is the faith diverse?" That is, why are there competing Christian churches, each with its own theology? The Muslim, expressing the anxieties of the Christian author or his audience, seems to contend that this diversity undermines all Christian claims to an authoritative interpretation of scripture.

John, however, has a reply at the ready. "Just as the Torah is one and the same and is accepted by us Christians and by you Hagarenes and by the Jews and the Samaritans, but each people differs in faith, so also concerning the gospel's faith: each sect understands and interprets it differently, and not like us." By "us," John refers to his own Miaphysite church, whose understanding of scripture he presents as being uniquely authoritative. The diversity of Christian interpretations of the gospels—Syria was home to both Miaphysites and Chalcedonians—is comparable to the diversity among religious communities that revere the Torah. The fact that rival communities misinterpret a shared sacred text does not invalidate the teachings of the one true religion, as the emir himself and, more importantly, the Christian reader would surely agree.

Notice how John simply asserts that Hagarenes, which is to say Muslims, revere the Torah. John takes this claim a step further in response to the emir's second challenge, regarding the nature of Jesus Christ: "When Christ, who you say is God, was in Mary's womb, who bore and governed the heavens and the earth?" That is, how could God have managed the affairs of the world in utero? Once again, however, John easily parries the emir's challenge: "When God descended to Mount Sinai and was there speaking with Moses for forty days and forty nights, who bore and governed the heavens and the earth? For you say that you accept Moses and his books." The emir, who evidently accepts John's depiction of Islam as an Old Testament religion, concedes that God governed the universe even while on Mount Sinai. This enables John to score his point by declaring that God did the same from within Mary's womb.

The emir continues to display his acceptance of the Torah in his third challenge. He enquires about the beliefs of Abraham and Moses and then pointedly asks why these and other biblical figures did not write openly about their faith in Christ. The patriarch responds with an argument long used in anti-Jewish disputations: Old Testament heroes only hinted at their Trinitarian faith because they feared that expressing it outright would cause average Israelites to believe that there are multiple gods. John illustrates these hints with the classic example of "Hear Israel that the Lord your God, the Lord is one" (Deuteronomy 6:4), emphasizing the verse's three references to the one God. Following up on this response, the emir demands proof from the Torah that Christ is God, that he was born from a virgin, and that God had a son, issues commonly raised in pre-Islamic apologies for Christianity. The author of *John and the Emir* reports that the patriarch provided evidence from the Old Testament for all these Christian doctrines but cites only one example: "The Lord brought down from before the Lord fire and sulfur upon Sodom and upon Gomorrah" (Genesis 19:24). The emir demands to see for himself that the word "Lord" appears twice in this verse, so the patriarch shows him the text in Greek and Syriac bibles. The emir then summons a Jewish "expert of scripture" to confirm the wording; the Jew, however, evasively professes his ignorance.

In his fourth and final challenge, the emir questions the scriptural basis of Christian law. The narrator, who does not provide the language of John's reportedly lengthy response, emphasizes that the patriarch delivered it in the presence of leaders from all the Christian cities and tribes, including not only fellow Miaphysites but also members of the rival Chalcedonian church. Even Chalcedonians, however, pray for the Miaphysite patriarch and recognize that the Holy Spirit itself filled John with true knowledge and graceful eloquence. Recall that the emir's opening challenge critiques the diversity of Christian beliefs; John's masterful command of scriptural interpretation implies that his beliefs are the most authoritative and that all Christians should therefore unite under the Miaphysite banner. Christian audiences of *John and the Emir* should not stray into Chalcedonian heresy, much less into the heresy of the Muslims who, like the Jews, fail to recognize the true signs of Christ embedded within the Old Testament.[5]

The Hagarenes portrayed in *John and the Emir* are clearly not Jews. They accept the Torah but not the biblical prophets, and the emir calls on a Jew to verify the biblical text. These Muslims are, however, similar enough to Jews that the author of this dialogue can simply recycle pre-Islamic arguments: John's prooftexts for biblical references to Christ and the accompanying interpretations derive from a sermon by the sixth-century Miaphysite patriarch Severus of Antioch.[6] By portraying Muslims as adherents of the Old Testament, the author of *John and the Emir* creates a compelling and relevant narrative through which to convey traditional theological arguments. In the process, he also suggests that Islam poses no new theological challenge to Christianity; as a variety of Judaism, it is utterly familiar and obviously inferior. While the emir may be more powerful than the patriarch, he cannot stump the Christian because Christians alone properly understand the Bible. The patriarch's remarks would not convince actual Muslims (or actual Jews, for that matter), but they were never intended to do so: *John and the Emir* seeks to bolster the faith of Christian audiences in the scriptural foundations of Miaphysite doctrines.

The same dynamic animates an eighth-century Arabic work by an anonymous Chalcedonian Christian, preserved at St. Catherine's

Monastery on Mount Sinai and published with the title *On the Triune Nature of God*. The ostensible purpose of this text is to persuade Muslims to accept Christian doctrines on matters such as the Trinity and the Incarnation (the belief that God became a human being), but its primary audience was actually fellow Christians whose convictions might waver. *On the Triune Nature of God* consists largely of proofs drawn from the Old Testament, and in this respect it belongs to a long-standing genre of testimony collections, which often present themselves as arguments against Jews. The author also cites a handful of quranic verses to support his theological claims, but manuscript expert James Rendel Harris aptly observes that this author imagines his Muslim addressee to be "a new kind of Jew" who likewise respects the authority of biblical evidence.[7]

Muslims of the seventh and eighth centuries did not in fact grant credence to the Jewish Bible, but *On the Triune Nature of God* nevertheless imagines that they do. Christian authors, after all, had long used Jewish foils to make the case to fellow Christians that Old Testament prophecies refer to Jesus Christ. Eighth-century Arabic-speaking Christians, however, regarded Muslims as far more relevant than Jews because they lived in a society that Muslims dominated. Rather than abandon the discourse of anti-Judaism, which played a fundamental role in the teaching of Christian doctrine, the author of this work simply addresses his testimony collection to a fictitious Bible-revering Muslim in the hopes that his actual Christian audience will continue to find classic anti-Jewish arguments convincing.

The author of *John and the Emir* likewise regards his quasi-Jewish Muslim foil as an especially effective vehicle for conveying traditional truth claims to contemporary Christians. A debate between John and a powerless rabbi would be far less compelling than one with a powerful Muslim governor, and the patriarch's victory would be much less satisfying. *John and the Emir* is written in the form of a letter to an unnamed addressee whom the opening sentence describes as "anxious and afraid on our behalf," eager to find out what transpired in the debate. Miaphysites and Chalcedonians alike "prayed for the life and the safety of the blessed lord patriarch." The author recognizes and takes full advantage of the dramatic potential that results from replacing the Jewish foil who traditionally appears in literary defenses of Christian doctrine with a Muslim foil.[8]

A similar dynamic appears in the *Disputation between a Muslim and a Monk of Bet Halé*, discussed in chapter 2 above. This apologetic text from the turn of the ninth century, by a member of the Church of the East, also emphasizes the high status of the Muslim notable who ultimately concedes that Christianity is superior to his own tradition. When the monk demands that the Muslim accept arguments based on the Torah and the prophets, the Muslim replies, "Truly, I will accept a proof (taken) from the Old (Testament)." Much of the conversation, in fact, focuses on demonstrating that the Jewish Bible, especially the Torah, supports Christian beliefs and practices. One would, for example, expect a real Muslim to challenge Christians on the basis of the Quran's depiction of Abraham, but in the *Bet Halé Disputation* the Muslim character debates the meaning of Genesis just as a Jewish disputant might. By constructing his debate in this manner, the author creates a contemporary vehicle for teaching Christian audiences time-honored lessons about how to properly interpret the Old Testament. If a powerful Muslim accepts Christian interpretations of the Old Testament, Christians have all the more reason to do the same.[9]

Even as Eastern Christian authors increase the dramatic tension within their texts by replacing Jewish foils with powerful Muslims, they also render Islam itself as unthreatening. Theologians, after all, had long since demonstrated that the Old Testament must be read through the lens of the New. The association of Muslims with Jews enables subjugated Christians to preserve a sense of confidence and religious superiority. Of equal significance, it also enables Christians to continue teaching their faith through the established discourse of anti-Judaism. Portrayals of Muslims as followers of the Old Testament reflect not a social reality of "Judeo-Hagarism" but rather the literary and rhetorical needs of Christian authors living in a society dominated by Muslims.

The presence of anti-Jewish tropes in early Christian texts about Muslims does not reflect a misunderstanding of Islam so much as a misrepresentation designed to bolster Christian faith through updated versions of tried and true arguments. We cannot know whether the authors of the works we have examined recognized the inaccuracy of their depictions, but they evidently regarded these depictions as sufficiently plausible and compelling to advance their goal of reinforcing Christian teachings about Christ and the true meaning of the Old Testament.

NEW ARGUMENTS WITH FAMILIAR FOILS

The works we have just examined employ pre-Islamic literary genres and traditional scriptural proofs in defense of Christian beliefs and practices: their anonymous authors simply change the target of their rhetoric from imaginary Jews to imaginary Bible-revering Muslims. New kinds of arguments on behalf of Christianity emerged in the late eighth century. This period was marked not only by greater familiarity with Islamic texts and beliefs but also by resurgent interest in Greek philosophy, as Christians and Muslims alike played active roles in the translation of Neoplatonic and Aristotelian works into Arabic. Some Christian apologists created testimony collections that find support for Christian truth claims not in the Old Testament but in the Quran. Many others offered philosophical proofs for doctrines such as the Trinity and Incarnation to supplement traditional arguments grounded in scripture.[10] Although these new philosophical arguments did not require Jewish foils, at least one author found value in branding Muslims as Jews nonetheless.

Timothy I, patriarch of the Church of the East from 780 to 823, is best known for his disputation with Caliph al-Mahdi, the most powerful Muslim ruler at the time. Timothy recounted this possibly fictional exchange in a Syriac letter composed between 782 and 785 that circulated widely in a number of medieval Arabic versions.[11] Shortly before writing that letter, the patriarch described another debate instigated by an unnamed and, perhaps, fictional Muslim philosopher in the caliph's court. This less familiar work, known as Letter 40, departs from earlier Eastern Christian literature both in its structure, which emulates contemporaneous Islamic works on God's unity, and in its use of philosophical reasoning as the primary means of demonstrating God's three-in-one nature as Father, Son, and Holy Spirit. In his introduction to Letter 40, however, Timothy frames the disputation in familiar terms by branding his Muslim foil as essentially Jewish. This setup primes Timothy's Christian audience to accept his novel arguments and reject contemporary critiques of Christian truth claims.[12]

The patriarch begins by reminding his audience that nothing is stronger than truth or weaker than falsehood and that victory and defeat are not always as they seem. He supports this claim by reference to the crucifixion of Christ, which Timothy blames on Satan and his Jewish minions. "When the prince of the world [that is, Satan] and his generals, the Jews, seemingly conquered [our Lord], in that moment they were conquered by him. When they seemed to put on the crown of victory, in that moment they were put to shame and disgraced with shame that can never be forgotten."

This anti-Jewish rhetoric activates strong emotions of disgust within Timothy's Christian audience that the patriarch quickly redirects toward his letter's rhetorical target: Muslims.

> Indeed, not only back in the days of Herod, Pilate, and the old Jews was there this sort of defeat and victory of truth and falsehood, but also now in our own times, in the days of the current rulers and the new Jews among us, the very same struggle and the very same contest persists between falsehood and truth. The stumbling block of the cross has not yet ceased. There is, however, nothing to fear from such strife and struggle because, as explained above, when it seems that truth is defeated the Shoot of Righteousness will demonstrate truth's victory in its full force.

Timothy declares (in the safety of a language that Muslims could not read) that Caliph al-Mahdi and his ministers are the contemporary equivalents of those who condemned Jesus while Muslims more broadly are "new Jews" who deny Christ's true significance. Through this anti-Jewish rhetoric, the patriarch frames his disputation with the Muslim philosopher as the latest round of a timeless struggle between truth and falsehood, exemplified respectively by Christians and by Jews old and new. Muslims may appear triumphant, but Christ, the "Shoot of Righteousness," will ultimately vindicate the Christians once more. Timothy—and, perhaps, his audience as well—appreciated this rhetoric about Muslims as "new Jews": in correspondence written at least fifteen years later, the patriarch seems to refer to Letter 40 as his treatise "against the new religion of the new Jews." Timothy used similar language in other works as well.[13]

What makes Muslims Jewish, according to Timothy, is "the stumbling block of the cross," to which the patriarch refers not only in the introduction to this disputation but also in its conclusion.[14] Timothy alludes to the words of Paul, who describes the proclamation of Christ crucified as "a stumbling block to Jews and foolishness to gentiles" (1 Corinthians 1:23). Timothy's use of Pauline language about Christ and the crucifixion, as well as his association of Muslims with Herod, Pilate, and the Jews of Christ's day, reflects the practice we explored in previous chapters of depicting Muslims in biblical terms.

Paul himself contrasts the so-called foolishness of faith in Christ with Greek ("gentile") wisdom, and he disparages the latter. Timothy, however, demonstrates in this disputation that there is no conflict between Aristotelian principles and Christian theology: Christian doctrines, he insists, are not in fact foolish on Greek terms. Muslims fail to accept

Christ as God not because of their admirable inclination toward philo-sophical wisdom but in spite of it. Timothy therefore makes a point of defining Muslims not as foolish gentiles but instead as stumbling Jews. The criterion of comparison by which he establishes the similarity of Muslims and Jews, notwithstanding their many differences, is that both stubbornly reject reasoned arguments in support of Christian faith.

The disputation itself revolves around themes foreshadowed by Tim-othy's introductory reference to "the stumbling block of the cross": the nature of Christ and the significance of the crucifixion. This debate begins with a philosophical discussion regarding how humans can obtain knowledge of God and then proceeds to an extensive conversa-tion about God's attributes. The Muslim affirms that, among these attributes, God is by nature one who knows. Timothy demonstrates that if this attribute characterizes God eternally (as it must if God is unchanging), then God must have been a knower possessing knowledge of a known prior to the creation of anything knowable. This is only possible, Timothy asserts, if God's nature is Trinitarian: the Father, the Son, and the Holy Spirit each know one another, are known by one another, and constitute the knowledge of one another. Timothy pro-ceeds to provide arguments from nature that one indivisible being can have three distinct modalities—a fruit, for example, simultaneously possesses taste, color, and smell—and only then offers proofs from the Old Testament and the Quran, such as references to God speaking in the first person plural. The debate subsequently turns to the Incarna-tion, the crucifixion, and reverence of the cross as the patriarch demon-strates that these distinctly Christian beliefs and practices are also con-sistent with philosophical principles.

There is no inherent reason to maintain that Timothy recounted—or, perhaps, invented—this disputation in order to dissuade Christians from converting to Islam, as the rate of conversion during the late eighth cen-tury was not especially high.[15] Rather, Timothy seems to fear that well-educated Christians might question core doctrines of their faith owing to their increasing familiarity with Greek philosophy or their exposure to Islamic critiques of Christian theology. This would account for why the patriarch focuses his attention not on Islam but on demonstrating that Christian doctrines withstand philosophical and Islamic scrutiny.

While Timothy obviously rejects Islamic critiques of Christian theol-ogy, he engages respectfully with his Muslim counterpart and, likewise, with the Quran both in Letter 40 and in his disputation with Caliph al-Mahdi. In the latter, the patriarch even praises Muhammad as one who "walked on the path of the prophets" by preaching not only mon-otheism but also, obliquely, Trinitarianism as well.[16] This respectfulness may reflect not only diplomatic tact but also and more importantly Timothy's awareness that his Christian audience already regarded the dominant elite and their beliefs favorably. Rather than challenge that perception, Timothy co-opts it by demonstrating that he can defeat his esteemed disputation partners on Islamic and philosophical terms alike, thus reinforcing the opening words of Letter 40: "There is nothing stronger than truth, and nothing weaker than falsehood" (a paraphrase of 1 Corinthians 1:25). Respectfulness notwithstanding, however, Timothy firmly declares in his introduction that those who reject core doctrines about Christ are no better than the eternally "disgraced" Jews.

By comparing esteemed Muslims with disgraced Jews, Timothy draws on the rich rhetorical tradition of anti-Judaism to reinforce his case that Christians should maintain their faith in Christ lest they too judaize. In fact, the very term he uses to describe Muslims, "new Jews," appears in earlier works that condemn the alleged heresy of rival Christians in the course of promoting what their authors regard as orthodox beliefs about Christ. Timothy does the same but now uses a Muslim foil to demonstrate how easy it is to fall into the falsehood known as Judaism. To crib from David Nirenberg's description of John Chrysostom's anti-Jewish rhetoric (discussed in chapter 1), Timothy "has not shifted his aim by turning from [Jews to Muslims]; he has merely changed ammunition."[17]

Chrysostom and Timothy alike aim to persuade audiences of fellow Christians regardless of whether they use Jews, fourth-century heretics, or eighth-century Muslims as their cannon fodder. Jews function in these works as the point of reference, the group Chrysostom and Timothy believe that Christians already despise and therefore the group to whom they compare their more sympathetic rhetorical targets. The assertion that rival Christians or Muslims are like Jews because they too lack faith in Christ gives Christians added incentive to differentiate themselves by cultivating proper faith.[18]

Both the patriarch and his Eastern Christian audience know that Muslims are not Jews and that Muslims in fact venerate Christ. For that reason, Timothy's polemical comparison of Muslims with Jews is shockingly scandalous. As historian Christina Brauner observes, comparisons of this nature "obtain their polemical edge by explicitly violating usual categories and standards of comparability—above all, by pointing out similarities in what is usually understood to be different or by comparing things commonly deemed incomparable."[19] Although Timothy's audience may not have regarded Muslims as Jews until now, they know that disdain for all things Jewish contributes to their own self-identification as Christians, and they are accustomed to anti-Jewish teachings that reinforce core Christian truth claims. Letter 40 features a Muslim disputant and a new style of philosophical argumentation, but through his polemical comparison the patriarch places this letter within the timeless contest between truth and falsehood that always pits Christians against "Jews." By employing the familiar rhetorical tradition of anti-Judaism, Timothy downplays the novelty of his argument in the hopes of increasing its persuasiveness. In this respect, his comparison is not only shocking but also deliberately cliché.

Timothy counts on his audience, now primed to perceive Muslims as quasi-Jewish, to assess his challenger accordingly. The Muslim philosopher ultimately earns the memorably disparaging title "new Jew" that appears in the introduction to Letter 40 by refusing to accept the patriarch's conclusions even though he cannot refute them. The fact that Muslims are unpersuaded by reasoned defenses of Christianity does not mean that Christian theology is unreasonable; rather, it reflects the Jewishness of the Muslims themselves. Christian audiences, therefore, should redouble their own faith knowing that it conforms not only to scripture but also to Aristotelian logic—and even, Timothy claims in his disputation with al-Mahdi, to the teachings of Muhammad. The patriarch's polemical comparison of Jews old and new gives fellow Christians further incentive to accept his teachings, lest they too come to resemble Jews.

A JEWISH MUSLIM FOIL FOR THE GOOD CHRISTIAN STUDENT

Theodore bar Koni, a teacher within Timothy's Church of the East, wrote his own dialogue between a Christian and a Muslim as the tenth chapter of the *Scholion*; Theodore added this chapter shortly after first publishing his popular instructional manual on the scriptural foundations of Christian theology in 792 with only nine chapters.[20] The *Scholion*'s Muslim, like the Muslims in *John and the Emir* and the *Bet Halé Disputation*, accepts the authority of the Old Testament, but he differs from them in crucial respects. In these other works, as well as in Timothy's disputations, all of which purport to recount actual dialogues, Christian heroes debate powerful Muslim officials whom Christian audiences fear or envy but can never truly emulate. Theodore, in contrast, constructs an explicitly fictional dialogue between a Christian teacher and a Muslim student—in a work written by an actual teacher for actual students. As a result, members of Theodore's Christian audience identify with the Muslim foil as a fellow student even as they presumably wish to differentiate themselves from him. This tension, which animates the entire dialogue, reaches its climax when the teacher polemically compares the Muslim student with Jews, the anti-Christians.

Theodore declares at the outset of chapter 10 that he wrote this dialogue to demonstrate the truth of Christian beliefs to those who accept the Old Testament and acknowledge the coming of Jesus Christ but reject the authority of the New Testament. He calls these people *hanpé*, a Syriac term that originally meant "pagans" but that also refers to generic non-Christians and, frequently, to Muslims. The dialogue's student, who represents these *hanpé*, is clearly a Muslim: he is a circumcised non-Jew, who, thanks to the teachings of a man born six centuries after Jesus, recognizes the importance of Christ but insists—paraphrasing the Quran—that God has neither a father nor a son. The student also voices ideas regarding Christianity commonly ascribed to Muslims, claiming, for example, that Christians falsified the text of the New Testament and that Jesus was not in fact crucified. At the same time, this fictional student serves as a pedagogical foil for the actual Christian students who studied Theodore's manual. To the extent that this literary character accepts the Church of the East's doctrines, readers of the *Scholion* should do the same. These readers, however, should also accept the teachings that the student resists.[21]

For much of the dialogue, the fictional student models appropriate behavior for actual students. He unswervingly accepts the authority of the Old Testament and shares his teacher's disdain both for the Jews and for Miaphysite and Chalcedonian theologies deemed heretical by the Church of the East. Not only is the student consistently attentive to the teacher, he also readily acknowledges the truth of his teacher's scriptural interpretations and accepts the teacher's arguments. In the first section of the dialogue, the teacher demonstrates that the Old Testament not only refers to Jesus Christ frequently but exists for the very purpose of preparing the Jews to recognize Christ upon his arrival. The student readily agrees with the teacher's interpretations of scripture but questions the scriptural foundations of core Christian practices that find no parallel within Islam: baptism, the Eucharist, and veneration of the cross. The teacher proceeds to marshal Old Testament evidence in support of these practices, which the student once again accepts. This student, however, repeatedly expresses doubts regarding two interrelated doctrines that contradict Islamic conceptions of monotheism: that Christ is the Son of God and that God comprises Father, Son, and Holy Spirit. Theodore reserves discussion of these doctrines—and his polemical comparison of Muslims and Jews—until the dialogue's climax.[22]

The teacher sets up his response to his student's doubts by asking the student to identify the difference between the teachings of Christ and those of Moses. The student struggles: after all, he has come to accept that there are no contradictions between the Old Testament and the New, which has been Theodore's point throughout the *Scholion*. The student lamely suggests, on the basis of Romans 14, that Christ abolished certain Old Testament practices related to dietary laws and holidays. "You still believe like a Jew!" the teacher retorts. The Jews, he explains, insist that the Messiah will not teach anything new, and by this point in the dialogue the student should realize that Moses himself foresaw the abolition of these practices. Yet Christ must have taught something new, for why else would God have sent him and the Old Testament foretold his arrival? The student, stumped, asks the teacher to identify Christ's distinctive lesson. "He taught about the Father, particularly that the Father has a Son who resembles him! But they [the Jews], like you, could not bring themselves to believe him and for that reason despised him." True to type, Theodore's Muslim student reiterates his inability to believe even after the teacher demonstrates that the Church of the East's doctrines regarding the Trinity and Incarnation align with Christ's own teachings, conform to logical reasoning, and find support within the Old Testament.[23]

For much of the *Scholion*'s tenth chapter, readers could imagine the student as a fellow Christian—after all, he assented to his teacher's every statement. Now, however, we discover to our surprise that this Muslim student is actually "Jewish" because he fails the crucial test. Real Muslims, of course, fail this test as well. In the end, it makes no difference whether or not Muslims actually accept the authority of the Old Testament: they do not accept Christ as God and, for that reason, they are no better than Jews.

Christian readers of the *Scholion* face the same challenge as its Muslim character because they too must decide whether or not to accept Christian doctrines regarding Christ and the Trinity. Theodore, like Timothy, does not seem especially worried that his students might convert to Islam. Rather, the doubts they might harbor regarding Christian truth claims place these students at risk of believing "like a Jew." Theodore's polemical comparison, like Timothy's, depicts the significance of belief in terms that are both stark and cliché, drawn as they are from the long-standing discourse of anti-Judaism: Muslims are like Jews because they too stumble over the nature of Christ and cannot accept irrefutable arguments in support of Christian theology. Actual Christian students should instead accept the teacher's arguments and cultivate proper faith in Christ. Theodore reinforces precisely this point: "Belief is foremost among the traits that one needs to acquire," his literary teacher declares in the final paragraph of chapter 10, apparently addressing the *Scholion*'s readers directly. This lesson sums up the message of the entire chapter, which Theodore describes as "an apology for our belief" in its opening sentence.[24]

Timothy I and Theodore bar Koni both seem to presume that Christians cannot bear the thought of becoming "new Jews" themselves. These authors mobilize their audiences' strong anti-Jewish sentiments to undercut Islamic critiques of Christian theology and inspire a reaffirmation of faith in Christ. Comparisons of Muslims with Jews appear precisely where Timothy and Theodore wish to emphasize the refusal of Muslims to accept Christian teachings about Christ and the Trinity. These comparisons clarify that one need not be part of the community that allegedly crucified Christ in order to stand in an antithetical relationship to Christianity: anyone who doubts Christian doctrines, notwithstanding their scriptural and rational foundations, judaizes. By creating a stark binary between truth and falsehood, proper faith and disbelief, Timothy and Theodore prod their audiences to accept Christian philosophical and exegetical arguments.

Foils that are simultaneously Muslim and Jewish enable Eastern Christian apologists—Miaphysites, Chalcedonians, and members of the Church of the East alike—to draw on traditional arguments and biblical frames of reference in support of longstanding truth claims. Christian audiences living under Muslim rule likely found the resulting rhetoric more relevant and more compelling than they would have if the foils were either Jewish or Muslim, notwithstanding the fact that the Jewish Muslims depicted in these works do not actually exist. These apologists also leverage the respect that Eastern Christians accorded to their Muslim overlords. The ability of Christian heroes to offer persuasive and irrefutable arguments to Muslim characters is significant precisely because Eastern Christian audiences perceived Muslims as formidable, and the authors themselves emphasize the power and the intelligence of their Muslim foils. In the next chapters, we will examine works whose authors employ a different rhetorical strategy: instead of implicitly acknowledging the respectability of misguided Muslims, they render Islam disreputable by alleging that its origins are irredeemably tainted with Jewishness.

CHAPTER 6

What Makes Islam Jewish? Allegations of Carnality and Irrationality

Eighth through Twelfth Centuries

Jews are to blame for Islam as we know it, at least according to Christian tales about Muhammad's Jewish associates. These Jews purportedly played a crucial role in creating a religion that promotes irrational beliefs and carnal (that is, physical rather than spiritual) practices—a religion, in short, that resembles what many premodern Christians imagined Judaism to be. Put differently, Christians used tales about Muhammad's Jewish associates to defame Islam by defining it, like Judaism, as the inverse of proper Christianity. Medieval Europeans, however, emphasized a different aspect of this binary opposition than their Eastern Christian predecessors. This difference reflects the distinct concerns and objectives of each set of polemicists as well as the fact that Eastern audiences, who lived within a Muslim-dominated society, already knew something about Islam while most European audiences did not.

The present chapter traces variations among Christian tales about Muhammad's Jewish associates as told across several centuries and regions. The same storytellers also ascribe differing roles to Muhammad himself and to another key associate, a Christian monk often called Sergius. This variety reflects the kaleidoscopic way Christians associated Islam not only with Judaism but also with paganism and various forms of Christianity. Tales about Muhammad's associates explain how allegedly pagan, Jewish, and Christian elements found their way into Islam, and they render Islam familiar by placing it within a biblically grounded framework of conceptualizing Christendom's enemies. These stories, like the tales about Bible-believing Hagarenes we encountered in chapter 5 and those about Muhammad we will examine in chapter 7, tell us nothing factual about Islam's origins. They do, however, shed valuable light on the ways in which their authors understand the challenges that confront fellow Christians.

We will begin with the oldest recorded Christian tale about Muhammad's Jewish associates, which appears in the early ninth-century *Chronicle* of Theophanes alongside several other disparaging reports about Muhammad and his teachings. These reports ascribe to Muslims the supposedly Jewish traits of carnality and irrationality. Ninth-century Eastern Christian polemicists stress the orientation toward fleshly pleasures and practices that Jews allegedly introduced into Islam, perhaps in order to counteract the attractiveness of the worldly privileges that Christians living under Muslim rule could obtain through assimilation and conversion. Twelfth-century Europeans living within a thoroughly Christian society, of course, had different concerns. These authors, worried that their well-educated readers might question the reasonableness of Christian theology, allege that Muslims fail to recognize that Christ is God because Muhammad's associates instilled Jewish irrationality into Islam. Eastern and European tales alike encourage Christians to cultivate the very characteristics that Muslims purportedly lack on account of their Jewishness.

DISPARAGING THE ORIGINS OF ISLAM

Theophanes, an early ninth-century monk who lived outside the Muslim world, preserved several distinct reports about Muhammad that circulated among Christians subject to Muslim rule. Cyril Mango, who translated Theophanes's *Chronicle* into English, contends that Theophanes himself did not compile these reports but rather copied a Greek translation of a collection assembled by an eighth-century Syriac chronicler. These brief reports disparage Islam by reworking in hostile fashion Islamic tales in praise of Muhammad and his followers.[1]

Theophanes's collection begins with a tale about Jews: "When [Muhammad] first appeared, the misguided Jews thought he was the messiah who is awaited by them, so that some of their leaders joined him and accepted his religion while forsaking that of Moses." These leaders—waiting in vain long after the arrival of the true messiah, Jesus Christ—discover their error when they see Muhammad sacrifice a camel and eat its meat in violation of biblical law. Too fearful to abandon

Muhammad's religion and at a loss for what to do, "those wretched men taught [Muhammad] illicit things . . . and remained with him." What exactly the Jews taught depends on how one interprets the ambiguous Greek text: "illicit things directed against us, Christians," but also, perhaps, "illicit things contrary to our Christian [religion]." The first translation blames Jews for Muslim hostility toward Christians, while the second blames Jews for ritual aspects of Islam that contradict Christian teachings, such as the practice of circumcision and principled abstention from pork. Theophanes himself may wish to portray both dimensions of Islam as Jewish.[2]

The notion that Jews tried to introduce false teachings into Islam already appears in Islamic tales—in which, of course, these efforts fail.[3] The Christian retelling, in contrast, demeans Muhammad by portraying him as incapable of resisting Jewish influence. The motif of Jewish-inspired hostility toward Christians already appears in the seventh-century *History of Sebeos*, which, as we saw in chapter 2, blames Jews for prompting Muslims to wage war against Christians and for trying to spark a massacre of Jerusalem's Christian population. Similarly, eighth-century polemicists alleged that Jews prompted Muslims to destroy Christian crosses and images.[4] Theophanes's tale about Muhammad's Jewish teachers accounts for the differences between Christians and their Muslim overlords as well as for the discrimination that Christians experience as members of a subject population.

The *Chronicle* proceeds to trace Muhammad's genealogy as a descendant of Ishmael and to describe his relationship with Khadija, the wealthy woman for whom Muhammad worked and whom he ultimately married. According to Islamic sources, Muhammad experienced divine revelations that made his body shake, and Khadija was the first to recognize Muhammad as a true prophet. The Christian tale counters this claim by alleging that Muhammad actually suffered from epilepsy, regarded at the time as a form of demonic possession. Muhammad, this tale reports, deceitfully told his wife that his seizures are prophetic revelations. Although Khadija was skeptical, "a certain monk living there, a friend of hers who had been exiled for his depraved doctrine," convinced her that Muhammad spoke truthfully. This heretical monk merely sought to ease his friend's distress, but the monk's false words proved to be at least as dangerous to fellow Christians as his false theology. The gullible Khadija became the first of the pseudoprophet's followers and persuaded others to do the same. The storyteller, channeling contemporaneous stereotypes about gender and rationality, emphasizes that Islam spread first among women, only later among men, and "in the last resort by war." The irrational faith that these early Muslims place in Muhammad's claim to prophethood parallels the Jews' misplaced belief that Muhammad is the messiah.[5]

Theophanes's *Chronicle* proceeds to explain that Muhammad preached mutual sympathy as well as aid for those who are wronged. It focuses, however, on Muhammad's depiction of paradise as a place of "carnal eating and drinking and intercourse with women," whose geography features "a river of wine, honey, and milk." The Christian author, most likely a celibate monk, characterizes this vision of paradise as "full of profligacy and stupidity." His account reflects both familiarity with certain Quranic teachings (see, for example, Quran 47:15, 52:17–28) and a readiness to draw sharp and caricatured contrasts between Christian and Islamic doctrines. This particular contrast hinges on the distinction between body and spirit already employed by Paul; Christians traditionally regard carnal practices as evil and, more specifically, as Jewish. Perhaps this, too, is an example of the "illicit things" that the Jews taught Muhammad, although the *Chronicle* does not explicitly ascribe this thoroughly un-Christian teaching to them.

Unlike the works we considered in chapter 5, which defend the validity of Christian teachings against critiques leveled by respectable Muslim foils, the tales that Theophanes preserves go on the offensive by rendering Islam despicable. Their compiler made no effort to unify these reports: the goal is simply to defame Islam by maligning its origins and teachings. Various later storytellers, however, reworked this material to make more pointed arguments about the Jewishness of Islam. Ninth-century Eastern Christian authors emphasized Islam's "Jewish" carnality, while twelfth-century European authors, familiar with a Latin translation of Theophanes's *Chronicle*, instead used stories about Muhammad's Jewish associates to allege that Islam, like Judaism, is irrational.[6] These choices, we will see, reflect the different audiences and objectives that each set of authors seeks to address.

THE CARNALITY OF ISLAM

Theophanes preserves distinct Christian tales about Muhammad that circulated in eighth-century Syria and Palestine. Other Eastern Christians told a different and more integrated story that also involves Muhammad, a monk, and one or more Jews. The set of traditions known today as the Legend of Sergius Bahira, which first took written form in the mid-ninth century, seeks to undermine Islam's appeal by emphasizing the carnal—and, more specifically, the Jewish—nature of Islamic beliefs and practices.[7]

The legend recounts that a monk named Sergius settled in the Arabian Desert as a solitary hermit after receiving a vision predicting the rise of an Arab empire. Sergius confidently informed his primitive, idolatrous neighbors that a powerful man would arise among them. These Arabs liked what they heard, so they called Sergius "Bahira," an honorific term for monks that means "the eminent" in Syriac, and they regularly visited the miraculous well near his home. One day, a young boy named Muhammad came along. Sergius Bahira immediately recognized and proclaimed Muhammad as the future leader of the Arabs. Knowing that Muhammad would soon gain immense power, Sergius secured a commitment from the boy that his successors would not harm Christians and proceeded to instruct Muhammad in the fundamentals of the Christian faith. Sergius also crafted a set of teachings for Muhammad to share with his followers and advised Muhammad to claim that he received this knowledge from the angel Gabriel. These teachings include a promise of paradise flowing with wine, milk, honey, and water and teeming with beautiful young women; an injunction to fast only during the day and only for one month in the year; basic norms regarding diet and morality; and a schedule of daily prayer. Sergius told Muhammad to proclaim that God would send down a book containing these teachings. In fact, Sergius himself wrote the book, "which they call 'Quran,'" and affixed it to the horn of a cow that appeared just after Muhammad delivered this prophecy. This sham miracle purportedly explains why Muslims also call the Quran "the Scripture of the Cow." (In fact, the Quran's longest chapter is named "The Cow" because of its subject matter.)[8]

Barbara Roggema, who edited and translated the Eastern Christian versions of the Sergius Bahira legend, aptly describes this legend as a work of "parasitical historiography": its creators adapted a tale told by Muslims themselves in order to attack Islam. In the Islamic version, Muhammad accompanied his uncle on a merchant caravan to Syria while he was still a young boy. The caravan stopped near the dwelling place of a solitary monk named Bahira, who noticed a miraculous cloud shading a member of the caravan; eager to understand this sign, he invited the group to a meal. The group left Muhammad behind to watch the bags, but the monk insisted that the boy come as well despite his apparent insignificance. Bahira recognized in Muhammad telltale signs marking him as the long-awaited prophet and warned Muhammad's uncle, "Take your nephew back to his country and guard him carefully against the Jews for—by God!—if they see him and know about him what I know, they will do him evil."[9]

In both the Islamic and Christian accounts, Muhammad's Arab companions dismiss the boy as young and insignificant while the monk recognizes miraculous signs of greatness that others fail to see. One version of the Christian legend even includes the monk's warning to protect Muhammad from the Jews, as Christians and Muslims alike alleged that Jews routinely sought to murder prophets.[10] The Christian account, however, emphatically ascribes the origins of Muhammad's teachings not to God but rather to Sergius (a.k.a. Bahira), who creates a watered-down version of Christianity suitable for the primitive Arabs. This religion is simply monotheistic, without the nuanced complexities of Trinitarianism, and it imposes lighter expectations with respect to fasting, food, prayer, and morality than those to which monks hold themselves. Sergius, accommodating the purportedly carnal nature of his Arab audience, even invents the vision of a physically pleasurable paradise that fellow monks regard with disgust. This tale, which likely circulated among Christian monks, accounts for the presence within the Quran both of passages that resemble Christian teachings, such as its description of Jesus Christ as "the Word of God and his Spirit" (Quran 4:171), and those that depart from it, including its depictions of paradise.[11]

The Quran, however, also contains passages that flatly contradict Christian teachings. Most versions of the Sergius legend present the monk as a thoroughly pious figure who would never introduce such content himself; these accounts blame a Jew for doing so after Sergius's death. In the words of the short Arabic version, "a man appeared who is known as Kab al-Ahbar, from the progeny of Abraham. He began to teach the Sons of Ishmael and to invalidate the word of Sergius. And he said to them, 'The one who will appear from amongst you [Muhammad], he is the Paraclete whom Christ mentioned as coming after him,' and he taught them many things from the Torah and the Prophets and also some of the stories of theirs."[12]

Kab al-Ahbar, like Bahira, features prominently in Islamic traditions. Kab, a Jewish scribe or rabbi, converted to Islam several years after Muhammad's death and played a prominent role in the transmission of traditions about biblical prophets within the early Muslim community. Some Islamic sources report that Kab sought to introduce into Islam certain false teachings from Judaism, but the caliphs who led the Muslim community firmly repudiated those teachings. These stories reassure

Muslims that their leaders effectively safeguarded Islam from corruption. Kab's inclination toward falsifying tradition reflects a broader tendency that the Quran ascribes to Jews, who allegedly distorted the text of their own Torah (5:13). The Christian authors of the Legend of Sergius Bahira agree with their Muslim counterparts regarding the danger that Jews pose, but in their version the Jew succeeds: Kab, they claim, corrupted the Quran that Sergius wrote for Muhammad.[13]

The specific teaching within the Quran that Christian authors ascribe to Kab relates to the "Paraclete," whom Jesus announces that God the Father will send after his Son's death (John 14:16–16:7). Christians traditionally understand this Greek term—which literally means advocate, helper, or comforter—in reference to the Holy Spirit, the third person of the Trinity. The Quran, however, reports that Jesus spoke of "a Messenger to come after me whose name is Ahmad" (61:6), and Muslim interpreters understood this verse to speak of Muhammad. This representation of Jesus's prophecy as referring to a flesh-and-blood person, which from a Christian perspective reflects a fundamental misunderstanding of God's true nature, exemplifies the false teachings that Kab the Jew purportedly inserted into the Quran. According to Syriac versions of the Sergius legend, Kab even declared that Muhammad, as Jesus's successor, would rise from the dead after three days; when his followers returned to check, however, they discovered a repulsive, rotting corpse. Nonetheless, these texts emphasize, Muslims continue to believe that Muhammad is the Paraclete and irrationally adhere to Kab's other teachings notwithstanding his evident lack of credibility.[14]

The East Syrian version of the legend adds further information about Kab's alterations to the Quran that Sergius wrote:

> After the death of Sergius, Kab the Scribe rose up and changed the writings of Sergius Bahira. He handed down another teaching to them and put in confusion, corruption, superstitions, ridiculous and arbitrary things, circumcision, ablution, "an eye for an eye and a tooth for a tooth" and "a killing for a killing" and divorce, and that when a woman is divorced, if another man does not take her in marriage, he cannot return to her. . . . Sergius gave them the New [Testament] and Kab the Old.[15]

Kab's teachings focus on physical rituals, corporal punishments, and sexual intercourse. Christians understand Old Testament references to these subjects spiritually, but Kab misreads these norms in a literal and carnal—that is, a purportedly Jewish—manner. Sergius taught Christianity while offering modest concessions to the fleshliness of the Arabs, but Kab allegedly transformed Islam into a variety of Judaism.

Given their excessive focus on the body, it is no wonder that Kab the Jew and the Muslims he misled are incapable of recognizing that the Paraclete is the Holy Spirit and that Jesus Christ is no mere human being. Muslims instead place their trust in Muhammad, even after they discover his rotting corpse. The fundamental errors of the Muslims, which the Legend of Sergius Bahira labels as Jewish errors, are that they fail to distinguish body from spirit and that they fail to understand the Trinity. Islam, in other words, is Jewish because of its purported carnality. Christians, implicitly, should differentiate themselves from Muslims by cultivating their own spirituality.

Eastern Christian versions of the Sergius Bahira legend display considerable knowledge of Islamic practices, beliefs, texts, and traditions, and their creators seem to presume similar familiarity on the part of their Christian audiences. Parasitical historiography, after all, only works to the extent that audiences recognize the relationship between the new accounts and the traditions they recast. Knowledge of and presumed familiarity with Islam are especially apparent in the Arabic versions of the legend, in which Sergius explains the hidden Christian meaning of numerous Quranic verses. The interactions between literate ninth-century Christians and Muslims that generated this familiarity may also have prompted concern about voluntary conversion to Islam, which carried worldly benefits in the form of elevated social status and reduced taxes. The legend's authors may seek to neutralize Islam's attractiveness by ascribing Christian roots to the religion's praiseworthy elements while countering Islamic claims about Muhammad's prophethood and the Quran's divine origins. The contention that Kab the Jew succeeded in corrupting Islam brilliantly advances such an agenda: it draws on familiar tropes about the falsehood and carnality of Jewish teachings while portraying Muslims as gullible quasi-Jews. Christians, schooled by Paul and countless subsequent teachers, should know better than to judaize for the sake of worldly—that is, carnal, not spiritual—benefits. Relatedly, this tale may seek to reinforce the commitment of Christian monks to subdue physical desires in pursuit of spiritual goals.[16]

Concern about conversion to Islam is explicit in the late-ninth-century *Apology of al-Kindi*: this Arabic text begins with a letter, ostensibly written by a Muslim, that invites Christians to convert. The anonymous Christian polemicist responds with a harsh refutation of Islam designed to make conversion thoroughly unappealing. He paints a highly unflattering picture of Muhammad, whose unchecked sexual appetite, hunger for power, military activities (along with battlefield losses), and inability to perform miracles disprove his false claims to prophethood. Muhammad, *al-Kindi* asserts, received guidance not from God but rather from Sergius, who converted Muhammad from idolatry to Christianity. "When the Jews perceived this, they revived an ancient feud and poured abuse upon him, as was the custom between them and the Christians." Muhammad's community would have remained Christian were it not for the malicious efforts of Kab and Abdallah ibn Salam, another Jewish figure familiar from Islamic traditions. These Jews deceitfully joined Muhammad's community, hiding from him their true objective to undermine Sergius's teachings. After Muhammad's death, Kab and Abdallah tampered with the original text of the Quran, which had been based on the Gospels alone. "They introduced passages from their own Torah and some of the laws and stories in their possession. In this way, they corrupted the whole, taking from it and adding to it as they chose, insinuating their own blasphemies into it."[17]

The *Apology of al-Kindi*, like the Legend of Sergius Bahira on which it draws, turns on its head the Islamic allegation that Jews corrupted the text of the Torah: the scripture that Jews corrupted was none other than the Quran itself. By portraying Islam as abhorrently Jewish, this work furthers the broader objective of rendering Islam despicable to Christians who might otherwise contemplate conversion. Unlike other Eastern Christian versions of the Sergius legend, however, *al-Kindi* does not specify what exactly is Jewish about Islam. This ambiguity provided an opening for European authors to take the tale in a new direction for their own purposes.

FAITH IN THE REASONABLENESS OF ROMAN CATHOLIC THEOLOGY

Eastern Christian polemicists used tales about Muhammad's Jewish associates to strengthen the resolve of Christians suffering under Muslim rule and to render Islam abhorrent to those who might otherwise contemplate becoming Muslims themselves. Petrus Alfonsi and Peter of Cluny, twelfth-century Europeans who discovered these tales in Theophanes's *Chronicle* and the *Apology of al-Kindi*, faced a fundamentally different challenge. In an era when schools began to focus increasing attention on the works of non-Christian authors like Aristotle, these European authors emphasized that human reason no less than the Bible exclusively supports Roman Catholic doctrines. In that respect, they pursued the same objectives as Timothy I, who demonstrated the validity of

Christian truth claims through philosophical dialogue with a respectable Muslim foil (see chapter 5; Timothy's work did not circulate in premodern Europe). Petrus Alfonsi and Peter of Cluny, however, adopted a different strategy for achieving their goal: they told tales about Muhammad's associates that emphasized the irrationality of Islam and Judaism, a secondary theme in Eastern Christian versions of the tale. European accounts of how Jews helped Muhammad create an unbiblical and irrational religion aim to bolster the confidence of Christian audiences in the foundations of their own faith.[18]

Alfonsi, a Jew who converted to Christianity in Aragon (in the northeast of present-day Spain), was the first European to adapt Eastern tales about Muhammad's associates. His *Dialogue against the Jews*, written around 1109, takes the form of a conversation between the author's current self, Petrus, and his former self, Moses, in which Petrus explains why he came to affirm Christian teachings—and, by extension, why members of his Christian audience should do the same. (If Alfonsi had wanted to reach a Jewish audience, he would not have written in Latin.) Alfonsi demonstrates the falsehood of Judaism and the truth of Christianity using both logical reasoning and scriptural evidence. After four chapters demonstrating that Judaism is "worthless and inconsistent" and before spending seven chapters defending Christianity, Alfonsi devotes his fifth chapter to Moses's question regarding why Petrus did not adopt "the faith of the Saracens, with whom you were always associated and raised." Perhaps Alfonsi felt the need to address Islam because Muslims constituted a sizeable portion of the early twelfth-century Iberian population; perhaps he did so because he and fellow Christian scholars regularly drew on scientific and philosophical works by Muslim authors. Petrus explains that Islam, like Judaism, is neither rational nor scriptural, and it is with this goal in mind that Alfonsi reimagines the *Apology of al-Kindi*'s tale about Muhammad's associates, which he read in the original Arabic.[19]

Petrus, Alfonsi's literary alter ego, begins his presentation of Islam with a biography of Muhammad, a poor orphan who wins the heart and wealth of his employer, Khadija. Muhammad then arrogantly seeks to become king of the Arabs by falsely claiming to be a prophet sent by God to this idolatrous people. To do so, however, he needs the assistance of local heretics, among them an excommunicated and embittered archdeacon whose name, according to one manuscript, was Sergius.

> Muhammad, supported by his advice, brought to a conclusion what he contemplated but still was unable to fulfill on his own. There were also two Jews among those heretics of Arabia whom we mentioned, named Abdallah and

Kab al-Ahbar, and these, indeed, attached themselves to Muhammad and offered their assistance to complete his foolishness. These three mixed together the law of Muhammad, each one according to his own heresy.

The *Apology of al-Kindi* and its predecessors depict Sergius as well-intentioned in his efforts to teach Christian truths to the primitive Arabs. Petrus, in contrast, portrays this figure as an unrepentant heretic who intentionally supported a false religion to rival Christianity. Alfonsi's archdeacon also conspires directly with Muhammad's Jewish associates to create the Quran. This, too, is a sharp departure from previous accounts: Eastern Christian and Islamic legends alike portray the monk as hostile toward Jews and Judaism, and in Eastern Christian accounts Kab can only corrupt Sergius's text after the monk's death. Muhammad himself also plays a more active and devious role in Alfonsi's tale. He now spearheads a conspiracy to deceive his followers, although the former pagan apparently cannot realize this ambition without the assistance of his Christian and Jewish associates. Eastern Christians familiar with earlier versions of this tale would not have found Alfonsi's retelling to be plausible, but Alfonsi knew that his European audience lacked such familiarity.

Alfonsi repeatedly emphasizes that the archdeacon, Kab, and Abdallah are all heretics. The archdeacon, he claims, instilled within Islam both the obsolete practice of circumcision and the heretical belief that Jesus Christ was a human being born of a virgin who was never crucified and did not die. Kab and Abdallah, he asserts, were among those "who embraced the law of Moses in a heretical way," so the unspecified elements they introduced into Islam are not even authentically Jewish. Having shown that Islam lacks proper scriptural foundations, Alfonsi then turns to arguments based on reason. He demonstrates, on what he believes to be purely logical grounds, that Muhammad could not have been a prophet, that Islamic rituals are a fig leaf for the underlying idolatry of traditional Arab worship, and that the Quran's permissive statements regarding sex and violence are not only carnal but irrational.[20]

Islam and Judaism alike, according to Alfonsi, cannot withstand either logical or scriptural critiques. Moses acknowledges at the start of the *Dialogue*'s sixth chapter that Petrus successfully confounded both Judaism and Islam on these grounds, so Petrus proceeds to employ biblical and rational arguments to defend Christian teachings. In the end, of course, Moses concedes the truth of Christianity, and Alfonsi hopes that his Christian readers will likewise come away confident that logic and scripture alike support Christian truth claims alone. The very purpose of his anti-Muslim and anti-Jewish polemics is to advance that pedagogical objective.

Alfonsi's *Dialogue against the Jews* was "the most influential and widely read of all medieval anti-Jewish tracts," and its fifth chapter "became one of the most frequently used sources for Latin writers on Islam."[21] Among its earliest users was Peter the Venerable, who served as abbot of the powerful Cluny monastery from 1122 until his death in 1156. Peter of Cluny was so committed to fostering anti-Muslim polemics that he commissioned the translation of key Arabic texts into Latin, including the Quran and the *Apology of al-Kindi*. Peter's *Summary of the Entire Heresy of the Saracens*, written in 1143 as an introduction to this collection of translated texts, includes an expansive depiction of Muhammad's associates. The abbot draws on Theophanes's *Chronicle* and, especially, on *al-Kindi* and Alfonsi, but his tale about the origins of Islam is far more hostile than those of his predecessors.[22]

Peter's Muhammad, like Alfonsi's, seeks to obtain political power by deceitfully persuading his fellow idolatrous Arabs that he is a prophet of the one true God. What happens next, however, differs in slight but significant ways from earlier accounts. "Satan bestowed success upon error, and he sent the monk Sergius, who had been expelled from the Church as a sectarian follower of the heretical Nestorius, to those parts of Arabia and united the monk-heretic with the false prophet." Sergius teaches Muhammad heretical interpretations of the Old and New Testaments that deny the divinity of Jesus Christ and, "completely filling him up with fables from apocryphal books, made him into a Nestorian Christian. And, in order that the complete fullness of iniquity should coalesce in Muhammad, and so that nothing should be lacking for his damnation or for that of others, Jews were joined to the heretic." Islam, in other words, was founded by a pagan (Muhammad), a Christian heretic (Sergius), and unnamed Jews. These figures collectively represent the full spectrum of Christendom's enemies; their collaboration, engineered by Satan himself, is essential for the creation of a truly perverse religion, the sum of all evil. Peter's emphasis on the role played by Satan may reflect his familiarity with contemporaneous Latin tales about Muhammad that we will explore in chapter 7.[23]

Unlike Alfonsi, Peter of Cluny specifies how the Jews contributed to the formation of Islam: "Lest he become a true Christian, the Jews whispered to Muhammad, shrewdly providing to the man who was eager for novelties not the truth of the scriptures but their own fables, which still today they have in abundance." Peter refers here to Talmudic literature, whose importance he discovered in part by reading Alfonsi's *Dialogue against the Jews*. Alfonsi condemns specific passages in the Talmud for containing unreasonable teachings that contradict philosophical and scientific truth, such as anthropomorphic representations of God and inaccurate explanations of meteorological phenomena. Peter of Cluny goes much further by alleging that the Talmud not only contains irrational elements but in fact transforms its students into irrational beasts—this, Peter contends in a later work, is why Jews refuse to accept compelling arguments on behalf of Christianity. After all, if human beings are defined by their use of logical reasoning and if reason demonstrates beyond doubt the validity of Christian truth claims, then those who nevertheless refuse to accept those claims must not be human. Islam, Peter alleges, lacks proper scriptural foundations because it rests on Sergius's heretical interpretations of the Bible, and it lacks rationality because of the Talmudic underpinnings introduced by the Jews whom Satan sent to Muhammad.[24]

Peter planned to elaborate on this claim in the last substantive chapter of his final work, *Against the Sect of the Saracens*. In the words of the outline drafted by his secretary, "The entirety of Muhammad's scripture is nothing other than the frightful dregs and the foul residue of heresies . . . and especially of that execrable book of the Jews, the Talmud." This is why the Saracens, "these animals and wretches," believe that Muhammad was a prophet notwithstanding compelling logical evidence to the contrary. What makes Islam Jewish, in short, is the Talmud, which transformed not only the Jews but also the Muslims into irrational beasts while drawing them away from truths conveyed in the Bible. Although Peter invites Muslims to accept his reasoned and biblically grounded arguments in the introduction to *Against the Sect of the Saracens*, this concluding chapter would have provided his Christian readers an advance explanation for why Muslims are unlikely to do so: Muslims judaize. The actual text of this work, however, is much shorter than the outline's projection and lacks this chapter about the relationship between the Talmud and the Quran. The most likely explanation for this omission is that Peter died before he could fully execute his original plan.[25]

Against the Sect of the Saracens, even in its current state, is a lengthy Latin treatise only accessible to well-educated Christians. Although ostensibly addressed to Muslims, its defense of Roman Catholic teachings actually seeks to shore up the faith of fellow monks. Peter claims to justify the pillars of Christian theology on rational and scriptural grounds that even Muslims ought to accept. If Christian readers doubt Catholic doctrines, they themselves must suffer from the plague of judaizing that prevents Muslims from accepting Christian truth claims. Historian John Tolan summarizes the thrust of Peter's work as follows: "If Muslims, Jews, and heretics could not be brought into the fold, at least their satanically-inspired errors could be dispelled from the minds of Christians." Branding Muslims as Jewish benefits Christians.[26]

Petrus Alfonsi and Peter of Cluny employ Jews and quasi-Jewish Muslims as literary foils within works whose primary objective is to reinforce claims about the rationality and scriptural foundations of Christianity. Their rhetoric about Jews and judaizers marks the bounds of proper Christian belief and raises the stakes of stepping beyond them by branding as Jewish all who doubt Christian truth claims. In the East, the claim that Muslims judaize enables Christians to make long-standing anti-Jewish arguments more relevant to Christians who live within an Islamic society. In Europe, that same claim makes anti-Muslim arguments more relevant to Christians who have no direct familiarity with Islam but who continue to understand their own beliefs and behaviors in opposition to Judaism. The tales about Muhammad that we will examine in the next chapter demonstrate even more clearly how European polemicists not only defamed Islam by defining it as Jewish but also prodded fellow Christians to differentiate themselves by cultivating the characteristics that Muslims and Jews alike allegedly disdain.

CHAPTER 7

Muhammad the Jew, and Other Moralizing Slurs

Twelfth through Seventeenth Centuries

No Eastern Christian polemicist ever alleged that Muhammad himself was Jewish—Christian audiences familiar with basic information about Islam's prophet would regard such a claim as absurd. In order to be persuasive, after all, polemical allegations need to be plausible. Some medieval Europeans, however, found value in portraying Muhammad as a fraudulent prophet who restored Old Testament practices that Christians commonly condemned as Jewish. Others alleged that Muhammad was himself Jewish by birth or upbringing. The figure they depict is not the historical Muhammad but rather a "European Muhammad," as John Tolan puts it in his study of such depictions: "a mirror for European writers, expressing their fears, hopes, and ambitions."[1] These writers rest their claims about Muhammad not on Islamic or even Eastern Christian sources but on the internal logic of their own worldviews. Their allegations regarding Muhammad's Jewishness are plausible because they confirm the preconceptions of those who define their own Christian identity in opposition to Jewishness. European Christians ridiculed Muhammad as a Jew and his followers as quasi-Jews in order to reinforce characteristics that Muhammad allegedly disdained, such as chastity, unity, faithfulness, and purity of lineage. The variety within these portrayals of Muhammad reflects the different characteristics that writers sought to foster within their own Christian communities.

This chapter examines the evolution of three different European portrayals of Muhammad as a Jew. We will first analyze a pair of fictional biographies in which Muhammad presents himself as a second Moses sent by God to restore Old Testament norms: the mid-twelfth-century *Otia de Machomete*, a Latin poetic narrative by Gautier (Walter) de Compiègne, and the expanded Old French version of this poem called the *Romans de Mahon*, composed by Alexandre du Pont in 1258.[2] These works ridicule Muhammad's followers for embracing his permissive sexual norms and, in so doing, they reinforce traditional Christian notions of chastity and monogamy. We will then turn our attention to twelfth- and thirteenth-century historians who identify Muhammad's mother or his mentor as a Jew. These unfounded claims account for features antithetical to proper Christianity that these historians ascribe to Islam. The final portion of this chapter examines ways in which historians and other writers of the fifteenth through early seventeenth centuries employ slanderous portrayals of Muhammad and his Jewish mother to reinforce their own conceptions of Christian society.

MUHAMMAD AS A FRAUDULENT MOSES

Multiple tales about Muhammad circulated in medieval Europe. Latin-literate Christians could read translations of Theophanes's *Chronicle* and, beginning in the mid-twelfth century, the *Apology of al-Kindi*, both discussed in chapter 6. Ninth-century Christians living under Muslim rule in present-day Spain wrote scathing biographies of Muhammad as well. These Latin works introduce two themes that remain prominent in later European accounts, including the *Otia* and *Romans:* that Muhammad was guided by the devil, and that he encouraged promiscuous sex.[3] The *Otia* and *Romans*, however, differ from other European tales about Muhammad because they depict him as a fraudulent Moses who claims to restore Old Testament norms. We can better recognize the significance of this atypical depiction by first examining a more representative tale.

Embrico of Mainz wrote an especially influential account of Muhammad's life around the turn of the twelfth century. Its nameless villain is a faithless Christian who employs magic and deception to gain public acclaim and corrupt the church. This scoundrel, an agent of the devil who hypocritically maintains the external appearance of a saintly monk, engineers Muhammad's rise from slavery to nobility by murdering Muhammad's master and arranging for Muhammad to marry the widow. The scoundrel then secures Muhammad's appointment as king by means of a ruse involving a ferocious bull that Muhammad secretly raises from infancy and publicly tames. Muhammad, following the pseudomonk's instructions, abolishes the "harsh law of the gospels" within his Christian kingdom by permitting adultery, incest, and all manner of sexual delights. God punishes Muhammad with epilepsy, but the pseudomonk persuades Muhammad's gullible followers that their king's seizures are in fact experiences of divine revelation. After Muhammad's death (pigs devour him during a seizure), the scoundrel performs one final trick: using a set of magnets, he arranges for Muhammad's iron coffin to float in mid-air as if by miracle.[4]

Embrico's account, John Tolan observes, is an "anti-hagiography," an inversion of tales commonly told about Christian saints. True saints flee from positions of power, preach chastity, and perform genuine miracles, while Muhammad and his mentor do the opposite. Tolan suggests that Embrico, writing at a time of heightened anxiety about heresy in Western Europe, sought to warn fellow Christians of the dangers posed by contemporary figures who, like the tale's nameless villain, only appear to be pious but in fact lead their followers into sin. Muslims are Christians who were led astray by heretics; Embrico's audience must take care to avoid the same fate. Similar lessons, also grounded in long-standing rhetoric about Christian heresy, underpin other twelfth-century tales about Muhammad as well.[5]

Gautier de Compiègne probably knew Embrico's work: his *Otia de Machomete* describes the magnetically suspended tomb and likewise identifies Muhammad as a slave rather than a poor orphan.[6] These similarities notwithstanding, the tale that Gautier tells, and that Alexandre du Pont later elaborates in his *Romans de Mahon*, differs sharply from its predecessors in that Muhammad is its sole protagonist. Instead of the villainous pseudomonk who drives every aspect of Embrico's tale, the *Otia* and *Romans* depict a pious hermit who foretells that Muhammad will subvert Christianity by replacing matrimony with adultery and spiritual baptism with carnal circumcision. This hermit, under duress, later affirms Muhammad's false claim that his epileptic seizures are actually divine revelations. Unlike other tales in which the monk functions as a mentor figure, this tale's Muhammad relies solely on his own thorough knowledge of Christianity and his devilishly innate talents.[7]

Gautier and Alexandre omit the antiheretical elements of Embrico's work because they choose instead to define Muhammad's religion as abhorrently Jewish. Muhammad, they claim, portrayed his teachings as the restoration of the Old Testament: "Let the law of Moses return, and everyone be redeemed! Let the new law [that is, the New Testament] be quashed and the old one restored, along with circumcision of the flesh, and let a man have ten wives, and one woman, ten husbands, without ever being accused of sin or deserving blame" (R. 1385–94; cf. O. 757–62). The hermit similarly prophesies that Muhammad "will get rid of the circumcision of the spirit, so that circumcision of the flesh will return" (O. 63–64); in Alexandre's version, the hermit associates this carnal practice with the "cursed people," which is to say, the Jews (R. 168). An attentive Christian, however, would immediately recognize that these teachings are not biblical. Muhammad's purported permission of multiple husbands, which Gautier and Alexandre repeat pointedly, contradicts Old Testament norms (and Islamic ones, too). From a Christian perspective, the physical circumcision that Muhammad promotes violates the Bible's true meaning as well. These authors also prime their audiences to recognize similarities between Muhammad and the Jews by reminding readers that the Jews put Christ to death because they did not understand the true meaning of their own scripture (O. 117–20 / R. 333–38). Muhammad is a patent fraud, but his followers—whom Gautier and Alexandre depict as gullible Christians—fail to recognize this.[8]

Gautier and Peter of Cluny, mid-twelfth-century monks from present-day France, both make a point of associating Muhammad with Jewishness, but they do so in very different ways. Peter, we saw in chapter 6, stresses the irrationality that Jews instilled within Muhammad's teachings and alleges that this Jewish influence is the reason why Muslims reject Christian ideas about God. His tale reinforces a binary distinction between Christians, whose faith in Christ finds support in reason no less than scripture, and non-Christians who are, in effect, subhuman because they cannot recognize that which reason demonstrates to be true. Gautier, in contrast, displays little interest in the debates over reason and faith taking place within elite intellectual circles. He focuses his tale on the carnality of Muhammad's teachings, which he pointedly associates with the Old Testament.[9] In doing so, however, Gautier's Otia makes a somewhat different point than the Eastern Christian Legend of Sergius Bahira that we also examined in chapter 6. The Eastern legend, written by and for Christians living under Muslim domination, defines Christianity as spiritual and Islam, like Judaism, as carnal; it takes for granted the social distinction between Christians and Muslims and disparages Islam as a means of preserving that distinction. Gautier, in contrast, portrays carnal impulses as a challenge that Christians themselves must confront. His tale, like his French society, contains no Muslims—only Christians whom Muhammad leads astray by misreading the Old Testament in a libertine and purportedly Jewish manner. Gautier's tale reinforces the importance of cultivating chastity and monogamy by portraying a society whose members abandoned these virtues—and, Alexandre adds, went to hell as a result (R. 1783–86).

The *Otia* and *Romans* alike emphasize Muhammad's efforts to portray himself as a second Moses. He leads his Christian followers up a mountain, reminding them that Moses received the Law in such a place. There, Muhammad reveals to his people channels of milk and honey, a familiar biblical motif, proclaiming them to be miraculous signs that God has replaced the New Testament's "harsh laws" with gentler and sweeter norms; the audience knows, however, that Muhammad prepared this ruse in advance. Muhammad then loudly prays to God, "who formerly gave the Law to Moses on Mount Sinai," to reveal this new law in written form. A well-trained, snow-white bull that Muhammad secretly raised from infancy heard his voice, ran toward its master, and kneeled before him, bearing between its horns a copy of the Quran that Muhammad himself, of course, had written (R. 1397–1546; quoted: 1488, 1492–94 / O. 765–860).

Audiences of the *Otia* and *Romans* likely laughed at the gullibility of Muhammad's followers. There is, however, a biting edge to this humor, especially in the *Romans*: Muhammad's community is uncomfortably similar to the French audience itself. Alexandre's tale, composed in Old French so as to be more widely accessible than Gautier's Latin original, is set in a familiar European landscape: the nameless lord and lady whom Muhammad initially serves possess "woods, meadows, and rivers; orchards, mills, ovens; castles, towns, and villages; along with knights, castellans, townsmen, and peasants" (R. 68–72; O. 28 merely states that the nobleman is "rich in castles and money and slaves"). To illustrate Muhammad's brilliance, Alexandre declares that "Through geometry he could find by visual means, if he wished, how many feet there are between Montaigu and Sauvoire," two landmarks near the author's hometown of Laon (R. 43–46). Alexandre's elite audience could readily imagine themselves at Muhammad's wedding feast, where guests identified by their medieval French social rank dined on French wine and fowl while listening to music played on European instruments and admiring "tapestries embroidered with sacred stories from the Old Testament" (R. 761–63).

While this wedding feast conforms to the ideals of medieval French elites, the marriage itself most certainly does not: Muhammad, though a slave by birth, marries the noble lady he formerly served following the death of her husband, his master. The lady initially rejects Muhammad's marriage proposal, worrying that her subjects would crudely exclaim,

"Our lady, who used to be on top, must lie underneath!" (R. 543–44; cf. O. 243–46). Muhammad, however, bribes the local barons to endorse this marriage and to pledge their own loyalty to him as their new lord. "The root of all sins is greed," Alexandre opines, emphasizing that the barons forsake fundamental social hierarchies in pursuit of horses, armor, and other worldly gifts (R. 605–12; cf. O. 295–301). A knight— elder and of noble birth, no less—draws on biblical texts to make the case that the institution of slavery stems from human sinfulness and that all faithful servants of God deserve to be free and noble (R. 676–736 / O. 349–78). Although twenty-first-century readers may applaud this argument for social equality, the medieval audiences for whom Gautier and Alexandre wrote would have scoffed. They would immediately recognize the knight's interpretation as a radical departure from normative Catholic teachings of the time, which enshrined social hierarchies as divinely ordained. Alexandre likely hopes, however, that members of his audience would also see in themselves the materialistic greed that motivates this self-serving misreading of scripture, as well as the lustfulness that makes Muhammad's purported teachings about sexual liberty so appealing.

According to the *Otia* and *Romans*, Muhammad's success rests on his ability to appeal to the base instincts of those around him through seductive misinterpretations of the Bible. French audiences who see themselves in their Muslim enemies ought to respond by recommitting themselves to proper Christian behaviors, especially with respect to chastity and monogamy, and to the doctrines of the Catholic Church rather than unauthorized interpretations of the Bible. Gautier and Alexandre reinforce this message by drawing not only on earlier tales about Muhammad but also on familiar themes of Christian anti-Judaism, especially the related allegations that Jews misread the Old Testament and focus unduly on the physical body rather than its spirit. The first Muslims, these authors assert, were Christians who judaized in pursuit of their passions, to their utter damnation; European Christians must take care not to make the same mistake.

Embrico, who fears that wolves in sheep's clothing might lead Christians into heresy, warns his audience to resist charismatic teachers with unorthodox teachings. Gautier and Alexandre, in contrast, teach their audiences to control their own sinful inclinations lest they, too, fall into the laughable, abhorrent state of their Muslim enemies. The discourse of anti-Judaism, a common feature in texts that promote normative Christian behavior, reinforces their morality tale especially well because all Christians are at risk of judaizing.

THE INVENTION OF MUHAMMAD'S JEWISH MOTHER
AND JEWISH MENTOR

Neither Alexandre nor Gautier claimed to be an historian: both educated their audiences through entertaining works of fiction. Alexandre freely adapts and greatly expands Gautier's *Otia* through his own creativity, and Gautier himself composes entire scenes that have no basis in earlier sources. He states that he learned about Muhammad third hand from a Muslim convert to Christianity as if through a game of telephone (*O.* 5–20; cf. *R.* 4–32). The distance that Gautier and other authors of fanciful tales about Muhammad place between themselves and their purported source of information enables them to deny any personal responsibility for historical accuracy and, as a result, gives them free rein to embellish their stories as they wish.[10]

Premodern historians display far greater fidelity to their sources than do Gautier and Alexandre. Even so, their preconceptions and worldviews, including their ideas about Judaism as the antithesis of Christianity, demonstrably shape the portrayals of Muhammad that appear in European works of history. Works that ascribe Jewishness to Muhammad's parents and upbringing exemplify the ways in which historical accounts about Muslims reinforce particular—and evolving—conceptions of Christian society by depicting Muhammad himself as embodying their inverse.

Islamic sources uniformly attest that Muhammad's parents, Abdallah and Amina, belonged to the tribe of Quraysh. During the sixth and early seventh centuries, some Arab tribes were entirely Jewish and some contained a mix of Jews and non-Jews. Quraysh, however, was entirely non-Jewish, and Islamic sources report that the tribe's commitment to its multiple deities fueled its members' hostile reaction to Muhammad's message of radical monotheism. Islamic sources trace Muhammad's ancestry directly to Abraham and Ishmael without any Jewish admixture, and no Eastern Christian author challenges this genealogy. European authors often reiterate the assertion found in Theophanes's *Chronicle* that Muhammad learned about Judaism and Christianity during his frequent trips to Palestine, and many repeat its allegation that Jews aided Muhammad in the creation of his false religion.[11] Some European historians, however, go further and assert that Muhammad himself was raised Jewishly. This claim has no factual basis, but European Christians regarded it as plausible nonetheless because it enables them to explain key differences they perceive between Christianity and Islam by means of anti-Jewish frames of reference.

Otto of Freising, who served as bishop of that town in the mid-twelfth century, demonstrates his commitment to accuracy when he pointedly rejects popular allegations that Muslims worship idols. He nevertheless declares in his *History of the Two Cities* that Muhammad was "of the stock of Ishmael by a gentile father and a Jewish mother." No earlier surviving source identifies Muhammad's mother as a Jew, but this claim nevertheless makes sense from a medieval Christian perspective. As we saw in chapter 1, Christians excluded from God's eternal covenant with Abraham not only the literal heirs of Hagar and her son Ishmael but also Hagar's figurative heirs, chief among them the Jews, because they fail to understand Christ's significance. Otto's genealogy reinforces this theological tradition: Muhammad is both a literal Ishmaelite through his father and a figurative heir of Hagar through his Jewish mother. (Although premodern Jews commonly defined Jewishness on the basis of maternal rather than paternal descent, there is no reason to presume that Otto or his successors perceived Jewish identity in the same fashion.)

From the bishop's perspective, this maternal lineage may also account for the similarities he perceives between Islam and Judaism. Saracens, Otto explains, are "worshippers of one God; they accept the Books of the Law and also the custom of circumcision" but deny that Jesus Christ is God or the Son of God. Otto asserts that Muhammad's principal teaching is "Wash yourselves, make yourselves clean," and that the Saracens, "in their stupidity, are accustomed to observe this precept by washing the hidden parts of the body daily." Like his claim about Muhammad's mother, this unfounded assertion reflects the Jewishness that Otto perceives in Islam. The words Otto ascribes to Muhammad, as the bishop and his readers knew, come from the book of Isaiah (1:16) and, according to the standard Christian interpretation, refer not to genital hygiene but rather to the blood of Christ and the water of baptism. The misinterpretation that Otto ascribes to Muhammad and his followers reflects their Jewish literalism and carnality. Christians, in contrast, appreciate the significance of baptism and the Eucharist, the ritual in which priests consumed the blood of Christ in the form of consecrated wine. What distinguishes Christians from Muslims (and Jews), Otto emphasizes, is not the worship of God but the reverence for Christ and the sacraments.[12]

Rodrigo Jiménez de Rada, archbishop of Toledo, probably had no access to Otto's *History of the Two Cities* and, in any case, pursued a different agenda when depicting Muhammad in his *History of the Arabs*, completed in 1245. This work, the oldest surviving Christian history of the Muslim world, draws heavily on Islamic sources. None of these sources, however, underpins Rodrigo's assertion that Muhammad's father, whom Rodrigo misnames "Ali," "vacillated between Catholic faith and the faithlessness of the Jews" owing to the negative influence of a nameless Jewish friend identified solely as a magician. Ali himself was away when his unnamed wife gave birth, but the Jewish magician was on hand and, by means of astrology, predicted Muhammad's glorious future. After Muhammad's parents died, his uncle placed the orphaned boy under the tutelage of this Jew, "who instructed him in the natural sciences, Catholic law, and the teachings of Jewish faithlessness. On this basis, [Muhammad] later usurped some elements from the Catholic faith and some from the Old Law for the support of his sect." Rodrigo's Muhammad, like that of the *Otia*, relies on his own knowledge rather than on outside assistance, but now Judaism profoundly taints his education and even his parentage.[13]

This unprecedented account of Muhammad's upbringing accords with what Lucy Pick, Rodrigo's biographer, describes as the archbishop's "theology of unity." Rodrigo believed that the ideal human state is to be unified under God and that humans suffer in this world on account of their religious, ethnic, and political diversity. The archbishop depicts Muhammad's origins within this conceptual framework: the divided loyalties of Muhammad's father, compounded by Muhammad's own unholy education in both Jewish and Catholic texts, prepared him to create his new sect. (Notice that Rodrigo blames both factors on a Jew.) At the time, Rodrigo observes, "Arabia and Africa were being pulled by conflicting desires, between Catholic faith, Arian heresy, Jewish faithlessness, and idolatry." This societal diversity, he explains, enabled Islam to spread rapidly, and Muslim armies soon shattered the Catholic kingdom of Spain. Division breeds further division. The proper response, Rodrigo believed, is to reunify the Iberian Peninsula under the dominion of the Church and to cultivate unwavering fidelity to Catholicism.[14]

Ali's unnamed friend, the magician who mentors Muhammad, calls to mind the nameless scoundrel depicted by Embrico of Mainz and other European storytellers. Rodrigo, however, identifies this figure as a Jew, not a Christian heretic, and he carefully avoids associating Muhammad with heresy. As Pick observes, Rodrigo sought "to create the theological grounding that would allow a place for Muslims and Jews to live under Christian rule. Identifying Muslims as heretics . . . would have undermined that place."[15] Heretics have no right to live within Christian society, and during Rodrigo's lifetime Catholic authorities violently eliminated heretical communities in present-day France. Jews, in contrast, had long lived peacefully within Christendom as a tolerated minority, and Rodrigo wanted to ensure that Muslims—who constituted a sizeable percentage of the population within the archbishop's domain—could do the same. Rodrigo's Muhammad embodies the inverse of the characteristics that the archbishop seeks to cultivate within his Christian society, but Muhammad's followers retain a rightful, albeit inferior, place within that society.

THE DEFAMATION OF MUHAMMAD'S JEWISH MOTHER

Otto and Rodrigo alike invent origin stories for Muhammad that conform to Christian theological worldviews. By the mid-fifteenth century, in contrast, many historians participated in the movement known as humanism, which sought to understand the world in secular terms rather than solely by recourse to theological frames of reference. One such historian, Flavio Biondo, uses Muhammad's ancestry to frame the relationship between Christians and Muslims primarily in terms of ethnopolitics: he reports that Muhammad's father was an Arab or a Persian. The Persians constituted the Roman Empire's great military rival until the Muslim conquests, when Arabs assumed that role. By associating Muhammad with these ethnic groups, Biondo emphasizes the geopolitical dimension of Islam precisely at a time when another Islamic empire, that of the Ottoman Turks, emerged as a military rival to European Christendom. This depiction of Islam implicitly reinforces a corresponding conception of Christian identity in ethnopolitical, even imperial, terms. Biondo, however, was unwilling to simply abandon the theologically oriented genealogy first offered by Otto of Freising, according to which Muhammad was an Ishmaelite with a Jewish mother. In Biondo's retelling, Muhammad's mother was "an Ishmaelite of the Hebrew people." Marcus Sabellicus, writing at the end of the fifteenth century, similarly describes Muhammad's father as either Arab or Persian and his mother as "an Ishmaelite, and therefore not ignorant of the Hebrew religion."[16]

The ethnic term "Hebrew" refers originally to Abraham and thus could in theory apply to Abraham's Ishmaelite and Jewish descendants alike, but it invariably refers to Jews alone. Biondo and Sabellicus nonetheless describe Muhammad's mother as simultaneously Jewish and Ishmaelite in order to incorporate information about Muhammad's ancestry found in earlier European histories even as they present Arab/Persian ethnicity as the primary—and, for that reason, paternal—element of Muhammad's identity. These humanist historians prioritized political dimensions of the rivalry between Christians and Muslims and, indeed, of Christian identity itself, but reference to the Jewishness of Muhammad's mother enables them to preserve the theological dimension of the contrast between Christianity and Islam.

Once Muhammad's mother, Amina, became a Jew within Christian historical literature, she stayed one. After all, it made sense to Europeans that the founder of a menacing rival to Christendom would have Jewish ancestry. False information like this could easily persist for centuries because most European authors and readers regarded Christian sources as more reliable than Islamic ones; repetition made this information seem even more reliable.[17]

The persistence of the claim that Amina was a Jew is especially striking among early modern scholars who had access to better information about Islam than their predecessors. Juan Andrés and Leo Africanus, early sixteenth-century converts to Catholicism from Islam, wrote influential and well-informed works about Islam and the Muslim world. Neither identifies Amina as a Jew, but some Northern European translators of their works saw fit to add that information nonetheless.[18] Theodor Bibliander published what Gregory Miller calls "a veritable sixteenth-century 'Encyclopedia of Islam,'" a massive compilation of translated Arabic texts (most notably the Quran) as well as Christian polemical, historical, and ethnographic works. To the best of my knowledge, none of these works describes Amina as in any way Jewish. Even so, Bibliander inaccurately asserts that Abdallah was a Persian idolater while Amina "was of the Ishmaelite people, who still acknowledged the teachings of Moses and would therefore circumcise sons and observe other Jewish practices."[19] Luis del Mármol Carvajal, whose late sixteenth-century work draws both on Leo Africanus and on decades of personal experience living among current and former Muslims, correctly identifies Abdallah as an Ishmaelite but relies on an inaccurate Christian source when he asserts that Amina was "Jewish by birth and by conviction." Mármol also repeats Rodrigo Jiménez de Rada's tale about the Jew who predicted Muhammad's greatness and taught him Jewish law, adding that this unnamed magician and astrologer was Amina's brother.[20]

Early modern Europeans routinely defamed Muhammad by slandering his Jewish mother. Louis Turquet de Mayerne, for example, layered multiple insults into his account of Muhammad's parentage: he identifies Abdallah as a pagan idolater and Amina as "his Jewish wife, a poor beggar bitch taken by Abdallah for love because he thought she was pretty." Because the term "Jew" was itself a slur while "Ishmaelite" was not, Turquet emphasizes the Jewish element of Muhammad's line-age at the expense of the Ishmaelite dimension. Joshua Notstock, Juan Andrés's English translator, similarly described Amina as "a Jewess, and of ill repute." The dishonorable nature of Muhammad's origins and, by extension, of Islam itself contrasts sharply with traditional depictions of Christ's holy family, and these slurs implicitly reinforce societal norms regarding sex and marriage.[21]

François Feuardent, a late sixteenth-century Catholic theologian, employs the by-now customary identification of Amina as a Jew to sup-port his conviction that Muhammad is none other than Antichrist. Euro-pean Christians had contended since the ninth century that Muhammad was one of many historical Antichrists or, stated differently, an especially significant precursor to the ultimate Antichrist who will appear at the end of days. An even older tradition maintains that Antichrist will descend from the Israelite tribe of Dan. Feuardent declares that Amina must belong to this tribe and then indulges in further speculation: "Who would bar one from saying that [Muhammad's] mother was an impure harlot who received adulterous seed from a man of her own tribe?" After all, Antichrist's mother ought to be the polar opposite of Christ's mother, the chaste Virgin Mary.[22]

Feuardent's argument is baldly circular: he draws on traditions about Antichrist to allege that Muhammad's biological parents were both Danite Jews and then uses that allegation to support his claim that Muhammad is Antichrist. This prompts the early seventeenth-century Spanish polemicist and historian Jaime Bleda to ridicule "the most learned and very famous Parisian professor" by proposing an even more elaborate and equally unsubstantiated account of Muhammad's parentage. "Muhammad, con-ceived through incestuous adultery, was a four-quarters Jew," Bleda jok-ingly suggests, because his true father was not Abdallah but rather Amina's brother, the Jewish magician/astrologer. Bleda warns that it would be a grave sin to lodge a similarly baseless accusation about the parents of an honorable Spaniard but, he says, Muhammad is so disreputable that call-ing him a Jew or even Antichrist cannot further damage his reputation.[23]

Bleda was a well-read and meticulous historian, as evidenced by his survey and evaluation of two dozen Christian statements regarding the date of Muhammad's birth. Bleda's own claims about Muhammad in his *Chronicle of the Moors of Spain*, however, are as inaccurate as those he rejects. He too reports that Amina was a Jew and also asserts that Muhammad himself expressed pride in his Jewish ancestry, something no self-respecting Spaniard would do in the early seventeenth century.

Bleda repeats Rodrigo's tale about the Jew who tutored Muhammad, follows Mármol in identifying this astrologer as Amina's brother, and for the first time provides a name for this Jew: Bahira, the figure also known as Sergius whose tales we traced in chapter 6. Bleda even opens his chronicle by identifying Muhammad with Antichrist. The only element of Feuardent's biography of Muhammad that Bleda rejects is the unsubstantiated claim that Amina engaged in adultery.[24]

Christian statements about Muhammad's parentage, like so many other Christian statements about Islam, reflect the profound impact of confirmation bias, the tendency to interpret new data in ways that align with one's preconceptions. What changes between the twelfth and seventeenth centuries is not the accuracy of these statements about Muhammad but the specific biases that they confirm—and, relatedly, the Christian norms they reinforce. Bleda's biases reflect his conception of Christian identity as profoundly ethnic, even racial, in nature.

Like other early modern Spaniards, Bleda embraced the notion of "blood purity," according to which any degree of Jewish ancestry renders one unfit to participate fully in Catholic society. The language Bleda uses in his tongue in cheek allegation about Muhammad—that he is "a four-quarters Jew," which is to say that all his grandparents were Jewish—reflects this racial conception of Jewishness and Christianness alike. Bleda's warning about baseless allegations against honorable Spaniards is also no idle remark: David Nirenberg observes with only slight exaggeration that "there is no leading sixteenth- or seventeenth-century Spanish writer or politician who entirely avoided being accused or accusing another of genealogical or cultural 'Jewishness.'"[25] Bleda's sober description of Muhammad's ancestry, no less than his intentionally over-the-top allegation, reflects the pervasive anxiety about Jewish ancestry within early modern Spain and reinforces the importance of safeguarding the reputation of one's own Christian lineage.

Depictions of Muhammad as a Jew persist across the centuries because European storytellers and historians, despite their differences, continued to see the world through the multifaceted lens of anti-Judaism. The scorn they heap on Muhammad and his followers powerfully reinforces characteristics they deem essential to being a good Christian. Premodern Europeans who portray Muhammad as a pagan, as a heretic, or even as a source of truth likewise seek first and foremost to shape the beliefs and practices of their Christian readers. These portrayals reflect not Muhammad himself but the concerns and agendas of European authors.[26]

CHAPTER 8

The Logic, and the Consequences, of Defining Muslims as Judaizers

Fourth through Seventeenth Centuries

Jews held a special place within the legal system of the Roman Catholic Church, known as canon law. From its fourth-century origins through the middle of the twelfth century, canonical sources consistently distinguish Jews from other non-Christians and express particular concern about the danger that Jews will corrupt the beliefs and behaviors of their Christian associates. European Christians perceived Muslims as especially threatening foreigners, but they nonetheless emphasized the Jews' unique legal status within Christian society. That changed in 1179 with the promulgation of a canon that treats Jews and Saracens alike— on the grounds, some explained, that Saracens judaize through their literal observance of circumcision and other Old Testament norms.

Within fifty years, it became common for canonists to subject Muslims to Jewry law, the largely pre-Islamic set of rules that Christians established to regulate the activity of Jews (not to be confused with the Jewish law that Jews created for their own communities). This development had far-reaching and potentially fatal consequences, particularly for Muslims who found themselves living within the expanding kingdoms of Christian Spain. The transformation of Muslims into quasi-Jews, however, does not stem from engagement with actual Muslims or Jews. Instead, it results from the internal logic of Roman Catholic canon law and the agendas of the authorities who shaped its development and application. These authorities feared that fellow Christians might adopt purportedly Jewish beliefs, practices, and interpretations of the Bible.

The allegation that Muslims judaize reflects the concern that Christians are liable to do the same if they interact with either Jews or Muslims. Christians are the intended beneficiaries of Jewry law, and the Jews and Muslims subjected to its application suffered collateral damage from an internal struggle to define and police Christendom.

This chapter begins with a brief survey of pre-Islamic Jewry law that focuses particular attention on canons that appear in the influential *Decretum Gratiani*, compiled around the year 1140. In this context, we will also examine early Latin statements about Muslims that found their way into the *Decretum* and other twelfth-century canon law collections. We will then analyze the process that unfolded between 1179 and 1229 through which Muslims became legally equivalent to Jews. This period witnessed many dramatic developments within Latin canon law, spurred not only by the increased legislative activity of popes and the councils of bishops they convened but also by the unprecedented efforts of scholastic lawyers to systematize disparate canonical sources. These canonists transformed Muslims into Jews through a process of legal alchemy that relates only tangentially to the beliefs and behaviors of actual Muslims and Jews. The results of this transformation appear both in the authoritative collection known as the *Liber extra* or *Decretals of Gregory IX*, published in 1234, and in the canons of local church councils.[1] The chapter concludes by examining the harsh consequences of this transformation for Muslims in Christian Spain and, especially, for their Catholic descendants, known as Moriscos.

THE DIFFERENCE BETWEEN JEWS AND SARACENS (PRE-1179)

The oldest surviving Latin canons, from early fourth-century Spain, already distinguish Jews from other non-Christians: they excommunicate Christians who marry their daughters to Jews but merely scold those whose daughters wed non-Christian "gentiles." This distinction between Jews and gentiles appears consistently in canon law literature through the mid-twelfth century. While authorities forbid the sale of Christian slaves to any non-Christian, for example, they regard bondage to Jews as "even worse"; for that reason, they mandate the liberation of Jewish-owned slaves but not slaves who serve pagan masters. In one of several letters on this subject, Pope Gregory I (r. 590–604) demands the liberation of Jewish-owned slaves "lest—God forbid—the Christian religion should be polluted by its subjection to Jews." This scenario involves more than the improper status inversion inherent when non-Christians exercise power over Christian slaves: what concerned Gregory is the timeless contest he perceived between the true Christian faith and the Jews, who not only reject Christianity but constantly seek to corrupt it. Similar concern prompts various councils of sixth- and seventh-century bishops to bar Jews from public office and even from appearing in public during the days that surround Easter, when the visible presence of those who reject Christ undermines the messages of rituals that commemorate Christ's death and resurrection.[2]

A canon issued in early sixth-century Gaul (present-day France) that forbids Christians from eating with Jews became a classic justification for distinguishing Jews from other non-Christians. This canon, known by its opening Latin word as *Omnes*, asserts that it is "unbecoming and sacrilegious" for Christians to participate in meals in which Jews who adhere to Old Testament dietary laws refuse to eat foods that Paul permitted. At stake in such meals is both the asymmetry that results from Jews holding themselves to more restrictive standards than Christians and, more fundamentally, the theologically freighted question of how one should interpret the Bible. The mid-twelfth-century canon law commentator Rufinus emphasizes this latter dimension of *Omnes*, explaining that its prohibition of shared meals applies solely to Jews "because through the abuse of scripture they subvert faith in Christ in various ways and condemn the food of Christians. Gentiles, however, are not like this, and therefore we are not prohibited from going to their table." What makes Jews more dangerous than other non-Christians, Rufinus and many others believed, is their adherence to—and misinterpretation of—the Bible.[3]

Muslims, in contrast, threatened European Christendom as invaders and gentile foreigners. References to Saracens within Latin canonical sources from the eighth and ninth centuries often appear in the context of rules governing the use of armed force in self-defense. Several authorities also express concern about the proximity of Muslim-controlled territory. In an incident that came to be seen as establishing a binding legal precedent, Pope Zacharias (r. 741–52) prevented the shipment of Christian slaves from Venice to "the pagan peoples in Africa." This and many other Latin texts erroneously imagine Muslims to be pagans, which is to say idolaters, perhaps solely because Muslims are clearly neither Jews nor heretical Christians, the other available categories within canon law. It is no surprise, then, that church authorities applied to Muslims existing norms related to pagans, such as the long-standing ban on selling Christian slaves to them, without also imposing Jewry law on Muslims. In fact, the only canon from before 1179 that refers to both Muslims and Jews emphasizes that each group bears a distinct legal status. "There is in fact a difference between the case of the Jews and that of the Saracens," insisted Pope Alexander II in 1063. "It is just to fight against the latter, who persecute Christians and expel them from their cities and their own residences. The former, however, are everywhere prepared to be subservient." Muslims and Jews alike threaten Christendom, but they do so in different ways that call for distinct Christian responses: Muslims pose a political and military challenge, while Jews pose a theological challenge.[4]

The conflation of Muslims and Jews that occurs in the late twelfth century is a significant departure from earlier legal discourse about these non-Christian communities. This change coincides not only with other dramatic developments in canon law but also with dramatic changes in Christian geography. At the start of Alexander II's pontificate in 1061, hardly any Muslims lived in lands subject to Christian rule. A century later, however, Christians governed majority-Muslim territories in the Holy Land, Sicily, and the Iberian Peninsula. Jewry law provided a ready-made template for establishing the legal status of these subject Muslims—but only to the extent that canonists could define Muslims as Jewish.[5]

THE CONFLATION OF JEWS AND SARACENS (1179–1229 AND BEYOND)

The Third Lateran Council, a gathering of three hundred bishops that Pope Alexander III convened in 1179, issued what seems at first glance to be a straightforward decree: "Jews and Saracens are not to be allowed to have Christian servants in their houses, either under pretense of nourishing their children or for service or any other reason." The reference to Saracens, however, is both unprecedented and odd. This canon, known by its opening words as *Iudaei sive Sarraceni*, is a miscellany of Jewry laws that mentions Muslims only in its initial sentence. After addressing the issue of domestic service (a status distinct from slavery), it turns to the subject of Christian testimony against Jewish defendants and from there to the property and inheritance rights of converts to Christianity, apparently referring to Jews by birth. A separate canon issued by the Third Lateran Council, which reflects long-standing concerns about Muslims as threatening foreigners, forbids the sale to Saracens of weapons or other materials and services that can be put to military use. The passing reference to Saracens in the canon devoted to Jewry law, in contrast, is out of place.[6]

Even in the context of *Iudaei sive Sarraceni*'s initial section, the reference to Saracens is anomalous. This section reiterates an earlier decree by Alexander III forbidding Christians "from placing themselves in ongoing service to Jews . . . This is because Jewish norms in no manner accord with our own and they, stirred by their hatred for the human race, would bend the simpleminded toward their superstition and faithlessness through ongoing conversation and constant intimacy." This papal decree refers solely to Jewish employers, draws on distinctly anti-Jewish tropes, and builds on a lengthy history of canonical concern about Christian subservience to Jews in particular. Why, then, does the Third Lateran Council apply its prohibition against domestic service to Jewish and Saracen employers alike?[7]

Historian Benjamin Kedar suggests that William of Tyre, whose crusade chronicle we encountered in chapter 3, is responsible for introducing the words "and Saracens" at a late stage in the drafting of this canon. William played a prominent role in the Third Lateran Council and wrote the official, now-lost record of the council's proceedings. As a bishop in the Latin Kingdom of Jerusalem established by European crusaders, he probably worried about the prospect of Christians working in Muslim homes. This simple and, perhaps, off-the-cuff emendation to the long-standing rule about Christian domestic servants addressed that practical concern. No one at the Third Lateran Council, however, could have anticipated how *Iudaei sive Sarraceni* would transform the ways in which legal scholars and practitioners thought about Jewry law as a whole.[8]

The most obvious impact of the canon's opening words—"Jews and Saracens"—is structural. We have seen that older canon law consistently distinguishes Jews from other outsiders and never associates Muslims with Jews. When Bernard of Pavia compiled his topically organized collection of canon law around the year 1190, however, he created a section called "On Jews, Saracens, and Their Servants." This set of canons, organized around the subject matter of *Iudaei sive Sarraceni*, includes in addition to this canon four others that address Jews alone and two that refer solely to Saracens. Subsequent collections of canon law, including the *Liber extra*, adopted both Bernard's organizational structure and this particular title. As a result, Jews and Muslims became permanently linked within European legal discourse.[9]

Bernard of Pavia associates Jewry law with what we might call Saracen law, but he does not equate Muslims with Jews or apply Jewry law to Muslims. On the contrary, Bernard follows in the footsteps of his predecessors by emphasizing the difference between Jews and those whom he regards as pagans. Jews, he explains, "observe the Law of Moses according to the letter by circumcising themselves and practicing other legalisms," while Saracens "accept neither the Old Testament nor the New." Bernard defines these communities in terms of their relationship to the Bible: Saracens, like other pagans, reject the Bible in its entirety; Jews accept the Old Testament alone; Christians, to whom Bernard implicitly contrasts these groups, accept Old and New Testaments alike. (Bernard also defines heretics in terms of their relationship to the Bible: they are Christians who interpret scripture incorrectly.) Because of this distinction, Christians may share meals with Saracens even though they may not eat with Jews. Echoing the mid-twelfth-century commentator Rufinus, Bernard emphasizes that "Jews, through the abuse of scripture and contempt of our food, attack our faith more" than Saracens do. Muslims, Bernard suggests, neither use nor abuse the Old Testament and thus pose no special challenge to Christians. As "pagans," Muslims remain exempt from Jewry law, with the anomalous exception of the Third Lateran Council's rule about domestic servants.[10]

Bernard transformed the structure of canon law, but he did not seek to change the ways in which canonists perceived Muslims. Huguccio, Bernard's contemporary and an equally influential canonist, did just that: perhaps in an effort to account for the Third Lateran Council's unprecedented association of Jews and Saracens, he collapsed the legal distinction between these groups. "Today," he asserted in the late 1180s, "there does not seem to be any reason for saying that servitude to pagans is different from servitude to Jews, for nearly all contemporary pagans judaize: they are circumcised, they distinguish among foods, and they imitate other Jewish rituals. There ought not be any legal difference between them."[11]

Huguccio acknowledges that the New Testament itself instructs Christian slaves to accept the authority of their pagan masters (1 Peter 2:18). He emphasizes, however, that twelfth-century "pagans"—that is, Muslims—are different from their predecessors because they adhere to "Jewish rituals" such as male circumcision and abstention from pork. Just as Christians may not serve Jews, Huguccio contends, so, too, they may not serve "judaizing pagans"—that is, Muslims. Canonists, after all, regarded literal observance of Old Testament law as a defining

feature of Judaism, and they would readily brand Christians who practice circumcision or distinguish among foods as judaizers; from this perspective, it follows naturally that Muslims judaize in their adherence to
these practices. By extension, Huguccio seems to suggest, Muslims are as
likely as Jews to corrupt the beliefs and behaviors of their Christian
slaves. Huguccio makes no reference to *Iudaei sive Sarraceni* in this passage; he is, after all, commenting on the *Decretum* rather than on the
canons of the Third Lateran Council, and the canon in question addresses
slavery rather than domestic service. His argument, however, elegantly
rationalizes the council's application of Jewry law to Saracens.

Huguccio, unlike Bernard, also forbids shared meals with Muslims
on the grounds that "nearly all Saracens at the present judaize because
they are circumcised and distinguish among foods in accordance with
Jewish norms . . . The reason for the prohibition [against Jewish food]
expressed in *Omnes* applies equally to both groups." According to
Huguccio's interpretation of *Omnes*, the sixth-century canon forbidding shared meals with Jews discussed above, exposure to Judaism is
dangerous because Christians might be tempted to adopt Old Testament practices. By this logic, interaction with Muslims is equally fraught
since they, too, observe Old Testament norms literally. Huguccio's
argument for avoiding shared meals with Jews and Saracens alike
appears in the influential Ordinary Gloss to the *Decretum*, the mid-
thirteenth-century commentary that regularly accompanied subsequent
copies of that collection.[12]

The trouble with Huguccio's argument, however, is that it mischar-
acterizes the danger that many canonists ascribed to Judaism. Rufinus
and Bernard, after all, understand *Omnes* to forbid shared meals with
Jews because of their so-called "abuse of scripture," not the mere fact
that Jews adhere to restrictive dietary laws. *Ecce vicit leo*, one of many
early thirteenth-century canon law commentaries whose author is now
unknown, highlights the difference between these canonists and argues
against Huguccio's position. "It is better to say that the reason for this
prohibition [of shared meals] is that Jews have the Law and by means
of it they can easily lead the simpleminded to their horrible ways if they
share meals with them." Saracens, this commentator asserts, are not as
capable of corrupting uneducated Christians because they cannot
appeal to the Law of Moses. For that reason, he seems to argue, Muslims do not meet the canonical definition of Jewishness and should not
be subject to Jewry law. *Animal est substantia*, another commentary
that makes the same observation with regard to food, transfers this

logic back to the case of slavery: the reason why Christians may in principle serve pagans but not Jews is that "Jews have the Law and for that reason can pervert Christian slaves more easily than gentiles who do not have the Law." This commentary instead justifies the prohibition of servitude to Saracens on narrower grounds, citing as precedent Roman laws that bar Jews and pagans alike from owning Christian slaves. *Iudaei sive Sarraceni*, this canonist suggests, does not impose Jewry law on Muslims but rather civil law. The author of *Animal est substantia* objects not to the practice of regulating subject Saracens but to the principle of equating Saracens with Jews: he seeks to preserve the unique role that Jews play in Christian thought as the people of the Old Testament. His workaround, however, proved unsatisfying to authorities who found value in treating Muslims like Jews in other respects.[13]

Pope Innocent III convened the Fourth Lateran Council in 1215; with 1,200 participants including four hundred bishops, it was the largest and most influential medieval gathering of its kind. This council adopted a novel approach to regulating Jews and Muslims alike: it asserted that Old Testament norms apply equally to both. In the canon known as *In nonnullis provinciis*, the council expresses deep concern over the prospect that Christians might inadvertently engage in sexual relations with "Jews or Saracens" whose dress is indistinguishable from the dominant Christian community. "In order that the offense of such a damnable mixing may not spread further under the excuse of a mistake of this kind, we decree that such persons of either sex, in every Christian province and at all times, are to be distinguished in public from other people by the character of their dress—seeing moreover that this very rule was enjoined upon them by Moses, as we read."[14] Pope Innocent III, to a far greater degree than his predecessors, maintained careful control over the canons approved at this council, so we need to presume that he not only intended this canon to refer to Jews and Saracens alike but also alleged that Moses enjoined rules upon all of "them."[15]

Innocent's claim about the Law of Moses, perhaps a reference to the biblical requirement that Israelites place fringes on their garments (Numbers 15:38 and Deuteronomy 22:12), is no mere afterthought, and his application of this claim to Muslims is not accidental. Thirteenth-century popes asserted the right to enforce on non-Christians the divine laws already incumbent on them, so the concluding assertion justifies the unprecedented claim that church authorities can directly regulate the dress of non-Christians. The notion that Moses imposed rules on Muslims and Jews alike also resolves the concerns expressed in *Ecce vicit leo* and *Animal est substantia*: both groups "have the Law," and for that reason both pose the same danger to simpleminded Christians and ought to be subject to the same canonical regulations.[16]

On what basis could the pope plausibly claim that Moses addressed Muslims? Perhaps, following Huguccio, he holds that Saracens are pagans who judaized and thus obligated themselves to observe biblical law in its entirety. Perhaps, like Bernard of Pavia, he confused Saracens with Samaritans, a religious community that does in fact regard the Five Books of Moses as scripture.[17] A more likely possibility, however, is that Innocent III took advantage of the decades-old association of Jews and Saracens first attested at the Third Lateran Council and enshrined in Bernard's widely adopted system of organizing canon law. Innocent seems to infer from this association that both communities share Jewish characteristics, of which the foremost is literal observance of Old Testament law. The expedience of this assertion, which justifies the pope's unprecedented claim of authority over non-Christians and facilitates their segregation within Christian society, matters far more than its accuracy.[18]

In the second half of *In nonnullis provinciis*, Innocent ascribes to Muslims another purportedly Jewish characteristic—namely, disrespect for Christ. This portion of the canon bars "them," which in this context refers to Jews and Saracens alike, from appearing in public at Eastertime lest they mock Christians or blaspheme Christ; the Fourth Lateran Council is the first to apply this classic element of Jewry law to Saracens. The following canon reiterates a sixth-century decree barring the appointment of Jews to public offices on the grounds that "It would be too absurd for a blasphemer of Christ to exercise power over Christians." It then adds, without precedent, "We extend the same thing to pagans," which in this context can only mean Saracens. Innocent III seems to presume that Muslims revile Christ simply because he associates Muslims with Jews. That association, in turn, stems from factors internal to canon law: the chapter headings created by Bernard of Pavia on the basis of the Third Lateran Council's canon about domestic servants, and the desire among canonists to impose the preexisting body of Jewry law on a relatively new group of subject non-Christians.[19]

The *Summula Conradi*, a synopsis of canon law written between 1226 and 1229, captures the transformation in the legal status of Muslims that began in 1179. After summarizing the various elements of Jewry law from late antiquity through the Fourth Lateran Council, the author simply declares, "That which is said regarding the Jews, understand it all regarding Saracens except, perhaps, that Christians are allowed to sit at the table of Saracens . . . perhaps for the reason that they do not have the Law with which to deceive the simpleminded, as do the Jews." This canonist duly notes the dispute between Huguccio and his detractors over the proper interpretation of *Omnes*, but he perceives consensus with respect to subjecting Muslims to every other facet of canonical Jewry law! The reverse, however, did not occur: no council or canonist subjected Jews to the limited number of laws originally imposed on Muslims alone. The association of Saracens with Jews did not expand the substance of Jewry law but rather the number of people to whom it applied. From the perspective of legal status, the Muslims who dwelled within Christendom had become "Jewish" and posed a danger to Christians for that very reason.[20]

The Fourth Lateran Council's canons had real and lasting impact on the lives of European Jews and Muslims.[21] These canons also influenced the course of subsequent ecclesiastical legislation: several dozen local church councils imposed Jewry law on Saracens during the thirteenth and fourteenth centuries, in keeping with the precedents established at the Lateran councils and the principle articulated in the *Summula Conradi*. In fact, more canons from local church councils regulate Jews and Saracens alike than Saracens alone. Some of these councils reiterated the Third Lateran Council's ban on domestic service or the Fourth Lateran Council's requirement of distinctive dress, both of which originally referred to Jews and Saracens simultaneously; many more forbade sexual relations with either Jews or Saracens. Various local councils also imposed on Jews and Saracens alike the Fourth Lateran Council's requirement that Jews pay church tithes on their lands and extended to baptized Jews and Saracens alike the Third Lateran Council's property protections, even though neither originally referred to Saracens. Some councils revised late antique laws related to food, doctors, and public baths by applying these restrictions to Saracens as well as Jews. Others articulated unprecedented restrictions regarding moneylending, attendance at non-Christian weddings or funerals, and the presence of non-Christians in or near churches and cemeteries. These canons reflect the underlying concern that social interactions with either Jews or Muslims—especially those in which Christians are subservient—might lead Christians themselves to judaize. The definition of Muslims as legally equivalent to Jews could also be used for other purposes: as we saw in chapter 3, the early fourteenth-century canonist Oldradus de Ponte drew heavily on this association when arguing for the conquest and expulsion of peaceful Jews and Muslims.[22]

There is no evidence that European Christian authorities systematically applied Jewry law to Muslims. Recall, for example, that Oldradus himself is selective and opportunistic when it comes to associating or distinguishing Muslims and Jews. While about sixty thirteenth- and fourteenth-century councils promulgated at least one canon that applies to Jews and Saracens alike, many of these councils also promulgated canons that relate to one group or the other; meanwhile, well over a hundred local councils issued canons that apply to Jews alone. The most significant impact of the principle that Muslims can be subjected to Jewry law is that it created the conditions under which Christian authorities could, when they wished, persecute Muslims along the same lines that they persecuted Jews in the name of protecting fellow Christians. Influential figures in early modern Spain seized this opportunity.

THE CONSEQUENCES OF JUDAIZING IN EARLY MODERN SPAIN

Church councils in the various Christian kingdoms of the Iberian Peninsula were especially likely to promulgate canons that imposed restrictions on Jews and Saracens alike. This comes as no surprise, since the region was home to numerous Jews and Muslims living under Christian rule. For that very reason, local Christians recognized the significant social and religious differences between Jews and Muslims. Even so, officials involved in the Spanish Inquisition often alleged that Muslims judaize, a charge with potentially deadly consequences. This allegation also features prominently in religious arguments from the turn of the seventeenth century in favor of expelling Spain's Moriscos, baptized Christians of Muslim ancestry.[23]

The Spanish Inquisition, which King Ferdinand and Queen Isabella established in 1478, primarily targeted Christians of Jewish ancestry. There were many such "New Christians" in fifteenth-century Spain because local Jews faced intense pressure to convert that occasionally included mob violence. Some converts and their descendants left their Jewishness behind, but others continued to observe familiar religious or cultural practices. Although Spanish Jews retained the right to practice Judaism, Jews who accepted baptism, even under duress, were legally defined as Christians for whom acts of judaizing constitute a severe canonical offense. The Inquisition sought to stamp out judaizing behavior within the Christian population through vigorous prosecution and public punishment. Because Christians associated Muslims with Jews, inquisitors also took aggressive steps to combat what they perceived as the judaizing practices of formerly Muslim New Christians.

Cristóbal de Gelba, a Muslim by birth, converted to Christianity but apparently did not abandon all his former practices or social ties. In 1486, this earned Cristóbal the unfortunate distinction of becoming the first Morisco to be convicted by the Spanish Inquisition. Inquisitors found him guilty of engaging in "Jewish ceremonies," as well as eating with Muslims and praying in a mosque. Inquisitorial records from the following year report that Cristóbal "judaized and passed to the law of Muhammad"—in other words, he practiced Islam. From the perspective of the Inquisition, living in accordance with Muhammad's teachings entails adherence to Jewish rites. Cristóbal's inquisitors even regarded his reversion to Islam as a Jewish practice. Cristóbal escaped, so the inquisitors could only burn him in effigy; others, however, were not so fortunate.[24]

We do not know the circumstances that prompted Cristóbal de Gelba to opt for baptism in the first place. A generation later, however, many Muslims converted to Christianity under duress. Although Ferdinand and Isabella granted Spanish Muslims the right to practice their religion as part of the terms for the surrender of Granada in 1492, these monarchs reneged on that pledge several years later. Their edict of 1502 expelling Muslims who refuse baptism cites as precedent the expulsion of Spain's Jews a decade earlier and offers the same justification: Muslims, like Jews, subvert the faith of former coreligionists recently converted to Christianity and, for that reason, must not dwell in Christian Spain. The country's Morisco population swelled, but everyone recognized that many of these New Christians continued to observe traditional practices. Sixteenth-century inquisitors sought to prevent former Muslims from backsliding, and in many cases they charged these Moriscos as "judaizers."[25]

The Moriscos of Granada were deeply concerned by this allegation. In 1529, their representatives demanded that inquisitors distinguish Muslim practices from Jewish ones and that they punish Moriscos only for adherence to practices mandated by the Quran. This petition, however, seems to have had little effect. Bernardo Pérez de Chinchón, writing in 1532, was among the many sixteenth-century Spanish polemicists who alleged that Muslims "keep the main part" of Jewish law. Of the 102 primarily Morisco individuals convicted by a Granadan tribunal in 1593, three quarters were forced to engage in public penance for the sin of judaizing. The following year, the papal nuncio Camillo Borghese (soon to become Pope Paul V) stated that the Moriscos, "although Christian, still judaize in many things." Moriscos, influential Christians believed, remain incorrigible in their Jewishness.[26]

This allegation also played a supporting role in the ultimately successful effort to persuade King Philip III (r. 1598–1621) to expel the Moriscos on the grounds that they posed a danger to Spain's Christian society. Martin de Salvatierra, a prominent bishop, emphasized that Moriscos do not belong in Spain because they are unwilling to give up the religious practices they adopted from the Jews. Jaime Bleda, the inquisitor whose account of Muhammad's Jewish ancestry we examined in chapter 7, bolsters that general allegation with specific examples in his *Defense of the Faith*, a polemical tract that Bleda distributed to notables as part of his tireless lobbying efforts on behalf of expulsion. Of the ninety-one numbered charges that Bleda lodges against Moriscos in the first portion of this lengthy work, roughly a dozen associate Moriscos with Jews. Not only do Moriscos allegedly practice circumcision and observe dietary laws as instructed by Moses, but they also fast "in Jewish fashion" when they observe Ramadan, draw on a Jewish interpretation of Abraham's near-sacrifice of Isaac when they celebrate Id al-Adha, adopt Jewish names, maintain a quasi-Jewish calendar whose holidays begin at sunset, and observe Jewish dining etiquette. Bleda, who presumes that Moriscos observe traditional Islamic practices in their entirety, defines these practices themselves as Jewish to make them more repulsive. He also alleges that Muslims, like Jews, engage in blasphemous behavior by mocking the cross and abusing the consecrated eucharistic host; we will return to the latter charge in chapter 9. By defining Moriscos as Jews rather than Christians, Bleda undermines arguments that Moriscos have a right to dwell within Christian Spain on account of their baptism.[27]

Juan de Ribera, Bleda's superior as the archbishop of Valencia, compared the Moriscos to the biblical Israelites whom God killed for worshipping the Golden Calf and argued that expulsion is a humane alternative to annihilation. Ribera challenged Philip III to offer "a demonstration of the king's greatness, which will deserve the title Catholic as his predecessor Ferdinand had earned when he expelled the Jews" in 1492. To be a true Catholic monarch, one must drive out Jews and judaizing Moriscos alike. Philip earned that title in 1609, when he decreed the expulsion of Spain's Moriscos, beginning with those in Valencia. The spurious allegations lodged against these Moriscos, including the charge of judaizing, ultimately uprooted several hundred thousand people from their homeland.[28]

The philosophers Max Horckheimer and Theodor Adorno, reflecting on Nazism, observed that "to call someone a Jew amounts to an instigation to work him over until he resembles the image." This description aptly describes not only the rhetoric of Spanish Christians but also that of all the authors we have considered in this book: they work over Muslims to render them as Jews.[29] The accuracy of the allegation is less relevant to achieving this goal than its plausibility to the intended audience. The same may be said regarding the imagined case of the political candidate who declares "My opponent is a pig!" Whether Jews or pigs constitute the negative reference point of a polemical comparison, what matters most to the polemicist is the objective of such rhetoric: to win an election in the imagined example, and to promote proper Christian beliefs and behaviors in the premodern cases this book explores. Representations of Muslims as judaizers serve not only to explain a rival community of relatively recent origin in terms derived from the Bible, but also, as we will see in the coming chapters, to define that community as the antithesis of Christendom itself.

PART THREE

Anti-Christian Muslims

CHAPTER 9

Muslims Killed Christ!? Theological Arguments and Political Agendas

Eleventh through Seventeenth Centuries

The allegation that Muslims killed Christ is shocking—and, for that very reason, a wide range of premodern European polemicists employed variations of it over the course of several centuries. This charge is literally preposterous, as it inverts chronological events by making "pre" what is actually "post." How could Muslims play a role in an event that occurred roughly six centuries before Islam emerged? The claim that Muslims killed Christ is also figuratively preposterous because it goes against common sense, contradicting not only the biblical narrative but also information about Islam familiar to some European and most Eastern Christians—namely, that Muslims revere Jesus as a servant of God and even as the messiah who will inaugurate the glorious end of days. One might add that this assertion is simply ridiculous, as premodern Christians blamed the Jews for killing Christ. By this point in the book, however, readers can likely guess the basis for alleging Muslim complicity in the crucifixion: polemicists branded Muslims themselves as Jewish.

The allegation "Muslims are Jewish," like our recurring example of the candidate for elected office who declares "my opponent is a pig," involves not only a target (Muslims) and a reference (Jews) but also a polemicist, a criterion of comparison, an objective, and an audience. We have seen in parts 1 and 2 that a wide range of Christian polemicists employed biblical criteria to brand Muslims as Jews with the objective of promoting specific beliefs and behaviors among their Christian audiences. Part 3, which focuses almost entirely on European sources, demonstrates the specific value that premodern Christians perceived in employing Muslims as their target and Jews as their reference: by applying the discourse of anti-Judaism, polemicists can ascribe theological dimensions to political conflicts between Christians and Muslims. This fusion of theological and political enmity generates explosive rhetorical energy that polemicists use to further their goal of promoting proper Christianity. The shock value of this metaphorical association—premodern Christians knew that Muslims are not Jews and did not literally kill Christ—also contributes to the power of this rhetoric. As historian Christina Brauner observes, polemical comparisons "play with scandalisation to gain attention and horrify (and at the same time entertain) the general public."[1]

Educated premodern Christians knew that Islam emerged long after Christ's lifetime; many knew that Muslims revere Jesus as a prophet; and some even addressed the Islamic conviction that no one killed Christ—according to the Quran, Jesus escaped the crucifixion unscathed, as befits a pious messenger of God (4:157).[2] Despite this knowledge, numerous European polemicists found it both plausible and useful to associate Muslims with Christ's killers, to allege that contemporary Muslims act as Christ-killers, or to ascribe purportedly Islamic characteristics to the biblical villains who played a role in the crucifixion. Christians also found it both plausible and useful to hold their living Jewish neighbors personally responsible for Christ's death many centuries before. Allegations like these made sense despite their flagrant disregard for basic chronology because Christians regarded the crucifixion not merely as an historical event but rather as a perpetual and timeless conflict between God's loving grace and those who utterly reject it—a conflict traditionally represented in terms of Jewish enmity toward Christ and Christians.

The very definition of Judaism as the antithesis of Christianity accounts to no small degree for the charge that biblical Jews killed Christ (in fact, as the Gospels make clear, Roman officials executed Jesus) and that contemporary Jews in some sense do the same. Allegations that target Muslims alongside Jews reinforce the notion that Islam is similarly antithetical to Christianity. The discourse of anti-Judaism, we have seen, provides a powerful means of motivating fellow Christians to make proper Christian choices regardless of whether it targets Jews, Muslims, or others because this discourse carries the implicit warning that all who make improper choices become "Jewish" themselves.

The present chapter begins by considering how and why European Christian writers of the eleventh and twelfth centuries associated Muslim warriors of their own era with Christ's Jewish antagonists. Such rhetoric, we will see, adds timeless theological significance to contemporary military conflicts and, in so doing, transforms the Christians who battle Muslims into religious heroes who avenge Christ's death. We will then examine a thirteenth-century work of art in which visual allusions to ongoing battles between Christians and Muslims reinforce a purely theological agenda. The artist promotes faithful devotion to the consecrated host, the wafer whose nature is transformed into the body of Christ during the ritual of the Eucharist, by portraying those who question its significance as simultaneously Jewish and Muslim. The chapter concludes with an analysis of Spanish allegations that local Muslims and Moriscos, like Jews, desecrate the eucharistic host and thus attack the body of Christ. Polemicists, we will see, redefined Moriscos—the baptized descendants of Muslims—not as Christians but rather as quasi-Jewish enemies of Christ in their theological arguments on behalf of political action: expulsion of the Moriscos from Spain. It seems, however, that these polemicists strategically refrained from alleging that Moriscos ritually kill Christ, perhaps because they sought to avoid provoking mass violence. The charge of Christ-killing, after all, carried serious implications for its targets, as European Jews knew all too well.

AVENGERS OF CHRIST

For several decades during the tenth century, Muslim brigands occupied the fortress of Fraxinetum (La Garde-Freinet), midway between Marseilles and Nice on the Mediterranean coast of present-day France. These brigands ravaged the surrounding region and often abducted travelers across the nearby Alps to ransom or sell as slaves. In 972, they captured Maiolus, abbot of the increasingly influential and wealthy monastery of Cluny, as he and his entourage returned from Rome. The Muslims received a sizeable ransom, but they did not have much time to enjoy it: Christian forces destroyed Fraxinetum soon thereafter, perhaps to avenge this particularly galling abduction of a prominent monk. Accounts of Fraxinetum's destruction exemplify various ways in which medieval Europeans depicted Muslims. Through comparison of these accounts, we can pinpoint an important function of rhetoric that brands Muslims as Jewish: those who identify contemporary Muslims with the killers of Christ can praise warriors who defeat Muslim foes as Christian, rather than merely secular, heroes.[3]

Most surviving tales about the Muslims of Fraxinetum were written by monks associated with Maiolus's monastery of Cluny, but we will begin our survey with an instructive account preserved in the *Chronicle of Novalese*, the history of a monastic community near Fraxinetum that suffered gravely from Muslim raids. The anonymous chronicler, who makes no mention at all of Maiolus, attributes Fraxinetum's destruction to divine justice and to a disgruntled Saracen named Aimo. Following a successful raiding expedition, a fellow brigand forcibly seized an espe-cially beautiful captive woman who by rights belonged to Aimo. God inspired the enraged Aimo to betray the fortress to Count Robald of Provence. The Novalese chronicler portrays Muslims not only as cruel, violent, and destructive but also lustful, immoral, and disloyal. The chronicler praises Robald and his brave men for routing the Saracens but credits the victory to Aimo's deception.[4]

Tales about Fraxinetum told by the monks of Cluny generally appear in works whose purpose is to promote Maiolus as a saint. Each account has its own emphasis. A biographer named Syrus, for example, stresses the difference between civilized Christians and barbarous Saracens, while the historian Ralph Glaber emphasizes that the Saracens recog-nized Maiolus's sanctity because they, too, revere the Bible, although they erroneously understand its prophecies as speaking of Muhammad rather than of Christ. Neither of these early eleventh-century authors employed biblical rhetoric to describe the Muslims of Fraxinetum, but both reported that the abbot himself did so in his ransom note: "Maio-lus, a captive, wretched and in chains, sends greetings to his lords and brothers, the monks of Cluny. The hordes of Belial have surrounded me; the snares of death have seized me. Please send a ransom payment for me and those held captive with me." The second sentence of this note is a direct quotation from Psalm 18:5, in which King David recounts his deliverance from enemies; it also calls to mind Paul's sharp contrast of Christ and Belial—that is, the devil (2 Corinthians 6:15). These references enable Maiolus to depict his Muslim captors as agents of Christ's timeless nemesis and enemies of Christ's present-day follow-ers. The abbot also alludes to the deliverance that he hopes to celebrate just as David once did.[5]

The biblical rhetoric of Maiolus's ransom note adds a theological dimension otherwise absent from most depictions of Fraxinetum's Mus-lims. Muslims can be lustful, cruel, barbarous, and misguided without being followers of the devil, and those who praise Maiolus as a saint need not portray him as a latter-day David or a Christ figure. Framing the abduction in biblical terms, however, transforms this event into an episode in the unending struggle between Christ and his enemies. We encountered a similar dynamic in chapter 5 when examining the way Timothy I depicts his disputation with a Muslim as the latest round in the timeless contest that pits Christians against Jews old and new. In both cases, the defeat of Muslims takes on added significance as a victory for Christ. Such rhetoric also elevates the stature of the Christian victors.

Odilo, who succeeded Maiolus as abbot of Cluny, does not quote the ransom note in his own *Life of Maiolus*, composed around the year 1033, but he too draws on the Bible to associate the Muslims of Fraxinetum with the Jews who caused Christ to suffer and die.

> Just as the Jews were exiled from their homeland on account of Christ's Passion, so too the Saracens were expelled beyond the borders of Christendom on account of their capture of Christ's most faithful servant, Maiolus. And just as God exercised vengeance on the Jews through Titus and Vespasian, rulers of the Romans, so too did God, on account of the merits of Saint Maiolus, remove from Christian shoulders the yoke of Saracen subjugation through William, the most illustrious man and most Christian ruler.[6]

Odilo, like others who wrote about Fraxinetum, depicts the Saracens as cruel and portrays their defeat as an act of divine justice prompted by Maiolus's merit. Only Odilo, however, glorifies the "most Christian ruler" who drove the Saracens out of Fraxinetum and the surrounding region. For the conquest of Fraxinetum to be "Christian," its Muslim inhabitants must be more than just cruel and barbarous: they must be enemies of Christ. Only by rendering Fraxinetum's Muslims as the contemporary equivalents of the Jews responsible for Christ's Passion, the suffering that culminated in Jesus's death, can Odilo portray Count William of Arles as an agent of divine vengeance in the model of the first-century emperors Titus and Vespasian, who destroyed the Jerusalem Temple. (The *Chronicle of Novalese* credits the destruction of Fraxinetum not to William but to his brother, Robald; Odilo's effusive praise of William might have something to do with William's generous donation to the monastery of Cluny.)[7]

Odilo associates present-day Muslims with Jewish Christ-killers in order to praise the warriors who defeated these Muslims as Christian heroes. His rhetoric was unusual in the early eleventh century, as the notion that soldiers could fight on behalf of Christ only gained widespread popularity several decades later with the emergence of crusade ideology. Earlier biographers of Maiolus saw no need to name, much less glorify, the secular lord who exercised divine justice by destroying Fraxinetum; the Novalese chronicler praises Robald and his men for their bravery, as befits soldiers, but does not portray their conquest as

in any way "Christian." Odilo's rhetoric about Muslims was also con-
troversial: a contemporaneous bishop ridiculed "King Odilo of Cluny"
for blurring the line between monks and soldiers by portraying military
engagement with Saracens as a Christian duty. Odilo, in other words,
needed to make a case for the theological significance of battling Muslims. By associating Muslims with the Jews who tormented and killed
Christ, Odilo frames attacks against them as righteous acts of vengeance rather than merely political conquests. Later works in praise of
Christian warriors do the same.[8]

Baldric, who served as abbot of the monastery in Bourgueil during
the First Crusade, makes especially powerful use of this trope when
imagining the sermon preached to crusaders just prior to their conquest
of Jerusalem in 1099:

> Rouse yourselves, members of Christ's household! Rouse yourselves, knights
> and foot soldiers, and seize firmly that city, our commonwealth! Give heed
> to Christ, who today is banished from that city and crucified; and with
> Joseph of Arimathea take him down from the cross; and lay up in the
> sepulchre of your hearts an incomparable treasure, that desirable treasure;
> and forcefully take Christ away from these impious crucifiers. For every time
> those bad judges, confederates of Herod and Pilate, make sport of and
> enslave your brothers, they crucify Christ. Every time they torment them and
> kill them, they lance Christ's side with Longinus.[9]

The Muslims of late eleventh-century Jerusalem allegedly kill Christ
anew through their maltreatment of Christians. As participants in the
timeless crucifixion, they are in the same league as the Jewish king, the
Roman governor, and the soldier at the foot of the cross who pierced
Christ's body with his lance. By avenging this contemporary crucifixion,
crusaders assume the role of Joseph of Arimathea, who attended to
Christ's body and arranged for its burial. Christian writers typically
associated Joseph with clergy performing the Eucharist, but now warriors, too, can participate in the ultimate Christian drama because that
drama unfolds not only in ritual but also on the battlefield. Through his
association of Jerusalem's Muslim defenders with biblical Christ-killers,
Baldric ascribes theological significance to military conquest.

The prologue of the *Chanson d'Antioche*, the first in a trilogy of Old
French epic poems recounting the First Crusade that crystallized in the
early thirteenth century, frames this military campaign against the Muslims in terms of vengeance for the crucifixion. "At the time when God
was first tortured by the Jews, broken and wounded by nails and the
lance," the crucified Jesus engaged in conversation with the thief dying

on the adjacent cross. "It is only right that you should be avenged for the treatment you have suffered at the hands of these cowardly Jews," the thief declares. Jesus replied,

> My friend, the race is not yet born who will come to revenge me for these sharp spear thrusts. They will come on my behalf and kill the wicked pagans who have repeatedly refused to obey my commandments; they will come to the aid of blessed Christianity, conquer my land and free my territory from tribute. . . . Not a single pagan will remain between here and the East: the Franks will liberate the whole land.

The term *Franks* refers in this context to the various European groups that participated in the crusade, many of whom lived in the region now known as northern France.[10]

The author of the *Chanson d'Antioche* does not explain how the crusaders' slaughter of "wicked pagans," which is to say Muslims, will avenge the acts of "cowardly Jews," but he doubles down on the association of contemporary Muslims and Jewish Christ-killers in the same fashion as Odilo of Cluny. The Roman emperors Titus and Vespasian, the poet declares with complete disregard for historical accuracy, "believed firmly in God the Son of the Virgin Mary" and destroyed Jerusalem when they learned what the Jews had done to Jesus on the cross. "And thus our Lord was avenged, and will be again. Anyone who goes to avenge him will be well rewarded: he will wear a crown in heavenly Paradise" (*laisses* 12–13).

Frankish crusaders, according to the *Chanson d'Antioche*, are Christian heroes in the mold of Titus and Vespasian, wreaking vengeance on Muslims as if these "pagans" are Jews. The specific charge leveled against the Muslims is that they wrongfully seized God's territory and even "wanted to put the Cross and the Holy Sepulchre up for sale" (*laisse* 14). This allegation of sacrilegious materialism, which refers to the very cross on which Jesus was crucified and to the place of his burial, resonates with contemporary complaints about French Jews, who allegedly tried to sell sacred objects stolen from churches or provided them as collateral for loans.[11]

A different relic—accompanied by different rhetoric about money—plays a key role in the final battle of the *Chanson d'Antioche*, as the Franks discover the very lance used to pierce Christ's side. "You have all heard God's command," declares Bishop Ademar of Le Puy as he rouses the Franks to combat. "We are the ones who have the lance, and we all know truly that it was with that lance he suffered torture and death for

FIGURE 14. *The Beam of the Passion*, on display at the Museu Nacional d'Art de Catalunya in Barcelona. The scenes depict the kiss of Judas and arrest of Christ, the flagellation, Christ on the road to Calvary, the crucifixion, Christ's followers removing his body, the entombment, and the return of the holy women to Christ's tomb. (For a clearer reproduction of the crucifixion scene, see fig. 15.) The unpainted rectangular blocks fill gaps created when the beam was put to new use, probably as part of a ceiling. Anonymous (Catalan?), early thirteenth century. (Photo: © Museu Nacional d'Art de Catalunya, Barcelona.)

us men when the villainous Jews put him cruelly to death. All of us are his sons: we shall avenge him" (*laisse* 294). When the bishop urges various noblemen to bear the lance rather than participate in the battle, each refuses with similar language. None will forsake the opportunity to kill Saracens for "all the gold in" various locales or for all the revenue of various French regions, so Ademar himself brings it onto the battlefield (*laisses* 307–14). In the climactic battle scene, the sultan's own son and heir appears with "thirty thousand Turks descended from Judas," the Jew who betrayed Jesus for thirty coins (*laisse* 347). The Franks who defeat these Judas-like forces do not engage in mere warfare, nor do they pursue the financial rewards that allegedly motivate Jews and Saracens. As true Christian heroes, these noblemen seek only to righteously avenge Christ's death by slaughtering the contemporary equivalents of Christ's killers.

The portrayal of Saracens as quasi-Jewish killers of Christ enables Christians not only to glorify those who defeat them in battle but also to inspire new military campaigns. The Muslim chronicler Izz al-Din Ibn al-Athir provides a vivid example of such rhetoric when recounting what happened after Muslim forces retook Jerusalem in 1187. Ibn al-Athir, perhaps drawing on firsthand knowledge, reports that the city's patriarch aroused fellow Franks to avenge this loss by making a picture of Jesus that "portrayed Christ (peace be upon him) along with an Arab, depicted as beating him. They put blood on the portrait of Christ and said to the people, 'This is Christ with Muhammad, the prophet of the Muslims, beating him. [Muhammad] has wounded and slain him.'" Ibn al-Athir inserts the customary Islamic honorific for

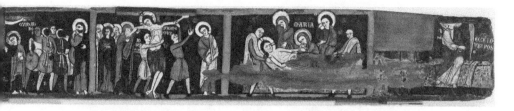

Jesus, whom Muslims revere as a messenger of God, but provides no further editorial commentary: he trusts that his Muslim audience will recognize the preposterous nature of the allegation that Muhammad killed Christ. Preposterous though it is, this propaganda builds on long-standing Frankish rhetoric associating Muslims with Christ's persecutors, and it provides powerful religious motivation for Christian warriors to avenge the maltreatment of their God. Ibn al-Athir credits this propaganda with raising "more men and money than there would be any way of counting" toward what academic historians call the Third Crusade; "even the women," he emphasized, "answered the call in great numbers." If Ibn al-Athir is reliable, he provides valuable evidence regarding the broad impact of religious rhetoric designed to appeal to a specific subset of Christian society, namely fighting men.[12]

DEVOTION TO CHRIST'S BODY

Monks like Odilo of Cluny and Baldric of Bourgueil, as well as the lay poets who created works like the *Chanson d'Antioche* and the artist whose imagery Ibn al-Athir describes, promote a model of Christian masculinity designed for knights and other warriors. Many Christian authorities, however, believed that clergymen ought to instead devote their lives to purely spiritual pursuits. For that reason, even proponents of the Crusades often discouraged monks and priests from joining the military campaigns. An early thirteenth-century work of art known as the *Beam of the Passion* (fig. 14) demonstrates how the association of contemporary Muslim warriors with biblical Jews can also encourage clerical audiences

FIGURE 15. The Crucifixion, with Moorish priests and elders on the right; detail from the *Beam of the Passion*. (Photo: © Museu Nacional d'Art de Catalunya, Barcelona.)

in their pursuit of religious objectives. In this case, these objectives relate to the Eucharist, the Christian ritual in which the priest's words and actions transform a simple wafer into the body of Christ.[13]

The *Beam of the Passion* originally hung above a eucharistic altar in or near Catalonia (presently in northeastern Spain). Given the dim lighting in premodern churches and the dimensions of the beam, which is just eight inches (20 cm) high, only members of the clergy participating in the Eucharist and related liturgical enactments would have been able to appreciate its seven scenes depicting key events related to Christ's death and entombment. The central scene, the crucifixion, features the Jewish priests and elders who conspired against Christ, and it reproduces their dismissive words about Christ's innocence, "What is that to us?" (Matthew 27:4; fig. 15). These and other villains, however, bear dark skin, distinctive sashes, and turban-like scarves that thirteenth-century viewers associated with "Moors" (*moros*), the pejorative Spanish term for African Muslims. The *Beam of the Passion* anachronistically conflates contemporary Muslims, especially those who fought in the armies of the nearby Almohad caliphate, with the Jews whom the Gospels associate with Christ's death.[14]

The crucifixion scene occupies the *Beam of the Passion*'s focal midpoint. Its artist also directs the viewer's gaze toward the sarcophagus (stone coffin) on which Christ's body rested before the resurrection (fig. 16) and, from there, toward the altar on which priests would place the consecrated wafer. All the scenes to the left of Christ's entombment con-

FIGURE 16. The Entombment and the Holy Women at the Tomb, detail from the *Beam of the Passion*. (Photo: © Museu Nacional d'Art de Catalunya, Barcelona.)

tain features that guide the viewer's eyes in a rightward direction, but the entombment scene itself is symmetrically arranged: Christ is framed by the men who lower his body onto the sarcophagus, Joseph of Arimathea and Nicodemus, while Christ's mother is framed by the women who join her in mourning. It is as if we have arrived at the work's intended destination: the sarcophagus, which the eucharistic altar beneath the beam symbolically represents. The angel who sits on the sarcophagus in the final scene gestures toward that altar as he says to the women who returned to Christ's tomb, "Behold the place where they laid him" (Mark 16:6)—which is to say, the place where the priests lay Christ's body in the form of the consecrated eucharistic host. Contemporary theorists of the Eucharist, including Pope Innocent III, identified these clergy with Joseph and Nicodemus.[15]

The *Beam of the Passion* dates from a period of intense theological discussion regarding the doctrine of transubstantiation, according to which the wafer consecrated during the Eucharist becomes the actual body of Christ. The beam's artist goads his clerical viewers toward faith in the Eucharist's efficacy and, especially, toward reverence of the consecrated host by suggesting that those who dismiss the host's significance—who say, as it were, "What is that to us?"—are equivalent to the enemies of Christ and Christendom.

The Moorish villains who appear at the crucifixion and in each of the preceding scenes stand juxtaposed with the holy women who revere Christ on the cross and who attend to his body in all subsequent scenes. Participants in the eucharistic liturgies that took place beneath the *Beam of the Passion* emulated these women as well as Joseph and Nicodemus.[16] By contrasting these faithful and visually pleasing followers of Christ with Christ's grotesque and despicable enemies, the artist inspires his clerical audience to identify with those who revere Christ's body and to revile those who abuse it. One need not battle Muslims to be an ideal Christian: saintliness results from devotion to Corpus Christi, a term that literally means "the body of Christ" but that refers to the consecrated eucharistic host.

The *Beam of the Passion* could have conveyed the same message using stereotypically Jewish figures as the representatives of Christ's enemies. Its artist instead departs from customary depictions of Christ's Passion—and the evident meaning of the biblical texts—by depicting these enemies as if they were soldiers in the Muslim armies that fought against the Iberian Peninsula's expansionist Christian kingdoms. We can be certain that the *Beam of the Passion*'s thirteenth-century viewers understood the difference between Jews and Muslims and recognized its depiction of Christ's biblical persecutors as anachronistic. This artist, however, presumably believed that the incorporation of Moorish foils in traditionally Jewish roles generates a more compelling case for devotion to Christ's body: those who dismiss the significance of the consecrated host, he warned, act not only like Jews but also like Christendom's Muslim enemies. Unlike Odilo and others who apply theological rhetoric to contemporary military confrontations, the *Beam of the Passion* employs imagery that evokes a contemporary conflict in order to advance his theological objective of bolstering faith in the Eucharist.

Manifest anachronisms, like the placement of thirteenth-century Muslims in biblical scenes, intensify the contemporary relevance of ancient stories. In this case, the anachronism reinforces not only the association of first-century Jews and present-day Muslims as the singular enemy of Christ but also the association of Christ's original followers with the contemporary Christians who emulate their faithful devotion. The *Beam of the Passion* invites its viewers to contemplate its simultaneously Moorish and Jewish figures for the purpose of bolstering their own Christian faith.[17]

A similar dynamic animates a sculpted image of the biblical priests who conspired against Christ; this image appears in the late twelfth-century cloister of Santa María la Mayor in Tudela, presently in northeastern Spain (fig. 17). As art historian Pamela Patton observes, the priests are dressed as twelfth-century Jews, and one displays a book whose unusual binding resembles volumes produced solely within the Islamic world. The book's modernity and foreignness serve to alienate Christ's Jewish enemies from the Old Testament, visually indicating that these Jews observe a newfangled postbiblical law, the Talmud, rather

FIGURE 17. Meeting of the Temple Priests and Pharisees in the House of
Caiaphas. The central figure displays a book with an "envelope-flap"
binding, in which a flap wraps around the fore-edge of the book (on the
viewer's left), overlaps the front cover, and fastens on the book's spine.
Cloister of Santa María la Mayor, Tudela, 1186–1200. (Photo: Pamela A.
Patton, courtesy of the photographer.)

than the words of their own prophets. The presence of an Islamic-style book in an image of biblical villains also links the Muslims who threatened Iberian Christendom with the Jews who sought Christ's death.[18]

The Tudela sculptor encourages his monastic viewers to perceive the ongoing conflicts between Christian and Muslim kingdoms—and, more locally, the tensions between Tudela's Christian, Jewish, and Muslim communities—within the timeless framework of the contest between Christ and his enemies. Here again, however, there is no suggestion that monastic viewers should take up arms against Muslims to avenge Christ's death. Perhaps the lesson for these monks is that they should devote themselves faithfully to preaching and teaching the Bible's true meaning within their religiously mixed society.

CHRIST'S CONTEMPORARY TORMENTORS

The *Beam of the Passion* was one of countless thirteenth-century works that promoted devotion to the body of Christ as manifest in the consecrated eucharistic host. One indication of the rising significance of the Corpus Christi within European Christendom is the rapid spread of its feast day: first celebrated in 1246, the Feast of Corpus Christi became universal within the Roman Catholic Church by the early fourteenth century. Another, darker indication of this rising significance is the emergence of host desecration allegations, according to which Jews obtain consecrated hosts so as to torture the body of Christ. This allegation, first lodged in 1290 against a Jew in Paris and then frequently repeated, sparked massacres and expulsions of Jewish communities throughout Central and Eastern Europe during the fourteenth and fifteenth centuries.[19] In the Iberian Peninsula, Christians invented their own host desecration allegations in which Muslims and Moriscos, the Catholic descendants of Muslims, play critical roles. Spanish polemicists, however, seem to refrain from accusing either Muslims or Moriscos of tormenting or attempting to kill Christ. Their allegations emphasize the theological divide that separates Christians from Muslims, but they do not ascribe to Muslims the same degree of enmity purportedly nurtured by Jews.

The Altarpiece of the Virgin that Jaume Serra and his workshop created between 1367–81 for the monastery of Santa María de Sigena (presently in northeastern Spain) provides both a classic image of Jewish host desecration and, next to it, the oldest surviving reference to a eucharistic tale involving a Muslim (fig. 18).[20] In the left-hand scene, which depicts the allegation lodged in Paris, a Christian woman seeking

FIGURE 18. Miracles of the Consecrated Host, detail from the *Altarpiece of the Virgin*. Workshop of Jaume Serra, 1367–81. Barcelona, Museu Nacional d'Art de Catalunya. (Photo: © Museu Nacional d'Art de Catalunya, Barcelona.)

release from her debt provides a consecrated host to her Jewish creditor in exchange for her pawned cloak. The Jew stabs the host, and it bleeds; he tries to destroy the wafer in a cauldron of boiling water, and an image of the Christ Child appears. The Jew himself remains obstinately blind to the miraculous evidence before his eyes, but his son and wife— along with the viewers—recognize through these miracles the truth of Christ's transubstantiation.

The adjacent scene is harder to decipher because the tale it depicts differs somewhat from the sole surviving written account, found in the avowedly misogynistic *Mirror* of Jaume Roig (ca. 1460). A Christian woman seeks an aphrodisiac from a Muslim, identifiable as such by his dark skin and turban; Roig describes the Muslim as a cleric and a sorcerer, which would account for the lavish attire he wears in Serra's image. The Muslim offers to aid the woman by means of a consecrated host, which she brings in a small box. When the Muslim opens the box, however, they discover a beautiful, glowing infant. In Roig's version of this tale, the shocked sorcerer instructs the woman to burn the box but, try as she might, she cannot destroy the baby. The Muslim confesses his sins and renounces Muhammad; the Christian is struck dead by lightning. Serra depicts a different ending in which, it seems, the eucharistic wafer itself recognizes the woman's sinfulness and miraculously slices through her throat when she next attempts to take communion.[21]

The Muslim in this tale differs fundamentally from the Jewish villain of the common host desecration narrative. As historian Miri Rubin observes, the Jewish perpetrator consistently procures a consecrated host in exchange for money or a pawned object, attacks the host with metal implements that call to mind the nails and lance of Christ's crucifixion, and then, when the host begins to bleed profusely, desperately struggles to destroy the indestructible wafer.[22] Roig's Muslim, in contrast, never even touches the consecrated host that the Christian woman sought to use for her own benefit: she is the one who pays the sorcerer for his services, and she then seeks in vain to destroy the host. This Muslim is not an enemy of Christ but rather a non-Christian who initially sees nothing wrong with putting a consecrated host to magical use. More significantly, this Muslim voluntarily confesses and converts; anti-Jewish host desecration narratives, in contrast, always conclude with the violent death of the Jewish perpetrator rather than his conversion. Neither Serra nor Roig portrays the Muslim kindly—Roig calls him an "evil dog"—but both recount the death of the Christian woman alone because she, not the Muslim, is the primary villain in their tales.

During Roig's lifetime, however, other polemicists began to lodge host desecration allegations against Muslims and Jews alike. Rebels who sought to overthrow King Enrique IV of Castile alleged in 1465 that, under the king's misrule, "some Jews and Moors sought on several occasions to obtain a consecrated host" and other sacred objects "in order to perform various evil rites to harm our Lord, his holy church, and our faith." The charge that secular rulers fail to adequately protect Christendom from Jewish assaults on the Christian faith dates to the Roman Empire and recurs frequently in premodern times, but Enrique's critics find value in expanding this allegation to encompass Castile's sizeable Muslim population. A truly Christian king, they suggest, would focus less on the tax revenues he receives from his non-Christian subjects and more on the harm they cause to the Catholic Church. Those who made this theological argument, however, clearly sought to advance a purely political objective: to depose their king.[23]

Isabella, Enrique's half-sister and successor as ruler of Castile, and her husband Ferdinand, king of Aragon, received the title of "Catholic monarchs" from Pope Alexander VI because they accomplished what Enrique did not: they conquered Muslim-held Granada, expelled the Jews, and established the Spanish Inquisition to root out judaizing among recent converts to Christianity. (Recall that Odilo of Cluny likewise dubbed William of Arles a "most Christian ruler" on account of his expulsion of the Muslims from Fraxinetum.) Ferdinand and Isabella also forced Spain's Muslims to choose between conversion and expulsion. As historian Yonatan Glazer-Eytan demonstrates, sixteenth-century inquisitors and polemicists alleged that former Muslims continued to disparage and desecrate the consecrated host. The Inquisition of Cuenca accused one such Morisco of purchasing stolen hosts and stringing them up in his latrine, a charge also lodged against former Jews. In another incident, Moriscos themselves allegedly stole consecrated hosts from a church and contemptuously cast them on the ground. Jaime Bleda, the proponent of Morisco expulsion whom we encountered in chapters 7 and 8, compared the harm that Moriscos inflict on the eucharistic wafer with that of the Jewish perpetrators in classic host desecration cases. Just as foreign rulers expelled the Jews of their domains in the wake of such incidents, Bleda argued, King Philip III should rid his land of Moriscos.[24]

Proponents of expulsion went out of their way to depict Moriscos as false Christians, inveterate Muslims, and, for that very reason, quasi-Jewish enemies of Spanish Christendom. These polemicists not only alleged that Moriscos engage in host desecration but also drew parallels to Northern European cases of host desecration that prompted expulsions of local Jewish communities. Glazer-Eytan's evidence, however, suggests two important and, perhaps, related differences between anti-Morisco allegations and their anti-Jewish precursors: Morisco perpetrators never torture or try to destroy the Corpus Christi, and their purported acts never spark violent responses. These differences likely stem not from the distinction between Jews and Muslims but from the motives that underpin the Spanish allegations. Anti-Jewish polemicists in Northern Europe often sought to stoke popular violence through their portrayals of Jews tormenting the eucharistic host. Bleda and his colleagues, in contrast, craft their polemics for the king and his counselors rather than the masses, and they promote expulsion rather than the massacres that often resulted from anti-Jewish host desecration charges. The relatively tame charges that these polemicists lodge against Moriscos—they cast consecrated hosts to the ground or place them in the latrine, rather than attacking the hosts with knives or trying to destroy them—seem calibrated so as not to spark acts of vengeance like those encouraged by the crusade-era authors with which this chapter began. Strategic thinking, as we already saw in the legal briefs of Oldradus de Ponte (chapter 3), informs many associations of Muslims with Jews precisely because those who link these groups employ such rhetoric in the service of specific political and theological objectives.[25]

Tales of host desecration, in all their various permutations, reflect acute awareness of the intertwined nature of theology and politics in premodern Europe, where Christian rulers regarded themselves as defenders of the faith. The charge that contemporaries disparage or seek to torment Christ's body calls for a forceful response whether the alleged perpetrators are Jews or Muslims. Note, however, that such rhetoric not only defines the Christian–Muslim conflict theologically but that it does so in thoroughly Jewish terms, as Jews remain the paradigmatic enemies of Christ with whom Muslims become associated. The case studies in the next chapter shed further light on this dynamic of defining Muslim enmity toward Christianity and Christendom not in terms of Islam but of Judaism: Jewish hostility toward Christ allegedly motivates anti-Christian assaults, while Muslim rulers provide the means that enable such acts.

CHAPTER 10

Conspiracy Theories: Muslim Agents of Jewish Malevolence

Seventh through Fourteenth Centuries

The Muslim ruler Yazid II (r. 720–24) ordered the destruction of all Christian images in the Abbasid Empire—and Eastern Christians placed the blame on a Jew. According to an account delivered at the Second Council of Nicaea in 787, "There lived a certain man in Tiberias, a ringleader of the lawless Jews, a magician and fortuneteller, an instrument of soul-destroying demons ... a bitter enemy of the Church of God. On learning of the frivolity of the ruler Yazid, this most-wicked Jew approached him ... saying, 'You will remain thirty years in this your kingship if you follow my advice'"—namely, to destroy all representational paintings. Yazid eagerly acted on this guidance; "abominable Jews and wretched Arabs" carried out the order because Christians refused to destroy the sacred images themselves.[1]

The most striking aspect of this narrative, found in both Greek and Latin accounts, is that it makes no reference to Islamic principles or even to Muslim hostility toward Christians.[2] Yazid acts for the sole purpose of securing a lengthy reign; his successor reportedly cancels the edict and kills the Jew simply because the prophecy failed. The Jew alone is "a bitter enemy of the Church of God," and the tale never explains this enmity because Christian audiences presuppose that Jews are, by definition, anti-Christian. The Muslim ruler is the willing agent of Jewish malevolence rather than an actor pursuing his own political or theological agenda. Put differently, the alleged motive behind this assault on Christian images is Jewish, while the Muslim ruler provides the means to enact it.

Similar rhetoric can also be found at the western end of the Mediterranean, where King Egica of Spain alleged in 694 that "those in regions across the sea call on fellow Hebrews [that is, the Jews of Spain] to act as one against the Christian people." Egica worried about the prospect of a Muslim invasion of his kingdom, as indeed occurred in 711, and he perceived these potential conquerors not as Muslims but as "Hebrews" acting out their longstanding Jewish malevolence toward Christians. In this allegation, both the means and the motive for an attack on Christendom are Jewish—because the king imagines the Muslims themselves to be Jews. Egica employs this charge to justify an unprecedented campaign of persecution against the Jews within his own kingdom.[3]

This chapter explores medieval allegations from present-day France that feature similar dynamics: Muslims and Jews purportedly collaborate in attacks against sacred targets and Christian kingdoms, and local Jews suffer the consequences. Islam, we will see, is entirely absent from these accounts, as their Muslim characters have no distinctive beliefs or practices. This is not to say that Muslims constitute merely political or military enemies of Christendom, however. Christians indeed imagine Muslims as theological enemies, and they do so by defining the motivation that drives this enmity in Jewish terms. Christian accounts regarding the alleged alliance between Jews and Muslims rest entirely on the discourse of anti-Judaism, not on "Islamophobia" if one understands that term literally as fear of Islam.[4]

FRENCH JEWS AND THE DESTRUCTION OF JERUSALEM'S CHURCH OF THE HOLY SEPULCHRE

Al-Hakim bi-Amr Allah, the Muslim ruler of North Africa and Palestine, destroyed Jerusalem's Church of the Holy Sepulchre in 1009—and Frankish monks placed the blame on the Jews of France. Ademar of Chabannes, writing in the 1020s, reports that "Western Jews and Saracens of Spain had sent letters to the East accusing the Christians of ordering armies of Franks to attack the Eastern Saracens." These letters, Ademar alleges, prompted the furious al-Hakim not only to destroy the Church of the Holy Sepulchre but also to compel all Christians under his rule to convert to Islam.[5]

Ralph Glaber, writing independently of Ademar during the late 1030s, offers a more elaborate account of how and why Jews persuaded al-Hakim to destroy the Church of the Holy Sepulchre. "Because of the fame of this monument," Glaber reports, "great multitudes of the faithful from all over the world" traveled to Jerusalem as pilgrims. "The devil, driven by envy, sought to pour out the venom of his malice upon the practitioners of the true faith by using his accustomed instruments, the Jews." The most "arrogant, envious, and insolent" of these Jews lived in Orléans, then the capital city of the Kingdom of France. These Jews "conceived a dastardly plot": they bribed a monk masquerading as a pilgrim to bring a letter to al-Hakim, written "in the Hebrew alphabet," alleging that the pilgrims would overrun al-Hakim's realm if the ruler did not act quickly to destroy Jerusalem's Christian "Temple." When the circumstances behind the Church of the Holy Sepulchre's destruction became known, Glaber continues, "all the Christians throughout the whole world decided unanimously to drive the Jews from their lands and cities. . . . Some were put to the sword, others were drowned in rivers, and many found other deaths; some even took their own lives in diverse ways."[6]

Although multiple sources indicate that Jews in Northern Europe suffered unprecedented persecution around the year 1009, academic historians disagree over whether events in Jerusalem played any role.[7] The allegation that local Jews bore responsibility for the destruction of the Church of the Holy Sepulchre circulated widely enough in monastic circles to reach both Ademar and Glaber, who lived in different regions and unrelated monasteries, but we cannot be certain to what degree political leaders or the masses also knew or accepted this charge. Although we know that the allegation about Jewish involvement in Yazid's campaign against Christian images circulated in Paris during the ninth century (see n. 2 above), there is no way to determine whether this allegation inspired efforts to blame Jews for the action of another Muslim ruler. We can, however, determine why Ademar and Glaber found the allegation compelling and what each hoped to achieve by recounting it in their respective histories. The plausibility of this allegation stems from the ways in which it confirms and reinforces beliefs about the impending end of days, and these authors regarded it as a useful means to promote specific Christian behaviors.

Ademar and Glaber were among those who firmly believed that Jesus Christ would return to earth in the year 1033, a millennium after his death and resurrection. This conviction prompted them to interpret events of the early eleventh century, such as extreme weather patterns and unusual astronomical events, as signs of the end-times foretold in the Bible and later apocalyptic literature. It comes as no surprise that they also understood al-Hakim's actions within this theological frame of reference. Glaber's repeated reference to the Church of the Holy Sepulchre as "the Temple" is especially telling: by linking this church to the structure that stood in the time of Jesus, Glaber can present al-Hakim's demolition as the fulfillment of Jesus's end-time prophecies about the Temple's destruction.[8]

The allegation that Jews participated in the destruction of the Church of the Holy Sepulchre provides crucial support for the assertion that al-Hakim embodies Antichrist, the figure whose emergence signals the onset of the end of days. Neither Ademar nor Glaber refers to al-Hakim by name; they instead call him "the Prince of Babylon" (Glaber) or "Nebuchadnezzar of Babylon" (Ademar). Ancient and medieval European writers often referred to Cairo, al-Hakim's capital city, as Babylon owing to the similar-sounding name of a nearby fortress, known in Arabic as Bab al-Yun. For monks steeped in literature about the end-times, however, "Babylon" represents the enemy of Christ in the final conflict between good and evil (Revelation 17–18). Apocalyptic texts maintained that Antichrist would come from Babylon and that Nebuchadnezzar, the Babylonian emperor who destroyed the First Jerusalem Temple in the days of ancient Israel, prefigures this ultimate tyrant. European Christians commonly identified Antichrist as a Jew, which accounts for why the Jews of Orléans could communicate with him in Hebrew. If al-Hakim is Antichrist, however, he must have Jewish followers: as we saw in chapter 4, Christians believed that Jews would flock to Antichrist on his arrival. This explains Ademar's factually incorrect report that "Jews and Saracens" in concert physically destroyed the Church of the Holy Sepulchre.[9]

Ademar and Glaber both ascribe a leading role not merely to Jews but more specifically to Jews in France. Given the fact that these monks wrote independently, this element must be part of the narrative that circulated widely in Frankish monastic circles. It reflects a deep-seated conviction that Franks—Jews and, especially, Christians—will be key players in the events of the end-times. Ademar, for example, believed that the emperor Charlemagne himself would rise from his tomb to lead Frankish forces to victory against Antichrist in Jerusalem. Beliefs like this surely contributed in some fashion to Frankish fervor for the Holy Land Crusades that began at the end of the eleventh century, as well as to the attacks on European Jews that occurred en route.[10]

Glaber actively promoted pilgrimage to Jerusalem during these end-times, and he recounts Jewish efforts to instigate the Church of the Holy Sepulchre's destruction in a manner that advances this goal. It was the "great multitudes of the faithful" visiting Christ's tomb, he asserts, that drove the envious devil to spur his Jewish minions into action in the first place. When the Jews of Orléans warn al-Hakim that the pilgrims would "occupy his whole realm, depriving him of all his power," they imply that pilgrimage also renders the devil himself powerless. Glaber concludes his account of this episode by reporting that "an incredible multitude of men from all over the world came exultantly to Jerusalem bearing countless gifts for the restoration of the house of God," and he returns to the theme of pilgrimage in subsequent sections of his *Histories*.[11]

Ademar joined the throng of Christian pilgrims who traveled to Jerusalem in 1033 in anticipation of Christ's triumphant return, but his account of al-Hakim's actions makes no reference to pilgrimage. Instead, Ademar frames this event in order to inspire faithfulness among his Frankish Christian readers. Whereas Glaber states that Christians expelled Jews from their cities to avenge the Church of the Holy Sepulchre's destruction, Ademar places an expulsion of Jews right before his account of this event. He reports that the bishop of Limoges, where Ademar lived at the time, required Jews to either adopt Christianity or leave the city. Although the bishop gave Christian teachers a month to persuade the Jews to convert, these efforts proved unsuccessful: most Jews chose to leave Limoges; some committed suicide to avoid forcible baptism; and only "three or four Jews became Christians." With this in mind, readers of Ademar's *Chronicle* learn that al-Hakim, enraged by the letter he received from Western Jews and Saracens, ordered the Christians in his realm to convert to Islam. Ademar disappointedly reports that only three Christians accepted martyrdom, while the rest converted; these Christians displayed far less resoluteness than the Jews of Limoges. Al-Hakim's forces then razed the Church of the Holy Sepulchre "because of our sins." Miracles, however, prevented the Saracens from destroying other sacred sites, and a terrible famine afflicted al-Hakim's realm in punishment for his deeds. According to Ademar, al-Hakim himself recognized these divine signs and sought penance. Through his account of these miracles, which Glaber does not mention, Ademar hopes to persuade Christian Franks to be more steadfast in their faith than their Eastern coreligionists and, in this respect, to emulate their Jewish neighbors.[12]

Neither Ademar nor Glaber ascribes any significance to the beliefs and practices of Muslims themselves, even though, as we saw in chapter 9, Glaber knew some basic tenets of Islam. According to their accounts, al-Hakim does not destroy the Church of the Holy Sepulchre out of

Islamic zeal; instead, he acts to safeguard his realm from the dangers posed by Frankish armies or Christian pilgrims. Those who bear enmity toward Christians are the Jews, who set the affair in motion. Even though al-Hakim plays the role of Antichrist, the devil still relies primarily on the Jews of France to accomplish his goals. These Jews, however, lack the power to harm Christian interests on their own. By positing an alliance between al-Hakim and the Jews, Frankish monks provide both a means and a motive for the attack on the Church of the Holy Sepulchre. Glaber's account of this alliance also serves to justify anti-Jewish violence notwithstanding the general norm that Christians should tolerate the presence of Jews in their midst. These Jews, he alleges, are more threatening to European Christendom than meets the eye because they draw not only on their own theological enmity toward Christ but also on the political might of the Muslim world.

ADD MUSLIMS AND STIR: THE WATER POISONING AFFAIR OF 1321

Lepers allegedly poisoned the waters of France—and many French officials placed the blame on Jews. In medieval France, individuals believed to be afflicted with the disease of leprosy were often forced to live in designated leper colonies out of concern that they would infect the broader population. On April 16, 1321, the mayor of Périgueux arrested all lepers in the vicinity on the grounds that they placed poison in the town's water supply to kill or make leprous the Christian populace. It is surely no coincidence that this was the date of Holy Thursday, which commemorates Jesus's Last Supper and his betrayal at the hands of Judas: the mayor, after all, accused local lepers of acting in Judas-like fashion. Officials in many other French towns quickly condemned and executed countless lepers on similar charges of water poisoning, notwithstanding the fact that no one fell ill or died as a result of the purported crimes. Mass arrests and executions of French Jews soon followed, prompted by charges that Jews and their Muslim allies played instrumental roles in the plot.[13]

The common denominator linking Jews and lepers, beyond their marginality within medieval French society, is that both were subject to the king's protection and sole jurisdiction. As part of their broader resistance to royal encroachment on local authority, several municipalities petitioned King Philip V in February 1321 to expel the Jews from France and to grant local jurisdiction over leper colonies and their assets. Some officials, like the mayor of Périgueux, used the water poisoning affair as an excuse to take matters into their own hands, while others pressured the king himself to punish the lepers and the Jews for their alleged crimes.

Between April and July of 1321, the motives that these officials ascribed to the alleged perpetrators grew increasingly elaborate and sensational. Lepers from across France conspired to seize control of the country! These lepers received support from foreign Muslim kings! The lepers acted on instructions from the Jews of France! Those Jews conspired with Muslim kings, offering to help Muslims conquer Paris in exchange for Jewish sovereignty over Jerusalem!! The Muslims who conspired with the Jews adopted Judaism themselves!?

What value did Christians perceive in alleging Muslim participation in the plot to poison France's waters? Muslims, we will see, played important roles not only politically, as rulers of rival kingdoms, but also theologically. The water poisoning allegation, after all, was simultaneously political and theological in nature from its very origins on Holy Thursday. Islam, however, plays no role whatsoever, as the Muslim figures in these allegations instead embody apostasy (that is, abandonment of Christianity), heresy, and, especially, Judaism. We will begin by examining an allegation that foreign Muslims colluded directly with French lepers and then turn to allegations regarding an alliance between those Muslims and the Jews of France, who purportedly employed the lepers as their agents.

The confessions of Guillaume Agasse, head of a leper colony in Pamiers, contain the earliest recorded reference to Muslim involvement in the affair. Even though Agasse makes no mention of Jews, his account deserves close attention because of the themes it introduces.[14] On June 4, 1321, after enduring torture, Agasse confessed to the bishop's deputy that two members of his colony poisoned the local water sources in the hopes of turning everyone in Pamiers into lepers. On June 11, Agasse confessed that he himself traveled to Toulouse to meet with other leper leaders and obtain the poison. These leaders, angered by the fact that healthy Christians disrespect and discriminate against lepers, conspired to make all Christians leprous and to seize control of local governments. Similar conspiracy theories circulated elsewhere in France at the time. Agasse adds, however, that the lepers sought support and protection from the king of Granada, the sole remaining Muslim-governed territory in Western Europe, who agreed to aid them. In other words, the motive behind the poisoning is leper resentment of fellow Christians, while Muslims provide the means.

On July 6, Agasse appeared before Bishop Jacques Fournier (the future Pope Benedict XII) and offered an even more elaborate depiction of the gathering in Toulouse. In this account, the leper leaders agreed to poison local waters so that "the sultans of Babylon and Granada would become lords of the whole land that Christians now possess once the Christians are dead or leprous." In return, the Muslim rulers promised the leper leaders riches, honors, and local lordships. The Muslims, however, demanded that these lepers "deny the faith and law of Christ" by spitting on and trampling the cross and the consecrated eucharistic host. An armed and helmeted Black man stood prepared to decapitate any who refused. Agasse and his fellow lepers dutifully denied Christ before collecting their shares of the poison, whose ingredients included "powder from the body of Christ," which is to say, a consecrated eucharistic host. In this account, the lepers and their foreign allies alike are enemies of Christ and Christendom.

Agasse ultimately pled guilty to charges of apostasy, blasphemous treatment of the cross and the consecrated host, and other heresies. These charges contain no reference either to Muslims or to water poisoning. As historian Carlo Ginzburg emphasizes, Agasse was not tried by municipal authorities but by the Inquisition, a religious court established to root out heresy: his judges were interested in offenses against the faith, like the denial of Christ, rather than murder and other civil crimes. Ginzburg suspects that the inquisitors pressured Agasse to provide a certain kind of confession, both through torture and, perhaps, by offering to spare Agasse from excommunication and a painful execution (they instead sentenced him to lifetime imprisonment).[15] It evidently took several tries, however, before Agasse provided the story his inquisitors wanted to hear. After realizing that he needed to do more than confirm the basic allegation of water poisoning, Agasse claimed a conspiracy of lepers to overthrow the government. In this context, the king of Granada functions as a plausible political ally for a band of French rebels. The theme of political conflict between Muslim and Christian rulers persists in Agasse's third confession, but this time Agasse emphasized the blasphemies that he and other lepers committed in accordance with the foreigners' demands, the crimes for which he was ultimately condemned.

The presence of a menacing African at the lepers' meeting may reflect the widespread conviction among Christians that Islam spread by the sword. Agasse, however, does not claim that the foreign rulers demanded conversion, and Islam itself plays no role in the anti-Christian behavior ascribed to Saracens and their allies. These enemies of Christendom demand nothing more (and nothing less) than the utter rejection of Christ, which constitutes proof that the lepers are themselves fellow enemies of their Christian neighbors. Within the context of the four-teenth-century Inquisition, it comes as no surprise that Agasse confesses specifically to maltreatment of the cross and the eucharistic host, objects that heretics allegedly disdained, or that Agasse was ultimately sentenced in the company of nonleprous heretics. His confessions portray Muslims as those who lead Christians into apostasy and heresy, not into Islam. As such, however, the Muslims themselves are irrelevant to the inquisitors. Not only are Muslims absent from the formal charges the inquisitors lodged against Agasse, but one of the judges who sentenced him, Bernard Gui, makes no reference to these Muslims when he later recounts the water poisoning affair in his chronicle.[16]

Meanwhile, the allegation that Jews played a behind-the-scenes role in the activity of the lepers circulated widely. Massacres and mass arrests of Jews occurred in various municipalities during the first half of June. Several chroniclers report that King Philip V was told in mid-June of a leper who confessed to receiving money from a Jew along with a poison made from human blood, urine, herbs, and a consecrated host.[17] When the king issued an edict on June 21 in response to the water poisoning affair, however, he focused his royal anger on the lepers alone. Philip was probably reluctant to take action against his Jewish subjects because of the substantial tax revenue he received from them. Lords and municipal officials, fully aware of this dynamic, stepped up their pressure on the king by alleging that French Jews conspired with foreign Muslims to kill the king himself and overthrow his kingdom.

THE JEWISH PLOT TO TRADE PARIS FOR JERUSALEM

The earliest dated allegations associating Jews with Muslims emerged on July 2, when a physician in Mâcon swore before local officials that he faithfully translated two letters about the water poisoning affair from Arabic into French. The author of these forgeries displays familiarity with Matthew Paris's *Chronica majora*, which alleges that in 1251 a Muslim sultan supplied French accomplices with powdered poisons, considerable sums of money, and letters written in Arabic.[18] The first of the Mâcon letters, from the king of Granada to "Samson, son of Elias, the Jew," provides evidence that the king had previously provided Samson with money and poison for the lepers to place in local water sources. "We have promised to return the Promised Land to you," the king of Granada wrote, "and we shall keep you up to date. I have also sent you something else for you to throw into the water that the king [of France] uses and drinks." This letter, in short, depicts the king of Granada as the mastermind of a plot to assassinate Philip V and kill many of his subjects, presumably so that Granada could conquer France more easily. The Jews participate in this plot in order to gain control of their biblical homeland, and they use money provided by foreign kings to corrupt the lepers.

In the second Mâcon letter, the king of Tunis likewise urges the Jews to act quickly to poison the Christians without concern for cost. "You are our brethren in law," he writes, expressing the notion that Muslims and Jews adhere to the same religion. The theme of brotherhood permeates this brief letter, in which the king of Tunis offers to care for the children of French Jews "like my own flesh." The portrayal of France's Jews as allies and even brethren of foreign Muslim kings renders the Jews themselves as disloyal foreigners with both the means and the motive to pose a serious threat to the king and his subjects. A truly Christian king of France would not protect the Jews but rather expel them; some chroniclers suggest that Philip V did just that in the wake of these allegations.[19]

Allegations regarding international funds transfers, a quid pro quo involving Jerusalem, and the brotherhood of Jews and Saracens also feature prominently in a complicated letter sent by Philip of Valois, Count of Anjou (and the future King Philip VI of France), to Pope John XXII.[20] There is no reason, however, to presume any direct connection between the authors of Philip's letter and whoever composed the Mâcon letters. Rather, these works attest independently to conspiracy theories that circulated widely among French political elites.

Philip's letter begins by recounting terrifying astronomical phenomena, earthquakes, fiery balls from the heavens, and a murderous dragon that all struck the counties of Anjou and Touraine on June 26. The people, believing that the end of the world was at hand, attacked the local Jews. They found in the home of a certain Bananias a ramskin document inscribed in Hebrew letters. Its unusually heavy seal, made of the purest gold, depicted "a monstrous Jew or Saracen atop a ladder leaning against the cross, in the act of defecating on the sweet face of the Savior."[21] Two baptized Jews revealed the contents of the document, which was then confirmed under torture by Bananias and fellow Jews before being translated into Latin.

There was indeed a near total solar eclipse in Anjou and Touraine that began shortly after dawn on June 26, 1321, making it seem as if "the sun became inflamed and blood-red."[22] Philip's letter goes on to falsely assert that "on the night of that day, the moon was disfigured and obscured as if by sackcloth"; solar eclipses, however, always coincide with the new moon, which is not visible at night. This account of the events of June 26 reflects, albeit in adapted form, an apocalyptic vision in the book of Revelation: "there came a great earthquake; the sun became black as sackcloth, the full moon became like blood, and the stars of the sky fell to the earth" (6:12–13). This is the first of several indications that Philip's ghostwriters, perhaps the three "Christian clerics expert in theological truth" credited with translating Bananias's document, possess both a vivid, biblically inspired imagination and a willingness to misrepresent recent events to better accord with the Bible.

These attributes become even more apparent in the opening lines of the purported translation, as Bananias professes his devotion and obedience to sultans and emirs who bear the names of Canaanite kings whom the biblical Israelites defeated and who rule over cities that those Israelites conquered. The name of Bananias's primary addressee, "Amicedich," means "my people is righteous" and alludes ironically to the prophecy, "Your people shall all be righteous; they shall possess the land forever" (Isaiah 60:21). From the author's perspective, of course, neither Muslims nor Jews are righteous, and neither deserves to possess the Holy Land over which Amicedich purportedly rules. The implicit message within these biblical allusions is that the truly righteous people, namely the Christians, will ultimately conquer that land just as biblical Israelites did.[23]

Bananias's letter recounts that Enoch and Elijah "publicly appeared on Mount Tabor to your people [that is, the Saracens], bequeathing to them our law and teaching it to them." The Saracens also discovered the original Ark of the Covenant, complete with the Ten Commandments and other contents described in the Old Testament. On account of these experiences, Amicedich reportedly established a perpetual alliance with the Jewish people through his agent, the viceroy of Granada, and declared his desire and that of his people to convert to Judaism. Medieval Christians identified the biblical figures Enoch and Elijah as the "two witnesses" who will prophesy at the end of days (Revelation 11:3), appearing just before the start of Antichrist's tyrannical reign. The traditional role of these witnesses, however, is to convert the Jews to Christianity, not to convert Muslims to Judaism. Christians, moreover, traditionally identify Mount Tabor as the site of the transfiguration, where Jesus appeared in the company of Moses and Elijah and a heavenly voice proclaimed, "This is my Son, the Beloved; listen to him!" (Mark 9:7 and parallels). Knowledgeable readers of Philip's letter, such as members of the papal court to whom he sent it, would immediately recognize as impossible the claim that Elijah taught Old Testament law rather than the teachings of Christ. Philip's equally knowledgeable ghostwriters may have placed this claim in Bananias's mouth to heighten the apocalyptic overtones already conveyed through remarks about the terrifying events of June 26: the appearance of Enoch and Elijah provides further evidence that the end of days is at hand. Christian readers of this letter should respond by mobilizing their forces to defeat Antichrist, Amicedich, and their Jewish minions.[24]

The apocalyptic language of Philip's letter and its references to the kingdoms conquered by biblical Israelites lend themselves perfectly to a call for crusade. In fact, Pope John XXII reproduced this letter for that exact purpose, despite whatever skepticism he may have had about its veracity. The pope—and, it seems, Philip of Valois—sought to pressure King Philip V to fulfill his long-standing vow to lead a crusade. The purported alliance between Muslims in the Holy Land and the Jews of France gives such a mission added urgency by introducing a dimension of national defense into what might otherwise seem like a pious but distracting undertaking.[25]

Philip of Valois, however, also seeks to justify action on the home front against local Jews: like the Mâcon letters, Philip's letter alleges that France's Jews seek to overthrow the king himself on behalf of their Muslim allies. Bananias asserts that Amicedich pledged not only to convert to Judaism but also to restore Jewish sovereignty over Jerusalem and its surroundings "provided that we [the Jews of France] enthrone you on the royal throne in Paris, the illustrious city of the Christians."[26] The Jews devised a plan to poison the waters of France with the aid of Christian lepers, whom they corrupted with money, but the simpleminded lepers were caught and revealed the plot. "We believe without a doubt that we would have been exterminated were it not for our great treasures, which hardened their greedy hearts: our gold and silver—and yours—redeemed us, as you must already know from your Granadan viceroy." Philip's audience would immediately identify the greediest of these hearts as that of King Philip V, who benefited the most from the Jews' money. Philip of Valois suggests, however, that the king's self-interest actually calls for removing these Jews from France.

In conclusion, Bananias reports that the Jews of France rejoice in their accomplishments to date and willingly suffer martyrdom for their cause. He asks Amicedich to send more gold and silver so that the Jews can fully implement their plan. At that time, Amicedich will take Paris, the

Jews will possess the Promised Land, "and we will all live together under one law and one eternal God" in accordance with the words of the psalmist, "How good and pleasant it is when brothers dwell in unity" (Psalm 133:1). As for the Christians, they will suffer the prophetic curse, "Their heart is divided and now they shall perish" (Hosea 10:2).

The most noteworthy feature of this elaborate account of a Jewish–Muslim conspiracy is that it lacks any committed Muslims: Amicedich and his followers declare their desire to convert to Judaism, and Banania refers to them as his brethren. Bananias corresponds with "sultans" and "emirs," but these titles are assigned to people with biblical names who encounter characters and artifacts from the Old Testament. Philip of Valois's account, in other words, renders the Saracens not as Muslims but rather as biblical. The term *Saracen* appears only once in Philip's letter, in reference to the figure on the gold seal who displays his utter disdain for the crucified Christ—but that figure appears in a quasi-biblical scene and, Philip reports, could be either a Saracen or a Jew. His letter portrays Jews and Muslims as indistinguishable, with the crucial exception being that Jews already live within France while their wealthy coconspirators merely aspire to do so. The same may be said regarding the portrayal of the Saracen kings in the letters from Mâcon.

Guillaume Agasse's report of a conspiracy between local lepers and foreign Muslims made no impact: his theologically oriented inquisitors focused solely on the alleged heresies of the lepers themselves. The allegation that Muslims conspired with France's Jews, in contrast, gained considerable traction. All fourteenth-century chronicles that report Jewish involvement in the affair state that they conspired with the king of Granada.[27] The allegations of an international conspiracy between Jews and Muslims also succeeded where the simpler allegation of a domestic plot among Jews and lepers failed: in mid to late July, Philip V issued a new order calling for the arrest and interrogation of all Jews on suspicion of their involvement in the poisoning of France's waters. The association of Muslims and Jews as enemies of Christendom generates a compelling framework within which to promote the fulfillment of Christian virtues—in this case, political action against the widely despised Jews of France.

As fans of mystery novels know, the detective needs to establish both motive and means to lodge a credible accusation: either alone is insufficient. The letters from Philip of Valois and Mâcon offer plausible allegations against the Jews of France precisely by involving Muslims in the plot. There were, of course, many anti-Jewish allegations that do not involve Muslims—for example, the charge that a Jewish moneylender in Paris pressured a penniless debtor to give him a consecrated host. The motive behind this alleged crime is Jewish enmity toward Christ, and Jews possessed the means to threaten impoverished debtors notwithstanding their own relative powerlessness within European society. French Jews were not, however, realistically capable of threatening the king, which is why those who lobbied Philip V to take action against them needed to include an alliance with Muslim rulers. These conspiracy theorists render the alliance itself plausible by portraying Muslims as Jewish and, thus, as motivated by the same anti-Christian animus as the Jews of France.

Recall from this book's introduction the observation by cultural theorist Gil Anidjar that Jews and Muslims, like religion and politics, are "distinct, but indissociable" within Christian Europe.[28] Polemicists and their audiences alike recognized the distinctions between these categories: they understood that Muslims are not Jews and that politics differs from theology. Polemicists, however, could render these categories rhetorically indissociable to the point that Muslims become Jewish; at times, their theologically grounded rhetoric possessed sufficient force to motivate political action.

Even so, European polemicists did not necessarily associate Muslims with Jews. The case of Guillaume Agasse exemplifies one alternative: Agasse, perhaps inspired by his inquisitors' interest in Christian heresy, portrays Muslims as those who reject and blaspheme Christ in heretical fashion. In Chapters 6 and 7, we encountered European tales in which faithless Christians, motivated by spitefulness, help Muhammad fashion a heretical alternative to authentic Christianity. Long before the invention of allegations that Jews sought to help Muslims conquer Paris, Frankish authors imagined that Saracens pursued this goal out of devotion to their own pagan deities; we will examine tales of this nature in the next chapter. Whether they brand Muslims as pagans, heretics, or Jews, these allegations ascribe theological motives to Muslims that have nothing at all to do with Islam. Only by associating Muslims with biblical enemies of Christ and Christendom can medieval European polemicists define Muslim aggression as fundamentally anti-Christian in nature.

CHAPTER II

How Muslims, Jews, and Romans Became Worshippers of Muhammad

Twelfth through Fifteenth Centuries

English, French, and Italian plays first performed during the fourteenth and fifteenth centuries contain a curious feature: the villains in their dramatizations of biblical episodes, including Jews, Romans, and Egypt's pharaoh, regularly call on Muhammad as their god. How could anyone familiar with the Bible believe that these diverse characters all worship the same deity? Although the answer is simple, its implications are profound and far-reaching. European Christians of the late Middle Ages perceived these biblical villains, along with contemporary Jews and Muslims, as enemies of the true God, which is to say, Christ. They often chose to present these distinct groups as constituting a singular enemy that we might call anti-Christendom. Invocations of a false god named Muhammad mark these biblical and contemporary villains as uniformly anti-Christian, notwithstanding the recognized differences among them—or the fact that the historical Muhammad postdates the Bible and made no claim to divinity.

Rhetoric about the diverse devotees of the false god Muhammad reflects widespread acceptance among Europeans Christians of three presumptions that, building on one another, crystallized during the twelfth, thirteenth, and fourteenth centuries, respectively:

1. Muslims are the inverse of Christians. Because Christians worship Christ as God, Muslims must worship Muhammad, imagined as Christ's antithesis.

2. Jews past and present do not merely misunderstand biblical prophecies identifying Christ as God, they knowingly reject God/Christ.
   It stands to reason that Jews instead worship Christ's antithesis, the
   false god named Muhammad.

3. All who actively oppose God/Christ, regardless of their ethnicity,
   must in effect adhere to anti-Christianity, whose god is Muhammad.

If one insists that a person's relationship to Christ constitutes the defining element of their theological identity, then the differences between
Muslims, Jews, Roman pagans, and so on become irrelevant: none
accept Christ as God. This binary worldview also lends itself to simple
and, for that reason, powerful rhetoric on behalf of self-differentiation
through the cultivation of faith in Christ.

The present chapter examines in turn each of the presumptions that
underpin this Christian binarism. The first of these presumptions is
especially important to this study of Jewish Muslims even though its
exemplars make a point of depicting Muslims as pagans rather than as
Jews. These sources offer instructive contrasts to contemporaneous
works that portray Jewish Muslims, and they also underpin later works
that depict Jews and other enemies of Christ as worshippers of Muhammad. Throughout, we will pay particular attention to the ways in which
evolving ideas about Muslims inform anti-Jewish rhetoric while evolving ideas about Jews transform anti-Muslim rhetoric.

MUHAMMAD-WORSHIP AS THE ANTITHESIS
OF CHRISTIANITY

"There is no god but God, and Muhammad is God's prophet." This
declaration of Islamic faith exemplifies the distinction that Muslims past
and present make between God and Muhammad: Muslims revere their
prophet as the ideal human being but most certainly do not regard him
as divine. Christians who interacted regularly with Muslims or who had
access to texts about Islam had much to say regarding Muhammad, as
we have seen in previous chapters, but they never suggest that Muslims
worshipped him. That notion first emerges in Frankish literature
recounting the First Crusade (1096–99), literature that portrays the conflict between Christians and Muslims not merely as political but also as
profoundly theological. The term *Franks* refers in this context to the
various European groups that participated in the crusade, many but not
all of whom came from the region now known as northern France.

While some Frankish authors made a point of learning about Islamic beliefs while on crusade, others simply imagined the faith of their Saracen enemies as the inverse of their own Christian beliefs. Because Franks worship Christ as the true God, some concluded that Saracens must worship the false god named Muhammad. This allegation derives not from the binary distinction between Christianity and Judaism but rather from a different pre-Islamic discourse that opposes Christianity to pagan idolatry.[1]

The crusade chronicle associated with Peter Tudebode, for example, depicts Saracens as worshippers of multiple deities, principally Muhammad. This devotion often manifests itself through invocations such as oaths taken "by Muhammad and by the power of all the gods." When the crusaders besieging Jerusalem held a procession of barefoot priests and bishops bearing crosses, Tudebode reports, Muslims on the city's walls likewise paraded an idol of Muhammad held aloft on a stick. This portrayal of Saracen devotion to Muhammad is a ludicrous inversion of genuine Christian convictions regarding the sanctity of the cross and the crucifix.[2]

According to Ralph of Caen, the heroic crusader Tancred discovered a huge statue in the Temple of the Lord (that is, the Dome of the Rock) that he could not immediately identify. "Perhaps it is an idol of Mars or Apollo," Tancred thought. "Could it be Christ? It does not bear the insignia of Christ—the cross, the crown of thorns, the nails, the pierced side—therefore, this is not Christ but rather the primordial Antichrist: Muhammad the depraved, Muhammad the pernicious!" The logic that Ralph ascribes to Tancred is telling: he does not rely on information provided by Muslims but instead deduces Muhammad's identity on the basis of a contrast with Christ imagery. More fundamentally, Tancred presumes that Saracens must worship Antichrist—in idolatrous fashion, no less—simply because they are the enemies of those who fight on Christ's behalf. As we observed in chapter 4, polemicists associated the Dome of the Rock with the Jerusalem Temple and contemporary Muslims with the ancient Greeks who placed idols in that Temple because these associations rendered the crusaders themselves as latter-day Maccabees, the biblical heroes who expelled the Greeks. Tancred entertains the possibility that Saracens similarly worship Greek gods, but he concludes that Muhammad must be their primary deity because he imagines Muhammad to be the antithesis of Christ. Ralph reports that Tancred's soldiers, like the Maccabees, eagerly destroyed the idol whose presence defiled the Temple of the Lord; in fact, no such statue ever existed. As medievalist Suzanne Conklin Akbari dryly observes, "The belief in Muslim idolatry absolutely requires that the charge be unprovable" because it is false. For that reason, those who make such allegations routinely report either that Christians destroyed the idols in question or that Muslims bar Christians from seeing the true objects of their worship.[3]

The identification of Muhammad as a god and an idol gained widespread currency through *chansons de geste*, Old French "songs of heroic deeds" in which valiant Franks defeat powerful Saracen foes. The authors of these popular works, first recorded in twelfth-century manuscripts, made no effort to represent Muslims accurately. As C. Meredith Jones observes in his classic study of the genre, "the French epic Saracen is a crude reversal of a French epic Christian. Everything that the Christian holds to be perverse, wicked, detestable, is presented as an integral part of Saracen doctrine, belief, or practice. He is offered as the natural enemy of Christendom." Just as Christians believe in the Trinity, Saracens in the *chansons de geste* worship three gods—Tervagant, Apollo, and Muhammad—who, of course, prove powerless in the face of armies that call on Christ. None of this has anything to do with the actual tenets of Islam; instead, it reflects Christian patterns of thought that predate the historical Muhammad.[4]

The *Song of Roland*, the foundational work of the *chanson de geste* genre, depicts a pair of fictional battles between Charlemagne's Frankish army and so-called pagans, whose king "does not love God" but rather "serves Muhammad and prays to Apollo" (lines 7–8). These battles, however, are not merely political: the title character's battle cry— "Pagans are wrong and Christians are right!" (line 1015)—encapsulates the fundamentally theological nature of the conflict. As Roland's vastly outnumbered troops prepare to face a Saracen ambush in the song's first battle, Archbishop Turpin rallies the Frankish warriors by invoking their loyalty to Charlemagne and Christ alike: "We must die well for our king—help sustain Christianity!" (lines 1128–29). Saracens, in contrast, frequently invoke Muhammad, only to discover that he and his fellow deities provide no aid. At the climax of the final battle, the pagan emperor "sees his pennant fall and Muhammad's standard brought low. The emir begins to realize that he is wrong and that Charlemagne is right" (lines 3551–54). Through its fusion of political and theological rhetoric, *Roland* defines Frankish identity itself in terms of Christianity: the Frankish emperor Charlemagne represents Christendom just as his Muhammad-worshipping counterpart represents the non-Christian world. Stated differently, *Roland* portrays Saracens as the inverse of Christian Franks and, for that very reason, as pagan worshippers of Muhammad.[5]

Charlemagne's victorious Franks, like Tancred's men in Jerusalem, smash the statues and idols they find in the Saracen *sinagoges* and *mahumeries* (line 3662). The latter term refers to Muhammad (whom Franks called "Mahum"), while the former, then as now, calls to mind Jewish houses of worship. Its passing reference to synagogues notwithstanding, *Roland* employs traditional rhetoric about the impotence of false deities rather than the discourse of anti-Judaism.[6] Many other crusade-inspired works of the twelfth and thirteenth centuries likewise frame the Christian-Muslim conflict in terms of the binary opposition between Christianity and paganism, defined as the worship of false gods, rather than the opposition between Christianity and Judaism.[7]

JUDAISM AS THE WILLFUL REJECTION OF GOD

There are, after all, multiple ways to define Christianity's binary inverse. European Christians customarily framed the contrast between themselves and Jews not in terms of whether one worships the true God or false deities but of whether one understands the Bible correctly or incorrectly. This long-standing conception of Judaism reflects the ideas expressed by the early fifth-century bishop Augustine, who taught that Jews attest to the authenticity of biblical texts that they themselves cannot comprehend.[8] Bernard of Clairvaux penned an especially eloquent version of this teaching in a letter promoting the Second Crusade of 1146. Bernard urges Christian soldiers to devote their bravery and love of combat to a glorious cause that will earn them eternal salvation—namely, battle against Muslim foes. Bernard insists, however, that "the Jews are not to be persecuted, massacred, or even put to flight" because they are "living letters" of the Old Testament, as Augustine taught. "It is an act of Christian piety both to vanquish the arrogant and also to spare the subjected, especially those who possess the Law, the promise, and the patriarchs, and from whom is Christ according to the flesh." Bernard insists that Muslims, whom he calls "enemies of the cross" and "gentiles" (that is, non-Jewish non-Christians), are fundamentally different from Jews.[9]

Beginning in the thirteenth century, however, European Christians increasingly portrayed Jews as knowingly and willfully rejecting God and the Bible alike. Historian Jeremy Cohen summarizes the new allegation as follows:

The Jewish leaders of the first century had indeed recognized Jesus as the messiah promised them by the prophets of the Old Testament. As they themselves understood, the Mosaic religion could no longer be maintained with honest intentions; either they had to accept Christianity, or they had to fabricate a qualitatively new religious system, removed from the biblical covenant. Concerned above all with their own power and stature, they chose the second alternative and maliciously engineered the murder of their real savior.[10]

We can appreciate both the magnitude of this shift in anti-Jewish discourse and its impact on anti-Muslim rhetoric by comparing the depictions of King Herod and his aides in the *Auto de los Reyes Magos*, a Castilian play from around the turn of the thirteenth century, with depictions of the same figures in English plays of the fourteenth and fifteenth centuries.

The *Auto de los Reyes Magos*, among the oldest surviving dramatizations of a biblical narrative (Matthew 2:1–18), contrasts the three wise kings (also known as magi) who seek out the newborn "Lord of the whole world" with Herod, king of the Jews, who refuses to entertain the possibility of any rival to his sovereignty. In the brief play's final scene, Herod summons his rabbinic advisors and demands to know what scripture has to say about the birth of such a figure. After the first rabbi declares that he can find no reference to it, the second retorts, "Praise Allah, how you are deceived! Why are you called a rabbi? You do not understand the prophecies which Jeremiah told us. By my Law, we have wandered . . . because we have not used the truth, nor is it found on our lips."[11]

Herod's advisors exemplify Augustine's conception of the Jews: they are devoted to the Bible, which proclaims the truth about Christ, but they cannot decipher its prophecies. The anonymous playwright associates these Jews with contemporary Muslims through the second rabbi's emphatic use of an Islamic phrase familiar to Spanish Christian audiences: *Hamihala*, a version of the Arabic expression *al-hamd li-llah*, "Praise be to God!"[12] Muslims, the playwright suggests, stand in the same relation to Christ as Herod and his rabbis: they prioritize their own earthly power over Christian truth, and they fail to understand biblical prophecies that would lead them toward this truth. The *Auto de los Reyes Magos* does not, however, suggest that either Jews or Muslims worship a false god, let alone that they worship Muhammad. Not only would such a claim be utterly implausible to Christians who interact regularly with Muslims, it does not align with the Augustinian notion that Jews unwittingly bless Christ, the true God, despite their failure to understand God or the Bible properly.[13]

This Augustinian notion is entirely absent from English, French, and Italian plays that depict Herod and other Jewish villains of the New Testament. Herod remains obsessively jealous for his own sovereignty, as he was in the *Auto de los Reyes Magos*, but fourteenth- and fifteenth-century plays define him and his aides not by their failure to understand scripture but by their devotion to a false god—namely, Muhammad. Exemplary in this regard are the Towneley plays, an English collection of uncertain origins. "To Mahowne and me all shall bow," Herod brashly declares in the Towneley *Offering of the Magi* (line 15). His messenger likewise proclaims that all must accept Herod alone as king and Muhammad alone as god (lines 79–84). According to the Gospel of Matthew (2:2, 16), Herod ordered the slaughter of all infant males in Bethlehem in the hopes of killing the newborn "king of the Jews." The Towneley play called *Herod the Great* recasts this episode as an attempt to eliminate not merely a rival to the throne but the rival of Herod's god. Herod's aide invokes "most myghty Mahowne" in the opening line and describes Herod himself as king of the Jews by grace of Muhammad (lines 14–16). Herod vows in Muhammad's name to provide women and riches to the soldiers who execute his order to kill all male infants (lines 621–26, 638–51, 662–63); as Michael Paull observes in his study of this play, Christians imagined that Muslims likewise recruited converts through offers of wealth and sensual pleasure. Although these and other biblical plays make no direct reference to Muslims, they imply that Muhammad's contemporary devotees are similarly eager to slaughter innocent Christians and impose the worship of Muhammad. Associations of Muslims with biblical villains, we have seen, infuse contemporary political conflicts with timeless theological significance.[14]

Just as the *Auto de los Reyes Magos* reflects the Augustinian conception of Jews widely accepted at the turn of the thirteenth century, English plays dramatize the ideas about Jews that circulated in the fourteenth and fifteenth centuries, according to which the Jews knew that Christ was God and killed him for that very reason. These new ideas reflect the culmination of developments in Christian thought that occurred over a period of several centuries. European theologians of the twelfth century increasingly relied on rational argumentation to prove that Christ is God, ultimately concluding that any reasonable person would inevitably recognize this truth. The Jews of Christ's day, they came to believe, must have recognized Christ's divine nature when they rejected and condemned him. Meanwhile, Petrus Alfonsi and Peter of Cluny, whom we encountered in chapter 6, drew attention to the fact that contemporary Jews do not follow the Old Testament literally but instead rely on the Talmud's interpretation of biblical texts (which does, in fact, differ significantly from biblical law itself). Thirteenth-century polemicists alleged that the rabbis of Jesus's day conspired to displace the Bible with the Talmud in order to prevent Jews from recognizing the truth about God. These polemicists supported their claim with Talmudic passages that purportedly demonstrate the Talmud's contradictions of biblical teachings, its blasphemous hostility toward Christ, and even its unwitting demonstration of Christ's divinity—the rabbis who composed the Talmud, these polemicists assert, could not hide all the evidence they sought to suppress.[15]

In tandem with these thirteenth-century theological developments, artists began to portray biblical Jews rejecting God in favor of false deities—such as Muhammad. A stained-glass window in Paris's Sainte-Chapelle, created between 1242 and 1248, depicts the prophet Isaiah reproaching Jews who worship an idol labeled "Mahomet" (fig. 19). An even more striking example is the image of the biblical Golden Calf incident on the *Hereford Mappa Mundi*, a map of the known world created in about 1300. This work depicts "Jews," labeled as such, worshipping a coin-defecating idol labeled "Mahū" (fig. 20). The artist distinguishes these Jews from the "people of Israel" whose route from Egypt to the Promised Land passes this scene and who ultimately become the faithful followers of Jesus Christ. Jews, in other words, encountered God at Mount Sinai alongside the true people of Israel but, unlike them, willfully rejected God (which is to say, Christ) in favor of idolatry—and money. The coin imagery on this English map reflects contemporaneous stereotypes about Jewish moneylenders, which grew increasingly vicious during the thirteenth century and contributed to the expulsion of England's Jews in 1290. The identification of Muhammad as an idol in these works follows in the tradition established within crusade chronicles and *chansons de geste*.[16]

The Jews who appear in *Jour de jugement*, an early fourteenth-century French dramatization of the events that will culminate in Christ's triumphant return to earth, also revere Muhammad. Much of this play focuses on the birth and reign of Antichrist, whom the play portrays as the offspring of a devil and a Jewish whore. This Jew, her attendant, and the devils invoke Muhammad's power and pray to him for a healthy

FIGURE 19. Isaiah reproaches Jews for worshipping an idol of Muhammad. Paris, Sainte-Chapelle, panel J-108 (1242–48). (Photo: © Reproduction Patrick Cadet / Centre des Monuments Nationaux.)

FIGURE 20. Jews ("Iudei") worshipping an idol of Muhammad ("Mahū") along the path of the Israelites toward the Promised Land; detail from the *Hereford Mappa Mundi* (ca. 1300). (Photo: © Hereford Cathedral.)

childbirth. Whether Muhammad himself is Antichrist or, as in this play, the deity worshipped by the Jews and devils who bring Antichrist into this world, he represents the antithesis of Christ. For that very reason, the Jews who hate Christ express their devotion to Muhammad instead.[17]

The notion that Jews past and present sought to torment and kill Christ while fully aware of his true identity as God also underpins the charge that Jews sought to torture and destroy consecrated eucharistic wafers. One must, after all, regard Christ as divine and accept the doctrine of transubstantiation to believe that an attack on the consecrated host inflicts harm on Christ himself. In several fourteenth- and fifteenth-century host desecration tales, the Jewish perpetrators invoke Muhammad as their god. The Jews of Brussels, sentenced to mass execution in 1370 on the grounds of host desecration, supposedly called out to Muhammad as they burned to death. The Jewish characters who engage in host desecration in French and English plays also invoke Muhammad. Paolo Uccello's fifteenth-century visual depiction of Jewish host desecration likewise marks the perpetrator as a devotee of Muhammad: the Jew's pawn shop features a prominent "Moor's head," an emblem commonly associated with Muslims during the fifteenth century. The association of these perpetrators with Muhammad follows from the presumption that Jews past and present are enemies of Christ who seize every opportunity to express their hostility through violence.[18]

The notion that Jews are inveterate enemies of Christ who knowingly crucified their own God in biblical times, currently seek to torture Christ's body in the form of the eucharistic host, and join with devils in anticipation of the reign of Antichrist developed for reasons unrelated to Christian ideas about Muslims. Thanks to works like the *Song of Roland*, however, Muhammad had already come to represent the primary or even sole god of Christendom's enemies within the popular European imagination. For that reason, late medieval artists and playwrights found it valuable to mark Jewish villains who reject Christ and act with violent hostility toward Christ's faithful followers as worshippers of Muhammad.

THE EQUIVALENCE OF THE ANTI-CHRISTIANS

The new conception of Judaism that emerged in the thirteenth century generated entirely new possibilities for the representation of Muslims. Working within the older conception of distinct pagan and Jewish antitheses of Christianity, crusade chronicles and *chansons de geste* portray Muslims, like pagans, as worshippers of a false deity while the *Auto de los Reyes Magos* instead associates Muslims with Jews in their failure to understand biblical prophecies. Late medieval playwrights, in contrast, can associate Muslims with Jews as the enemies of God, a more all-encompassing—and more terrifying—inverse of Christianity than either idolatry or biblical misinterpretation. English, French, and Italian plays reflect both the long-standing notion that Muhammad is the antithesis of Christ and the more recent notion that Jews, because they hate Christ, must worship Muhammad instead of God. By ascribing invocations of Muhammad to Jewish and non-Jewish villains alike, these dramatizations of biblical scenes also reinforce a third and broader presumption: that all enemies of Christ revere Muhammad as their god.

This pattern is especially pronounced in the Towneley plays, which portray not only Herod as a devotee of Muhammad but also the Old Testament's pharaoh and the Roman rulers Caesar Augustus and, especially, Pontius Pilate, who sentenced Jesus to death. The Towneley Pilate brags about his own evil doings and credits Muhammad, his god, as their inspiration. This Roman governor proudly proclaims himself to be the prince of the Jews and expresses horror at Jesus's behavior in "our" Temple as he vows in Muhammad's name that Jesus will suffer the consequences. Pilate also worries that Jesus will "destroy our law," which is to say the Law of Moses.[19]

The Towneley plays depict Pilate as a paradigmatic adherent of Judaism: even his rejection of Christ in favor of Muhammad is in keeping with other fourteenth- and fifteenth-century portrayals of Jews. By implication, contemporary Muslims who allegedly worship Muhammad instead of Christ also practice Judaism. To state the same conclusion differently, the Towneley playwright and his contemporaries portray Roman villains, Jews, and Muslims alike as "anti-Christians," a group characterized primarily by enmity toward Christ whose tenets also include devotion to Muhammad and literal observance of Old Testament laws. These portrayals have minimal relation to the actual beliefs and practices of Romans, Jews, or Muslims; rather, they reflect the inverse of normative Christian beliefs and practices.

The Towneley plays depict Christ's suffering, death, and resurrection as a contest between the true God and the false god named Muhammad, whom Pilate and his henchmen repeatedly invoke as they condemn and torment Christ. These and other English plays frame sacred history as a timeless contest between Muhammad's devotees, on the one hand, and Christ and his followers, on the other. The former are selfish, violent, and obsessed with this-worldly power, traits that European Christians also commonly associated with Muslims. The latter, in contrast, are selfless and serene, confident that they will triumph despite the adversity they face. Invocations of Muhammad link Christ's biblical enemies to one another as well as to contemporary Muslims: they are all anti-Christians notwithstanding their obvious differences.[20]

This approach to retelling sacred history may in part reflect increasing concerns among European Christians about the rising military might of the Muslim Ottoman Empire, which captured Constantinople in 1453 and proceeded to conquer territory within Europe as well. The objective of these references to Muhammad, however, is not to praise or motivate Christian warriors, as was the case in the crusade-era rhetoric that we examined in chapter 9. Late medieval plays instead encourage ordinary citizens to see themselves as part of the timeless drama of Christianity and to differentiate themselves from this drama's villains. Not only were the plays in fact performed by volunteers from various craft guilds, but they model patterns of righteous and wicked behavior, such as selflessness and selfishness, relevant to daily life. Audiences and actors alike should recommit themselves to proper Christian faith and practice because, in the end, Christ will emerge victorious no matter what happens on distant battlefields. More to the point, anyone can become an anti-Christian, so everyone must instead strive to be a good Christian.

Once Christians began to imagine Christ's first-century enemies as devotees of Muhammad, it seems a small step to place Muslims themselves into these scenes. The plays we have examined do not include explicitly Muslim characters, but other writers and artists took the liberty of anachronistically introducing such figures. The Holkham Bible, an early fourteenth-century English manuscript, depicts Jesus offering his famous lesson, "render unto Caesar the things that are Caesar's," to "Saracen knights."[21] According to one manuscript of the fourteenth-century Book of John Mandeville, Saracens participated alongside Jews in the conspiracy to arrest and kill Jesus and were among those to whom Judas returned his payment for betraying Christ.[22] Various artists of the fourteenth through sixteenth century placed recognizably Muslim figures or emblems associated with Muslims at Christ's crucifixion and in other biblical scenes. To cite only one example: the Chapel of the Crucifixion at Sacro Monte di Varallo, created by Gaudenzio Ferrari in the early sixteenth century, features several figures whose faces, headgear, and weapons call to mind Turkish Muslims, as well as a banner with Islamic crescent moons (fig. 21). The creators of works such as this, like

FIGURE 21. The Chapel of the Crucifixion at Sacro Monte di Varallo. Fresco with terracotta figures by Gaudenzio Ferrari, 1523–28. (Photo: © A. Dagli Orti / © DeAgostini Picture Library / Bridgeman Images.)

the artist of the *Beam of the Passion* we analyzed in chapter 9, employ obviously anachronistic imagery to relate contemporary political concerns to timeless theological lessons and, in so doing, intensify the relevance of biblical scenes. These works make no reference to the worship of Muhammad, but they emphasize that Muslims, Jews, and Christ's Roman executioners are all anti-Christians.[23]

In a sense, we have come full circle to the binary worldview that Paul articulates to the Galatians through his table of opposites (see chapter 1). Paul's rivals allegedly persecute the true followers of Christ but cannot escape their own state of cursedness. Those who adhere to Paul's teachings, in contrast, stand on the proper side of this table on account of their faith in Christ and, for that reason, can look forward with confidence to God's covenantal promises. Paul himself did not have Muslims in mind when he wrote his Letter to the Galatians; in fact, Paul did not even define his own community of Christ-followers in opposition to Judaism. Later Christian readers, however, had no trouble applying Paul's teachings to Jews and Muslims alike thanks to the discourse of anti-Judaism: all who behave in purportedly Jewish fashion fall on the wrong side of this binary. Once European Christians defined Judaism as the rejection of Christ rather than the misinterpretation of scripture, they could render all non-Christians as Jewishly anti-Christian.

The next and final chapter in our study of premodern Christian conceptions of Jewish Muslims focuses on Martin Luther (1483–1546), who drew heavily on this rhetorical tradition of oppositional binarism. Like his medieval predecessors, Luther often associated Muslims with Jews, although he alleged that these anti-Christians worship the devil rather than Muhammad (whom Luther regarded as a false prophet, not a false god). What most distinguished Luther from his predecessors is that he focused his polemics primarily against Roman Catholics in the course of promoting a form of Christianity that he called Evangelical— that is, gospel-oriented—and that many today call Protestant.[24] Luther's orientation toward the Bible, especially Paul's letters, shapes not only his conception of Christianity but also his frequent allegation that rival Christians, Jews, and Muslims alike fall on the wrong side of Paul's binary and, for that reason, do not worship the true God.

CHAPTER 12

Luther's Rivals and the Emergent Discourse of Anti-Islam

Sixteenth Century

> Even if the last age of this world is overwhelmed by an enormous multitude
> of idols—those of the Jews, of Muhammad, and of the Papists—still let us
> sound forth the voice of the gospel and bear witness that the crucified and
> risen Jesus Christ, whom the apostles show us, truly is the Son of God and
> the Savior, and let us curse all their errors that conflict with the gospel.

Martin Luther encapsulates many of his core teachings in this sentence
from his Preface to the Quran, written in 1542 toward the end of
Luther's prolific career.[1] Luther, who believed that God would soon
bring an end to the world as we know it, preached that gospel-oriented
(literally, evangelical) Christians should bear witness to Jesus Christ as
revealed within the Bible while condemning all teachings to the contrary. His list of those who adhere to idolatry, which is to say the worship of false gods, begins with the Jews and culminates with the
"Papists," Luther's disparaging term for those who allegedly follow the
Catholic pope instead of Christ. Luther places the teachings of Muhammad in the same category as Judaism and Catholicism, and he subjects
them to the same critique—namely, that they contradict the Bible. Also
noteworthy is the extensive attention that Luther devotes to Jews and
Catholics (as well as rival Protestants, although they are absent from
the quoted sentence) in a work whose primary focus is the Quran.

The sheer volume of Martin Luther's anti-Muslim rhetoric may
eclipse that of all previous Christian authors combined. The Preface to
the Quran is one of six works that Luther wrote about Muslims, whom

he usually called "Turks," but the vast majority of Luther's roughly 4,500 references to Muslims appear in lectures and publications devoted to other topics. Luther frequently associates Muslims with Jews and Catholics, to whom he devoted even more attention. Over five hundred references to *Turks* appear in close proximity to *Jews*, and over seven hundred appear near terms related to *pope* (including "Papists"); all three terms appear in close proximity on at least four hundred of these occasions.[2]

Luther is not, chronologically speaking, the last premodern author whose work appears in the present study. He merits our sustained attention in this concluding chapter not because of when or even how frequently he wrote about Muslims but because of the ways in which he did so. Luther was especially proficient in deploying the discourse of anti-Judaism against Muslims, among others, and in that respect his works represent a summation and a climax within the history of the dynamics we have explored throughout this book. In addition, and of greater lasting significance, Luther inaugurated a new anti-Islamic discourse grounded in the Bible itself. This discourse, like anti-Judaism, brands as "Islamic" specific characteristics (ideas, practices, traits, etc.) that non-Muslims purportedly display in order to critique those characteristics while promoting their opposites as normative. Luther's rhetoric powerfully demonstrates the degree to which Christian ideas about Muslims—like Christian ideas about Jews—derive from classic Christian texts, engage timeless Christian concerns, and advance core Christian objectives. These ideas, which predate the rise of Islam, have little to do with the beliefs and practices of actual Muslims.

Before we proceed, I need to address a terminological issue. In the introduction, I explained that anti-Judaism differs from antisemitism because antisemitism condemns what Jews allegedly *are*, inherently, while anti-Judaism condemns what people (Jews and non-Jews alike) *think or do*. Of the two, only anti-Judaism advances the goal of moral exhortation: this discourse presumes that people can choose whether or not to display Jewish characteristics, and it places those who allegedly make the wrong choice beyond the pale in order to reinforce opposing characteristics. A similar distinction between two dimensions of Islamophobia, which one might call *anti-Islam* and *antimuslimism*, facilitates a deeper understanding of negative rhetoric regarding Muslims. Just as antisemitism condemns Jews as Jews, antimuslimism is a form of racist essentialism that condemns Muslims as Muslims. The discourses of anti-

Judaism and anti-Islam, in contrast, condemn allegedly Jewish or Islamic characteristics and their bearers, whoever they might be, and motivate self-differentiation rather than discrimination. The discourse of anti-Judaism is already explicit within the New Testament, and Luther makes the case that, implicitly, the discourse of anti-Islam appears there as well.[3]

Luther's condemnations of Islam, we will see, served first and foremost as a means to condemn Catholics, who constituted the most relevant foil against which Luther defines proper Christianity. His polemical references to Turks, in other words, often do not target Muslims themselves. The same may be said regarding much of Luther's anti-Jewish rhetoric. Because comparison constitutes an especially powerful rhetorical weapon, Luther employs Muslims and Jews as ammunition in his intra-Christian polemics. Luther's opponents fired back in kind: for example, they maligned Lutherans by equating them with Turks.[4] Real Muslims and, especially, real Jews got caught in the Christian crossfire. Luther gave voice not only to anti-Judaism but also to virulent antisemitism when he condemned Jews, as Jews, on account of their allegedly intrinsic characteristics and when he advocated for persecuting Jews specifically. This rhetoric appears in its sharpest form in Luther's treatise *On the Jews and Their Lies,* which Luther wrote concurrently with his Preface to the Quran; this work, which had little impact in the sixteenth century, served as a source of inspiration for Nazis and other modern antisemites. Luther's anti-Islamic rhetoric also contributed to modern Islamophobia in significant and enduring ways.[5]

This chapter begins by examining the use of anti-Judaism to condemn Muslims and fellow Christians in one of Luther's earliest works, a lecture on Psalm 74 delivered in 1514. We will then turn to the parallel discourse of anti-Islam that Luther develops in his first work focused on Muslims, *On War against the Turks* (1529). In this treatise, Luther employs biblical interpretation to establish Islam as a theological enemy of Christendom in its own right, and he uses Muhammad's purported teachings as the reference with which to polemicize against the pope. Luther proceeds to draw strategically on both anti-Judaism and anti-Islam in subsequent works, promoting certain characteristics as truly Christian by branding Christians who allegedly display the opposite traits as Jew-ish or Muslim-ish. The chapter's final section shows how Luther grounds this rhetoric in the oppositional binary that Paul articulated in his Letter to the Galatians, the work we examined at the beginning of chapter 1.

ANTI-JUDAISM IN LUTHER'S RHETORIC ABOUT TURKS

To say that Martin Luther lived an eventful life would be a gross under-statement. When he began his teaching, preaching, and writing career as a professor at the University of Wittenberg in 1513, Luther was a Roman Catholic monk. His acerbic critique in 1517 of indulgences, grants by which the pope releases a soul from purgatory to heaven in exchange for a donation toward specific papal initiatives, quickly mushroomed into a condemnation of the papacy as an institution, and the pope branded Luther a heretic in 1520. During the following years, Luther decisively rejected Catholicism in favor of what he called Evangelicalism (his detractors called it "Lutheranism"). Luther also found himself at odds with rivals who preferred a more radical reformation of Christian faith and society, including those who founded what today are known as Reformed (or Presbyterian) and Baptist churches. These events and many others, among them the failed but terrifying Turkish Siege of Vienna in 1529, left their imprint on Luther's thought and writings. In certain respects, however, "the whole later Luther is already present in the Lec-tures on the Psalms" that Luther delivered as a newly installed professor of biblical theology. Luther's lecture on Psalm 74, which he presented in 1514, exemplifies both the manner in which Luther thought about Jews and the ways in which he used the discourse of anti-Judaism throughout his career to criticize Muslims and, especially, fellow Christians.[6]

Psalm 74, at first glance, laments the destruction of the Jerusalem Temple by God's enemies. Luther, however, asserts that this is merely a superficial understanding of the psalm's literal meaning. The psalmist, he explains, employs figurative language depicting the destroyed Tem-ple in order to bemoan the "spiritual devastation" wrought by Christ's Jewish enemies as the psalmist cries out against "the faithlessness through which ungodly Jewish interpreters corrupt scripture." The con-ception of Jews that Luther expresses here and throughout his career follows that of his late medieval predecessors who, as we saw in chapter 11, alleged that Jewish leaders intentionally rejected God and deliber-ately obscured the true meaning of biblical prophecies.[7]

According to Luther, Psalm 74 literally condemns the Jews who lived from the time of Jesus through the present day. At the same time, the psalm speaks allegorically of Turks and Christian heretics, "because that which the faithlessness of the Jews did and does to the people of the synagogue all heretics and, even more so, the Turks did and do to the people of the church."[8] Just as the leaders of the Jews willfully block their followers from recognizing and accepting Christ as God, so, too, heretics and Turks prevent Christians from following Christ properly: heretics through their allegedly false teachings and Turks through their alleged refusal to allow any sort of Christian teaching. Luther regards Muslims as political enemies of the church, but his association of Turks with Jews enables Luther to emphasize the theological dimensions of this enmity. Muslims, like the Jews of Jesus's day, purportedly use their worldly power to stifle Christian faith.

Luther repeatedly associates Turks and heretics with Jews as he progresses verse by verse through Psalm 74. The psalmist, Luther explains, cries out against "that which is incorrigible, obstinate, and desperate, which fights even against the known truth . . . a defense of one's own righteousness and a stubborn vindication of one's own thought, as in the case of the Jews, heretics, and Turks." Heretics and Turks, no less than the Jews, have torn down "faith in Christ and the works of faith" and instead "set up their own faith, their own belief, their own meaning, their own works." The long-standing discourse of anti-Judaism shapes Luther's understanding of the psalmist's words and also provides the negative reference point with which, by analogy, Luther associates Muslims and heretics.[9]

In one respect, Luther declares, Muslims are even worse than Jews:

> With every device, with every use of the tongue, [Jews] are active in persuading their people not to believe in Christ. This is what it means to cut down the gates of the soul with axes and hatchets [Luther refers here to verse 6]. The Turk, however, does this not only by means of the tongue and the word, but also through the sword and death he forbids the hearing of Christ's Word. By this means, he utterly destroys the very gates of salvation.

The enmity of the Turks is more all-encompassing than that of contemporary Jews because it is political as well as theological; as Luther alleges in his lecture on Psalm 80, the Turk "compels all to adopt his faith by the force of arms." At this stage of his career, however, Luther does not ascribe any particular content to the Turks' faith.[10]

Luther, like countless predecessors from as early as the second century (see chapter 1), also criticizes members of his own Christian community by describing their behavior as Jewish in nature. He explains that Psalm 74:4 describes the Jews, who "observe the externalities of the holy day and do not defile the letter of the Sabbath, but in its innermost midst they defile it in the worst way." Immediately, however, Luther pivots. "Christians now act similarly: taking leave from toilsome work [on holy days], they devote themselves to works of sinners." By comparing sinful Christians to Jews, Luther encourages his audience to observe holy days in pious fashion.[11]

Luther returns to this point in the lecture's climactic conclusion. The entire psalm, he explains, "can also be interpreted as referring to our own extremely bad morals, for we are as bad as the Turks or worse in the way we profane sacred things." Jews exemplify that which is bad, Turks are at least as bad as Jews, and we Christians are at least as bad as Turks! Here, Luther addresses neither the literal meaning of the psalm, which in his reading refers to Jews as the enemies of Christ, nor its allegorical message, which refers to heretics and Turks as enemies of the collective Church. Rather, this portion of the lecture explains the moral lessons embedded in Psalm 74; Luther regarded this layer of the Bible's meaning, which medieval interpreters called its "tropological" sense, as "the primary sense of scripture" because it addresses the individual Christian believer.[12]

Luther condemns fellow monks and priests for their willful misuse of church property, their prideful pursuit of luxury, their rash administration of sacraments and canonical justice, and their abuse of holy days as occasions for sinful activities. This is not a critique of Catholicism as such—those critiques first emerged several years later—but of sinful Christians who fail as individuals to live as they should. Turks, Luther reminds his students, destroy the gates of salvation with their words and swords "while we do it spiritually . . . not through heretical teachings but rather offensive words and deeds, to such an extent that the Word of God would now seem to be preached in vain because there are no gates through which it might enter."[13]

Earlier in the lecture on Psalm 74, Luther associates Christians who abuse their holy days with Jews. In this sermonic climax, however, he instead makes a point of associating Christians who engage in this and other offensive practices with Turks, the political rivals whom his audience feared and despised. This shocking comparison strengthens Luther's rhetoric regarding the severity of Christian sinfulness and the importance of addressing it, lest God use the Turks to punish European Christendom through military conquest.[14] Turks themselves, however, are only relevant in the context of this lecture because Luther branded them as Jewish by analogy.

"IF YOU COMPARE THE TURK AND THE PAPISTS": ANTI-JUDAISM WITHOUT JEWS

In his lecture on Psalm 74, Luther associates Turks and errant Christians with Jews, whom Luther regards as the biblical text's sole literal subject. Luther's treatise *On War against the Turks*, published in January 1529, differs in two crucial ways: Luther now alleges that the Bible itself condemns Islam, and he employs Muslims as the primary negative reference with which to condemn errant Christians without first branding these Muslims as Jewish. Luther, in other words, employs a discourse of anti-Islam that is structurally and functionally equivalent to the long-standing discourse of anti-Judaism.

On War against the Turks explains the nature and magnitude of the danger that Turks pose to European Christendom in an effort to promote what Luther believed to be the proper Christian response to their aggression. "The Turk is the rod of the wrath of the Lord our God and the servant of the raging devil," Luther declares. For that reason, he insists, Christians should first and foremost repent and pray for God to restrain the devil. After all, "if the Turk's god, the devil, is not beaten first, there is reason to fear that the Turk will not be so easy to beat." In order to inspire passionate prayer, Luther makes the case that Turks, as agents of the devil, seek not only to conquer Christians but also, through the imposition of Muhammad's teachings, to destroy the traditional pillars of Christian society: church, civil government, and the household. The impending Turkish invasion, Luther insists, is not merely political in nature but also and more profoundly a theological assault against the very foundations of Christianity. This novel claim about the nature of Muhammad's teachings rests neither on the Quran itself nor on the earlier polemical works from which Luther derived his information about Islam but rather on Luther's interpretation of the Bible.[15]

Luther emphasizes that the Quran, although it praises Christ, understands him to be a prophet rather than God. "From this anyone can easily see that Muhammad is a destroyer of our Lord Christ and his kingdom, for if anyone denies the articles concerning Christ, that he is God's Son, that he died for us and still lives and reigns at the right hand of God, what has he left of Christ?" According to Luther's definition, Muslims reject Christ and, by extension, God; this is why Luther insists that Muslims instead serve the devil. These claims resonate with texts we examined in previous chapters, which also allege Muslim enmity toward Christ and associate Muslims with the devil and the worship of false gods solely because Muslims are not Christians. "Once Christ is no more," Luther declares, "what remains is Muhammad with his doctrine of works and, especially, of the sword."[16]

Luther alleges that the Quran itself commands Turks to destroy Christian forms of government by sword. "Thus the Turk is really nothing but a murderer or bandit, as his deeds show." To support this claim about Muslims, however, Luther relies not on accounts of their deeds but on pre-Islamic sources: Augustine and, especially, the Bible. He explains, for example, that murder inevitably follows from the rejection of Christ, "for Christ says in John 8 that the devil is a liar and a murderer. . . . Thus, when the spirit of lies had taken possession of Muhammad, and the devil had murdered men's souls with his Quran and had destroyed the faith of Christians, he had to go on and take the sword and set about to murder their bodies." The Bible, in other words, purportedly demonstrates that, because Muslims tell lies about the nature of Christ, they must be murderers. The passage in the Gospel of John to which Luther refers actually condemns Jews, to whom Jesus declares, "You are from your father the devil, and you choose to do your father's desires. He was a murderer from the beginning and does not stand in the truth . . . for he is a liar and the father of lies" (8:44). Luther, however, implies that Jesus himself spoke of Muslims no less than of Jews.[17]

Finally, Luther claims that "Muhammad's Quran has no regard for marriage" because it permits polygamy and divorce in violation of Christian norms. Luther repeats widespread (but false) allegations that Turkish men commonly have ten to twenty wives whom they sell at will "like cattle." On this basis, he declares that Muslims do not engage in marriage at all "because none of them takes or has a wife with the intention of staying with her forever, as though the two were one body, as God's word says [in Genesis 2:24]." In sum, "what good can there be in the government and the whole Turkish way of life when according to their Quran these three things rule among them, namely, lying, murder, and disregard of marriage?" Because Islam allegedly revolves around the rejection and abolition of core Christian characteristics—faith in Christ, interpersonal morality, and marital fidelity—Christians must do everything in their power to prevent the further expansion of the Turkish Empire within Europe.[18]

Many of the polemicists we encountered in previous chapters brand Muslims as Jews (or pagans) in order to read Muslims into the Bible as timeless enemies of Christ. Luther does the same in his lecture on Psalm 74, which relies on the allegorical association of Turks with Jews. In *On*

War against the Turks, however, Luther asserts that scripture itself directly condemns Turks just as it directly condemns contemporary Jews. This method of portraying Muslims as biblical enemies enables Luther to associate his Christian rivals with Muslims just as he and his predecessors associate their rivals with Jews.

Having defined Islam as antithetical to Christianity, Luther goes on to polemically compare Islam with Catholicism, which Luther identifies as the cause of much Christian sinfulness. Summarizing his argument about the nature of Islam, Luther alleges that the Turk "does not think it a sin to overthrow Christ, lay government waste, and destroy marriage. The pope also works at all these things, though in other ways—with hypocrisy, while the Turk uses force and the sword." Luther goes on to declare that the pope closely resembles Muhammad: "He, too, does not rule with the gospel, or word of God, but has made a new law and Quran, namely, his decretals, and these he enforces with the ban just as the Turk enforces his Quran with the sword." Luther defines Turk and pope alike as both theological and political enemies of true Christians because they promote false beliefs and sinful behaviors while seeking to destroy the foundations of Christian society.[19]

Luther returns to these associations repeatedly in subsequent works. "If you compare the Turk and the Papists," he declares in 1532, "they are very dissimilar and wish to be so. But they agree on this one thing: that they fight against Christ and wish to see this teaching [about Christ's ultimate judgment] put down." To cite another example from 1539: "The Turk set Christ aside and accepted Muhammad; the pope rejects Christ and holds to his canon laws." Both are not only liars but also murderers: "today the Turk is abducting our people in droves, murdering and tormenting them; so does the pope, who is banishing, hanging, burning, beheading, and drowning us" (1537). In *Prayer against the Turks* (1541), Luther reprises his allegation that Papists and Turks alike desecrate and destroy marriage. "The pope, under the pretense of chastity, has forbidden marriage and condemned it as sinful; the Turk tears man and wife apart and sells the women as though they were mere cows or calves. . . . In brief, both the papacy and the Turkish kingdom are doing nothing else than destroying the authority of home, city, and church."[20]

Luther makes no reference to Jews in these polemical comparisons. Jews, after all, do not "set Christ aside" because they never claimed to accept him, and they possess neither the power to murder Christians with impunity nor the reputation of selling wives. Even so, Luther's rhetoric about Turks and Papists closely resembles the discourse of anti-Judaism that we have examined throughout this book. Luther constructs the Islam he purports to describe by drawing on foundational Christian principles and texts: his rhetoric about "home, city, and church" channels long-standing Christian political thought, and his claims about the nature of Islam's alleged teachings rest explicitly on the Bible. Like countless predecessors, Luther addresses an audience of fellow Christians and seeks to promote a thoroughly Christian agenda through the comparison of his rhetorical target with a despised reference. Now, however, Islam serves as a derogatory reference in its own right by means of which Luther can disparage the pope. The discourse of anti-Islam plays the role that anti-Judaism plays in other polemical comparisons because Luther contends that the Bible itself condemns Islamic characteristics just as it condemns Jewish ones. This contention is a natural corollary of Luther's conviction that Christians need not seek guidance from any source beyond scripture.

Luther's newfound ability to disparage his Christian rivals by means of polemical comparisons that employ Turks as a negative theological reference may account for the dramatic increase in his association of Turks and Papists. In works published before 1529, about 10 percent of references to Turks appear in close proximity to words such as *pope* and *Papist*; that rate more than doubles in works published after that year. The rate of association between Turks and Jews, in contrast, remained fairly consistent (at about 13 percent) throughout Luther's career. The discourse of anti-Judaism, after all, was part of Luther's polemical arsenal from the start and retained its rhetorical potency. The discourse of anti-Islam constitutes a complementary weapon that Luther, a master polemicist, often found to be even more useful given contemporary concerns about Turks.[21]

LUTHER'S REREADINGS OF GALATIANS

The difference between Luther's early and mature rhetoric regarding Jews, Turks, and Catholics is especially apparent in his two sets of lectures on Galatians. Luther ascribed special importance to this book of the Bible, as his own theology rests on Paul's insistence that "a person is reckoned as righteous not through works of Law but through faith in Jesus Christ" (Galatians 2:16). Recall from chapter 1 that, although Paul condemned rivals within his own Christ-believing community, early Christian interpreters understood the Letter to the Galatians as a condemnation of Judaism. A similar distinction applies to Luther's lectures. Luther published his earlier lectures on Galatians in 1519 as a faithful believer critiquing fellow members of the Roman Catholic Church. By the time he delivered his later lectures on Galatians in 1531, however, Luther had broken decisively from Catholicism and insisted that Paul himself condemned it as well.

The 1519 lectures illustrate the ways in which the early Luther critiqued errant Christians by means of polemical comparisons with Jews and, separately, with Turks. Luther's rhetoric about Christian abuse of holy days provides a clear example. Recall that, in his lecture on Psalm 74, Luther faulted Christians for their idleness and their sinful behavior on the Catholic Church's many feast days by comparing these Christians to Jews. In the published version of the earlier Galatians lectures, Luther instead faults bishops and priests who, out of deference to the pope, feel the need to promote extraneous holy days that do more harm than good. "The commandment of the Roman Church is not binding if it cannot be kept to the honor and glory of God," Luther declares as he berates those who allegedly "place reverence for a person ahead of reverence for God and, in the name of the pope and St. Peter, crown and even worship the devil within the church of Christ." Luther goes on to describe such obedience as "far worse than the tyranny of the Turks . . . The Turk, of course, will kill our bodies and rob us of our land, but we are killing souls and depriving them of heaven" by providing opportunities for sinfulness. Luther's predecessors might be shocked by the target of his polemic, but they would recognize his comparative rhetoric as similar in nature to their own.[22]

This passage exemplifies the inflammatory manner in which Luther addressed the papacy, which he associates with Judaism, Turkish conquerors, and the devil himself. To cite another example from the 1519 lectures, Luther declares that papal laws are similar to those of the Talmud and are even worse than Turkish dominion: "since the tyranny of laws oppresses consciences, it far exceeds the tyranny of the Turks, which oppresses only bodies." Turks constitute the political enemies of Christian Europe while Judaism represents the theological inverse of Christianity. Luther alleges that the papacy is anti-Christian in both respects, but at this stage of his career he needs two separate comparisons to make this case.[23]

By the time he returned to Galatians in 1531, Luther not only rejected Catholicism but also adopted a simpler and more forceful way to disparage his rivals. Going far beyond earlier interpreters, Luther now understood Paul himself to condemn not only postbiblical Jews but also Turks, Papists, and "sectarians," Luther's derisive term for those affiliated with what we would today call rival Protestant denominations.

These later lectures, which circulated widely and exercised considerable influence, emphasize that only Luther's Evangelical community adheres to Paul's teachings: no one else is actually Christian or even a worshipper of God, as everyone else falls on the wrong side of Paul's table of opposites.[24]

Luther opens his later lectures by explaining why he needs to teach Galatians once again: "there is a clear and present danger that the devil may take away from us the pure doctrine of faith and may substitute for it the doctrines of works and of human traditions." Luther distinguishes this doctrine of faith, which he calls "Christian righteousness," from human systems of righteousness, all of which rest on the active performance of deeds, or "works." Christian righteousness, in contrast, is entirely passive, "for here we work nothing, render nothing to God; we only receive and permit someone else to work in us, namely God." It is human nature, Luther observes, to rely on our own worthiness, to try through our own actions to overcome our sinfulness, but these efforts are doomed to fail because humans are inherently sinful. The only solution is to receive the grace that God the Father grants through Jesus. Christ alone can accomplish what humans cannot, but the devil constantly seeks to prevent humans from receiving Christ's gift of grace by persuading them to rely on works instead of faith.[25]

"If the doctrine of [passive] righteousness is lost," Luther declares, "the whole Christian doctrine is lost. And those in the world who do not teach it are either Jews or Turks or Papists or sectarians, for between these two kinds of righteousness—the active righteousness of the Law and the passive righteousness of Christ—there is no middle ground." Luther's claim does not rest on the teachings of rival faith communities but on binary reasoning: anyone who does not espouse "Christian righteousness" must by definition espouse a form of works-based righteousness because no alternative exists. Luther does not claim that these rival communities are similar in nature, merely that they are equivalent in their essence. "The Turks perform different works from the Papists, and the Papists perform different works from the Jews, and so forth. But although some do works that are more splendid, great, and difficult than others, the content remains the same . . . for they are still works." The devil, Luther implies, has many means of drawing humans away from faith in Christ, but they all differ from true Christianity in the same way and they all achieve the same end: damnation.[26]

The later lectures on Galatians reinforce the core principles of Luther's mature theology:

1. Humans can be reckoned as righteous before God by means of divine grace alone.

2. Divine grace comes through Christ alone.

3. Christ dispenses grace on the basis of faith alone.

4. Those who have faith in Christ should rely on the authority of scripture alone.

Luther also presses a related claim: these doctrines characterize Evangelical Christianity alone. "The pope, the Turks, the Jews, and all the sectarians . . . put Christ the Mediator out of their sight," he alleges (commenting on Galatians 1:3). "Whoever falls away from the doctrine of [passive] righteousness is ignorant of God and is an idolater. Therefore it is all the same whether he then returns to the Law or to the worship of idols; it is all the same whether he is called a monk or a Turk or a Jew or an Anabaptist. For once this doctrine is undermined, nothing more remains but sheer error, hypocrisy, wickedness, and idolatry" (commenting on 4:9). When Paul declares that "if you receive circumcision, Christ will be of no advantage to you" (5:2), Luther explains, he condemns "whoever teaches that anything beyond the Gospel of Christ is necessary to attain salvation, whether he be a Papist, a Jew, a Turk, or a sectarian." Muslims and Catholics, no less than Jews, allegedly adhere to religions that do not revolve around Christ, that rely on works-righteousness, and that prioritize postbiblical sources (the Quran, canon law, and the Talmud, respectively).[27]

Like Paul, Luther addresses and seeks to persuade his own followers while harshly condemning his rivals, whose counterarguments he silences without engagement. This silencing rests on the consistent use of derogatory terms for Christian rivals and on Luther's consistent association of them with the already despised Jews and Turks, much as Paul tars his own rivals by associating them with Hagar and Ishmael. In both his earlier Galatians lectures and the lecture on Psalm 74, however, Luther compares Christians to a negative reference point: their practices on holy days are even worse than those of the Jews, and the pope's tyrannical laws are even more destructive than those of the Turks. These comparisons presuppose and implicitly reinforce the distinction between Christians and non-Christians. In the later lectures on Galatians, Luther instead conflates Catholics and rival Protestants with Turks and Jews to create a singular antithesis of Evangelical Christianity. This rhetoric is shocking because Luther violates widely accepted distinctions: he declares that the well-known differences among these groups are irrelevant because they all share the same defining feature. Late medieval polemicists engaged in similar rhetoric regarding those who reject Christ as God. Luther shifts the defining common denominator to rejection of the doctrine that grace depends on faith alone and, in so doing, places his Christian rivals in the devil's camp alongside Muslims and Jews.

In his earlier lectures, Luther understands biblical texts as referring literally to Jews and only allegorically to Turks, heretics, and sinful Christians. Allegory, however, plays no role in the later lectures on Galatians: Luther insists that Paul himself condemns not Jews or specific Christ-believing rivals but rather works-righteousness in all its forms. The practices of Catholics, Muslims, and Jews alike, Luther explains, run afoul of Paul's declaration that "through works of Law no fleshly creature will be reckoned as righteous" (Galatians 2:16). In effect, Luther not only grafts his own table of opposites onto the one that Paul created but also ascribes it to Paul himself.

The Preface to the Quran with which this chapter began illustrates how Luther continued to employ not only traditional anti-Jewish rhetoric but also this broader binary distinction between Evangelical Christians and everyone else.[28] The first third of this brief work focuses not on Islam but on Judaism because Luther wishes to remind his readers that "when faithful minds compare the testimony of the prophets to the delirium and blasphemies of the Jews, they are greatly strengthened in faith and in love for the truth of the Gospel and are provoked to a righteous hatred of Jewish perversity." So, too, Luther insists, pious Christians should familiarize themselves with the Quran: "when Muhammad's book has been brought forward and all its parts thoroughly examined, all faithful persons will more easily discern the madness and venom of the devil," whose teachings differ from those of biblical prophets and apostles. Luther values the discourse of anti-Judaism—and, likewise, anti-Islam—because he believes that properly framed comparisons foster proper Christian beliefs and practices. Luther concludes his preface, however, by condemning his rivals collectively.

> We must fight everywhere against the armies of the devil. How many different enemies have we seen in our own time? The defenders of the pope's idols, the Jews, a multitude of Anabaptist monstrosities, the [Unitarian] party of Servetus, and others. Let us prepare ourselves against Muhammad as well.

Luther devoted his preaching and writing to battles against many theological enemies, but he ultimately reduces this diversity to a simple binary: Muslims, Jews, Catholics, and other rivals are all followers of the devil, while only those who believe as Luther does truly worship God.

Paul, the first-century Jew, did not employ either anti-Judaism or anti-Islam. Paul's successors, however, emulated his use of polemical comparison and his method of promoting proper beliefs and behaviors through binary opposition to the purported characteristics of one's rivals. The discourse of anti-Judaism that emerged shortly after Paul's death, and the discourse of anti-Islam that emerged nearly 1,500 years later in the works of Martin Luther, reflect the enduring influence and motivational power of Paul's oppositional rhetoric.

Afterword: Rhetoric about Muslims and Jews Today

Rhetoric about Jewish Muslims did not end with Martin Luther. We encountered early seventeenth-century works from both Catholic Spain and Protestant England that pointedly associate Muslims with Judaism; later examples include future British Prime Minister Benjamin Disraeli's mid-nineteenth-century quip that Arabs are "Jews upon horseback."[1] I leave to those with more directly relevant expertise the task of analyzing how Christians and others in modern times employed the discourse of anti-Judaism in their anti-Muslim rhetoric. It seems, however, that polemicists today no longer find value in using the metaphor "Muslims are Jewish": this allegation, which persisted for well over a thousand years, is now evidently neither plausible nor useful.

Even so, contemporary polemicists continue to employ the discourses of anti-Judaism and anti-Islam for the same reason as their predecessors: to persuade members of their own communities to differentiate themselves not only from Jews or Muslims but also from others who allegedly bear purportedly Jewish or Islamic characteristics. The resulting rhetoric promotes not only discrimination but also and more importantly the adoption of a contrasting set of beliefs and practices. For that reason, it is important to analyze not only the claims that contemporary polemicists make about their Jewish or Muslim targets but also the ways in which they seek to motivate their non-Jewish or non-Muslim audiences. Attention to the similarities and differences between select examples of twenty-first-century American rhetoric and the premodern rhetoric we examined in this book's core chapters sheds light both on what has changed in recent decades—namely, ideas about Jews—and what has, unfortunately, persisted.

ABRAHAM'S HEIRS

Many people today refer to Christianity, Islam, and Judaism collectively as "Abrahamic religions," emphasizing that adherents of all three traditions revere the biblical figure of Abraham and claim him as a biological or spiritual ancestor. Those who employ this rhetoric within the context of interfaith relations seek to inspire present-day Christians, Jews, and Muslims to work toward a more harmonious future as equal members of a common family that shares fundamental values. Advocates for the notion of Abrahamic religions pointedly reject the anti-Jewish and anti-Muslim discourses that underpin premodern Christian depictions of Hagar's heirs. Like Paul and his successors, however, those who promote this concept seek to motivate audiences to differentiate themselves from their rivals, who refuse to include Islam within a pluralistic conception of admirable faiths similar to Christianity.[2]

In this respect, among others, *Abrahamic* is an expanded successor to *Judeo-Christian*. The latter term rose to prominence in the 1930s and 1940s within politically and religiously progressive circles as a means of combatting widespread antisemitic sentiments through the promotion of alternative beliefs and practices. Those who defined the United States as embodying Judeo-Christian values contested rival efforts by the Ku Klux Klan, Nazi sympathizers, and others to define America as Christian (read: white Protestant). During the Cold War, prominent Americans from across the political and religious spectrum contrasted the country's Judeo-Christian nature with "godless communism" in an effort to foster engagement in faith communities and interfaith activities. The term *Abrahamic* rose to prominence in an effort to combat a new set of ideological rivals: politically and religiously conservative Americans who promoted Islamophobia in response to the Iranian Revolution of 1979 and, especially, the Al-Qaeda terrorist attacks of September 11, 2001 ("9/11"). Abrahamic rhetoric, no less than the earlier Judeo-Christian rhetoric, motivates self-differentiation from those whose intolerance allegedly renders them unworthy heirs of Abraham.[3]

Some contemporary Christians reject the claim that Islam is fundamentally similar to Christianity. Unlike their premodern predecessors, however, these figures often link Judaism with Christianity rather than with Islam. Consider, for example, the remarks that evangelical pastor John Hagee delivered to an American pro-Israel conference in 2007:

> If a line has to be drawn, draw the line around both Christians and Jews: we are united; we are indivisible; we are bound together by the Torah—the roots of Christianity are Jewish. We are spiritual brothers, and what we have in common is far greater than the things we've allowed to separate us over the years.

Muslims, perceived as a threat to both the State of Israel and Judeo-Christian civilization, fall on the other side of Hagee's line.[4]

Christian Zionists regard the Jewish State of Israel as the fulfillment of God's covenantal promises to Abraham. Like Paul nearly two thousand years earlier, they appeal to biblical tales about Abraham's sons to bolster their claims and refute their rivals—now including those who promote visions of Abrahamic coexistence and Palestinian statehood. The root of the Israel/Palestine conflict, according to Hagee, is that "the Jews are descended from Isaac; the Arabs are descended from Ishmael." As such, the conflict has no resolution and Jews clearly enjoy divine favor. Just as Paul's rhetoric about Hagar and Sarah motivates Galatians to differentiate themselves from rival believers in Christ, American Christian Zionist rhetoric about Muslims motivates fellow Christians to adopt beliefs and actions that set them apart from their nonevangelical and non-Zionist rivals within American society.[5] (Similarly, it seems, the anti-Israel rhetoric of progressive American activists often motivates supporters of the Palestinian cause to differentiate themselves from local political and ideological rivals, such as progressive Zionists.)

As Hagee himself implicitly acknowledges, the notion that Jews belong in the same category as Christians rather than in the category of anti-Christians is a radical departure from premodern Christian thought. This notion is now widespread (albeit not universally accepted) within evangelical, mainline Protestant, and Roman Catholic circles. Many conservative Christians, however, continue to regard Muslims as paradigmatic anti-Christians. Modern and contemporary Islamophobic polemicists regularly reiterate Martin Luther's allegations that Muslims do not worship God, seek to destroy Western forms of government, and treat women in an appalling fashion. To return to the terminological distinction I made at the start of chapter 12, this rhetoric often takes the form of *antimuslimism*: it condemns Muslims as such for purportedly bearing these characteristics inherently. At other times, Luther's successors follow in his footsteps by using the discourse of *anti-Islam* to condemn fellow non-Muslims—for example, Mormons in plural marriages—who purportedly bear these characteristics as well.[6]

ISLAMOPHOBIA AND ANTI-IMMIGRANT SENTIMENTS

Virgil Goode is among these successors to Martin Luther. As a Republican congressman from Virginia, he published an opinion piece titled "Save Judeo-Christian Values" (*USA Today*, January 2, 2007) in response to news that Keith Ellison, a Minnesota Democrat and the first Muslim elected to the House of Representatives, would take his oath of office over the Quran.

> If American citizens don't wake up and adopt the Virgil Goode position on immigration there will likely be many more Muslims elected to office and demanding the use of the Quran. . . . Let us remember that we were not attacked by a nation on 9/11; we were attacked by extremists who acted in the name of the Islamic religion. I believe that if we do not stop illegal immigration totally, reduce legal immigration and end diversity visas, we are leaving ourselves vulnerable to infiltration by those who want to mold the United States into the image of their own religion, rather than working within the Judeo-Christian principles that have made us a beacon for freedom-loving persons around the world.

This rhetoric falls into the pattern we have seen throughout this book: Goode (polemicist) associates Ellison (target) with Islamic extremists (reference) on the grounds that both revere the Quran (criterion of comparison) for the express purpose of persuading American citizens (audience) to adopt a highly restrictive position on immigration (objective). Goode does not claim that the United States is inherently superior to other nations as a beacon of freedom. To the contrary, he insists that Americans must actively preserve that distinction in the face of threats posed not only by foreign Muslims but also and more urgently by fellow Americans, particularly Democrats like Ellison, who maintain that immigration and diversity enrich the country. In this respect as well, Goode's rhetoric resembles that of Luther and other premodern polemicists who worried first and foremost about the beliefs and behaviors of fellow Christians. Unlike these predecessors, however, Goode makes no appeal to the discourse of anti-Judaism; he seeks, after all, to save "Judeo-Christian" values.

Robert Bowers is among those Americans who adopted "the Virgil Goode position on immigration" but, unlike Goode, he also espoused long-standing negative ideas about Jews. Bowers, whose social media bio began with the declaration that "Jews are the children of satan. (john 8:44)" [sic], massacred worshippers at the Tree of Life Synagogue in Pittsburgh, Pennsylvania, on October 27, 2018. He explained his motivation in an online forum popular among white nationalists: "HIAS [a Jewish organization that aids refugees] likes to bring invaders in that kill our people. I can't sit by and watch my people get slaughtered. Screw your optics, I'm going in." Bowers railed against immigrants and HIAS in previous posts as well, including a repost of a telling statement by another user: "Open you Eyes! It's the filthy EVIL jews Bringing the Filthy EVIL Muslims into the Country!!" [sic].[7]

Bowers alleged that Muslims are "invaders" who seek to destroy American society through violence and that Jews undermine Western civilization by using their power and money to influence government policy and popular culture. These charges resemble those made against Jews and Muslims in fourteenth-century France—Muslims as aspiring infiltrators, Jews as well-funded and well-connected insiders—but neither Bowers nor other contemporary polemicists suggest a conspiratorial alliance between these purported enemies of America. While it is common for those who express antisemitic beliefs to also espouse Islamophobic ideas, there is no evidence that one set of ideas informs the other, let alone that Islamophobic antisemites present Muslims as Jewish. Because the negative characteristics that these individuals ascribe to Jews, on the one hand, and Muslims, on the other, differ radically, rhetoric about Jewish Muslims is neither plausible nor useful to them.[8]

Bowers's online activity exemplifies not only antisemitism but also the discourse of anti-Judaism, which, we have seen, seeks first and foremost to inspire specific behaviors within an audience of fellow non-Jews. His polemics motivate white Americans ("my people") to resist the "propaganda war against Western civilization" that Jews allegedly wage through permissive immigration policies and through the promotion within popular culture of diversity as a societal value. Bowers condemned not only Jews but all who allegedly bear or even tolerate these purportedly Jewish characteristics; President Donald Trump was among those whom Bowers placed in this category.[9]

Bowers and Trump differed in many respects, but both employed similar rhetoric about the danger Muslim immigrants allegedly pose to America. At the time of the Tree of Life shooting, the primary immigration-related news story related not to Muslims but rather to a caravan of migrants from Guatemala and Honduras passing through Mexico on its way toward the US border. Several days before the attack and, it seems, with an eye on the upcoming midterm elections, Trump alleged that the caravan included "criminals and unknown Middle Easterners." This allegation amplified baseless claims circulating in right-wing media that Bowers and others in his online circle accepted as fact. Trump and fellow polemicists associated Latin American migrants and refugees with Islamist terrorism in order to motivate their audiences to vote for Republicans who support building a wall on the border with Mexico. The target and reference have changed, but this polemical comparison closely resembles premodern rhetoric that branded Muslims as enemies of Christendom and likewise inspires audiences to differentiate themselves from members of their own society who do not conform to the polemicists' norms.[10]

THE PERSISTENCE OF SELF-DIFFERENTIATION

Well-meaning critics of Islamophobic and antisemitic sentiments sometimes call on Muslims and Jews to do a better job of proving themselves to their detractors. If only Muslim American organizations condemned Islamist terror attacks more loudly, one such argument goes, people would not accuse Muslim Americans of supporting these attacks. Arguments of this nature mistakenly assume that anti-Muslim and anti-Jewish discourses are grounded in fact-based reasoning. We have seen that this is emphatically not the case regarding premodern discourses, and the same may be said about contemporary rhetoric.

The persuasiveness of rhetoric about Muslims, Jews, and other out-groups rests not on its accuracy but on its plausibility, and plausibility depends not on facts but on the way in which one sees the world. Many Christians who understood human history as the timeless conflict between Christ and his enemies and who numbered Jews among those enemies considered it perfectly plausible that Jews of their own era would reenact the crucifixion on eucharistic wafers or the bodies of Christian children. This claim has no grounding in fact, but it is not baseless: it rests on core Christian teachings and, for that reason, it retained its plausibility well into the twentieth century.[11] Conceptions of Muslims as un-American also have deep roots impervious to evidence of patriotism among Muslim Americans. Not only are these false claims plausible within certain audiences, but they reinforce the self-identity of those audiences as truly faithful Christians or patriotic Americans who recognize dangers that others naively dismiss.[12]

Another common response to antisemitism, Islamophobia, and similar ideologies is to dismiss their adherents as unintelligent and delusional, or to brand ideologues as cynical manipulators of popular ignorance in pursuit of power or wealth. Historical evidence belies these stereotypes: some of the greatest thinkers of premodern Europe—and also of modern Europe and America—espoused antisemitic, Islamophobic, and other racist ideas. The inability of these figures to recognize the ways in which their preconceptions determined their perceptions testifies to their all-too-human limitations. To understand why many people past and present maintain ideas of this nature, we need to take seriously the logic that underpins their worldviews and the blinders that accompany these perceptions of reality.

None of this is to say that facts are irrelevant or that education is pointless. We encountered several cases in this study where widespread exposure to accurate information rendered long-standing claims implausible. Eastern Christian apologists, for example, changed the ways in which they portrayed Islam as their audiences became more familiar with actual Muslims, and European polemicists revised their conception of Jewish engagement with the Bible as they discovered the importance of rabbinic literature to medieval Jews. The latter example, however, also illustrates the tendency to replace one set of inaccurate ideas with another. Medieval Christian ideas about Jews, after all, remained grounded not in fact but in the logic of anti-Judaism. When ideas about proper Christianity shifted, ideas about Jews followed suit: Jews, for example, changed from being poor readers of scripture to eager killers of Christ to proponents of works-righteousness for no reason other than that Christians came to define themselves in new ways. What did not change—until recently—was the Christian practice of using the discourse of anti-Judaism to motivate self-differentiation.

"Gods change up in heaven, gods get replaced, prayers are here to stay." This observation about the relationship between theology and human behavior, by Israeli poet Yehuda Amichai, captures the intrinsic nature of anti-Judaism, Islamophobia, and similar discourses.[13] The specific claims about Jews and Muslims change, even the ideologies that these claims reinforce succeed one another in relentless fashion. The practice of defining "Us" in contrast with a Jewish or Muslim "Them," and of employing that contrast to promote specific beliefs and behaviors, endures. As a product of human culture, this practice need not persist indefinitely: contemporary shifts in attitudes toward Jews demonstrate the possibility of abandoning even the most well-trod rhetorical paths. Change of this nature, however, ultimately depends neither on facts nor on worldviews but on the commitment not to ground one's own identity in opposition to the identity of others. A commitment, in other words, to employ comparison more thoughtfully and compassionately.

Acknowledgments

Books may look like the work of a single author, but they in fact reflect the contributions of many people—in this case, hundreds. While I take sole responsibility, these individuals deserve a portion of the credit. I cannot possibly list them all by name, but I am nonetheless deeply grateful to each one.

I stumbled on the concept of Jewish Muslims through collegial conversations during a 2012 National Endowment for the Humanities Summer Institute on the Muslim-Christian-Jewish medieval Mediterranean. In retrospect, however, my research into the ways Christians used ideas about Jews to think about Muslims began in 2000 with a paper I wrote for a graduate seminar on medieval canon law. This book rests on knowledge and skills I gained thanks to my teachers and colleagues at the Columbia University Department of Religion and at the many other educational institutions that have formed me as a scholar and a person—perhaps most importantly the institution at which I teach, Colby College. I am also indebted to my current colleagues and to members of Colby's administration for the support and flexibility they provided during the process of researching, writing, and revising this work.

Dozens of colleagues, current and former students, friends, and family members have offered invaluable feedback on draft chapters over the years. Specialists helped me refine my analyses of sources in their areas of expertise, saving me from numerous errors (although some, no doubt, remain). No less importantly, nonacademic readers helped me find ways to communicate my ideas more effectively. I also received helpful feedback when test-driving book-related material at conferences organized by the American Academy of Religion, Association for Jewish Studies, Center for Medieval and Renaissance Studies at the University of California Los Angeles, Center for Religious Studies at the Ruhr-Universität Bochum, Middle East Studies Association, Universität Bielefeld, and Verein für Reformationsgeschichte/Society for Reformation Research, as well as invited lectures at Claremont School of Theology, Cornell University, Denison University, Middlebury College, New York University, and Pomona College.

Librarians are the unsung heroes of academic research. I could not have written this work without the aid of librarians at Colby College, throughout the State of Maine, and well beyond. They enabled me to consult thousands of articles and books, even in the midst of the COVID-19 pandemic. I am also grateful to Harvard and, especially, Princeton University for providing in-person access to their collections before the pandemic, and to the Lillian Goldman Law Library at Yale Law School for loaning microfilms from the collection of the Stephan Kuttner Institute of Medieval Canon Law during the pandemic.

Eric Schmidt, an acquisitions editor at the University of California Press, championed this project from the start and provided wise counsel throughout the decade it took for this book to move from conception to reality. I am grateful as well to everyone else associated with the press who expertly guided this book through the production process. Lisa Moore, a freelance development editor, went above and beyond in her feedback on the complete manuscript, which is much stronger as a result.

Sara Kahn Troster, my partner, has been a steadfast support since before I even began my academic studies and professional career. Our children, Ren and Jacob, have provided a wonderful mix of encouragement, understanding, and distraction. Neither words nor the dedication of this book to the three of them can adequately express my love and appreciation.

July 28, 2022
Portland, Maine

Chronology

Bold entries refer to individuals or works discussed in this book; bracketed numbers refer to the chapters in which they receive substantive attention. Key events to which multiple individuals or works respond appear in italics.

PRE-ISLAMIC

Crucifixion of Jesus: ca. 30 CE.

Paul (40s–50s) [1, 3, 12]: foundational figure who inaugurates the use of binary rhetoric—including rhetoric about Hagar, Sarah, and their figurative descendants—as a means of motivating followers of Christ to differentiate themselves from their rivals.

Gospel of Matthew (80s) [1]: account of Jesus's life, death, and resurrection in which John the Baptist dismisses the significance of claims that Jews descend from Abraham.

Gospel of John (late first/early second centuries) [1, 12]: account of Jesus's life, death, and resurrection in which Jesus alleges that Jews are descendants of the devil.

Tertullian (late second century) [1]: influential early Christian thinker who popularizes the interpretation of Paul's binary rhetoric as contrasting Christianity with Judaism.

Hippolytus of Rome (early third century) [4]: foundational theorist of Antichrist who asserts that Antichrist will rebuild the Jewish Temple in Jerusalem and persecute Christians at the urging of his Jewish followers.

Eusebius (early fourth century) [4]: historian who exemplifies the early Christian portrayal of the Jerusalem Temple's destruction as divine punishment for the Jews' crucifixion of Christ and as proof that God favors Christians.

Cyril of Jerusalem (mid-fourth century) [4]: preacher (and future bishop) who explains that Antichrist will win over the Jews by rebuilding the Jerusalem Temple.

John Chrysostom (late fourth century) [1]: provocative preacher who exemplifies the early Christian discourse of anti-Judaism, which he employs to motivate proper Christian behaviors through contrast with behaviors ascribed to Jews and "judaizing" Christians.

Jerome (late fourth century) [1]: translator of the Bible into Latin who crystallizes the early Christian consensus that Judaism is the binary opposite of Christianity and thus that Jews are anti-Christian; defines Arabs, whom he calls Saracens, as violent and idolatrous heirs of Hagar.

Augustine (d. 430) [1, 3, 11]: influential bishop and theologian who insists that Jews ought to live within Christendom because they attest to prophecies about Christ and demonstrate the punishment that befalls those who misinterpret these prophecies; applies Paul's allegory of Hagar and Sarah to justify persecution of rival Christians.

***Omnes* (506) [8]:** canon from Gaul (present-day France) that provides the classic legal justification for distinguishing Jews from other non-Christians— namely, that Jews misinterpret the Bible.

Cyril of Schythopolis, *Life of Euthymius* (sixth century) [1]: biography of a fifth-century saint that depicts Arab converts as "no longer Hagarenes and Ishmaelites but descendants of Sarah."

EASTERN CHRISTIAN

Muhammad establishes the Muslim community, ca. 610–632.
Muslim conquests beyond the Arabian Peninsula begin in 634.

Sophronius (r. 634–ca. 638) [2]: Patriarch of Jerusalem who portrays the Muslim conquest unfolding in his lifetime as the consequence of Christian sins that he defines as "Jewish."

***History of Sebeos* (ca. 655) [2, 4]:** Armenian chronicle that associates Muslims with Jews as descendants of Hagar and as allies in the conquest of Palestine and the persecution of Christians.

***Apocalypse of Pseudo-Shenute* (late seventh century) [4]:** originally Coptic work that portrays the construction of the Dome of the Rock as a sign that Antichrist will soon arrive.

***John and the Emir* (ca. 700) [5]:** Miaphysite Syriac text that features a Muslim who accepts the authority of the Old Testament, to whom the hero reiterates long-standing anti-Jewish arguments on behalf of Christian doctrines.

***On the Triune Nature of God* (eighth century) [5]:** Chalcedonian Arabic text that presents traditional biblical prooftexts in support of Christian doctrines to a Bible-believing Muslim foil instead of the customary Jewish foil.

Second Council of Nicaea (787) [10]: proceedings include the allegation that a Jew instigated the destruction of Christian images by the Muslim ruler Yazid II (ca. 723).

Timothy I (r. 780–823) [5]: Patriarch of the Church of the East who portrays Muslims as "new Jews" in order to frame novel arguments on behalf of Christianity in familiar yet shocking terms.

Theodore bar Koni (790s) [5]: theologian and educator within the Church of the East who compares a fictional Muslim student with a Jew because the student does not accept Christ as God.

Disputation between a Muslim and a Monk of Bet Halé (ca. 800) [2, 5]: Syriac text from the Church of the East stressing that Muslims, notwithstanding their high status in this world, cannot enter the heavenly kingdom because they are heirs of Hagar rather than believers in Christ; portrays Muslims as adherents of the Old Testament.

Theophanes (early ninth century) [4, 6]: Byzantine Greek chronicler who portrays the Muslim conquest of Jerusalem as a fulfillment of the Bible's apocalyptic predictions; compiles Eastern Christian tales about Muhammad that emphasize supposedly Jewish traits of irrationality and carnality.

Legend of Sergius Bahira (mid-ninth century) [6]: Eastern Christian tale, in Syriac and Arabic versions, that attributes positive aspects of Islam to a pious Christian monk who mentored Muhammad and negative aspects of Islam to a Jew.

Apology of al-Kindi (late ninth century) [6]: Anti-Islamic polemic in Arabic that depicts Jews corrupting the Quran, which had previously conformed to Christian teachings.

EUROPEAN CHRISTIAN

Egica (r. 687–702) [10]: Visigothic king who alleges that Muslims called on local Jews to act as one against the Christians of Spain.

Charlemagne (d. 814) [4, 10, 11]: first Holy Roman Emperor, commissions art and architecture that call to mind Solomon's biblical Temple by employing design elements found in the Dome of the Rock. Later Christians believe that Charlemagne will rise from his tomb to lead Frankish forces to victory against Antichrist and depict him as a character in the *Song of Roland*.

Council of Paris (825) [10]: reiterates the allegation lodged at the Second Council of Nicaea that a Jew instigated Yazid II's destruction of Christian images.

Maiolus (r. 954–94) [9]: abbot of Cluny and the subject of numerous tales regarding his capture by the Muslims of Fraxinetum in 972.

The Muslim ruler al-Hakim bi-Amr Allah destroys the Church of the Holy Sepulchre in Jerusalem, 1009.

Ademar of Chabannes (d. ca. 1034) [10]: chronicler who alleges that "Western Jews and Saracens of Spain" instigated al-Hakim's destruction of the Church of the Holy Sepulchre.

Ralph Glaber (d. 1047) [9, 10]: historian who blames the Jews of France for inspiring al-Hakim's destruction of the Church of the Holy Sepulchre; recounts the capture of Maiolus without depicting the Muslim captors in biblical terms and does not associate this event with the subsequent conquest of Fraxinetum.

Odilo (r. 994–1049) [9]: abbot of Cluny who associates Maiolus's Muslim captors with the Jews who killed Christ in order to portray the military conquest of Fraxinetum as "Christian."

Chronicle of Novalese **(mid-eleventh century) [9]:** non-Cluniac account of the conquest of Fraxinetum that makes no reference to Maiolus and does not depict the conquerors as "Christian" in nature.

Christian campaigns against Muslim-ruled regions of Spain begin in earnest, late eleventh century.

Pope Alexander II (r. 1061–73) [3, 8]: insists, in a letter to Spain's bishops, that it is just to fight against Muslims but not against subservient Jews.

Pope Urban II (r. 1088–99) [3, 9]: calls for a military campaign to liberate Jerusalem and Eastern Christians from Muslim domination. Some accounts of his inspirational sermon employ anti-Jewish tropes to depict Muslims.

First Crusade to the Holy Land begins in 1096, culminates in the conquest of Jerusalem in 1099.

Embrico of Mainz (ca. 1100) [7]: depicts Muhammad as the puppet of a faithless Christian scoundrel who seeks to lead Christians into heresy and sinfulness.

Lamb Tympanum, Church of San Isidoro, León (ca. 1100) [3]: depicts Hagar and Ishmael as contemporary Muslims, legitimating military campaigns against Spain's Muslim kingdoms in terms of the timeless conflict between Christianity and its rivals.

Song of Roland **(ca. 1100) [11]:** foundational work of the *chansons de geste* poetic genre that depicts Muslims as worshippers of a trinity of gods including Muhammad.

Saewulf (ca. 1102) [4]: early and exemplary European pilgrim to the Latin Kingdom of Jerusalem who portrays the Dome of the Rock as the biblical Temple.

Albert of Aachen (early eleventh century) [3]: chronicler who reports that knights understood their massacres of European Jews as part of their crusade against the enemies of Christianity.

Peter Tudebode (early eleventh century) [11]: participant in the First Crusade who alleges that Muslims worship multiple deities, including Muhammad.

Baldric of Bourgueil (ca. 1105) [4, 9]: chronicler who justifies the conquest of Jerusalem by alleging that Muslims reenact the crucifixion of Christ through their persecution of Christians; among those who depict the Dome of the Rock as the biblical Temple.

Robert the Monk (ca. 1106) [3]: chronicler whose version of Urban II's call for crusade depicts Saracens forcibly circumcising Christians.

Petrus Alfonsi, *Dialogue against the Jews* (ca. 1109) [6]: convert from Judaism who depicts Islam as the invention of Jewish and Christian heretics; contends that Islam, like Judaism, contradicts both logical reasoning and scriptural evidence.

Ralph of Caen, *Tancredus* (ca. 1112–18) [11]: biographer who reports that Tancred discovered a huge idol of Muhammad in the Dome of the Rock.

Liber Floridus (1120) [4]: encyclopedic work that depicts Christ's favor toward the Church and rejection of the Synagogue; its visual depiction of this rejection may represent not only the Jews but also the Muslims of the Holy Land.

Melisende Psalter (ca. 1131–43) [4]: illuminated manuscript that depicts Christ's entry into Jerusalem as if he is visiting the crusaders' Temple of the Lord (that is, the Dome of the Rock) and that portrays Muslim worship as idolatrous.

South Tympanum, Abbey Church of Saint-Gilles-du-Gard (mid-twelfth century) [4]: represents the Christian-Muslim military conflict in terms of the timeless contest between Church and Synagogue.

Mid-twelfth-century Psalms commentaries [3]: anonymous commentators layer anti-Muslim interpretations of Psalm 5 on top of long-standing anti-Jewish interpretations.

Gautier (Walter) de Compiègne, *Otia de Machomete* (mid-twelfth century) [7]: literary work that portrays Muhammad as a fraudulent second Moses who claims to restore Old Testament norms while in fact enjoining carnal practices that Christians themselves might find tempting.

Bernard of Clairvaux, letter promoting the Second Crusade (1146) [11]: insists that Christian soldiers ought to vanquish Muslims but spare Jews in keeping with Augustine's teachings.

Peter of Cluny (r. 1122–56) [6]: abbot who depicts Islam as the diabolical invention of a pagan, a heretic, and Jews, the last of whom introduced Talmudic irrationality into Islam.

Otto of Freising (d. 1158) [7]: chronicler who is the first to identify Muhammad's mother as a Jew; emphasizes that Muslims, like Jews, worship one God, accept the authority of the Bible, and observe carnal rituals literally.

Iudaei sive Sarraceni (Third Lateran Council, 1179) [8]: first canon to equate Muslims with Jews for legal purposes.

William of Tyre (1130–86) [3, 4, 8]: bishop and historian whose version of Urban II's call for crusade justifies the enterprise with reference to Paul's allegory of Hagar and Sarah and to the Maccabees' liberation of the Jerusalem Temple from Greek idolaters; played a leading role at the Third Lateran Council and may be responsible for introducing the reference to Saracens in *Iudaei sive Sarraceni*.

Muslims regain control of Jerusalem, 1187.

Huguccio (late 1180s) [8]: scholar of canon law who applies Jewry law to Muslims on the grounds that Muslims practice circumcision, dietary restrictions, and other Jewish rituals.

Bernard of Pavia (ca. 1190) [8]: scholar of canon law who creates the enduring legal category "On Jews, Saracens, and Their Servants" but maintains the traditional legal distinction between Jews and Muslims.

Cloister of Santa María la Mayor, Tudela (1186–1200) [9]: contains a sculpted image in which the biblical priests who conspired against Christ wear the clothing of twelfth-century Jews and bear an Islamic-style book.

Auto de los Reyes Magos **(ca. 1200) [11]:** Castilian play that depicts Herod's rabbinic advisors employing an Islamic phrase as they acknowledge their inability to decipher biblical prophecies.

The Beam of the Passion **(early thirteenth century) [9]:** work of art that anachronistically conflates contemporary Muslims with the Jews whom the Gospels hold responsible for Christ's death.

Chanson d'Antioche **(early thirteenth century) [9]:** French epic poem that frames the crusaders' military conquest of Muslims in terms of vengeance for the crucifixion of Christ.

Ecce vicit leo **and** *Animal est substantia* **(early thirteenth century) [8]:** exemplary of canon law commentaries that seek to preserve the traditional legal distinction between Jews and Muslims, in contrast to the argument of Huguccio.

Pope Innocent III (r. 1198–1216) [3, 8]: author of Jewry law who, at the Fourth Lateran Council of 1215, asserts the right to apply such discriminatory regulations to Muslims, in part on the grounds that Moses himself imposed rules on Muslims.

Summula Conradi **(between 1226 and 1229) [8]:** captures the new consensus among scholars of canon law that Jewry law applies to Muslims.

Izz al-Din Ibn al-Athir (d. 1233) [9]: Muslim chronicler who reports that Christians created an image of Muhammad killing Christ to rally support for the Third Crusade following the Muslim reconquest of Jerusalem in 1187.

Rodrigo Jiménez de Rada (d. 1247) [7]: bishop and historian whose *History of the Arabs* (1245) depicts a Jewish magician as exercising a profound influence on Muhammad and his parents, to the point that Muhammad incorporated aspects of the Old Testament into his teachings.

Sainte-Chapelle, Paris (1242–48) [11]: contains a stained-glass window in which the biblical prophet Isaiah condemns Jews who worship an idol of Muhammad.

Frontispiece of the First Book of Maccabees, Arsenal Old Testament (1250–54) [4]: represents Muslims as idolaters in order to portray crusaders as latter-day Maccabees.

Alexandre du Pont, *Romans de Mahon* (1258) [7]: Old French version of Gautier de Compiègne's *Otia de Machomete* that motivates French elites to control their own sinful inclinations.

First host desecration allegation (in Paris), 1290.

Hereford Mappa Mundi (ca. 1300) [11]: depicts Jews worshipping a coin-defecating idol of Muhammad.

Jour de jugement (early fourteenth century) [11]: French play that depicts both Antichrist's Jewish mother and the devils praying to Muhammad for a healthy childbirth.

Holkham Bible (early fourteenth century) [11]: depicts Jesus teaching "Saracen knights."

Water poisoning affair in France, April 1321.

Guillaume Agasse (June–July 1321) [10]: head of a leper colony who confesses that lepers rejected Christ and poisoned local water sources with the aid of Muslim rulers.

Mâcon letters (July 1321) [10]: forged correspondence from Muslim rulers to French Jews documenting a conspiracy to poison the waters of France so that Muslims could rule Paris in exchange for Jewish rule over the biblical Land of Israel.

Letter from Philip of Valois to Pope John XXII (July 1321) [10]: contains an elaborate forgery that depicts an alliance between Jews and Muslims who themselves seek to covert to Judaism; the purported objective of this alliance is to secure Muslim rule over Paris in exchange for Jewish rule over Jerusalem.

Oldradus de Ponte (d. ca. 1337) [3]: lawyer in the papal court who selectively associates Muslims and Jews as Hagar's heirs when arguing that Paul's teachings authorize military aggression against Muslims as well as the expulsion of Jews and Muslims from Christian kingdoms.

Eyewitness to the Execution of the Jews of Brussels (1370) [11]: reports that these Jews, convicted on the charge of host desecration, invoked their god, Muhammad, as they burned to death.

Workshop of Jaume Serra, *Altarpiece of the Virgin* (1367–81) [9]: depicts both the Paris host desecration allegation of 1290 with its Jewish villain and, adjacent to it, a host desecration allegation involving a Muslim.

Melchior Broederlam, Champmol Altarpiece (1393–99) [4]: depicts the Temple of Jesus's day using visual elements associated with the Dome of the Rock, including an Islamic crescent.

Towneley plays (written during the fourteenth or fifteenth century) [11]: an English collection that portrays Herod and Pontius Pilate, among other biblical villains, as worshippers of Muhammad.

Book of John Mandeville (Cotton Manuscript, ca. 1410–20) [11]: states that Saracens participated alongside Jews in the conspiracy to arrest and kill Jesus.

Flavio Biondo (d. 1463) [7]: humanist historian who defines Muhammad's ancestry primarily in ethnopolitical terms (Arab or Persian) but retains a theological dimension by identifying Muhammad's mother as a Jewish Ishmaelite.

Jaume Roig, *Mirror* (ca. 1460) [9]: misogynistic work that recounts a host desecration allegation involving a Christian woman and a Muslim cleric.

Rebels against Enrique IV of Castile (1465) [9]: allege that the king fails to safeguard consecrated eucharistic wafers from Jews and Muslims who seek to perform evil rites with them.

Paolo Uccello, *Miracle of the Profaned Host*, Corpus Domini Altarpiece (1467–68) [11]: depicts the Jewish perpetrator of a host desecration as a devotee of Muhammad.

Spanish Inquisition established, 1478.

Cristóbal de Gelba (1486) [8]: first Christian of Muslim ancestry subjected to the Spanish Inquisition, on the grounds that he allegedly engaged in judaizing behavior.

Marcus Sabellicus (d. 1506) [7]: humanist historian who, like Flavio Biondo, identifies Muhammad's father as a Persian or Arab and his mother as a Jewish Ishmaelite.

King Ferdinand and Queen Isabella expel from Spain Muslims who refuse baptism, 1502.

Gaudenzio Ferrari, Chapel of the Crucifixion, Sacro Monte di Varallo (1523–28) [11]: exemplifies the placement of Muslims in the crucifixion of Christ and other biblical scenes.

Petition by the Moriscos of Granada (1529) [8]: demands that inquisitors punish Moriscos only for adherence to practices mandated in the Quran, not for allegedly Jewish practices.

Martin Luther (1483–1546) [12]: foundational figure in the Protestant Reformation who draws on both the long-standing discourse of anti-Judaism and a new parallel discourse of anti-Islam to condemn not only Jews and Muslims but also Catholics and rival Protestants.

> **Lecture on Psalm 74,** delivered in 1514 (unpublished in Luther's lifetime).

> **Early lectures on Galatians,** published in 1519 (originally delivered in 1516–17): only the version prepared after the indulgence controversy of 1517 contains hostile references to the pope and to Turks.

> *On War against the Turks,* published in 1529: Luther's first work devoted to Turks, prepared in anticipation of the Turkish assault on Vienna that year.

> **Later lectures on Galatians,** delivered in 1531 (first published in 1535)

> **Preface to the Quran,** written in 1542, published in Theodor Bibliander's edition

Theodor Bibliander (d. 1564) [7]: prepares the first printed Latin translation of the Quran, which he publishes in 1543 alongside numerous other works about Islam; depicts Muhammad's mother as a Jewish Ishmaelite.

Bernardo Pérez de Chinchón (d. ca. 1556) [8]: one of many sixteenth-century Spanish polemicists who allege that Muslims observe Jewish practices.

Luis del Mármol Carvajal, *Descripción general de Africa* (1573) [7]: Spanish chronicle that depicts Muhammad's mother as "Jewish by birth and conviction" and identifies the Jewish magician who tutored Muhammad as her brother.

François Feuardent (late sixteenth century) [7]: theologian who alleges that Muhammad is Antichrist, partly on the speculative grounds that his Jewish mother committed adultery with a fellow Jew.

King Philip III of Spain decrees the expulsion of Moriscos, 1609.

Jaime Bleda (d. 1622) [7, 8, 9]: tireless proponent of the Morisco expulsion from Spain who alleges that these Christians of Muslim ancestry observe Jewish practices and inflict harm on the eucharistic wafer; identifies Muhammad's mother and tutor as Jews.

Louis Turquet de Mayerne and Joshua Notstock (early and mid-seventeenth century) [7]: historians who defame Muhammad by slandering his Jewish mother.

Notes

INTRODUCTION

1. In the eleventh-century words of Albert of Monte Cassino, "It is the function of metaphor to twist, so to speak, its mode of speech from its property; by twisting, to make some innovation; by innovating to clothe, as it were, in a wedding dress; and by clothing, to sell, apparently at a decent price." Translation adapted from Nirenberg, *Neighboring Faiths*, 189.

2. Cohen, *Living Letters*, 2 (emphases in the original); Lipton, *Dark Mirror*; Boyarin, *Judaism*, esp. 105–29; Nirenberg, *Anti-Judaism*, 6.

3. On the latter term, see Kendi, *How to Be an Antiracist*.

4. There are many competing definitions of antisemitism. On account of its simplicity, I quote the 2021 Jerusalem Declaration on Antisemitism, accessed June 15, 2022, https://jerusalemdeclaration.org. On the different spellings of this term, see Lipstadt, *Antisemitism Here and Now*, 22–25.

5. Murphy, *Representing Religion*, 144, 148 (emphases in the original).

6. Gavin Langmuir devoted much of his scholarship to critiquing the widespread association of anti-Judaism with theology and antisemitism with racism; his alternative proposal, that anti-Judaism is nonrational whereas antisemitism is irrational, is also problematic. See *Toward a Definition of Antisemitism*, and, for an assessment, Chazan, *Medieval Stereotypes and Modern Antisemitism*, 125–34. George Fredrickson is among those who distinguishes anti-Judaism from antisemitism on the basis of whether the goal is conversion or elimination; in *Racism: A Short History*, he presents antisemitism as a paradigmatic form of racism. On premodern European racism, see Heng, *Invention of Race*, chapters 2 and 3 of which examine the impact of such racism on Jews and Muslims, respectively.

7. Nirenberg, *Anti-Judaism*, 2–5, 430–39, on Karl Marx, "On the Jewish Question" (1844). A translation of Marx's essay, which does not appear in

most English-language anthologies of his works, can be found in the Marxists Internet Archive, accessed June 15, 2022, https://www.marxists.org/archive /marx/works/1844/jewish-question/.

8. "Jews will not replace us," a variation on "You will not replace us," gained widespread notice following a 2017 rally in Charlottesville, Virginia, whose stated purpose was to "Unite the Right" in support of white nationalist ideas and policies; the discourse of anti-Judaism furthered that motivational objective. On the rhetoric employed at this rally, see Neiwert, "When White Nationalists Chant"; Feshami, "Fear of White Genocide." An image attacking 2016 Democratic presidential candidate Hillary Clinton that featured a six-pointed star and piles of money likewise employs the discourse of anti-Judaism: it motivates voters to oppose a (non-Jewish) candidate by associating her with Jewishness in a derogatory fashion.

9. The term *Islamophobia* gained widespread use thanks to *Islamophobia: A Challenge for Us All*, a 1997 report by the Runnymede Trust, a British antiracist think tank. This report defined the term as "a useful shorthand way of referring to dread or hatred of Islam—and, therefore, to fear or dislike of all or most Muslims" (p. 1), implying that attitudes toward Islam drive attitudes toward Muslims. Runnymede's 2017 follow-up report, *Islamophobia: Still a Challenge for Us All*, instead declares that "Islamophobia is anti-Muslim racism" (p. 1), dropping the term's religious dimensions entirely. This latter definition is now widespread; see, for example, Love, *Islamophobia and Racism in America*. For a history of the term, with particular attention to debate over the original Runnymede definition, see Green, *Fear of Islam*, 9–33.

10. The quoted synopsis of Said's classic study, *Orientalism*, is that of Katharine Scarfe Beckett (*Anglo-Saxon Perceptions*, 10). Said himself devotes only limited attention to premodern sources, but his work has informed those of numerous premodernists. Scarfe Beckett offers valuable critical reflections on the applicability of Said's theory of Orientalism to premodern anti-Muslim discourse. See also, among others, Akbari, *Idols in the East*. My understanding of discourses as heterogeneous and my emphasis on analyzing individual statements within their broader discursive contexts align with the ideas expressed by Freiberger, *Considering Comparison*, 167–97.

11. Portrayals of Islam as a form of paganism and as a Christian heresy are well documented. See Tolan, *Saracens*, which builds on but does not entirely supersede the classic studies of Daniel, *Islam and the West*, and Southern, *Western Views of Islam*. Akbari, *Idols in the East*, analyzes geographic approaches to thinking about Muslims that derive from Greek sources as well as theological approaches grounded in the Bible.

12. Anidjar, *The Jew, the Arab*; on the plural yet singular nature of the enemy, see esp. 30–33.

13. David Nirenberg (*Anti-Judaism*) makes clear that anti-Judaism is not solely a Christian discourse: non-Christian and post-Christian thinkers also employ Judaism as a powerful foil against which to define their own communities and with which to promote their own ideologies. The same may be said regarding certain aspects of Islamophobia.

14. Soskice, *Metaphor and Religious Language*, 26.

15. Brauner, "Polemical Comparisons." On the influence of the "literati" in shaping medieval Christian attitudes toward Jews, heretics, and lepers, see Moore, *Formation of a Persecuting Society*.

16. Anidjar, *The Jew, the Arab*, xi.

17. Smith, *Drudgery Divine*, 51.

18. On the significance of juxtaposition within the comparative process, see Freiberger, *Considering Comparison*, 150–60; on taxonomic and illuminative modes of comparison, see 126–31. See also Freidenreich, "Comparisons Compared," esp. 88–94.

19. Tolan, *Faces of Muhammad*, 3; similarly, see Dimmock, *Mythologies*, xi–xiv.

CHAPTER 1. PAUL'S RIVALS AND THE EARLY CHRISTIAN DISCOURSE OF ANTI-JUDAISM

1. Countless books examine Paul's life and works, and scholarship on this crucial figure evolved dramatically in the late twentieth century. For an accessible survey that reflects these developments, see Sanders, *Paul: A Very Short Introduction*.

2. Paul's use of the term *judaize* here is unique in the New Testament. On the meaning of this and related terms in classical Greek, Jewish, and Christian sources, see Cohen, *Beginnings of Jewishness*, 175–97. On the passage in which this term appears and, more broadly, on Paul's vision of a Christ-following community whose Jewish and gentile members adhere to different standards because Jews alone are bound by biblical law in its entirety, see Freidenreich, *Foreigners and Their Food*, 87–100.

3. The phrase "ex-pagan pagans" is that of Paula Fredriksen, whose interpretation of Galatians (*Paul: The Pagans' Apostle*, 94–130) informs but differs from the one offered here. On Paul's belief that only certain biblical laws, later known as "Noahide laws," are universally binding, see Van Zile, "Sons of Noah."

4. On Paul's ideas about Abraham, see Thiessen, *Paul and the Gentile Problem*; on the ideas that Paul's rivals likely held, see esp. 26–32.

5. Tables of opposites appear frequently in Greek rhetoric; see Martyn, *Galatians*, 402–6, 438–39, and, on a much earlier period, Lloyd, *Polarity and Analogy*. Michele Murray (*Playing a Jewish Game*, 34–36) demonstrates that Paul's rivals in Galatia likely include gentile Christ-followers who had already adopted circumcision themselves and who sought to persuade fellow gentiles to do the same.

6. Paul is not the only member of his generation to interpret Sarah and Hagar allegorically. The Jewish philosopher Philo of Alexandria (d. ca. 50 CE) understands Sarah to represent pure virtue or wisdom while Hagar represents the school learning that prepares one to achieve this elevated state. See Bos, "Hagar and the *Enkyklios Paideia*."

7. On Paul's use of the term "Jerusalem," see Martyn, *Galatians*, 457–66.

8. This notion, absent from Genesis itself, appears in various early Jewish interpretations of Genesis 21:9; for another example, see *Genesis Rabbah* 53.11.

9. On Paul's Jewishness see, for example, Ambrose, *Jew among Jews*. The oldest surviving contrast between the terms *Judaism* and *Christianity* appears in the works of Ignatius of Antioch, active in the early second century; on his use of these terms, see Boyarin, *Judaism*, 112–18.

10. For a broader survey of early Christian interpretations of Hagar, see Clark, "Interpretive Fate," esp. 128–29.

11. My understanding of the relationship that early Christians likely perceived between Abrahamic rhetoric in Galatians and the Gospels is informed by Nirenberg, *Anti-Judaism*, 48–86.

12. Tertullian, *Against Marcion* 5.2, 5.4 (trans. Evans, 513, 531). Jerome, *Commentary on Galatians* 4:21–31 (trans. Cain, 187, 191–92). Galatians does not in fact refer to Jews who do not follow Christ, but Paul does so in his Letter to the Romans, esp. 2:17–3:8, 9:1–11:32. Twenty-first-century scholars differ sharply in their interpretations of these crucial passages. Various early Christian sources, and many twentieth-century scholars as well, contend that Jews persecuted second- and third-century Christians, but these allegations are unfounded; see Taylor, *Anti-Judaism and Early Christian Identity*, 78–114.

13. Chrysostom, *Discourses against Judaizing Christians* 1.4 (trans. Harkins, 16); the medieval title ascribed to these sermons is *Against the Jews*. On similar rhetoric in the work of Jerome, see Newman, "Jerome's Judaizers." On the term *judaize*, see n. 2 above.

14. Epiphanius of Cyprus (d. 403), in his catalogue of Christian heresies, routinely defines their teachings in terms of Judaism or "Hellenism" (that is, paganism). See Berzon, *Classifying Christians*, 130–44; on the distinction Epiphanius and other fourth-century Christians drew between these heresies and Judaism (or paganism) itself, see also Boyarin, *Border Lines*, 203–11. On Chrysostom and other early Christians who accuse heretics of preaching Judaism, see Nirenberg, *Anti-Judaism*, 87–134.

15. The identification of Arabs as Ishmaelites already appears in Jewish works from the second century BCE and features prominently in the late first-century CE writings of the Jewish historian Josephus. See Eph'al, "'Ishmael' and 'Arab(s)'"; Millar, "Hagar, Ishmael, Josephus." In Greco-Roman antiquity, *Arabia* referred not only to the Arabian Peninsula but also to the desert region stretching from the Sinai Peninsula into present-day Jordan.

16. Augustine, Letter 196.13, in *Corpus Augustinianum Gissense*.

17. Cyril of Schythopolis, *Life of Euthymius*, in *Kyrillos von Skythopolis*, ed. Schwarz, 21 (trans. Lamoreaux, "Early Eastern Christian Responses to Islam," 10).

18. Early Christian references to Arab circumcision include the *Letter of Barnabas* (9.6, which refers to Arabs rather than Ishmaelites), Origen's *Contra Celsum* (5.48), and Eusebius's *Praeparatio Evangelica* (6.11). These and similar works may draw on Josephus, *Antiquities* 1.214. Sozomen (*Historia Ecclesiastica* 6.38.11) asserts that Ishmaelites "practice circumcision like the Jews, refrain from the use of pork, and observe many other Jewish rites and customs" on account of their shared Abrahamic ancestry (trans. Stroumsa, *Barbarian Philosophy*, 77). See, further, Millar, "Hagar, Ishmael, Josephus," and, more broadly, Jacobs, *Christ Circumcised*.

19. On the term *Saracen*, see Retsö, *Arabs in Antiquity*, 505–25; Shahid, *Rome and the Arabs*, 123–41. More broadly, see Ward, *Mirage of the Saracen*.

20. Jerome's interpretation of Genesis 16:12 appears in his *Hebrew Questions on Genesis* (trans. Hayward, 49). His explanation of the term "Saracen" appears in his commentary on Ezekiel 25:1–7; this translation is by Tolan, "Wild Man," 517. See also the references in the following note. Anthony Hilhorst observes that Joseppus, the otherwise unknown author of the *Hypomnesticon biblion*, may have been the first to claim that Ishmaelites call themselves Saracens in order to usurp for themselves the name of Sarah (*Patrologia Graeca* 106:164); see Hilhorst, "Ishmaelites, Hagarenes, Saracens," 429.

21. On Jerome's references to Saracens and their European afterlives, see Tolan, "Wild Man"; Scarfe Beckett, *Anglo-Saxon Perceptions*, esp. 90–115, 134–37, and 198–217; Ogle, "Petrus Comestor, Methodius, and the Saracens."

22. One example of a premodern rejection of allegations that Muslims worship idols, discussed in chapter 7 below, is Otto of Freising, *Chronica* 7.7 (trans. Mierow, *Two Cities*, 412). One example of the allegation that Muslims practice idolatry in Mecca, discussed in chapter 6, is Petrus Alfonsi, *Dialogue against the Jews* (trans. Resnick, 157–58).

CHAPTER 2. MAKING SENSE OF THE MUSLIM CONQUESTS

1. Kennedy, *Great Arab Conquests*, 70. See also Hoyland, *In God's Path*, which draws extensively on seventh- and eighth-century Christian sources. On the rise of Islam, see Donner, *Muhammad and the Believers*.

2. Population figures for late antiquity are always estimates. This one comes from Sidney Griffith (*Church in the Shadow of the Mosque*, 11), who cites as his source Valognes, *Vie et mort des chrétiens d'orient*; I have not, however, been able to identify the basis for Jean-Pierre Valognes's estimate.

3. For broader studies of early Christian responses to the Muslim conquests, see Griffith, *Church in the Shadow of the Mosque*, 23–44; Penn, *Envisioning Islam*, 15–52. Michael Penn emphasizes that many Christian writers did not describe their Muslim conquerors, perhaps in a conscious effort to downplay their significance. See also Hoyland, *Seeing Islam*.

4. This translation of Sophronius's letter is by Robert Hoyland, *Seeing Islam*, 69; more broadly, see 67–74, and, especially, Olster, *Roman Defeat*, 99–115. David Olster addresses Christian responses to the seventh-century Persian conquest in other chapters.

5. Usener, "Weihnachtspredigt des Sophronios"; the translations and discussion that follow are informed by Sophronius, *Fêtes chrétiennes*, 31–51 (a complete French translation); Hoyland, *Seeing Islam*, 70–71; Olster, *Roman Defeat*, 106–11.

6. Cohen (*Living Letters*, 2–3) defines the term as follows: "the Jew as constructed in the discourse of Christian theology, and above all in Christian theologians' interpretation of scripture." See further Nirenberg, *Anti-Judaism*, esp. 48–134.

7. Papadopoulos-Kerameus, ed., *Analekta Hierosolymitikēs Stachyologias*, 5:151–68. The translations and discussion that follow are informed by

Sophronius, *Fêtes chrétiennes*, 61–86; Hoyland, *Seeing Islam*, 71–73. Anti-Jewish rhetoric appears in many of Sophronius's sermons. In one, the patriarch offers a table of opposites inspired by Paul's Letter to the Galatians; this table includes a contrast between the Jews as the fleshly descendants of Abraham and Christians as his children by faith. Unlike later Christians, however, Sophronius does not incorporate Saracens into this table. See *Fêtes chrétiennes*, 104.

8. The *Apocalypse of Pseudo-Methodius*, which makes no reference to post-biblical Jews, circulated widely not only among Eastern Christians but also in Greek and Latin translations. For an introduction to this text with an English translation of relevant passages, see Penn, *When Christians First Met Muslims*, 108–29. On the *History of Sebeos*, see below. The Coptic *Apocalypse of Pseudo-Shenute*, discussed in chapter 4, is exceptional among seventh-century works of this genre in its association of Muslims with contemporary Jews.

9. The *History of Sebeos* was once ascribed to a bishop of that name, but internal evidence does not support this attribution. For a brief overview and a comprehensive bibliography, see Greenwood, "History of Sebeos." For more in-depth analysis, see especially Greenwood, "Sasanian Echoes"; Howard-Johnston, *Witnesses to a World Crisis*, 70–102. *Sebeos* draws on Daniel's prophecy of the fourth beast (Daniel 7:4–7, 23–24) on three occasions, including in its account of the Muslim conquest of Persia and its conclusion; on this rhetoric, see Greenwood, "Sasanian Echoes," 375–88.

10. Translations of the *History of Sebeos* are slightly adapted from those of R. W. Thomson (*Armenian History Attributed to Sebeos*, 1: 95–98); I am grateful to Zara Pogossian for her careful reading of the Armenian original on my behalf. The terms "free woman" and "slave woman" (Thomson captures the Armenian more precisely as "handmaiden") are the same as those used in the standard Armenian translation of Galatians 4:22. *Sebeos'* account of the Muslim conquest of Palestine and its aftermath draws on one or more Palestinian sources. James Howard-Johnston (*Armenian History Attributed to Sebeos*, 2:238–40) and Tim Greenwood ("Sasanian Echoes," 365–66) disagree regarding the degree to which the Armenian historian adapted or simply copied his source material, but both ascribe the introductory language quoted here to that historian.

11. On Syriac accounts of Jewish resistance in Edessa and Jewish flight from that city, which differ considerably from those found in the *History of Sebeos*, see Hoyland, "Sebeos, the Jews," 90.

12. The ninth-century Syriac chronicler Dionysius of Tel-Mahre offers a similar account of Muhammad's rallying cry; see Hoyland "Sebeos, the Jews," 96–97. The ascription to Arabs of overstated claims about their Abrahamic ancestry is common. The eighth-century Syriac *Revelations and Testimonies about Our Lord's Dispensation*, for example, provides a retort that Christians can offer "if the wicked Jews or the Arabs say to you, 'Abraham is the father of the Jews, and the heathens' father is Ishmael, son of Abraham. And you, Syrian Christians, who is your father?'" See Debié, "Muslim–Christian Controversy," 228. Maximus the Confessor, writing between 634 and 640, describes the Arabs as "a Jewish people . . . whom God hates, though they think they are worshipping God." See Maximus' Epistle 14 in *Patrologia Graeca* 19:540; this translation is by Lamoreaux, "Early Eastern Christian Responses," 14.

13. On Ghewond's history, composed in the late eighth or late ninth century, see Greenwood, "Reassessment," esp. 133–42. Greenwood contends that Ghewond reworked the account of the Muslim conquests found in *Sebeos*; Howard-Johnston (*Armenian History Attributed to Sebeos* 2:241), in contrast, maintains that Ghewond drew independently on the same source material. For the relevant portion of Ghewond's work, see, in Armenian and French, *Łewond Vardapet, Discours historique*, 2–9; a less precise English translation appears in *History of Lewond*, 48–49.

14. This passage of *Sebeos* is ambiguous. Thomson understands it to mean that twelve thousand Ishmaelite soldiers emulated the biblical Israelites in their battle against the Romans (*Armenian History Attributed to Sebeos*, 1:96), while Hoyland interprets it as indicating that the Ishmaelites distributed twelve thousand Israelites among their troops ("Sebeos, the Jews," 89).

15. Some seventh-century Greek sources, including Epistle 14 of Maximus the Confessor and the *Doctrina Jacobi*, also report that Jews aided or at least cheered on the Muslim conquerors of Palestine; on the relevant passages of these texts, see Olster, *Roman Defeat*, 89–90, 171. Portrayals of Jews as supporters of invading forces are commonplace in Christian sources and can be found, for example, in accounts of the Persian conquest of Palestine. The historicity of these anti-Jewish allegations is suspect, not least because these allegations echo the longstanding notion that Jews are the prime enemies of Christendom. See Cameron, "Blaming the Jew."

16. *Armenian History Attributed to Sebeos*, 1:102–3. On this Ishmaelite house of prayer, located on the site of the former Jewish Temple, see chapter 4 below. It is unclear whether the *History of Sebeos* or its source already recognizes that Muslims regard pigs as abhorrent or whether, like the fifth-century historian Sozomen (*Historia Ecclesiastica* 6.38.11), it ascribes this abhorrence to Ishmaelites on account of their Abrahamic ancestry and purported affinity to Judaism. This report may also draw on Jewish traditions about how Romans used pigs to defile the Jewish Temple; on those traditions, see Rosenblum, "Why Do You Refuse to Eat Pork?," 103–7. On a later Eastern Christian tale about Jews who sought to spark a Muslim massacre of Christians, see Minov, "Christians, Jews, and Muslims"; I am grateful to Barbara Roggema for drawing my attention to this work.

17. David Taylor ("Disputation") introduces his edition with a detailed discussion of the work's date and place of origin. Translations that follow are slightly adapted from Taylor's. On the *Bet Hālē Disputation*, see also Penn, *Envisioning Islam*, 36–39; Reinink, "Political Power and Right Religion."

18. Taylor, "Disputation," 204. On the term *ṭayyāyā*, see Penn, *Envisioning Islam*, 56–59.

19. Taylor, "Disputation," 208–11 (quotations: 209, 211).

20. On the *Bet Hālē Disputation*'s use of earlier anti-Jewish works, see chapter 5, n. 9.

21. Taylor, "Disputation," 229–32 (Jews: 231, quotation: 232). Taylor observes that the author draws some of his language and cross imagery from the *Apocalypse of Pseudo-Methodius*; he frames its relevance, however, in terms of the present day rather than the end-times.

22. Taylor, "Disputation," 238–40. The monk quotes the Syriac version of Hebrews 12:6, 8; the Greek original explicitly refers to illegitimate children.

23. Taylor, "Disputation," 240–41. Taylor observes that the contrast between the son and the hired hand may stem from Jesus's parable of the prodigal son (Luke 15:19), which emphasizes that sons are always treated better than mere laborers.

CHAPTER 3. "DRIVE OUT THE SLAVE AND HER SON"

1. Some early New Testament manuscripts, probably influenced by the text of Genesis, end Paul's quotation in Galatians 4:30 with "my son, Isaac," instead of "the son of the free woman." In its new context, that phrase would still refer to present-day circumstances because Paul identifies his followers with Isaac. All manuscripts omit the pronoun "this" in both references to the slave: inclusion of that word would undermine Paul's argument for the contemporary relevance of Sarah's instructions.

2. Augustine, *Homilies on John*, 224 (Homily 11.13); Augustine speaks here of the Donatists. See Clark, "Interpretive Fate," 141–43.

3. Fredriksen, *Augustine and the Jews*; Cohen, *Living Letters*. The latter focuses primarily on the reception of Augustine's teachings about Jews and the challenges to these ideas that emerged in the twelfth and thirteenth centuries. On this latter period, see also Cohen, *Friars and the Jews*.

4. The definitive study of the Lamb Tympanum and its political rhetoric remains that of John Williams ("Generationes Abrahae"), whose insights underpin the present analysis. In this article, Williams contests the general attribution of this work to the period of Urraca (d. 1101), sister of King Alfonso VI. Subsequently, however, he affirms the consensus that the work dates to around 1100; see the postscript to the Spanish translation, 177–79. On the history and iconography of the Church of San Isidoro, see Martin, *Queen as King*, 30–95. On Isidore, see Tolan, *Saracens*, esp. 4–16; on Pelagius, see 94, 106–8.

5. Devorah Schoenfeld (*Isaac on Jewish and Christian Altars*) discusses the influence of Isidore's anti-Jewish rhetoric (81–84) and translates the *Glossa ordinaria*'s distillation of his remarks on Genesis 22 (161–63).

6. On the significance of Romanesque church portals as sites of visual communication to the general public, see Altman, "Medieval Marquee." On the social, rather than sacral, significance of the Lamb of God in the Lamb Tympanum, see Williams, "Generationes Abrahae," 5, 10. On the rarity of iconographic depictions of Galatians 4:22–31, see Williams, "Generationes Abrahae," 7; Moralejo Alvarez, "Pour l'interprétation iconographique," 140–41. Deeana Klepper ("Historicizing Allegory," 332–38) presents twelfth- and thirteenth-century illuminated manuscripts that depict the banishment of Hagar as representative of the banishment of the Jews; on the Lamb Tympanum, see 319–21.

7. On the depictions of Ishmael and Hagar in the Lamb Tympanum, as well as the licentiousness ascribed to Muslim women, see Williams, "Generationes Abrahae," 6–9. On the depiction of contemporary Muslim warriors in eleventh- and twelfth-century Iberian art, see more broadly Monteira Arias, "Seeking the Origins."

8. *Liber denudationis* 10.5, in Burman, *Religious Polemic*, 342–45; Thomas Burman suggests that this originally Arabic work was written in Toledo between 1085 and 1132 (49–53).

9. *Tathlith al-wahdaniyah*, as cited in al-Imam al-Qurtubi, *Al-I ʿlām*, 217; the anonymous author of this early thirteenth-century Arabic work sharpens his polemic by citing a prooftext from the Quran (9:98) as evidence that the nomadic Arabs who descend from Hagar are especially disbelieving and hypocritical. On this work and its date of authorship, see Burman, *Religious Polemic*, 70–80 (on Ishmael and Hagar, see 75), and Burman, "When I Argue."

10. For the full text of the pope's letter, along with similar letters sent to Narbonne in present-day France, see Simonsohn, *Apostolic See and the Jews*, 1:35–36. On Alexander II's encouragement of Frankish participation in Leonese expeditions, see O'Callaghan, *Reconquest and Crusade*, 24–27.

11. For a brief account of the rise of the crusading movement, see Riley-Smith, *Crusades: A Short History*, 1–17. On the term *Holy Land* as an invention and condensation of Crusade ideology, see Mastnak, *Crusading Peace*, 119–20.

12. *Robert the Monk's History*, 79–80. This particular allegation also appears in the spurious letter of Emperor Alexius Comnenus I to Count Robert of Flanders that commonly circulated with Robert the Monk's history (p. 219). Both works, which Carol Sweetenham tentatively dates to ca. 1106, sought to inspire participation in further crusading efforts (4–7, 215–18). On the various early versions of Pope Urban II's sermon, none of which accurately reflects the original, see Cole, *Preaching of the Crusades*, 1–36. On the allegation that Jews forcibly circumcised Christians, see Tartakoff, *Conversion, Circumcision, and Ritual Murder*.

13. *Albert of Aachen's History*, 1:37; Riley-Smith, "First Crusade and the Jews," 67.

14. *Willemi Tyrensis Archiepiscopi Chronicon* 1.15; this translation is adapted from *History of Deeds*, 89–90. Of all the prooftexts on which William draws, Galatians 4:30 is the only one that calls for action resembling a war of liberation; to the best of my knowledge, however, no other version of Urban's sermon cites this verse. William's reliance on Galatians rather than Genesis is evident in his use of the term "free woman" and his reference to "the slave" instead of "this slave."

15. William's condemnation of anti-Jewish assaults appears in *Chronicon*, 1.29; on contemporaneous figures who made this distinction in the context of the Second Crusade, see chapter 11, n. 9. On the Middle English *Siege of Jerusalem* and its relation to a vernacular version of William's chronicle, see Akbari, *Idols in the East*, 124–35.

16. *Patrologia Latina* 116:210, which erroneously attributes this commentary to Haymo of Halberstadt. Klepper ("Historicizing Allegory," 318–19) discusses this passage but misattributes it to Haymo of Halberstadt's ninth-century contemporary, Haimo of Auxerre. For evidence that this is in fact a twelfth-century commentary, see Gross-Diaz, *Psalms Commentary*, 118–20, and the bibliography cited there.

17. On the Latin text of Psalm 5's inscription, see Klepper, "Historicizing Allegory," 317. Jerome, whose translation follows the ancient Greek version of

the psalm rather than the Hebrew original, addresses this inscription in his Homily 2 on the Psalms; see *Homilies of Saint Jerome*, 1:15. There is no critical edition of the Interlinear Gloss, which achieved stable form in the twelfth century; I consulted *Biblia cum glossa ordinaria*, 2:461a. My translation conjoins two adjacent glosses, on the terms "her" and "obtains." A slightly different version of that gloss appears in the Eadwine Psalter (Cambridge, Trinity College, R.17.1, 9v) in conjunction with a prologue, a more thorough commentary, and an illumination depicting the psalm's contents. On the psalm prologues in this historically significant manuscript, see Gibson, "Latin Apparatus," 111–12. A more thoroughgoing anti-Muslim interpretation of Psalm 5 from the early fourteenth century appears in Nicholas of Lyra, *Postilla moralis*, 3:92v–93v.

18. The key portion of Alexander II's statement on Jews and Saracens appears in the *Decretum* as C. 23 q. 8 c. 11; the relevant Justinianic text is Cod. 1.11.6. On this canon and its twelfth- and thirteenth-century commentaries, see Herde, "Christians and Saracens," at 58–61. More broadly, see Freidenreich, "Muslims in Western Canon Law, 1000–1500," and chapter 8 below.

19. Oldradus wrote hundreds of consilia on a wide range of topics. Norman Zacour (*Jews and Saracens*) provides texts and translations of eight consilia regarding Jews or Muslims, along with a general introduction. The following discussion analyzes all four consilia that address both Jews and Muslims. Quotations of Oldradus are adapted from Zacour's translations, which place Oldradus's many embedded citations in footnotes for ease of reading.

20. For the text of Consilium 72, see Zacour, *Jews and Saracens*, 80–82 (Latin), 47–53 (English).

21. Oldradus endorses the expansive position of Henry of Segusio (d. 1271), the canon law commentator known as Hostiensis, that non-Christians have no right to exercise political sovereignty. See further Muldoon, *Popes, Lawyers, and Infidels*, 3–28.

22. Oldradus here follows in the footsteps of Hostiensis, who likewise applies Innocent III's decree (promulgated in 1205) to Jews and Saracens alike; see Kaplan, *Figuring Racism*, 141–46. On the use of Hagar rhetoric by Innocent and by Oldradus, see, further, Klepper, "Historicizing Allegory," 309–10, 340–42. On Innocent's decree in its original context, see Tolan, "Of Milk and Blood."

23. Oldradus cites Augustine's Homily 11 on John (quoted above at n. 2) as excerpted in *Decretum* C. 23 q. 4 c. 39, as well as an additional Augustinian passage excerpted in C. 23 q. 4 c. 42. (On the *Decretum Gratiani* and its citation system, see references in chapter 8, n. 1.)

24. Zacour, *Jews and Saracens*, 83–84 (Latin), 54–58 (English).

25. Consilium 264: Zacour, *Jews and Saracens*, 86–89 (Latin), 62–67 (English). Consilium 51: 85 (Latin), 42–43 (English). William Stalls ("Jewish Conversion to Islam") contends that Oldradus's consilium on this subject relates to actual cases in the Crown of Aragon (presently in northeastern Spain). The legality of conversion between Judaism and Islam remained a live question in that region into the fifteenth century, when various legal authorities strictly forbade it; see Nirenberg, *Neighboring Faiths*, 35–54.

CHAPTER 4. IMAGINING THE DOME OF THE ROCK AS THE
BIBLICAL TEMPLE

1. Pamela Berger's *Crescent on the Temple* provides an indispensable overview of Christian and Jewish visual depictions of this building as the Jewish Temple; on fig. 5, see pp. 185–87. On the building itself, see Grabar, *Dome of the Rock*.

2. Blair, "What is the Date"; Shani, "Iconography of the Dome of the Rock."

3. Hughes, *Constructing Antichrist*, 6; for a broader history of this concept, see McGinn, *Antichrist*.

4. Eusebius, *Life of Constantine*, 3.33, trans. Cameron and Hall, 135. On Justin, Origen, and Eusebius, see Gregerman, *Building on the Ruins of the Temple*, 19–136. On Constantine as a latter-day Solomon for his construction of the Church of the Holy Sepulchre, see Nibley, "Christian Envy," 112–14.

5. Levenson, "Emperor Julian's Attempt." For broader perspective on the significance that Christians ascribed to Jerusalem and the dangers they perceived in Jewish efforts to reclaim it, see Jacobs, *Remains of the Jews*, 139–99.

6. I am grateful to Jos van Lent for sharing a prepublication draft of his critical edition and translation of the *Apocalypse of Shenute* (cited: verses from chapter 5 of van Lent's translation), forthcoming under the working title *Two Shenoutean Apocalyptic Homilies from the Islamic Period*, as well as for his thoughts on the relationship between this passage's references to the Temple and to Antichrist. Van Lent ("*Apocalypse of Shenute*") dates this work (which survives only in a medieval Arabic translation) to 692–95, in part because he believes that it refers to the construction of the Dome of the Rock. For other references to Arab construction efforts on the Temple Mount in late-seventh-century apocalyptic literature, see Reinink, "Early Christian Reactions."

7. *Armenian History Attributed to Sebeos*, 1:102. Arculf's account appears in *De locis sanctis* by Adomnan of Iona (1.1.14); the translation is that of Hoyland, *Seeing Islam*, 221.

8. This account originally appears in the eighth-century *Chronicle* by Theophilus of Edessa; although this work no longer survives, its contents can be reconstructed from several works that draw extensively on it. See Hoyland, *Theophilus of Edessa's Chronicle*, 126–27. Anastasius of Sinai, writing in the 680s, contends that Muslims were aided in their construction efforts not by Jews but rather by demons; see Flusin, "L'Esplanade du Temple," 25–26.

9. Theophanes, *Chronicle*, 471. Theophanes's account of the encounter between Umar and Sophronius likely derives at least in part from Theophilus; see Hoyland, *Theophilus of Edessa's Chronicle*, 114–17. On tales of this meeting, see Sahas, "Face to Face Encounter."

10. Newsom, *Daniel*, 308. Dunbar, "Hippolytus of Rome," esp. 331–35; on the lasting impact of ideas found in Hippolytus's commentary, see Hughes, *Constructing Antichrist*. Cyril of Jerusalem, Lenten Lecture 15.15, in *Works*, 62. On Cyril's remarks in the context of sources about the subsequent effort to rebuild the Jewish Temple, see Parmentier, "No Stone upon Another?"

11. *Chronicle of Zuqnīn*, 240, cf. 233; I am grateful to Jan van Ginkel for drawing this source to my attention.

12. For that reason, the authors of Christian apocalyptic literature had to revise their conceptions of the Dome of the Rock itself. The *Apocalypse of Peter—Book of Rolls,* composed no earlier than the late ninth century, ascribes the following words to Christ: "Remember, O Peter, what I told you before the day when I taught the Jews in the Temple that 'there shall not be left one stone upon another in Jerusalem that shall not be thrown down'? Know, O Peter, that I will make the House that Solomon built in my name a dwelling place for my opponents, the wild asses. And next I will make it a ruin." Recall that Genesis 16:12 describes Ishmael, progenitor of the Arabs, as a "wild ass." See Roggema, "Biblical Exegesis," 148. I am grateful to the author for drawing my attention to this work.

13. Writing to Charlemagne in 798, Alcuin refers to Aachen as "Jerusalem, your chosen homeland, where the Temple of the wisest Solomon is being built masterfully for God." See Bianca Kühnel, "Jerusalem in Aachen," esp. 96. On the Dome of the Rock as one of the models for the Palatine Chapel, see further Gustav Kühnel, "Aachen, Byzanz." Similarly, Louis IX's Sainte-Chapelle, dedicated in 1248, incorporates references to architectural elements of the Aqsa Mosque, which Latin Christians called "Solomon's palace." These elements reinforce the king's claim to be a latter-day Solomon with Paris as the New Jerusalem. See Weiss, *Art and Crusade,* 65. Medieval artists and architects often incorporate only certain features of a building in their "copies" of it; see Krautheimer, "Introduction."

14. Pamela Berger (*Crescent on the Temple*) collects dozens of exemplars of biblical scenes in which representations of the Dome of the Rock appear; on the Harley Golden Gospels image, see 57–59.

15. *Bible moralisée;* the translation appears on p. 131. On the contrast between the Gothic architecture of the church and the pre-Gothic architecture of the Temple, see below.

16. Berger, *Crescent on the Temple.* European artists even adopted this convention in representations of the rebuilt Temple designed for Jewish viewers: see 197–223.

17. Cole, "Theme of Religious Pollution."

18. Wilkinson, *Jerusalem Pilgrimage;* Saewulf's remarks about the Temple appear on pp. 104–5, and the reference to the "Saracen chieftain," by the Russian abbot Daniel, is on p. 132. (Daniel misidentifies the builder as Umar, perhaps drawing on the work of Theophanes.) Achard of Arrouaise, who served as prior of the Temple of the Lord church from 1112–36, was among the first to allege that a Byzantine emperor—or, perhaps, Emperor Constantine's mother, Helena—built the building; several pilgrimage accounts echo this claim, with varying degrees of credulity. Michelina Di Cesare ("Prophet in the Book," 26) identifies several additional pilgrimage narratives that attribute the building's construction to Muslims. See further Kedar and Pringle, "The Lord's Temple"; Weiss, "Image of the Temple."

19. On Fulcher of Chartres and Raymond D'Aguilers, see Nibley, "Christian Envy," 229. For an English translation of Fulcher's remarks, see Peters, *First Crusade,* 92–93. Baldric, *Historia Ierosolimitana,* 7; William of Tyre, *Chronicon* 1.15 (trans. *History of Deeds,* 90).

20. Raymond D'Aguilers, *Historia Francorum*, 128. His term "Temple of Solomon" could refer either to the Dome of the Rock or to the Aqsa Mosque. See further Kedar, "Jerusalem Massacre." On literary depictions of Saracen idolatry associated with the Crusades, see Tolan, *Faces of Muhammad*, 25–29. On visual depictions, see Camille, *Gothic Idol*, 129–64. On fig. 8, see also Weiss, *Art and Crusade*, 163–66. On Muslims as pagans, see further Tolan, *Saracens*, 105–34.

21. Domed, cross-topped representations of the Jerusalem Temple also appear in the Melisende Psalter's depictions of the Presentation in the Temple and the Temptation of Christ (London, British Library, Egerton MS 1139, fol. 3r and 4r). See Berger, *Crescent on the Temple*, 80–84. On manifest anachronism within European art, see Nagel and Wood, *Anachronic Renaissance*. On the concurrent representation of Islam as paganism, Judaism, and heresy, see Akbari, *Idols in the East*, 200–247.

22. Bernard the Monk, *Journey to the Holy Places and Babylon* (870), in Wilkinson, *Jerusalem Pilgrims*, 266. The ascription of synagogues to Muslims already appears in the *Narratives* of Anastasius of Sinai, compiled ca. 660; see Hoyland, *Seeing Islam*, 99.

23. On the history of the conflict between Church and Synagogue, see Rowe, *The Jew, the Cathedral, and the Medieval City*, esp. 40–78; Rubin, "*Ecclesia* and *Synagoga*." More broadly, see Lipton, *Dark Mirror*. On the *Liber Floridus*, see Akbari, *Idols in the East*, 75–89, esp. 76–77; and, in depth, Derolez, *Making and Meaning of the Liber Floridus*.

24. On this work, see O'Meara, *Iconography of the Façade*, esp. 95–132; O'Meara addresses the *Liber Floridus* image on pp. 101–8.

25. On the Champmol Altarpiece in the context of other works that depict the Temple using both Gothic and pre-Gothic architecture, see Pinson, "Iconography of the Temple," 149–58. See also, with particular attention to the crescent, Berger, *Crescent on the Temple*, 159–66.

CHAPTER 5. "NEW JEWS": MUSLIMS AS FOILS FOR EDUCATING EASTERN CHRISTIANS

1. On the social context of Eastern Christianity during this period, see Tannous, *Making of the Medieval Middle East*. On anti-Jewish rhetoric among Eastern Christians, see Becker, "Syriac Anti-Judaism"; Rosenkranz, *Die jüdischchristliche Auseinandersetzung*. On the function of such rhetoric during the seventh century, see Cameron, "Blaming the Jews"; Olster, *Roman Defeat*; O'Sullivan, "Anti-Jewish Polemic."

2. For an analysis of these works that focuses particular attention on their rhetorical elements, see Freidenreich, "You Still Believe." Sidney Griffith ("Jews and Muslims") offers a valuable survey of these and other relevant sources; see also Jakob, *Syrisches Christentum und früher Islam*, 258–81. I cite more focused studies below.

3. Crone and Cook, *Hagarism*; "Judeo-Hagarism" is the title of chapter 1. On this book and its reception, see Donner's retrospective review as well as Shoemaker, *Death of a Prophet*, 1–3.

4. Penn, "*John and the Emir.*" Quotations below, including those of scriptural verses, follow Penn's translation. Penn observes that the emir's questions are common to most early Syriac literature on Islam (68). On Syriac terms for Muslims, see Penn, *Envisioning Islam*, 56–63. Crone and Cook (*Hagarism*, 14) cite *John and the Emir* as evidence that proto-Muslims revered the Torah alone.

5. Gerrit J. Reinink ("Beginnings of Syriac Apologetic Literature") emphasizes the significance of rhetoric about Chalcedonians within *John and the Emir.*

6. Severus of Antioch, Homily LXX, in Brière, *Homiliae cathedrales*, 26 and 29 (see also 21). This observation was first made by Nau, "Un colloque," 259n1 and 260n2; see also Reinink, "Beginnings," 177n71.

7. Gibson, ed., *On the Triune Nature*; Harris, "Tract," 76. On this work as a testimony collection, see Swanson, "Beyond Prooftexting," and Bertaina, "Development of Testimony Collections." Martin Albl (*Scripture Cannot be Broken*) concludes his survey of testimony collections by observing that "the form of the dialogue between a Jew and a Christian seems to be a literary fiction; the aim was to instruct Christians" and, indeed, these collections "were evidently part of the basic instruction of many Christian groups" (158). On the continued use of traditional anti-Jewish rhetoric in Christian works addressing Islam, see also Griffith, "Jews and Muslims," 82–84.

8. On the dramatic elements of this narrative framework and their impact on the reception of *John and the Emir*, see Penn, *Envisioning Islam*, 125–26.

9. Taylor, "Disputation," 225. The Muslim declares that "Scripture bears witness to [Abraham's] righteousness," an allusion to Genesis 15:6, and he stresses that God commanded Abraham to practice circumcision, a reference to Genesis 17:9–14 (212). Neither of these elements of the Abraham story appears in the Quran. The Muslim's reference to observance of "the sacrifices of Abraham" (208), however, may allude to the Islamic ritual that commemorates Abraham's deed: in his reply, the monk stresses that Abraham's near sacrifice of his son is merely a symbol for the actual sacrifice of Christ, the Son of God. On this work's discussion of that near sacrifice, see Reinink, "Lamb and the Tree." Crone and Cook (*Hagarism*, 12–13) cite the *Bet Hālē Disputation* as evidence that circumcision and sacrifice were core elements of Hagarism because they presume that this work was composed in the early eighth century; for Taylor's argument that the work actually dates to the turn of the ninth century, see "Disputation," 190–200. Robert Hoyland (*Seeing Islam*, 469–70) emphasizes the relationship between the *Bet Hālē Disputation* and the late-seventh-century anti-Jewish *Trophies of Damascus.*

10. See, for example, the disputation text attributed to Theodore Abu Qurra, discussed in Bertaina, "Testimony Collections," 168–71.

11. Timothy I, *Disputation*. For an English translation and early edition of this disputation, also known as Letter 59, see Mingana, "Apology of Timothy." For a summary and brief analysis, see Hunter, "Interfaith Dialogues."

12. Timothy I, *Die Briefe 40 und 41*; the passages cited below appear on pp. 3–4 of both the edition and the German translation. When preparing my own translation, I also consulted Hurst, "Letter 40." For a summary and analysis, with particular attention to elements of Letter 40 that resemble contempo-

raneous works by Muslim philosophers, see Griffith, "Syriac Letters," 105–15. See also Penn, *Envisioning Islam*, 79–83. On the dates of Letters 40 and 59, see Berti, *Vita e studi*, 56–57.

13. This later correspondence is known today as Letter 24, which Vittorio Berti (*Vita e studi*, 62) dates to the years 800–805; see *Die Briefe 3–29*, 1:123 (Syriac), 2:94 (German). For citations of other works by Timothy that refer to Muslims as "new Jews," see Freidenreich, "You Still Believe," at n. 6. Sidney Griffith, who opens his foundational study of Eastern Christian rhetoric about Muslims and Jews with this passage from Letter 40, speaks of "the 'new Jews' theme" in Eastern Christian sources even as he acknowledges that only Timothy uses this phrase with respect to Muslims; see "Jews and Muslims," 65 and 84.

14. Timothy I, *Die Briefe 40 und 41*, 1:64 (Syriac), 2:50 (German).

15. Widespread Christian conversion to Islam began no earlier than the ninth century and, quite possibly, much later; see chapter 6, n. 16.

16. On Timothy's rhetoric about Muhammad, with translations of the relevant passages, see Penn, *Envisioning Islam*, 108–10. Timothy draws on the classic anti-Jewish trope of biblical prophets hiding their own Trinitarian convictions from Israelites prone to polytheism (exemplified, for example, in *John and the Emir*) in his depiction of Muhammad's approach to teaching polytheistic Arabs; see Roggema, "Muslims as Crypto-Idolaters," 16–17.

17. Nirenberg, *Anti-Judaism*, 115. For references to fifth- and sixth-century works that refer to rival Christians as "new Jews," see Freidenreich, "You Still Believe," n. 6. On similar rhetoric that predates the Council of Chalcedon, see Shepardson, *Anti-Judaism and Christian Orthodoxy*, 118–56.

18. On the distinction between the rhetorical target about whom polemicists speak and their actual target—namely, their audience—see further Freidenreich, "You Still Believe."

19. Brauner, "Polemical Comparisons," para. 3.

20. Still later, Theodore appended an eleventh chapter on a tangentially related subject: Christian heresies. The *Scholion* survives in a dozen manuscripts representing two text families. For a text of chapter 10, see *Liber scholiorum*, 2:231–84; for a French translation, see *Livre des Scolies*, 2:172–211. On this work, see Griffith, "Chapter Ten"; Griffith, "Theodore bar Kônî's *Scholion*."

21. Michael Penn (*Encountering Islam*, 83–86) translates the key passages of the introduction to chapter 10 into English and makes a somewhat different point about Theodore's representation of the student. On the term *ḥanpē*, see also Penn, *Encountering Islam*, 67–69 and 165–66, as well as Griffith, "Prophet Muḥammad," 118–22. For the original text of Theodore's introduction, see *Liber scholiorum*, 231–32.

22. See further Griffith, "Chapter Ten," 171–74 and 185–86.

23. Theodore, *Liber scholiorum*, 276.

24. Theodore, *Liber scholiorum*, 283 and 231. The Syriac root I consistently render as "belief" or "believe" (*h.y.m.n.*) also means "faith" and "think," among other synonyms used by Griffith and Penn in their discussions of the *Scholion*.

CHAPTER 6. WHAT MAKES ISLAM JEWISH? ALLEGATIONS OF
CARNALITY AND IRRATIONALITY

1. On the origins of this collection of tales, see Theophanes, *Chronicle*, xliii–
lv, lxxxii–lxxxvii. On the relationship of these tales to Islamic sources, see Conrad, "Theophanes."

2. Theophanes, *Chronographia*, 333. Mango and Scott (*Chronicle*, 464) provide the first translation of the ambiguous phrase *kath' hēmōn tōn Christianōn*;
their interpretation accords with the eighth-century Latin translation by Anastasius Bibliothecarius (Yolles and Weiss, *Medieval Latin Lives*, 16–17). The second
translation, which is mine, understands the Greek phrase to include an implicit
indirect reference to "religion" (*tēn thrēskeian*). This term appears twice in the
passage, accompanied both times by the same verb and, in the first case, by an
explicit indirect reference: the Jews accepted Muhammad's *religion* while *forsaking* (*aphēsai*) *that of* Moses; later, they feared to *forsake* Muhammad's *religion*
and taught Muhammad matters contrary to [*that of*] the Christians. The tenth-
century Constantine Porphyrogenitus, quoting Theophanes, reports both that
Jews taught Muhammad to act against Christians and that they taught him aspects
of Torah such as circumcision; see *De administrando imperio* 80–81 (§17). My
understanding of this passage as hinging on Muhammad's sacrifice of a camel—
and my suspicion that the term "religion" refers specifically in this context to ritual practices—follows Hoyland, *Seeing Islam*, 506. I am grateful to Todd Berzon
and, especially, David Jorgensen for their thoughts on the meaning of this passage.
The allegation that Jews associated Muhammad with the long-awaited messiah
already appears in *Doctrina Jacobi*, a seventh-century Christian text; for a translation and discussion of the relevant passage, see Hoyland, *Seeing Islam*, 55–61.

3. Muhammad Ibn Ishaq (*Life of Muhammad*, 239–40) offers a classic
example of the Islamic stories that Theophanes's source may have known. Jews
living in Muslim lands also told stories about rabbis who wrote the Quran and,
in the process, embedded hidden messages testifying to the work's nature as a
forgery rather than a divine scripture. On these traditions, which may postdate
Theophanes, see Firestone, "Muhammad."

4. For examples, see chapter 4, n. 8, and chapter 10, nn. 1–2.

5. Theophanes, *Chronographia*, 333–34 (*Chronicle*, 464–65). John of
Damascus, writing in 743 or shortly afterwards, also associates Muhammad
with a heretical monk; see Sahas, *John of Damascus*, 132–33 (text), 73–74
(discussion). On the association of epilepsy with demonic possession, see Temkin, *Falling Sickness*, 86–92.

6. On Anastasius Bibliothecarius's translation of Theophanes's *Chronicle*
and its influence, see chapter 7, n. 3, below.

7. Barbara Roggema (*Legend of Sergius Baḥīrā*) provides editions and translations of two Syriac and two Arabic versions of this legend along with detailed
analysis of the relations among these versions, with Islamic sources, and with
later Christian tales. A Latin version of this legend, which contains no reference
to Muhammad or his Jewish associates, appears (without translation) in
Bignami-Odier and Levi della Vida, "Une version latine." On the relationship
among the various versions of this legend, see also Szilagyi, "Muhammad and
the Monk."

8. This summary encapsulates shared elements in the East Syrian, West Syrian, and short Arabic versions of the legend, labeled sections 5–6 and 10–16 in Roggema's editions; the long Arabic version departs somewhat from its counterparts. See Roggema, *Legend of Sergius Baḥīrā*, 266–85, 330–55, 388–409, 444–97. References to "the *surah* of the Cow," apparently understood to be distinct from the Quran itself, and to "Sergius Bahira" also appear in the *Bet Halé Disputation*; see Taylor, "Disputation," 192–93. In Syriac, the word *bḥīrā* is not a proper name but rather an honorific title often associated with monks; for that reason, Syriac storytellers needed to explain why Arabs referred to the monk simply as Bahira. On the use of these names, see Roggema, *Legend of Sergius Baḥīrā*, 56–60; Szilagyi, "Muhammad and the Monk," 197–202.

9. Ibn Ishaq, *Life of Muhammad*, 79–81 (quoted: 81, with slight adaptation). On this and other Islamic tales, see Roggema, *Legend of Sergius Baḥīrā*, 37–52; Roggema proceeds to demonstrate that the Christian legend is secondary to the Islamic one (52–60). On "parasitical historiography," see 30–31. For a comparative study of Islamic, Christian, Samaritan, and Jewish versions of the tale, see Freidenreich, "Muḥammad, the Monk, and the Jews."

10. Roggema, *Legend of Sergius Baḥīrā*, 394–95. On anti-Jewish themes in the short Arabic version of this legend, see Griffith, "Muḥammad and the Monk Baḥîrâ," 166; more broadly, see Reynolds, "Jews as 'Killers of the Prophets.'" On allegations that Jews sought to murder Muhammad, see Teipen, "Jews in Early Biographies."

11. On appeals to this quranic verse in Christian tales about Sergius, see Roggema, *Legend of Sergius Baḥīrā*, 105–13. In the short Arabic version of the legend, Sergius himself expresses disgust with the vision of paradise he teaches to Muhammad (404–5).

12. Roggema, *Legend of Sergius Baḥīrā*, 391; for Syriac parallels, both of which include reference to the Paraclete, see 268–69, 332–35. The long Arabic version, in contrast, contains no reference to Kab, and instead ascribes the Quran's scandalous passages to Sergius himself; see 508–25. On the saintliness ascribed to Sergius in Syriac versions, see Roggema, "Salvaging the Saintly Sergius."

13. On this figure, see Tottoli, *Biblical Prophets*, 90–91; Wolfensohn, *Ka'b al-Aḥbār*. On an Islamic tale about Kab's false teachings, see Halperin and Newby, "Two Castrated Bulls." On the Islamic allegation that Jews (and Christians) falsified the text of their own scripture, see Nickel, *Narratives of Tampering*.

14. Roggema, *Legend of Sergius Baḥīrā*, 269, 303, 335, cf. 391. On the association of Muhammad and the Paraclete, see Anthony, "Muḥammad, Menaḥem, and the Paraclete"; on Eastern Christian responses, see Griffith, "Prophet Muḥammad," 138–41.

15. Roggema, *Legend of Sergius Baḥīrā*, 303–5, slightly adapted. According to this text, Kab not only endorses the Old Testament's permission of divorce, a practice that Jesus and Paul condemn, but also invents a requirement that a divorcée must marry someone other than her ex-husband before he is allowed to marry her again. This Islamic rule, which various Christian polemicists ridicule, seeks to prevent husbands from summarily divorcing their wives. The roughly contemporary chronicle by Dionysius, Miaphysite patriarch of

Tel-Mahre (r. 818–845), also emphasizes that Muhammad enjoined circumcision and ablution while permitting divorce. For a reconstruction of the relevant portion of this now-lost text, see Jacobs, "Rise of Islam," 223–26.

16. There is no reliable demographic information regarding medieval conversion to Islam. Richard Bulliet (*Conversion to Islam*) sought to address this issue by tabulating distinctly Islamic first names found in the genealogical records of individuals notable enough to be included in later biographical dictionaries; on the basis of this data, he estimated that the majority of conversions to Islam in Iraq and Syria took place in the ninth and tenth centuries. Unfortunately, this data set is inherently nonrepresentative and also fails to distinguish families who gave their sons Islamic names to reflect their new religious identity from those who simply hoped to help their sons pass as Muslims. See the critique in Tannous, *Making of the Medieval Middle East*, 342–46, and, more broadly, Carlson, "When Did the Middle East Become Muslim?" For our purposes, however, what matters is not overall conversion rates but rather the perception of Christian authors that a significant number of community members found Islam to be attractive. Bulliet's data, which presumably oversamples literate elite circles, lends weight to the supposition that the creators of the written Sergius legends had reason to worry about Islam's attractiveness to contemporary Christians.

17. *Apology of al-Kindi*, 454; I revised Anton Tien's translation in light of *Risālat al-Kindī*, 83–85. For the somewhat different Latin version of this work with an English translation, see Yolles and Weiss, *Medieval Latin Lives*, 216–515, at 346–51. For a summary of the *Apology of al-Kindi*, see Tolan, *Saracens*, 60–64. On the textual history and authorship of this work, see van Koningsveld, "Apology of al-Kindî." Similar claims about the roles that Sergius Bahira, Kab al-Ahbar, and Abdallah ibn Salam played in the formation of Islam appear in the *Apocalypse of Peter—Book of Rolls*; see Roggema, *Legend of Sergius Baḥīrā*, 166–68. According to Islamic tradition, Abdallah ibn Salam was a highly respected rabbi who embraced Islam during Muhammad's lifetime. For a classic account, see Ibn Ishaq, *Life of Muhammad*, 240–41; for a thorough study, see Stafford, "Creation of Arabian Jewish Tradition."

18. On the conceptions of rationality that emerged in northwestern Europe during the late eleventh and early twelfth centuries, with particular attention to their implications for Christian conceptions of Jews, see Sapir Abulafia, *Christians and Jews*. John Tolan (*Saracens*, 135–69) surveys a wide range of twelfth-century European depictions of Muhammad, including those discussed below; more broadly, see Tolan, *Faces of Muhammad*.

19. Petrus Alfonsi, *Dialogue against the Jews*, 146–63; quoted: 146 and, in the next paragraphs, 151–52, checked using *Petri Alfonsi Dialogus*, 192, 200–202. On Alfonsi, the *Dialogue*, and its reception, see Tolan, *Petrus Alfonsi*; on the *Dialogue*'s fifth chapter, see esp. 27–33. On Alfonsi's portrayal of Islam as fundamentally Jewish in nature, see Halevi, "*Lex Mahomethi*."

20. On Alfonsi's portrayal of Islam as idolatrous, see Septimus, "Petrus Alfonsi on the Cult at Mecca."

21. Tolan, *Petrus Alfonsi*, 95–131 (quoted: 95, 109).

22. The translations that follow are slightly revised versions of Peter the Venerable, *Writings against the Saracens*, 38–40, checked using the edition and

translation in *Schriften zum Islam*, 6–9. On this passage, see also Kritzeck, *Peter the Venerable and Islam*, 129–32. On Peter's anti-Islamic writings more broadly, see Bruce, *Cluny and the Muslims*, 70–99, and Iogna-Prat, *Order and Exclusion*, 323–57.

23. Peter's conception of Islam's origins proved influential. Oliver of Paderborn (d. 1227) states in his *Historia Damiatina* that the devil dictated the contents of the Quran to Sergius and Muhammad. In a letter to the Egyptian sultan al-Kamil urging conversion, he tones down this rhetoric somewhat by ascribing the Quran to "some Jew and Sergius the apostate monk." See Di Cesare, *Pseudo-Historical Image*, 215–19. Juan de Torquemada (d. 1468) repeats verbatim Peter's account of the Jew joining with the heretic to create the sum of all evils in his *Tractatus* (p. 15).

24. For Peter of Cluny's critique of the Talmud, see book 5 of *Against the Inveterate Obduracy of the Jews*. On Peter's rhetoric about the Talmud, much of which postdates his *Summary of the Entire Heresy of the Saracens*, see Resnick, "Peter the Venerable." See further Cohen, *Living Letters*, 245–70; Iogna-Prat, *Order and Exclusion*, 275–322. On Alfonsi's critique of the Talmud, see Cohen, *Living Letters*, 210–16; Tolan, *Petrus Alfonsi*, 22–25.

25. Peter the Venerable, *Writings against the Saracens*, 171. This outline, in the form of abstract-like chapter headings, was drafted by Peter of Poitiers in 1155; Peter of Cluny died the following year. On the relationship between the outline, which envisioned four books, and the surviving work, which contains only two books, see *Writings against the Saracens*, 16, and Bruce, *Cluny and the Muslims*, 93–94.

26. Tolan, "Peter the Venerable," 367.

CHAPTER 7. MUHAMMAD THE JEW, AND OTHER MORALIZING SLURS

1. Tolan, *Faces of Muhammad*, 263; the French title of this book, tellingly, is *Muhammad l'Européen*.

2. Yvan Lepage (*Le Roman de Mahomet*) provides editions of both the *Romans de Mahon* and the *Otia de Machomete,* the latter edited by R.B.C. Huygens. Julian Yolles and Jessica Weiss (*Medieval Latin Lives*) reprint Huygens's edition of the *Otia* with English translation (104–77). Reginald Hyatte (*Prophet of Islam*, 37–95) provides an English translation of the *Romans*. I am grateful to my student, Sarah Shoer, for her insights into the *Romans*. Quotations from the *Romans* and the *Otia*, abbreviated as R. and O. respectively, cite them by line number and generally follow the published translations.

3. For the Latin text of these works with English translation, see Yolles and Weiss, *Medieval Latin Lives*, 2–21, 216–551. On the Iberian texts, see further Wolf, "Earliest Latin Lives of Muḥammad." On the influence of Anastasius Bibliothecarius's Latin translation of Theophanes's *Chronicle* in his *Chronographia tripertita* (written 871–74), see Kedar, *Crusade and Mission*, 33–35, 86–89.

4. Text and translation: Yolles and Weiss, *Medieval Latin Lives*, 24–101 (quoted: line 711).

5. Tolan, "Anti-Hagiography." Similar twelfth-century tales are offered by Adelphus (Yolles and Weiss, *Medieval Latin Lives,* 180–213) and the crusade chronicler Guibert of Nogent (*Deeds of God,* 32–36); on these works, see the following note.

6. Alexandre Eckhardt ("Le cercueil flottant") credits Embrico as the inventor of Muhammad's floating coffin; see more broadly Tolan, "Mangled Corpse." I am unaware of any author prior to Embrico who identifies Muhammad as a slave. Tolan discusses Gautier's *Otia* alongside the works of Embrico, Adelphus, and Guibert in *Saracens,* 135–47; he examines the *Otia* at greater length in "European Accounts," 228–32. On elements common to the works of Embrico, Gautier, and Alexandre, see Akbari, *Idols in the East,* 224–27. See also, with particular attention to the *Romans de Mahon,* Akbari, "Rhetoric of Antichrist."

7. The role played by the hermit in the *Otia* (35–70 and 576–634) and *Romans* (93–180, 1054–1157) resembles that of Theophanes's monk: both falsely confirm Muhammad's claim to prophecy. On the influence of Theophanes's *Chronicle* (in Anastasius's Latin translation) on the *Otia,* see Cambier, "Quand Gauthier," 539. No other Latin source, however, portrays the monk as pious or able to predict the future. These elements within the *Otia* and *Romans* call to mind Sergius in Eastern Christian legends (see chapter 6), which crusaders and other travelers may have encountered in the Holy Land.

8. Gautier's emphasis on the restoration of circumcision, as well as the tale described below about a well-trained bull bearing a copy of the Quran, may reflect familiarity with Guibert's work (see nn. 5–6 above).

9. Gautier may, however, indirectly critique the value of the emerging liberal arts curriculum by depicting Muhammad as thoroughly schooled in its elements: grammar, rhetoric, logic, arithmetic, astronomy, music, and geometry (*O.* 23–24; cf. *R.* 38–62). Peter of Cluny also condemns Muhammad for allegedly promoting circumcision and sexual promiscuity, but he does not associate these elements of Muhammad's teachings with Jews or the Old Testament; see, for example, *Writings against the Saracens,* 44.

10. See Tolan, *Saracens,* 137–39.

11. For numerous examples, see the texts collected by Di Cesare, *Pseudo-Historical Image.*

12. Otto of Freising, *Chronica,* 5.9 and 7.7 (trans. *Two Cities,* 337 and 412 [adapted]); these are the only two passages about Muhammad in Otto's chronicle. For the standard Christian interpretation of Isaiah 1:16, see *Biblia cum glossa ordinaria,* 3:4a.

13. Rodrigo Jiménez de Rada, *Historia arabum* 1–2, in *Historiae minores,* 88–89.

14. Pick, *Conflict and Coexistence,* 73–79; in this paragraph, I use Pick's translation of Rodrigo's words in *Historia arabum* 1. On Rodrigo's biography of Muhammad, see also Maser, "Rodrigo Jiménez de Rada."

15. Pick, "What Did Rodrigo Jiménez de Rada Know," 231.

16. Biondo, *Historiam,* 123; Biondo completed this work in 1444. Sabellicus, *Enneades* 8.6, 34r; Sabellicus, who first published this work in 1498, seems to rely on Biondo. Biondo encountered the tradition regarding Muhammad's Jewish mother in Godfrey of Viterbo's late-twelfth-century *Pantheon,* which

repeats Otto's genealogy verbatim; see Di Cesare, *Pseudo-Historical Image*, 180 (and, for Otto's work, 169). On the medieval circulation of Otto's *Two Cities* and Godfrey's *Pantheon*, see Weber, "Historical Importance," 154–58. On the geopolitical orientation of Biondo's work and his strategic association of distinct ethnic groups into a single Oriental enemy, see Meserve, *Empires of Islam*, esp. 187.

17. On the role that repetition plays in European biographies of Muhammad, see Dimmock, *Mythologies*, 24–25; the accounts that Dimmock surveys, however, make no reference to Muhammad's Jewish parentage. For examples of European scholars who took Islamic sources seriously, see Burman, *Reading the Qur'ān*.

18. Juan Andrés (*Confusión*, 89) identifies both of Muhammad's parents as Ishmaelite idolaters. The introductions to early Dutch and English translations of this work, however, identify Amina as a Jew: see *De zeer wonderlijcke ende*, ii; *Confusion of Muhamed's Sect*, unpaginated preface by Joshua Notstock. John Pory's English translation of Leo Africanus's *La descrittione dell'Africa* includes supplemental material drawn from various sources; for Pory's account of Muhammad's parentage, see Leo Africanus, *Geographical Historie*, 380.

19. Miller, "Sixteenth-Century 'Encyclopedia' of Islam," 243. I was unable to find any reference to Amina as a Jew in either a cursory search of Bibliander's 600-page anthology or in closer readings of many of its underlying sources. Bibliander, who may draw on Sabellicus, addresses Muhammad's parentage and its significance in *Ad nominis Christiani* (unpaginated; p. 24 of the PDF). Heinrich Knaust, Bibliander's contemporary, reports both that Muhammad's mother was a Jew and that he was educated by the Jewish astronomer who befriended his father; see *Von geringem herkommen*, b2a–3b, summarized by Miller, *Turks and Islam*, 52–53.

20. Mármol Carvajal, *Descripción general de Africa* 1:53r–v.

21. Turquet de Mayerne, *Histoire générale d'Espagne*, 202, first published in 1608. In order to work an Ishmaelite dimension into Muhammad's biography, Turquet asserts that the young Muhammad was captured by Arabs and sold into slavery to an Ishmaelite master. Joshua Notstock: see n. 18 above; Notstock derived his information about Amina's Jewishness from Baudier, *Histoire générale*, 14. For similar accounts, see d'Avity, *Les estats, empires, et prinicipautez du monde*, 1279; Purchas, *Purchas His Pilgrimage*, 199. See also Sandys, *Relation of a Journey*, 52. On English sources, see further Parker, "Preposterous Conversions," 8, and, more broadly, Dimmock, *Mythologies*.

22. François Feuardent, commenting on Irenaeus's *Adversus haereses* 5.30. In this passage, Irenaeus expresses confidence that the letters of Antichrist's earthly name, when assigned traditional numerical values, will add up to 666 (Revelation 13:18), but he cautions that the names of many people who are not Antichrist also correspond with that number. Feuardent, however, throws caution to the wind. He first identifies Martin Luther as an Antichrist—by spelling his name "Martin Lauter"—and then does the same for "Maometis." Feuardent offers no fewer than twelve proofs that Muhammad is an Antichrist, of which the numerical value of his name is the first and Muhammad's Jewish parentage the fourth. These proofs appear in identical form in both the first edition of Feuardent's

commentary, published in 1576 (372–74), and the revised second edition, published twenty years later (487–89). In the latter, Feuardent adds that in 1593 he was summoned to a hearing that challenged the orthodoxy of his claims about Muhammad. Feuardent states that the hearing resulted in the complete vindication of his arguments, but the mere existence of this challenge is telling. Irenaeus also discusses Antichrist's Danite ancestry in the passage on which Feuardent comments. On this tradition, see Bousset, *Antichrist Legend*, 171–74; Emmerson, *Antichrist in the Middle Ages*, 79–80. Eulogius and Alvarus, proponents of the mid-ninth-century Cordoban martyrs movement, were the first to allege that Muhammad was a precursor of Antichrist; see Tolan, *Saracens*, 90–93. On fourteenth-century English associations of Muhammad with Antichrist, see Paull, "Towneley Cycle," esp. 190–92. On other medieval associations of Muhammad with Antichrist, see Akbari, "Rhetoric of Antichrist." On early modern associations, with particular attention to Spanish sources, see Magnier, *Pedro de Valencia*, 151–61.

23. Bleda, *Corónica*, 5. My reading of Bleda as speaking tongue in cheek differs from that of Grace Magnier (*Pedro de Valencia*, 141–43), who understands him to endorse both Feuardent's allegation and its elaboration. I am grateful to my student, Alex Rhodes, for working through the text of Bleda's *Corónica* with me. On Bleda's rhetoric about Muhammad, see further Boase, "Morisco Expulsion," 21–22.

24. Bleda on Muhammad's year of birth: *Corónica*, 2–3; on Amina and Bahira: 3; on Muhammad's pride in his Jewish ancestry: 19. On p. 1, Bleda describes Muhammad as "the worst precursor of Antichrist," using that term to refer solely to the supernatural figure who will arrive at the end of days.

25. Nirenberg, *Anti-Judaism*, 244 (more broadly, see 212–45); Boase, "Morisco Expulsion," 23.

26. See further Tolan, *Faces of Muhammad*, which devotes particular attention to positive portrayals of Muhammad within European literature. Tolan, however, is only able to offer two premodern cases in which Christians portray Muhammad favorably: some Catholics argued that Muhammad attested to the Immaculate Conception of the Virgin Mary (126–31), and Michael Servetus appealed to Muhammad's teachings in support of his doctrine of Unitarianism (113–18).

CHAPTER 8. THE LOGIC, AND THE CONSEQUENCES, OF DEFINING MUSLIMS AS JUDAIZERS

1. The *Decretum Gratiani* and the *Liber extra*, as interpreted through their twelfth- and thirteenth-century commentaries, remained normative within the Roman Catholic Church until the early twentieth century. The standard edition of these texts is Friedberg, *Corpus iuris canonici*. For a brief introduction to these collections and related texts, see Brundage, *Medieval Canon Law*, 44–69; on the citation systems used to refer to specific laws within these collections, see 190–202. At greater length, see Hartmann and Pennington, *History of Medieval Canon Law*.

2. For comprehensive references to early medieval Latin canonical legislation regarding Jews, with comparison to canons regarding pagans and heretics, see

Freidenreich, "Jews, Pagans, and Heretics." For the relevant primary sources, see Linder, *Jews in the Legal Sources*; for in-depth analysis, with particular attention to the reception of these laws among twelfth- and thirteenth-century canonists, see Pakter, *Medieval Canon Law and the Jews*. On the canons associated with the early fourth-century Council of Elvira, see "Jews, Pagans, and Heretics," 76–79, and the citations there, esp. Laeuchli, *Power and Sexuality*. The phrase "even worse" appears in canon 9 of the mid-seventh-century Council of Chalon, which forbids the sale of Christian slaves beyond the bounds of the local Christian kingdom lest they come to serve non-Christian masters (Linder, *Jews in the Legal Sources*, 481–82). Pope Gregory I: Letter 3.37 (trans. Linder, 425). This letter appears in the *Decretum* as D. 54 c. 13.

3. *Omnes* was promulgated as canon 40 of the Council of Agde, convened in 506; it appears as C. 28 q. 1 c. 14 in the *Decretum*. On this and other Gallic canons about shared meals, see Freidenreich, *Foreigners and Their Food*, 113–18; on the interpretation of *Omnes* and related canons by commentators on the *Decretum*, see 203–7 and, esp., Freidenreich, "Sharing Meals." The latter includes texts and translations of both *Omnes* (47–48) and Rufinus's *Summa decretorum* on C. 11 q. 3 c. 24 (52).

4. See Freidenreich, "Muslims in Canon Law, 650–1000," and "Muslims in Western Canon Law, 1000–1500." Bernard of Pavia incorporates an account of Pope Zacharias's intervention into his *Breviarium extravagantium*, a late twelfth-century compilation of canon law also known as *Compilatio prima* (1 Comp. 5.5.2), but this particular text does not appear in the subsequent *Liber extra*; see Friedberg, *Quinque compilationes antiquae*, 55. On Pope Alexander II's distinction (preserved in the *Decretum* as C. 23 q. 8 c. 11), see chapter 3 above at n. 10.

5. Muslims also lived as a minority community in Hungary from the Christianization of that country in the year 1000 through the thirteenth century. The experience and legal status of those Muslims, however, differs from the rest of European Christendom. See Berend, *At the Gate of Christendom*.

6. Translation: Tanner, *Decrees*, 223–24. *Iudaei sive Sarraceni* appears as a single textual unit in every undamaged manuscript tradition of the Third Lateran Council's canons; it is customarily listed as canon 26 of the Third Lateran Council, but this council's canons circulated in widely varying sequences during the Middle Ages. See Summerlin, *Canons of the Third Lateran Council*, 147–51, 156, 161–66. On pp. 71–75, Danica Summerlin discusses *Iudaei sive Sarraceni* within the broader context of Jewry law but without any analysis of the canon's reference to Saracens. That term is clearly original, however: the definitive Latin edition contains no reference to manuscripts that omit "and Saracens" from the text of this canon (*Conciliorum oecumenicorum generaliumque decreta*, 145). On the council's ban against certain kinds of commerce with Saracens (*Ita quorundam*, customarily listed as canon 24) and its important afterlife, see Stantchev, *Spiritual Rationality*. For a brief treatment of the Third Lateran Council and its canons, see Duggan, "Conciliar Law," 333–41.

7. Alexander III, *Ad haec*; an extract of this letter appears in the *Liber extra* (X) as 5.6.8. See also *Quia super his* (an extract of which appears as X 5.6.4), in which the same pope worries that Christian servants who live with their Jewish employers will "be converted to the faithlessness of Judaism through

conversation with them." Alexander III may allude in these letters to a sixth-century letter by Pope Gregory I (4.21, X 5.6.2) that exhorts a fellow bishop "on account of your position and in consideration of the Christian religion to leave no opportunity for the simpleminded to become subject in any manner to Jewish superstition." Medieval interpreters understood Gregory's letter and *Iudaei sive Sarraceni* alike to forbid Jews from employing Christians in their homes; see the Ordinary Gloss to X 5.6.2, *retinere,* and, from the first decade of the twelfth century, *Animal est substantia* on D. 54 c. 13, *polluatur.* (On the latter work, see n. 13 below.)

8. Kedar, "*De Iudeis et Sarracenis.*"

9. Bernard of Pavia, *Breviarium extravagantium,* book 5, title 5; the equivalent section within the *Liber extra* is 5.6. On the relationship between Bernard's title and the Third Lateran Council, see Kedar, "*De Iudeis et Sarracenis,*" 207.

10. Bernard of Pavia, *Summa decretalium,* 210–11 (definition of heretics: 213); Bernard composed this work, an explanatory summary of his *Breviariam decretalium,* in the 1190s. Bernard, following Jerome (see chapter 1 above), erroneously asserts that "Saracens" call themselves by this name to claim descent from Abraham's wife Sarah and thus hide their descent from her slave, Hagar; he also employs the term "pagans" when referring to Muslims. For overviews of Roman Catholic "Saracen law," see the references in n. 4 above.

11. Huguccio, *Summa decretorum,* on D. 54 d.a.c. 13, transcribed and discussed in Freidenreich, "Sharing Meals," 60; see also Pakter, *Medieval Canon Law,* 119. On this work, see Müller, "*Summa decretorum* of Huguccio." Unfortunately, most of the *Summa decretorum* is only available in unpublished medieval manuscripts.

12. Huguccio, *Summa decretorum,* on C. 11 q. 3 c. 24; transcribed and discussed in Freidenreich, "Sharing Meals," 59–64.

13. *Ecce vicit leo* on C. 11 q. 3 c. 24, transcribed and discussed in Freidenreich, "Sharing Meals," 62; the second recension of this commentary, on which this transcription is based, was written ca. 1210. *Animal est substantia* (ca. 1206–1216) on D. 54 c. 13, *Mancipia,* as edited by E.C. Coppens; the commentator cites Codex Justinianus 1.10.1 and 1.3.54. Coppens's incomplete and unpublished edition, available online (the Radboud Repository, accessed June 15, 2022, https://repository.ubn.ru.nl/handle/2066/197926), does not include C. 11 q. 3 c. 24, but the version of that comment in MS Liège Bibl. de l'Université 127 E, fol. 142v, also contains a version of the passage quoted from *Ecce vicit leo.* I was unable to consult *Ecce vicit leo* on D. 54 c. 13.

14. Translation: Tanner, *Decrees,* 266. Of the twenty manuscripts that underpin García y García, *Constitutiones Concilii quarti Lateranensis,* 107, six omit the clause about Moses. This clause is also absent from the version of this canon that appears in the *Liber extra* (5.6.15), perhaps because its editor, Ramon Penyafort, was personally knowledgeable about Islam; this explanation may likewise account for the omission of the clause in some manuscripts. I am grateful to Rowan Dorin for his insights regarding this canon.

15. On the Fourth Lateran canons and the pope's personal role in drafting them, see Duggan, "Conciliar Law," 341–52, esp. 343; Moore, *Pope Innocent III,* 228–51, esp. 237. More broadly, see Chazan, "Pope Innocent III and the

Jews." Ten years before the Fourth Lateran Council, however, Innocent III did not seize an obvious opportunity to similarly associate Jews with Saracens. In a letter to Alfonso VIII of Castile, the pope reprimands the king for favoring his non-Christian subjects in their financial dealings with church officials. "While the Synagogue waxes, the Church wanes, and the slave woman is placed before the free." Innocent associates Hagar with the Jews alone when he could easily have included Saracens as well. A few sentences later, he contrasts the Church with "the Synagogue and the Mosque," making clear that, as he sees it at the time, Muslims are distinct from Jews. For the full text, see Simonsohn, *Apostolic See and the Jews*, 1:85–86; for an abridged text with English translation, see Grayzel, *Church and the Jews*, 112–13. (The translation above is mine.)

16. Pope Innocent IV (r. 1243–54) articulates most clearly the claims that thirteenth-century popes made regarding their authority over non-Christians; see Muldoon, *Popes, Lawyers, and Infidels*, esp. 10–11.

17. Bernard of Pavia, *Summa Decretalium*, 210; Bernard makes no effort to reconcile his assertion that Samaritans are Saracens with his definition of Saracens as those who reject both Old and New Testaments.

18. On the influence of canon law scholarship on Innocent III's legislation, see Pennington, "Innocent III," 2.

19. The Fourth Lateran Council's canon on public office (c. 69, X 5.6.16) is known as *Cum nimis absurdum* (trans. Tanner, *Decrees*, 266–67). Unlike the previous canon, this one requires no special claim of authority because it regulates the behavior of the Christians who make appointments to public office rather than the non-Christians who might hold such office. I am not aware of any subsequent work of ecclesiastical legislation that seeks to restrict the appearance of Muslims in public during the Easter season. To the best of my knowledge, only two local church councils—both held in cities with sizable Muslim populations—extended to Saracens the prohibition against holding public office: Buda 1279, c. 125, and Valladolid 1322, c. 22. For these and other works of local ecclesiastical legislation, see Corpus Synodalium: Local Legislation in Medieval Europe, accessed June 15, 2022, https://corpus-synodalium.com.

20. Renard, *Trois sommes de pénitence*, 2:87. More broadly, see Stantchev, "Apply to Muslims." Stafan Stantchev (*Spiritual Rationality*, 91–104) demonstrates that the papal practice of forbidding certain kinds of commerce with Muslims eventually inspired similar bans on commerce with Jews, heretics, Baltic pagans, and various Christian polities, but these later bans do not rest on a claim that the proscribed groups are equivalent to Saracens.

21. See Resnick, "The Jews' Badge"; Echevarria, "Marks of the Other."

22. This paragraph summarizes data gleaned from a preliminary study of Jews and Saracens in local canon law; I look forward to publishing further details in the future. See also Szpiech, "Saracens and Church Councils."

23. On Christian ideas about Moriscos, see Constable, *To Live like a Moor*; Tueller, *Good and Faithful Christians*; Perceval, *Todos son uno*.

24. "Memoria de diversos autos" (Philadelphia, University of Pennsylvania Ms. Codex 1484), 7v, 13v; Monter, *Frontiers of Heresy*, 24–25.

25. For the text of Ferdinand and Isabella's edict, see Carrasco Manchado, *De la convivencia a la exclusión*, 233–37. On the efforts of Granada's bishop,

Hernando de Talavera, to instill proper Christian practice among former Muslims, see Scotto, "Conflation of Judaism and Islam." Davide Scotto demonstrates that Talavera employed the same methods when preaching to Christians of Muslim and of Jewish ancestry even though he did not regard Islam and Judaism as equivalent. It seems unlikely that Talavera himself would have accused Moriscos of judaizing.

26. See Stuczynski, "Two Minorities," at 138–39, and the sources to which he refers.

27. Salvatierra: Boronat y Barrachina, *Los moriscos españoles*, 1.618, 632. Bleda, *Defensio fidei*; see esp. 28 (quoted), 32–36, 38, 44–45, 48, 57–64, 100, 102–3, 106. On this work, see Glazer-Eytan, "Conversos, Moriscos, and the Eucharist," at 286–89. What makes Islamic fasting Jewish, according to Bleda, is the practice of abstaining from all food and drink rather than adopting a restricted diet.

28. For Juan de Ribera on Catholic kings, see Tueller, *Good and Faithful Christians*, 121. For Ribera on Moriscos as Israelites, see Feros, "Rhetorics of the Expulsion," 75. Similarly, Pedro Aznar Cardona (*Expulsion justificada*, 175v–176r) appeals to Psalm 78:21–22. On the use of biblical texts in rhetoric promoting expulsion of the Moriscos, see Boase, "Morisco Expulsion." More broadly, see Magnier, *Pedro de Valencia*.

29. David Nirenberg (*Anti-Judaism*, 217–45) demonstrates the applicability of this observation to Spanish Christian rhetoric about fellow Christians; the quotation from Horkheimer and Adorno appears on p. 240.

CHAPTER 9. MUSLIMS KILLED CHRIST!? THEOLOGICAL ARGUMENTS AND POLITICAL AGENDAS

1. Brauner, "Polemical Comparisons," para. 1. On the roles of Jews and Muslims—and also of religion and politics—in the formation of European identity, see further Anidjar, *The Jew, the Arab*, discussed in the introduction above.

2. John of Damascus (d. 749) was the first to address this issue; thirteenth-century Latin authors who did the same include Mark of Toledo, Ramon Martí, and Thomas Aquinas. For references, see Tolan, *Saracens*, 52, 183, 237, 244. More broadly, see Robinson, *Christ in Islam and Christianity*.

3. For a detailed study of Maiolus's abduction, Cluniac tales about it, and the long-term impact of these tales, see Bruce, *Cluny and the Muslims*. On the Muslim community itself, see Ballan, "Fraxinetum."

4. Clark, *Chronicle of Novalese*, 92–93 (English), 209–10 (Latin). This chronicle, which dates from the mid-eleventh century, is similar to other non-Cluniac sources regarding Fraxinetum's destruction in that none of these sources mentions Cluny's abbot. See Zerner, "La capture de Maïeul."

5. On Cluniac tales about the abduction of Maiolus, see Bruce, *Cluny and the Muslims*, 41–62; on the ransom note, which Scott Bruce plausibly attributes to Maiolus himself, see 34–39. I cite Bruce's translation of Syrus, *Life of Maiolus* 3.5. This author bolsters the contrast he draws between civilized Christians and barbarous Saracens by using imagery from the *Aeneid*, Virgil's classic epic about the origins of Rome. Text: Iogna-Prat, *Agni immaculati*, 247–60. Ralph

Glaber added an account of Maiolus's abduction to his *Histories* (1.4.9) after spending time at Cluny between 1030 and 1035, where he probably encountered Syrus's work among other relevant sources. Text: Glaber, *Histories*, 18–23; date: xxxiv–xlv. R. W. Southern (*Western Views of Islam*, 28) identifies this passage as the first reference to Muhammad by a Northern European.

6. Odilo, *Vita sancti Maioli*, 289; for a French translation, see Iogna-Prat, et al., *Saint Maïeul*, 37–38.

7. William donated to Cluny properties he gained through the defeat of the Saracens of Fraxinetum in what he described in his bequest as "war in the name of Saint Maiolus"; see Iogna-Prat, *Agni immaculati*, 120–21. Reference to William as the liberator of Fraxinetum also appears in subsequent Cluniac sources, including Glaber's *Histories*, but William is absent from the non-Cluniac sources of the tenth and early eleventh centuries discussed in Zerner, "Capture de Maïeul"; on William's donation, see p. 210 of Zerner's article. (Modern historians commonly credit the victory to both William and Robald.) Glaber, unlike the various Cluniac biographers of Maiolus, does not suggest any causal relationship between the abduction of the abbot and the destruction of Fraxinetum, nor does he indicate that God inspired William's attack.

8. Mastnak, *Crusading Peace*, 1–54; on Bishop Adalbero of Laon's critique of Odilo (quoted: *Carmen ad Rotbertum Francorum regem*, line 115), see 24–25. See also Iogna-Prat, *Agni immaculati*, 361–62.

9. Baldric, *Historia Ierosolimitana*, 108 (trans. Riley-Smith, "First Crusade and the Persecution of the Jews," 68). This sermon stems from Baldric's own imagination rather than from the testimony of crusaders. On the theme of vengeance in other crusade chronicles, see chapter 3 above. The New Testament speaks of multiple Jewish kings named Herod. The most famous, Herod the Great, is said to have massacred innocent children in his effort to kill the newborn Jesus (see chapter 11 below). Baldric, however, may refer to Herod Antipas, son of Herod the Great; according to Luke 23:7–12, this Herod mocked Jesus during his final trial and became friends with Pilate.

10. *Chanson d'Antioche*, trans. Edgington and Sweetenham; the quotations in this paragraph are from *laisses* (roughly: verses) 8–11. The *Chanson d'Antioche* ascribes to Jews the roles that Romans played in the New Testament's depictions of the crucifixion, which makes it easier for the poet to portray the Roman emperors—and, by extension, the European crusaders—as Christ's faithful avengers.

11. Peter of Cluny, for example, lodged this allegation against the Jews in 1146; see Chazan, *From Anti-Judaism to Anti-Semitism*, 123–24.

12. Ibn al-Athir, *Chronicle*, 363–64, slightly revised. I am unaware of Christian sources related to the Third Crusade that refer to such propaganda, but I see little reason to question the reliability of Ibn al-Athir's report about its existence.

13. For a detailed study, see Freidenreich and Plesch, "What is That to Us?" I am grateful to Véronique Plesch and to our student, Anna Spencer, for their insights into this work.

14. On the stereotypes evident in the *Beam of the Passion* and their association with Muslim soldiers, see Monteira Arias, "Seeking the Origins," esp. 97–102; see also Patton, *Art of Estrangement*, 113–19.

15. On the association of Christ's sarcophagus with the eucharistic altar beginning in the mid-twelfth century, see Graeve, "Stone of Unction," 230–31. On the association of Joseph of Arimathea and Nicodemus with the clergy who perform the Eucharist, see Izbicki, *Eucharist in Medieval Canon Law*, 106, 112.

16. Flanigan, "Liturgical Context."

17. On manifest anachronisms, see Nagel and Wood, *Anachronic Renaissance*.

18. Patton, "Islamic Envelope-Flap Binding"; see also "Cloister as Cultural Mirror." On Jewish adherence to the Talmud rather than the Old Testament, see chapter 6 above and chapter 11 below.

19. Miri Rubin (*Gentile Tales*) traces the roots and legacy of the Paris host desecration allegation (on which, see 40–48). On the Feast of Corpus Christi, see Rubin, *Corpus Christi*, esp. 164–287.

20. These scenes appear to the right of the Last Supper, in which Christ instituted the Eucharist ritual; to the left of the Last Supper, Serra depicts two other classic tales of miracles performed by the consecrated host. On these images, see Rodríguez Barral, *La imagen de judío*, 197–203; Glazer-Eytan, "Jews Imagined and Real," 49–53; and below.

21. Roig, *Mirror*, 304–6. On Serra's depiction and its relations both to Roig's version and to a thirteenth-century tale in which there is no Muslim character, see Glazer-Eytan, "Conversos, Moriscos, and the Eucharist," 270–80; I am grateful to the author for sharing a pre-publication version.

22. Rubin, *Gentile Tales*, 71–73.

23. See *Memoria de don Enrique IV de Castilla*, 2:476–77; see further Glazer-Eytan, "Conversos, Moriscos, and the Eucharist," 282. On the use of anti-Jewish rhetoric to critique secular rulers, see Nirenberg, *Anti-Judaism*. For another dimension of the association that polemicists drew between Enrique IV and Muslims, see Constable, "Food and Meaning."

24. Glazer-Eytan, "Conversos, Moriscos, and the Eucharist," 285–87.

25. Contrast the incendiary—and, originally, anti-Jewish—charge lodged by a city councilor of Toledo that a Morisco doctor systematically killed his Christian patients; see Soyer, "Myth of *El Vengador*." In at least some communities, average Spaniards were unpersuaded by anti-Morisco polemics and resisted royal efforts to round up and expel local Moriscos. See Dadson, *Tolerance and Coexistence in Early Modern Spain*, esp. chapter 6; Vincent, "Geography of the Morisco Expulsion."

CHAPTER 10. CONSPIRACY THEORIES: MUSLIM AGENTS OF JEWISH MALEVOLENCE

1. Vasiliev, "Iconoclastic Edict," 28–30 (the translation is Vasiliev's). Stephen Gero (*Byzantine Iconoclasm*, 62–67) makes the case that this tale about a Jewish magician's promise of lengthy rule originally referred not to Yazid but to the Byzantine emperor Leo III, who initiated his own campaign of iconoclasm in 726. No reference to Jewish influence appears in the Syriac, Arabic, or Armenian sources on Yazid's edict surveyed by Alexander Vasiliev. Several Syriac sources do, however, blame Jews for the Muslim practice of tearing down

crosses, which they trace to the advice Jews offered when Muslims sought to rebuild the Jerusalem Temple; see chapter 4, n. 8, above, and Hoyland, *Theophilus of Edessa's Chronicle*, 126–27. For an historical account of Yazid's edict and its motives, see Sahner, "First Iconoclasm in Islam"; on Islamic attitudes toward images more broadly, see Flood, "Iconoclasm."

2. For Greek sources, including Theophanes's *Chronicle*, see Vasiliev, "Iconoclastic Edict," 26–35, and Gero, *Byzantine Iconoclasm*, 59–84; for Latin, including an account presented at the Council of Paris in 825, see Vasiliev, 35–37. On anti-Jewish and anti-Muslim polemics in later works promoting the veneration of icons, see Corrigan, *Visual Polemics*.

3. Texts and translations of the relevant passages from the Seventeenth Council of Toledo appear in Linder, *Jews in the Legal Sources*, 529–38. The quoted material appears on p. 530; the translation is mine.

4. The argument of this chapter inverts that of Cutler and Cutler, *Jew as Ally of the Muslim*. As reviewers of that book uniformly observed, Allan and Helen Cutler failed to support their thesis that "anti-Muslimism" was the driving force behind Christian hatred of Jews. These authors did, however, provide an invaluable service by drawing scholarly attention to the relationship between Jews and Muslims in medieval Christian thought and to many of the primary sources that associate these groups with one another. Chapters 9–11 of the present book offer fresh analyses of these sources, among others. On the term *Islamophobia*, see n. 9 of the introduction above. On a fifteenth-century polemical work from present-day Spain that alleges an alliance of Jews and Muslims while depicting Islam itself as a form of Judaism, see the *Disputa del Bispe de Jaen contra los jueus*, discussed by Szpiech, "Prisons and Polemics," 282–83; I am grateful to Ryan Szpiech for drawing my attention to this work.

5. Ademar, *Chronicon* 3.47, ed. Bourgain, 166–67 (translation by Callahan, "Al-Hākim, Charlemagne," 42). See also Frassetto, "Image of the Saracen as Heretic." On al-Hakim's actual motivation, see Canard, "La destruction de l'Église de la Résurrection." Al-Hakim did not in fact compel Christians or Jews to convert.

6. Glaber, *Histories*, 132–37; I have slightly modified John France's translations of *Histories* 3.7.24–25 to more precisely reflect the Latin original. On the date of this passage, see xlii.

7. For a thorough survey of the debate, description of the relevant primary sources, and argument in favor of the thesis that the destruction of the Church of the Holy Sepulchre prompted the persecution of European Jews, see Landes, "Massacres of 1010." An important counterargument not mentioned by Richard Landes is that hardly any eleventh-century Frankish authors other than Ademar and Glaber make reference to this destruction, which suggests that knowledge about it was not widespread; see France, "Destruction of Jerusalem."

8. Callahan, "Ademar of Chabannes."

9. On the apocalyptic dimensions of the depictions of al-Hakim offered by Ademar and Glaber, see Landes, "Massacres of 1010," 97–98. On Cairo as "Babylon," see Scheil, *Babylon under Western Eyes*, 258. Al-Hakim in fact persecuted Jews and Christians alike. On traditions that ascribe Jewish ancestry to Antichrist, see the references above, chapter 7 n. 22.

10. Callahan, "Al-Hākim, Charlemagne."

11. On the significance of pilgrimage, see Callahan, "Jerusalem in the Monastic Imaginations."

12. Ademar, *Chronicon* 3.47 (the translation is mine). Ademar also differs from Glaber by incorrectly dating the destruction of the Church of the Holy Sepulchre to 1010. Landes ("Massacres of 1010," 83–86) makes the case that Ademar intentionally postdated al-Hakim's action so as to dissociate it from the expulsion of Jews from Limoges. One could, however, argue that Glaber postdated the persecutions of European Jews so as to explain them as justifiable revenge for events in Jerusalem.

13. On the water poisoning affair, see Nirenberg, *Communities of Violence*, 43–68; Ginzburg, *Ecstasies*, 33–62; Barber, "Lepers, Jews, and Moslems." (See also Barzilay, *Poisoned Wells*, published too recently to inform my analysis.) Malcolm Barber and Carlo Ginzburg provide extensive summaries of the primary sources, while David Nirenberg provides especially insightful analysis; the following discussion builds on the foundations they laid. On persecution of medieval lepers, with particular attention to parallels with anti-Jewish persecution, see Moore, *Formation of a Persecuting Society*. More broadly, see Rawcliffe, *Leprosy in Medieval England*. On the Jews of France, with particular attention to their political and fiscal significance, see Jordan, *French Monarchy and the Jews*.

14. Jean-Marie Vidal ("La poursuite des lépreux," 456–78) provides the full text of the inquisitorial records in Latin; the relevant passages appear on pp. 466–67. For a French translation, see Duvernoy, *Le régistre d'inquisition de Jacques Fournier*, 2:633–43.

15. Ginzburg, *Ecstasies*, 21–24.

16. The relevant passage from Bernard Gui's *Flores chronicorum* appears in Baluze, *Vitae paparum Avenionensium*, 1:164–65.

17. The most significant of these chronicles, often echoed by others, is *Chronique latine de Guillaume de Nangis*, ed. Géraud, 2:31–36, at 32. The earliest recorded reference to Jewish involvement in the affair (translated by Nirenberg, *Communities of Violence*, 93) appears in a June 2 letter by the king of Mallorca, who reports information gleaned previously in the papal court of Avignon.

18. Vidal, "La poursuite des lépreux," 449–51, provides the complete French text of both letters, along with Latin attestations to the authenticity of the translation by notaries and city officials. Ginzburg (*Ecstasies*, 47–48) provides a detailed summary of the first letter and a translation of nearly all the second. (Translations here are mine.) Paris, *Chronica majora*, 5:252.

19. On royal treatment of the Jews in the aftermath of the water poisoning affair, see Brown, "Alleged Expulsion of 1322." See also, and more broadly, Jordan, "Home Again." Deeana Klepper ("Historicizing Allegory," 340–41) suggests that Oldradus's opinion in favor of expelling subject Jews may have played a role in deliberations on this subject.

20. Philip's letter survives because the pope quotes it in full; see Mansi, *Sacrorum conciliorum*, 25:569–72.

21. This quotation is Ginzburg's paraphrase (*Ecstasies*, 45) of the Latin, which goes into greater scatological detail; all other quotations are my translations of the original text.

22. For details on this solar eclipse, I consulted the NASA Eclipse Website, accessed June 15, 2022, https://eclipse.gsfc.nasa.gov/solar.html. The letter's description matches observations of the sun and sky during other near-total eclipses.

23. The names of the sultans and emirs in this letter derive, albeit in garbled form, from Joshua 11–12. Given the biblical nature of the other names within this letter, "Bananias" may allude to Ananias, the high priest who sought to kill Paul (Acts 23).

24. The events Bananias describes purportedly occurred in the year 6294 from the creation of the world. Jews in medieval France used a creation-based calendar, but this date falls nowhere near the fourteenth Christian century by any Jewish or Christian calculation. On Enoch and Elijah, see Emmerson, *Antichrist in the Middle Ages*, 95–101.

25. On tensions between Philip V and the papacy regarding the promised crusade, see Taylor, "French Assemblies and Subsidy in 1321." Neither Philip V, who died in early 1322, nor his successors ever went on crusade.

26. French epic poems often portray Muslims as eager to conquer Paris, a city frequently portrayed as the New Jerusalem. See Comfort, "Literary Role of the Saracens," 648–50; Pysiak, "Saint Louis as a New David."

27. Ginzburg (*Ecstasies,* 54n9) provides references to the primary sources, among which the most significant is the continuation to the *Chronicle* of Guillaume de Nangis, cited in n. 17 above. Many of these sources also blame Jews (rather than Muslims, as Agasse alone claims) for causing the lepers to blaspheme Christ and for creating the poison out of consecrated hosts. Bernard Gui, who participated in Agasse's trial, is the only chronicler to make no reference to either Jews or Muslims in his account of the affair (see n. 16 above).

28. Anidjar, *The Jew, the Arab*, xi.

CHAPTER 11. HOW MUSLIMS, JEWS, AND ROMANS BECAME WORSHIPPERS OF MUHAMMAD

1. See Tolan, *Saracens,* esp. 105–34, and *Faces of Muhammad,* esp. 19–43. See also Akbari, *Idols in the East.* On the term *Franks*, see Bartlett, *Making of Europe*, 101–5.

2. Tudebode, *Historia de Hierosolymitano itinere*; the cited passages appear on pp. 137 and 148 of the edition, 115 and 126 of the somewhat loose translation (the translation here is mine). The passage about the crusader procession is the only one in this history for which Tudebode himself takes credit; see Rubenstein, "Who was Peter Tudebode?," esp. 202.

3. Ralph of Caen, *Tancredus,* 107 (lines 3641–45). Ralph likely composed this work between 1112–18; see *Gesta Tancredi,* 3–4 (and, for another translation of the cited passage, 144). On this passage, see Camille, *Gothic Idol,* 142–45; Tolan, *Saracens,* 119–20. Akbari, *Idols in the East,* 242.

4. Jones, "Conventional Saracen," 203. On *Roland*'s depictions of Saracen gods, idols, and houses of worship, see Akbari, *Idols in the East,* 206–10; Tolan, *Faces of Muhammad,* 30–35. The French name "Apollin" may refer not to the Greek god Apollo but rather to the angel of destruction "Apollyon" mentioned

in Revelation 9:11; the origins of the French name "Tervagan" are unknown. See McClure, "In the Name," 422n12.

5. Text: Brault, *Song of Roland.* Gerard Brault dates this work to ca. 1100 (1:4 and n. 19). On Frankish self-definition in *Roland,* see Kinoshita, *Medieval Boundaries,* 15–45. On the Trinitarian dimensions of Frankish Christian identity and their Saracen antithesis, see McClure, "In the Name," esp. 433–35, 443. On Saracens as representatives of the entire non-Christian world, including the pagans of Northern Europe, see Comfort, "Literary Role of the Saracens," 630–31.

6. For earlier references to Muslim "synagogues," see chapter 4, esp. n. 22. The mid-twelfth-century *Chronica Adefonsi Imperatoris,* which recounts the deeds of Alfonso VII of León-Castile, also consistently uses this term when speaking of Muslim houses of worship: see Barton and Fletcher, *World of El Cid,* 180n103. (I am grateful to Paola Tartakoff for drawing my attention to this reference.) The term could also be used in the context of other despised communities: writing in the 1180s, Walter Map (*De nugis curialium* 1.30, pp. 118–21) refers to the gathering places of Cathars, a Christian community that Map deemed heretical, as "synagogues." On portrayals of Jews in the *Song of Roland* and related works, see Herman, "Note on Medieval Anti-Judaism."

7. The *Jeu de saint Nicolas,* a play composed ca. 1200 in which the saint's icon demonstrates its power while an idol of Tervagant proves to be impotent, exemplifies the portrayal of the Christian-Muslim conflict in terms of paganism; see Akbari, *Idols in the East,* 210–13. Anti-pagan discourse also underpins associations of Muslims with biblical Philistines, who likewise discovered the impotence of their false gods. An early thirteenth-century *Bible moralisée* depicts the Philistine idolaters of 1 Samuel 5:2–4 as "Saracens" who worship in a "mahommerie"; see Camille, *Gothic Idol,* 162–64; Strickland, *Saracens, Demons, and Jews,* 171–72. Some Europeans branded the Muslims who regained control of Jerusalem in 1187 as the "new Philistines"; see Siberry, *Criticism of Crusading,* 82.

8. Recall, for example, that the late twelfth-century canon lawyer Bernard of Pavia defined Jews as those who "observe the Law of Moses according to the letter," whereas Christians follow the spiritual meaning of the Old Testament as revealed through the New Testament (chapter 8 above, at n. 10). On the influence in medieval Europe of Augustine's rhetoric about Jews, see Cohen, *Living Letters.*

9. For a translation and discussion of Bernard's Letter 363, see Cohen, *Living Letters,* 233–45. The translation here is based on Cohen's, revised in light of *Sancti Bernardi opera,* 8:316–17. The quoted material refers not only to Augustine's teachings but also to *Aeneid* 6.853 and Romans 9:4–5. Peter of Cluny also wrote a letter regarding the Second Crusade that, notwithstanding its significantly more hostile attitude toward the Jews, maintains an absolute distinction between Jews and Muslims; see Cohen, *Living Letters,* 245–54. On these letters, see also Chazan, *From Anti-Judaism to Anti-Semitism,* 109–35.

10. Cohen, "Jews as the Killers of Christ," 25. In *Living Letters of the Law,* Jeremy Cohen emphasizes the crucial role of twelfth-century thinkers in laying the foundations for these thirteenth-century allegations. I focus on the thirteenth century in this chapter because allegations that Jews worship Muhammad first appear then.

11. *Auto de los Reyes Magos*, lines 138–47. I use the translation of Lucy Pick; see the discussion in *Conflict and Coexistence*, 182–203. Pick, who questions the customary dating of the *Auto* to the late twelfth century, argues that this work constitutes part of a broader effort by Archbishop Rodrigo Jiménez de Rada to portray the Battle of Las Navas de Tolosa (1212), in which the armies of three Christian kings defeated a Muslim king, as a contemporary reiteration of the biblical narrative about the three wise kings.

12. MacDonald, "*Hamihala.*" Pick (*Conflict and Coexistence*, 197) speculates that costumes may have reinforced the association of Herod and his advisors with local Muslims.

13. For evidence that Spanish Christians understood the monotheistic nature of Islamic oaths, see Vicens, "Swearing by God." Augustine's assertion that Jews bless Christ appears in *City of God* 16.37, discussed in Cohen, *Living Letters*, 32.

14. *Towneley Plays*, ed. Epp. Paull, "Towneley Cycle," esp. 193–97. Other English plays of the period ascribe such invocations not only to Herod but also to the Jews who conspire against Christ, torment him, and have him crucified: see Paull, "Middle English Literature," 196–229. On invocations of Muhammad by non-Jewish villains, see below. Herod and his associates also invoke Muhammad—and Tervagant—in the French *Passion de Semur*, line 3870, and in Arnoul Gréban's *Mystère de la passion*, e.g., line 6086. For references to such invocations in the Italian *Passion* of Revello, which I was not able to consult, see Bulard, *Le scorpion*, 226n1.

15. See Cohen, *Friars and the Jews*, and *Letters of the Law*. In the latter book, Jeremy Cohen also contends that the association of Jews with Muslims contributed to the change in Christian conceptions of Jews; for a brief version of this argument, see "Muslim Connection." My argument here is the reverse: changing Christian conceptions of Jews generated new ways of associating Jews with Muslims. On the use of Talmudic evidence by Christian polemicists, see also Chazan, *From Anti-Judaism to Anti-Semitism*, 136–69.

16. Di Cesare, "Reading the Bible through Glass." On the *Hereford Mappa Mundi* image, see Strickland, "Meanings of Muhammad," esp. 151–52; Leshock, "Religious Geography," 205–12. Sara Lipton (*Images of Intolerance*, 40–43) highlights the relationship between depictions of Jewish idolatry and Jewish avarice. On the Jews of England and their expulsion, see Mundill, *The King's Jews*.

17. Emmerson and Hult, trans., *Jour de Jugement*, lines 316, 378, 413, 419, 443, 454. On this play, see Emmerson, *Antichrist in the Middle Ages*, 172–80. Michelina Di Cesare ("Reading the Bible through Glass") contends that the Sainte-Chapelle image referenced above depicts Jews worshipping Muhammad as Antichrist rather than as a deity. On Muhammad as Antichrist, see also chapter 7 above.

18. See Chemers, "Anti-Semitism," including, on the Brussels affair, 42–46, and, on the French *Mistère de la saincte hostie*, 46–47. On Uccello's work, which draws on an unpublished Italian host desecration play, see Lavin, "Altar of Corpus Domini in Urbino." On the Moor's head in this image, see Bulard, *Le scorpion*, 193–95, 232–34. On host desecration narratives in general, including discussion of the primary sources mentioned here, see Rubin, *Gentile Tales*.

19. "Prynce of all Jury [Jewry], Sir Pilate I hight [am called]": *The Crucifixion,* line 23. "In oure tempyll? The dwill, what dyd he thare? That shall he by [pay for], by Mahouns blode": *The Conspiracy,* lines 180–81. "Dystroy oure lawe": *Conspiracy,* line 601. All quotations from *Towneley Plays,* ed. Epp. The depiction of Pilate in the Towneley plays differs sharply from other English plays of the period, which portray Pilate sympathetically and for that reason do not associate him with Muhammad. They too, however, ascribe invocations of Muhammad to both the Jews and the Roman soldiers who contribute to Christ's suffering and death. See Paull, "Middle English Literature," 219–26. One of Pontius Pilate's Roman soldiers already invokes Muhammad in the early fourteenth-century French *Passion du Palatinus,* line 1688; such invocations become far more frequent and widespread in later works.

20. See Paull, "Towneley Cycle"; Leshock, "Representations of Islam"; Chemers, "Anti-Semitism."

21. *Holkham Bible,* f. 27v (transcription and translation: p. 71). Matthew 22:15–22 in fact identifies Pharisees and Herodians as the members of Jesus's audience.

22. *Mandeville's Travels,* 1:61; see Leshock, "Religious Geographies," 218–19.

23. For discussion of Ferrari's Chapel of the Crucifixion among numerous other examples, see Bulard, *Le scorpion,* 225–34; Cutler and Cutler, *Jew as Ally of the Muslim,* 103–7, summarize and supplement Marcel Bulard's discussion. See also Strickland, *Saracens, Demons, and Jews,* 176–77. On the depiction of biblical Jews wearing headgear or clothing associated with Muslims, see Kalmar, "Jesus Did Not Wear a Turban." On manifest anachronisms more broadly, see Nagel and Wood, *Anachronic Renaissance.*

24. In the United States, the church that Luther most directly inspired is still formally called the Evangelical Lutheran Church of America. Most American evangelicals today, however, are not Lutheran in the narrow sense of that term, and the ELCA itself is a "mainline" (not an "evangelical") Protestant denomination. On Luther, with particular attention the significance he ascribed to the devil, see Oberman, *Luther.*

CHAPTER 12. LUTHER'S RIVALS AND THE EMERGENT DISCOURSE OF ANTI-ISLAM

1. Throughout this chapter, I employ (with modifications) the translations that appear in *Luther's Works,* a still-growing series commonly cited as *LW;* Luther's "Preface to the Quran" appears in *LW* 60:286–94 (quoted: 291). My own analyses also draw on the Latin and German texts in *Luthers Werke,* the comprehensive critical edition of Luther's Latin and German works known as the *Weimarer Ausgabe* after its place of publication and commonly cited as *WA* (here: *WA* 53:570). This preface first appeared within Theodor Bibliander's edition of the Quran and other texts related to Islam, which we encountered in chapter 7. On the controversy surrounding publication of Bibliander's work and Luther's involvement in its resolution, see Clark, "Publication of the Koran in Latin." On Luther's polemics against the Quran, see Francisco, *Martin Luther and Islam,* 175–210; Francisco addresses Luther's Preface to the Quran

on pp. 211–17. See also, and more broadly, Edwards, *Luther's Last Battles*, 97–114.

2. Luther's writings contain over 14,000 references to Jews (many to those who lived in biblical times) and over 14,000 terms related to the word *pope*, to say nothing of other terms associated with Catholicism. I have calculated these figures using Luthers Werke im WWW, a digital version of the *Weimarer Ausgabe,* last accessed June 15, 2022, https://luther.chadwyck.com. Total figures for each set of terms reflect texts (excluding editorial material) in Luther's *Schriften,* his publications excluding the German Bible translation. (The *Weimarer Ausgabe* also includes Luther's private letters and his "table talk," accounts of his remarks over meals; these sections, along with the German Bible glosses, contain an additional nine hundred or so references to Muslims.) For Muslims, I searched for the German and Latin equivalents of *Turks, Saracens,* and *Muhammad,* including spelling variants and suffix permutations. Only about six hundred of these 4,500 references appear in works devoted to Turks: *On War against the Turks* (1529), *An Army Sermon against the Turks* (1529), Preface to the *Tract on the Religion and Customs of the Turks* by George of Hungary (1530), *Appeal for Prayer against the Turks* (1541), Preface to the Quran (1542), and a translation of Riccoldo da Monte di Croce's *Refutation of the Quran* with preface and afterword (1542). To calculate the total number of references to Jews, I manually selected relevant terms beginning with "iud" and "jud," and also included variants of *synagogue.* Proximity figures (within twenty words of variants and permutations of *Turk*) are conservative estimates because the search engine's capacity to handle multivariable proximity searches is insufficient to yield precise figures. On the staggering volume of Luther's total literary output in both absolute and relative terms, see Edwards, *Printing, Propaganda, and Martin Luther,* 1–2. More broadly, see Pettegree, *Brand Luther.*

3. On the term *Islamophobia,* see n. 9 of the introduction. I have no strong opinion on whether to refer to *antimuslimism* or *anti-Muslimism* and employ the former simply to parallel *antisemitism.* (There are indeed people who self-identify as Muslims, but Jews do not self-identify as Semites.)

4. For examples of rhetoric from both sides, see Miller, *Turks and Islam,* 61–65.

5. On Luther's rhetoric about Jews, see Kaufmann, *Luther's Jews,* esp. 94–124; Nirenberg, *Anti-Judaism,* 246–68. Andrew Pettegree (*Brand Luther,* 298) observes that *On the Jews and Their Lies* was rarely published during Luther's lifetime. On the legacy of Luther's anti-Muslim rhetoric, see n. 6 of the afterword below.

6. Quotation: Karl Holl, as cited by Gordon Rupp (*Righteousness of God,* 138). David Nirenberg (*Anti-Judaism,* 252–56) likewise finds the core of Luther's anti-Judaism in these lectures, which Luther himself did not publish. I refer to this psalm using the Hebrew numbering system that is now standard in all languages; Luther, who used Jerome's Latin translation, knew this text as Psalm 73.

7. LW 10:431 (WA 3:492; 55.2:464). Luther's understanding of Psalm 74 both draws on and departs from that of the fourteenth-century commentator Nicholas of Lyra, whose allegorical interpretation also focuses on Muslims; see

Postilla moralis, 3:190r–192r. Luther's explanation of Psalm 74 conforms to his general practice of interpreting the literal sense of the biblical text with reference to Jews and its allegorical sense with reference to the church, the collective body of Christians. See further Ebeling, "Beginnings of Luther's Hermeneutics."

8. *LW* 10:431 (*WA* 3:492; 55.2:465), commenting on verses 3–4.

9. *LW* 10:435–37 (*WA* 3:495–97; 55.2:468–71); Luther elaborates further on these phrases toward the end of the sermon, pp. 450–53.

10. *LW* 10:442 (*WA* 3:500; 55.2:475), on Psalm 74:6; *LW* 11:98 (*WA* 3:608; 55.2:593), on Psalm 80:14; see also *LW* 11:339, on Psalm 104:4.

11. *LW* 10:437 (*WA* 3:496; 55.2:470).

12. *LW* 10:453 (*WA* 3:509; 55.2:482). "Primary sense of scripture": Luther's lecture on Psalm 77, *LW* 11:12 (*WA* 3:531; 55.2:508). On Luther's understanding of the senses of scripture, see Ebeling, "Beginnings of Luther's Hermeneutics," 460–64.

13. *LW* 10:454 (*WA* 3:510; 55.2:483).

14. Like Sophronius of Jerusalem in the earliest days of the Muslim conquests (see chapter 2 above), Luther consistently blames Christian sinfulness for the military threat that Muslims pose: God would easily overpower Christendom's political rivals if only Christians were more righteous. Gregory Miller (*Turks and Islam,* 99–107) shows that such rhetoric was commonplace in the sixteenth century.

15. Quotations: *LW* 46:170 (*WA* 30.2:116). For discussion of *On War against the Turks* in the context of Luther's understanding of church, government, and household, see Francisco, *Martin Luther and Islam,* 131–49. None of Luther's most significant sources about Islam—the refutations of the Quran by Riccoldo da Monte di Croce and Nicholas of Cusa, and Gregory of Hungary's *Tract on the Religion and Customs of the Turks*—make reference to this tripartite framework. On Luther's engagement with these works, see Choi, "Martin Luther's Response to the Turkish Threat"; Grafton, "Martin Luther's Sources."

16. *LW* 46:177 (*WA* 30.2:122). More broadly, see Miller, *Turks and Islam,* 49–51.

17. *LW* 46:178–79 (*WA* 30.2:123–24). Luther also cites Augustine's allegation that Donatists killed Catholics as well as other purported examples of murderous heretics, the implication being that false belief inevitably leads to homicide. On contemporaneous rhetoric about Turkish violence, see Miller, *Turks and Islam,* 80–82.

18. *LW* 46:181–82 (*WA* 30.2:126–27). On contemporaneous rhetoric about Turks and marriage, see Miller, *Turks and Islam,* 82. Luther already alleges that "the Turk considers women as beasts" in his 1528 Lectures on 1 Timothy (2:11, *LW* 28:277, *WA* 26:46); in that context, he also disparages the manner in which Jews purportedly treat their wives.

19. *LW* 46:184, 197–98 (*WA* 30.2:129, 142); Luther also associates Turks with some of his Protestant rivals in this context.

20. 1532: Lecture on Psalm 2:9 (*LW* 12:65; *WA* 40.2:275); see also, from the same year, Lecture on Psalm 45:6 (*LW* 12:232). 1539: Sermon on John 3:32 (*LW* 22:464, *WA* 47:176; see also *LW* 22:467–68). 1537: Sermon on John 1:51 (*LW* 22:204–5, *WA* 46:714–15); when addressing John 1:17, Luther declares

that the pope and the Turk alike "converted Christ into a Moses: they still labor under the illusion that they can keep the Law" (*LW* 22:148, *WA* 46:665). *Prayer against the Turks*: *LW* 43:239 (*WA* 51:620–21); see also Luther's afterword to his translation of Riccoldo's *Refutation of the Quran* (*LW* 60:265). Catholic polemicists likewise condemned Luther for allegedly engaging in the same destructive practices as the Turks; for examples, see Bohnstedt, *Infidel Scourge of God*, 24.

21. For further information on these proximity searches, see n. 2 above. I conducted proximity searches for variants of "Turk" within 20 words of "iuda*," "iude*," or "jude*" for Luther's entire *Schriften* and for the periods 1509–16, 1517–26, 1527–36, and 1537–46, finding no significant variation in the rate of association.

22. *LW* 27:296–97 (*WA* 2:541). When Luther delivered these lectures in 1516 and 1517, before the controversy over indulgences erupted, he made no reference to either the pope or the Turks: all of the cited passages, including those in the following paragraph, are absent from the original lecture notes (published in *WA* 57).

23. Quotation: *LW* 27:237 (*WA* 2:501), on Galatians 2:19. Similarly, Luther declares in his introductory dedication that "for kings, princes, and whoever could do so to resist the Roman Curia would be a matter of far greater piety than to resist the Turks themselves" (*LW* 27:159, *WA* 2:449). The comparison with the Talmud appears in the context of Galatians 2:17 (*LW* 27:226–27); see also Luther's remarks on 3:25 (*LW* 27:279).

24. Luther first published his later lectures on Galatians in 1535; the text was prepared by a disciple on the basis of lecture notes. Versions of these lectures were published on at least twenty occasions during the sixteenth and early seventeenth centuries in Latin, German, and English. See Kolb, "Influence of Luther's Galatians Commentary"; see also *LW* 26:x.

25. *LW* 26:3–6 (*WA* 40.1:39–43).

26. *LW* 26: 9–10 (*WA* 40.1:48–49).

27. *LW* 26:28, 395–96; 27:9 (*WA* 40.1:76, 602; 40.2:10).

28. *LW* 60:289–94 (*WA* 53:569–72).

AFTERWORD

1. Disraeli, *Tancred*, 253. Disraeli himself, who portrayed Jews in a positive fashion, does not engage here in anti-Jewish discourse, but most fellow Christians in his day did not share his high regard for either Jews or Muslims. See further Schweller, "Mosaic Arabs."

2. Bruce Feiler's *Abraham: A Journey to the Heart of Three Faiths* is paradigmatic of this pluralistic rhetoric. For a history of the term *Abrahamic religions*, see Silk, "Abrahamic Religions as a Modern Concept."

3. On the term *Judeo-Christian* and its proponents, see Silk, "Judeo-Christian Tradition." More broadly, see Schultz, *Tri-Faith America*, and, with particular attention to evangelical circles, Hummel, *Covenant Brothers*, 40–58.

4. John Hagee, keynote speech to the AIPAC Policy Conference, Washington, DC, March 11, 2007, as quoted by Durbin, "Mediating the Past," 111; see

further Hummel, *Covenant Brothers,* esp. 207–8. On American evangelical attitudes toward Islam and Muslims, see also Spector, *Evangelicals and Israel,* 50–110, and the works cited in the following two notes.

5. See Durbin, *Righteous Gentiles,* esp. chapter 5. Quotation: Kidd, *American Christians and Islam,* 154.

6. There are evident similarities between Luther's rhetoric about Muslims and ideas expressed by American Christians. See, for example, Kidd, *American Christians and Islam,* esp. chapter 1 on the colonial era; Marr, *Cultural Roots of American Islamicism,* esp. chapter 4 on the application of anti-Islamic rhetoric to Mormon targets. See also Heise, "Marking Mormon Difference." I am not aware of scholarship that traces the history of Luther's influence in this regard.

7. Beckett, "Pittsburgh Shooting"; Roose, "On Gab." Note that, unlike Bowers, many white nationalists do not associate their ideology with Christianity; see Berry, *Blood and Faith.*

8. For example: Daniel Freeman and his collaborators ("Coronavirus Conspiracy Beliefs") found a high correlation between individuals who agree with the statement, "Jews have created the virus to collapse the economy for financial gain," and those who agree that "Muslims are spreading the virus as an attack on Western values." In personal correspondence, however, Freeman explained this correlation as resulting from survey respondents' "general tendency toward conspiracy ideas (regardless too much of precise content)." Similarly, Simon Weaver ("Rhetorical Discourse Analysis") found that even websites that contain both anti-Muslim and antisemitic jokes reflect profound differences in the stereotypes ascribed to each target.

9. Amend, "Analyzing a Terrorist's Social Media Manifesto"; Katz, "Inside the Online Cesspool."

10. Qiu, "Trump's Evidence-Free Claims." See further Romero and Zarrugh, "Islamophobia"; Braunstein, "Muslims as Outsiders."

11. See, for example, Teter, *Blood Libel,* and, on an incident in New York State in 1928, Berenson, *The Accusation.*

12. See, for example, Curtis, *Muslim American Politics,* esp. chapter 5; Elfenbein, *Fear in Our Hearts.* On early American conceptions of Muslims as un-American, see Spellberg, *Thomas Jefferson's Qur'an.*

13. Amichai, "Gods Change, Prayers are Here to Stay," in *Open Closed Open,* 39. For a similar observation about anti-Judaism that draws on Friedrich Nietzsche's notion of "masks," see Nirenberg, *Anti-Judaism,* 9–10.

Bibliography

Ademar of Chabannes. *Chronicon*. Edited by Pascale Bourgain. Turnhout: Brepols, 1999.

Akbari, Suzanne Conklin. *Idols in the East: European Representations of Islam and the Orient, 1100–1450*. Ithaca, NY: Cornell University Press, 2009.

———. "The Rhetoric of Antichrist in Western Lives of Muhammad." *Islam and Christian–Muslim Relations* 8, no. 3 (1997): 297–307.

Albert of Aachen. *Albert of Aachen's History of the Journey to Jerusalem*. Translated by Susan B. Edgington. Aldershot: Ashgate, 2013.

Albl, Martin C. *"And Scripture Cannot be Broken": The Form and Function of the Early Christian* Testimonia *Collections*. Leiden: E. J. Brill, 1999.

Altman, Charles. "The Medieval Marquee." *Journal of Popular Culture* 14, no. 1 (1980): 37–46.

Ambrose, Kimberly. *Jew among Jews: Rehabilitating Paul*. Eugene, OR: Wipf and Stock, 2015.

Amend, Alex. "Analyzing a Terrorist's Social Media Manifesto: The Pittsburgh Synagogue Shooter's Posts on Gab." *Hatewatch* (blog), Southern Poverty Law Center, October 28, 2018. https://www.splcenter.org/hatewatch/2018/10/28/analyzing-terrorists-social-media-manifesto-pittsburgh-synagogue-shooters-posts-gab.

Amichai, Yehuda. *Open Closed Open: Poems*. Translated by Chana Bloch and Chana Kronfeld. New York: Harcourt, 2000.

Andrés, Juan. *Confusión o confutación de la secta mahomética*. Edited by Elisa Ruiz García. Mérida: Regional de Extremadura, 2003.

———. *The Confusion of Muhamed's Sect*. Translated by Joshua Notstock. London, 1652.

———. *De zeer wonderlijcke ende warachtighe historie van Mahomet*. Antwerp, 1580.

Anidjar, Gil. *The Jew, the Arab: A History of the Enemy.* Stanford, CA: Stanford University Press, 2003.

Anthony, Sean W. "Muḥammad, Menaḥem, and the Paraclete: New Light on Ibn Isḥāq's (d. 150/767) Arabic Version of John 15:23–16:1." *Bulletin of the School of Oriental and African Studies* 79, no. 2 (2016): 255–278.

The Armenian History Attributed to Sebeos. Translated, with notes, by R. W. Thomson. Historical commentary by James Howard-Johnston. 2 vols. Liverpool: Liverpool University Press, 1999.

Augustine. *Corpus Augustinianum Gissense.* Edited by Cornelius Mayer. Basel: Schwabe, 1995.

———. *Homilies on the Gospel of John 1–40.* Translated by Edmund Hill. Hyde Park, NY: New City Press, 2009.

Aznar Cardona, Pedro. *Expulsion justificada de los Moriscos españoles.* Huesca, 1612.

Baldric of Bourgueil. *The Historia Ierosolimitana of Baldric of Bourgueil.* Edited by Steven Biddlecombe. Woodbridge: Boydell & Brewer, 2014.

Ballan, Mohammad. "Fraxinetum: An Islamic Frontier State in Tenth-Century Provence." *Comitatus: A Journal of Medieval and Renaissance Studies* 41 (2010): 23–76.

Baluze, Etienne, ed. *Vitae paparum Avenionensium.* Paris, 1693.

Barber, Malcolm. "Lepers, Jews, and Moslems: The Plot to Overthrow Christendom in 1321." *History* 66, no. 216 (1981): 1–17.

Bartlett, Robert. *The Making of Europe: Conquest, Colonization and Cultural Exchange, 950–1350.* Princeton, NJ: Princeton University Press, 1993.

Barton, Simon, and Richard Fletcher, trans. *The World of El Cid: Chronicles of the Spanish Reconquest.* Manchester: Manchester University Press, 2000.

Barzilay, Tzafrir. *Poisoned Wells: Accusations, Persecution, and Minorities in Medieval Europe, 1321–1422.* Philadelphia: University of Pennsylvania Press, 2022.

Baudier, Michel. *Histoire générale de la réligion des Turcs.* Paris, 1626.

Becker, Adam H. "Syriac Anti-Judaism: Polemic and Internal Critique." In *Jews and Syriac Christians: Intersections across the First Millennium*, edited by Aaron Michael Butts and Simcha Gross, 47–66. Tübingen: Mohr Siebeck, 2020.

Beckett, Lois. "Pittsburgh Shooting: Suspect Railed Against Jews and Muslims on Site Used by 'Alt-Right.'" *Guardian,* October 27, 2018. https://www.theguardian.com/us-news/2018/oct/27/pittsburgh-shooting-suspect-antisemitism.

Berend, Nora. *At the Gate of Christendom: Jews, Muslims, and "Pagans" in Medieval Hungary, c. 1000–c. 1300.* Cambridge: Cambridge University Press, 2006.

Berenson, Edward. *The Accusation: Blood Libel in an American Town.* New York: W. W. Norton, 2019.

Berger, Pamela C. *The Crescent on the Temple: The Dome of the Rock as Image of the Ancient Jewish Sanctuary.* Leiden: E. J. Brill, 2012.

Bernard of Clairvaux. *Sancti Bernardi opera.* 9 vols. Rome: Editiones Cistercienses, 1957–77.

Bernard of Pavia. *Summa decretalium*. Edited by Ernest Laspeyres. 1860. Reprint, Graz: Akademische Druck- u. Verlagsanstalt, 1956.

Berry, Damon T. *Blood and Faith: Christianity in American White Nationalism*. Syracuse, NY: Syracuse University Press, 2017.

Bertaina, David. "The Development of Testimony Collections in Early Christian Apologetics with Islam." In *The Bible in Arab Christianity*, edited by David Thomas, 151–73. Leiden: E.J. Brill, 2007.

Berti, Vittorio. *Vita e studi di Timoteo I († 823), patriarca cristiano di Baghdad: ricerche sull'epistolario e sulle fonti contigue*. Paris: Association pour l'avancement des études iraniennes, 2009.

Berzon, Todd S. *Classifying Christians: Ethnography, Heresiology, and the Limits of Knowledge in Late Antiquity*. Oakland: University of California Press, 2016.

Bible moralisée, Codex Vindobonensis 2554, Vienna, Österreichische Nationalbibliothek. Commentary and translation by Gerald B. Guest. London: Harvey Miller, 1995.

Bibliander, Theodor. *Ad nominis Christiani socios consultatio*. Basel, 1542. https://doi.org/10.3931/e-rara-1995.

Bignami-Odier, J., and M.G. Levi della Vida. "Une version latine de l'Apocalypse Syro-Arabe de Serge-Bahira." *Mélanges d'archéologie et d'histoire* 62 (1950): 125–48.

Biondo, Flavio. *Historiam ab inclinatione Romanorum libri XXXI*. Basel, 1531.

Blair, Sheila S. "What is the Date of the Dome of the Rock?" In *Bayt al-Maqdis: ʿAbd al-Malik's Jerusalem*, part 1, edited by Julian Raby and Jeremy Johns, 59–85. Oxford: Oxford University Press, 1992.

Bleda, Jaime. *Corónica de los moros de España*. Valencia, 1618. Reprint, Valencia: Biblioteca Valenciana, 2001.

———. *Defensio fidei*. Valencia, 1610.

Boase, Roger. "The Morisco Expulsion and Diaspora: An Example of Racial and Religious Intolerance." In *Cultures in Contact in Medieval Spain: Historical and Literary Essays Presented to L.P. Harvey*, edited by David Hook and Barry Taylor, 9–28. London: King's College London Medieval Studies, 1980.

Bohnstedt, John W. *The Infidel Scourge of God: The Turkish Menace as Seen by German Pamphleteers of the Reformation Era*. Philadelphia: American Philosophical Society, 1968.

Boronat y Barrachina, Pascual. *Los moriscos españoles y su expulsión: estudio histórico-critico*. Valencia: Vives y Moro, 1901.

Bos, Abraham P. "Hagar and the *Enkyklios Paideia* in Philo of Alexandria." In *Abraham, the Nations, and the Hagarites: Jewish, Christian, and Islamic Perspectives on Kinship with Abraham*, edited by Martin Goodman, George H. van Kooten, and Jacques T.A.G.M. van Ruiten, 163–75. Leiden: E.J. Brill, 2010.

Bousset, Wilhelm. *The Antichrist Legend: A Chapter in Christian and Jewish Folklore*. Translated by A.H. Keane. London: Hutchinson, 1896.

Boyarin, Daniel. *Border Lines: The Partition of Judaeo-Christianity*. Philadelphia: University of Pennsylvania Press, 2006.

———. *Judaism: The Genealogy of a Modern Notion*. New Brunswick, NJ: Rutgers University Press, 2019.

Brault, Gerard J., ed. and trans. *The Song of Roland: An Analytical Edition.* 2 vols. University Park: Pennsylvania State University Press, 1978.

Brauner, Christina. "Polemical Comparisons in Discourses of Religious Diversity." *Entangled Religions* 11, no. 4 (2020). https://doi.org/10.46586/er.11.2020.8692.

Braunstein, Ruth. "Muslims as Outsiders, Enemies, and Others: The 2016 Presidential Election and the Politics of Religious Exclusion." *American Journal of Cultural Sociology* 5, no. 3 (2017): 355–72.

Brière, Maurice, ed. and trans. *Les Homiliae cathedrales de Sévère d'Antioch: Traduction syriaque de Jacques d'Édesse (Homélies LXX à LXXVI). Patrologia orientalis*, vol. 12. Paris: Firmin-Didot, 1919.

Brown, Elizabeth A. R. "Philip V, Charles IV, and the Jews of France: The Alleged Expulsion of 1322." *Speculum* 66, no. 2 (1991): 294–329.

Bruce, Scott G. *Cluny and the Muslims of La Garde-Freinet: Hagiography and the Problem of Islam in Medieval Europe.* Ithaca, NY: Cornell University Press, 2015.

Brundage, James A. *Medieval Canon Law.* London: Longman, 1995.

Bulard, Marcel. *Le scorpion, symbole du peuple Juif dans l'art réligieux des XIVe, XVe, XVIe siècles.* Paris: Boccard, 1935.

Bulliet, Richard W. *Conversion to Islam in the Medieval Period: An Essay in Quantitative History.* Cambridge, MA: Harvard University Press, 1979.

Burman, Thomas E. *Reading the Qur'ān in Latin Christendom, 1140–1560.* Philadelphia: University of Pennsylvania Press, 2007.

———. *Religious Polemic and the Intellectual History of the Mozarabs, c. 1050–1200.* Leiden: E. J. Brill, 1994.

———. "'When I Argue with Them in Hebrew and Aramaic': *Tathlīth al-waḥdanīyah,* Ramon Martí, and Proofs of Jesus's Messiahship." In *Polemical Encounters: Christians, Jews, and Muslims in Iberia and Beyond,* edited by Mercedes García-Arenal and Gerard Wiegers, 25–43. University Park: Pennsylvania State University Press, 2019.

Callahan, Daniel F. "Ademar of Chabannes, Millennial Fears and the Development of Western Anti-Judaism." *Journal of Ecclesiastical History* 46, no. 1 (1995): 19–35.

———. "Al-Ḥākim, Charlemagne, and the Destruction of the Church of the Holy Sepulcher in Jerusalem in the Writings of Ademar of Chabannes." In *The Legend of Charlemagne in the Middle Ages: Power, Faith, and Crusade,* edited by Matthew Gabriele and Jace Stuckey, 41–57. New York: Palgrave Macmillan, 2008.

———. "Jerusalem in the Monastic Imaginations of the Early Eleventh Century." *The Haskins Society Journal: Studies in Medieval History* 6 (1994): 119–27.

Cambier, Guy. "Quand Gauthier de Compiègne composait les Otia de Machomete." *Latomus* 17, no. 3 (1958): 531–39.

Cameron, Averil. "Blaming the Jews: The Seventh-Century Invasions of Palestine in Context." *Travaux et Mémoires* 14 (2002): 57–78.

Camille, Michael. *The Gothic Idol: Ideology and Image-making in Medieval Art.* Cambridge: Cambridge University Press, 1989.

Canard, Marius. "La destruction de l'Église de la Résurrection par le calife Ḥākim et l'histoire de la descente du feu sacré." *Byzantion* 35, no. 1 (1965): 16–43.

Carlson, Thomas A. "When Did the Middle East Become Muslim? Trends in the Study of Islam's 'Age of Conversions.'" *History Compass* 16, no. 10 (2018). https://doi.org/10.1111/hic3.12494.

Carrasco Manchado, Ana Isabel. *De la convivencia a la exclusión: imágenes legislativas de Mudéjares y Moriscos. Siglos XIII—XVII.* Madrid: Silex, 2012.

Chazan, Robert. *From Anti-Judaism to Anti-Semitism: Ancient and Medieval Christian Constructions of Jewish History.* New York: Cambridge University Press, 2016.

———. *Medieval Stereotypes and Modern Antisemitism.* Berkeley: University of California Press, 1997.

———. "Pope Innocent III and the Jews." In *Pope Innocent III and His World*, edited by John C. Moore, 187–204. Aldershot: Ashgate, 1999.

Chemers, Michael Mark. "Anti-Semitism, Surrogacy, and the Invocation of Mohammed in the *Play of the Sacrament.*" *Comparative Drama* 41, no. 1 (2007): 25–55.

Choi, David Sukwon. "Martin Luther's Response to the Turkish Threat: Continuity and Contrast with the Medieval Commentators Riccoldo da Monte Croce and Nicholas of Cusa." PhD diss., Princeton Theological Seminary, 2003.

Chrysostom, John. *Discourses against Judaizing Christians.* Translated by Paul W. Harkins. Washington, DC: Catholic University of America Press, 1979.

Clark, Elizabeth A. "Interpretive Fate amid the Church Fathers." In *Hagar, Sarah, and Their Children: Jewish, Christian, and Muslim Perspectives*, edited by Phyllis Trible and Letty M. Russell, 127–47. Louisville, KY: Westminster John Knox Press, 2006.

Clark, Elizabeth Artemis. "The Chronicle of Novalese: Translation, Text and Literary Analysis." PhD diss., University of North Carolina Chapel Hill, 2017.

Clark, Harry. "The Publication of the Koran in Latin: A Reformation Dilemma." *Sixteenth Century Journal* 15, no. 1 (1984): 3–12.

Cohen, Jeremy. *The Friars and the Jews: The Evolution of Medieval Anti-Judaism.* Ithaca, NY: Cornell University Press, 1982.

———. "The Jews as the Killers of Christ in the Latin Tradition, from Augustine to the Friars." *Traditio* 39 (1983): 1–27.

———. *Living Letters of the Law: Ideas of the Jew in Medieval Christianity.* Berkeley: University of California Press, 1999.

———. "The Muslim Connection, or On the Changing Role of the Jew in High Medieval Theology." In *From Witness to Witchcraft: Jews and Judaism in Medieval Christian Thought*, edited by Jeremy Cohen, 141–62. Wiesbaden: Otto Harrassowitz, 1996.

Cohen, Shaye J. D. *The Beginnings of Jewishness: Boundaries, Varieties, Uncertainties.* Berkeley: University of California Press, 1999.

Cole, Penny J. "'O God, the Heathen Have Come into Your Inheritance' (Ps. 78.1): The Theme of Religious Pollution in Crusade Documents, 1095–1198."

In *Crusaders and Muslims in Twelfth-Century Syria*, edited by Maya Shatz-miller, 84–111. Leiden: E.J. Brill, 1993.

———. *The Preaching of the Crusades to the Holy Land, 1095–1270.* Cambridge, MA: Medieval Academy of America, 1991.

Comfort, William Wistar. "The Literary Role of the Saracens in the French Epic." *Proceedings of the Modern Language Association* 55, no. 3 (1940): 628–59.

Conrad, Lawrence I. "Theophanes and the Arabic Historical Tradition: Some Indications of Intercultural Transmission." *Byzantinische Forschungen* 15 (1990): 1–44.

Constable, Olivia Remie. "Food and Meaning: Christian Understandings of Muslim Food and Food Ways in Spain, 1250–1550." *Viator* 44, no. 3 (2013): 199–236.

———. *To Live like a Moor: Christian Perceptions of Muslim Identity in Medieval and Early Modern Spain.* Edited by Robin Vose. Philadelphia: University of Pennsylvania Press, 2018.

Constantine Porphyrogenitus. *De administrando imperio.* Edited by Gy. Moravcsik. Translated by R.J.H. Jenkins. Rev. ed. Washington, DC: Dumbarton Oaks, 1967.

Corrigan, Kathleen. *Visual Polemics in the Ninth-Century Byzantine Psalters.* Cambridge: Cambridge University Press, 1992.

Crone, Patricia, and Michael Cook. *Hagarism: The Making of the Islamic World.* Cambridge: Cambridge University Press, 1977.

Curtis, Edward E., IV. *Muslim American Politics and the Future of US Democracy.* New York: New York University Press, 2019.

Cutler, Allan Harris, and Helen Elmquist Cutler. *The Jew as Ally of the Muslim: Medieval Roots of Anti-Semitism.* South Bend, IN: University of Notre Dame Press, 1986.

Cyril of Jerusalem. *The Works of Saint Cyril of Jerusalem.* Translated by Leo P. McCauley and Anthony A. Stephenson. Washington, DC: Catholic University of America Press, 1970.

Dadson, Trevor J. *Tolerance and Coexistence in Early Modern Spain: Old Christians and Moriscos in the Campo de Calatrava.* Woodbridge: Tamesis, 2014.

Daniel, Norman. *Islam and the West: The Making of an Image.* Edinburgh: Edinburgh University Press, 1960.

D'Avity, Pierre. *Les estats, empires, et prinicipautez du monde.* Paris, 1613.

Debié, Muriel. "Muslim–Christian Controversy in an Unedited Syriac Text: *Revelations and Testimonies about Our Lord's Dispensation.*" In *The Encounter of Eastern Christianity with Early Islam*, edited by Emmanouela Grypeou, Mark Swanson, and David Thomas, 225–35. Leiden: E.J. Brill, 2006.

Derolez, Albert. *The Making and Meaning of the Liber Floridus: A Study of the Original Manuscript, Ghent, University Library MS 92.* London: Harvey Miller, 2015.

Di Cesare, Michelina. "The Prophet in the Book: Images of Muhammad in Western Medieval Book Culture." In *Constructing the Image of Muhammad in Europe*, edited by Avinoam Shalem, 9–32. Berlin: De Gruyter, 2013.

———. *The Pseudo-Historical Image of the Prophet Muhammad in Medieval Latin Literature: A Repertory.* Berlin: De Gruyter, 2011.

———. "Reading the Bible through Glass: The Image of Muhammad in the Sainte-Chapelle." In *The Image of the Prophet Between Ideal and Ideology: A Scholarly Investigation*, edited by Christiane J. Gruber and Avinoam Shalem, 187–99. Berlin: De Gruyter, 2014.

Dimmock, Matthew. *Mythologies of the Prophet Muhammad in Early Modern English Literature.* Cambridge: Cambridge University Press, 2013.

Disraeli, Benjamin. *Tancred.* 1847. Reprint, New York: Routledge, n.d.

Donner, Fred M. *Muhammad and the Believers at the Origins of Islam.* Cambridge, MA: Belknap Press, 2010.

———. Retrospective review of *Hagarism: The Making of the Islamic World*, by Patricia Crone and Michael Cook. *Middle East Studies Association Bulletin* 40 (2006): 197–99.

Duggan, Anne J. "Conciliar Law 1123–1215: The Legislation of the Four Lateran Councils." In *The History of Medieval Canon Law in the Classical Period, 1140–1234: From Gratian to the Decretals of Pope Gregory IX*, edited by Wilfried Hartmann and Kenneth Pennington, 318–66. Washington, DC: Catholic University of America Press, 2008.

Dunbar, David G. "Hippolytus of Rome and the Eschatological Exegesis of the Early Church." *Westminster Theological Journal* 45, no. 2 (1983): 322–39.

Durbin, P.T., and Lynette Muir, eds. *Passion de Semur.* Leeds: University of Leeds Centre for Medieval Studies, 1981.

Durbin, Sean. "Mediating the Past through the Present and the Present through the Past: The Symbiotic Relationship of American Christian Zionists' Outsider and Insider Enemies." *Political Theology* 15, no. 2 (2014): 110–31.

———. *Righteous Gentiles: Religion, Identity, and Myth in John Hagee's Christians United for Israel.* Leiden: E.J. Brill, 2019.

Duvernoy, Jean, trans. *Le régistre d'inquisition de Jacques Fournier (Évêque de Pamiers), 1318–1325.* 3 vols. Paris: Mouton, 1978.

Ebeling, Gerhard. "The Beginnings of Luther's Hermeneutics." Translated by Richard B. Steele. *Lutheran Quarterly* 7, nos. 2–4 (1993): 129–58, 315–38, and 451–68.

Echevarria, Ana. "The Marks of the Other: The Impact of Lateran IV in the Regulations governing Muslims in the Iberian Peninsula." In *Jews and Muslims under the Fourth Lateran Council: Papers Commemorating the Octocentenary of the Fourth Lateran Council (1215)*, edited by Marie-Thérèse Champagne and Irven M. Resnick, 183–98. Turnhout: Brepols, 2019.

Eckhardt, Alexandre. "Le cercueil flottant de Mahomet." In *Mélanges de philologie romane et de littérature médiévale offerts à Ernest Hoepffner*, 77–88. Paris: Belles Lettres, 1949.

Edgington, Susan B., and Carol Sweetenham, trans. *The Chanson d'Antioche: An Old French Account of the First Crusade.* Farnham: Ashgate, 2011.

Edwards, Mark U., Jr. *Luther's Last Battles: Politics and Polemics, 1531–1546.* Ithaca, NY: Cornell University Press, 1983.

———. *Printing, Propaganda, and Martin Luther.* Berkeley: University of California Press, 1994.

Elfenbein, Caleb Iyer. *Fear in Our Hearts: What Islamophobia Tells Us about America*. New York University Press, 2021.

Emmerson, Richard Kenneth. *Antichrist in the Middle Ages: A Study of Medieval Apocalypticism, Art, and Literature*. Seattle: University of Washington Press, 1981.

Emmerson, Richard Kenneth, and David F. Hult, trans. *Antichrist and Judgment Day: The Middle French* Jour du Jugement. Asheville, NC: Pegasus Press, 1998.

Eph'al, Israel. "'Ishmael' and 'Arab(s)': A Transformation of Ethnological Terms." *Journal of Near Eastern Studies* 35, no. 4 (1976): 225–35.

Epp, Garrett, P. J., ed. *The Towneley Plays*. Kalamazoo, MI: Medieval Institute Publications, 2017.

Eusebius. *Life of Constantine*. Translated by Averil Cameron and Stuart G. Hall. Oxford: Clarendon Press, 1999.

Feiler, Bruce. *Abraham: A Journey to the Heart of Three Faiths*. New York: Morrow, 2002.

Feros, Antonio. "Rhetorics of the Expulsion." In *The Expulsion of the Moriscos from Spain: A Mediterranean Diaspora*, edited by Mercedes García-Arenal and Gerard Wiegers, translated by Consuelo López-Morillas and Martin Beagles, 60–101. Leiden: E. J. Brill, 2014.

Feshami, Kevin A. "Fear of White Genocide." *Roundtable* (blog). *Lapham's Quarterly*, September 6, 2017. https://www.laphamsquarterly.org/roundtable/fear-white-genocide.

Feuardent, François. *Divi Irenaei, Lugdunensis episcopi, et martyris, Adversus Valentini, et similium Gnosticorum Haereses, libri quiunque*. 1st ed. Paris, 1576. 2nd ed. Cologne, 1596.

Firestone, Reuven. "Muhammad, the Jews, and the Composition of the Qur'an: Sacred History and Counter-History." *Religions* 10, no. 1 (2019). https://doi.org/10.3390/rel10010063.

Flanigan, C. Clifford. "The Liturgical Context of the *Quem Queritis* Trope." *Comparative Drama* 8, no. 1 (1974): 45–62.

Flood, Finbarr Barry. "Iconoclasm." In *Encyclopaedia of Islam*. 3rd ed. Brill online, 2019. https://doi.org/10.1163/1573-3912_ei3_COM_32363.

Flusin, Bernard. "L'Esplanade du Temple à l'arrivée des Arabes, d'après deux récits byzantins." In *Bayt al-Maqdis: 'Abd al-Malik's Jerusalem*, part 1, edited by Julian Raby and Jeremy Johns, 17–31. Oxford: Oxford University Press, 1992.

France, John. "The Destruction of Jerusalem and the First Crusade." *Journal of Ecclesiastical History* 47, no. 1 (1996): 1–17.

Francisco, Adam S. *Martin Luther and Islam: A Study in Sixteenth-Century Polemics and Apologetics*. Leiden: E. J. Brill, 2007.

Frank, Grace, ed. *Passion du Palatinus*. Paris: Librairie Honoré Champion, 1970.

Frassetto, Michael. "The Image of the Saracen as Heretic in the Sermons of Ademar of Chabannes." In *Western Views of Islam in Medieval and Early Modern Europe*, edited by David R. Blanks and Michael Frassetto, 83–96. New York: St. Martin's Press, 1999.

Fredrickson, George M. *Racism: A Short History*. Princeton, NJ: Princeton University Press, 2002.

Fredriksen, Paula. *Augustine and the Jews: A Christian Defense of Jews and Judaism*. New York: Doubleday, 2008.

———. *Paul: The Pagans' Apostle*. New Haven, CT: Yale University Press, 2017.

Freeman, Daniel, Felicity Waite, Laina Rosebrock, Ariana Petit, Chiara Causier, Anna East, Lucy Jenner, et al. "Coronavirus Conspiracy Beliefs, Mistrust, and Compliance with Government Guidelines in England." *Psychological Medicine* 52, no. 2 (2022): 251–63. https://doi.org/10.1017/S0033291720001890.

Freiberger, Oliver. *Considering Comparison: A Method for Religious Studies*. Oxford: Oxford University Press, 2019.

Freidenreich, David M. "Comparisons Compared: A Methodological Survey of Comparisons of Religion from 'A Magic Dwells' to *A Magic Still Dwells*." *Method and Theory in the Study of Religion* 16, no. 1 (2004): 80–101.

———. *Foreigners and Their Food: Constructing Otherness in Jewish, Christian, and Islamic Law*. Berkeley: University of California Press, 2008.

———. "Jews, Pagans, and Heretics in Early Medieval Canon Law." In *Jews in Early Christian Law: Byzantium and the Latin West, 6th–11th Centuries*, edited by John Tolan, Nicholas de Lange, Laurence Foschia, and Capucine Nemo-Pekelman, 73–91. Turnhout: Brepols, 2013.

———. "Muḥammad, the Monk, and the Jews: Comparative Religion in Versions of the Baḥīrā Legend." *Entangled Religions* 13, no. 2 (2022). https://doi.org/10.46586/er.13.2022.9644.

———. "Muslims in Canon Law, 650–1000." In *Christian–Muslim Relations: A Bibliographical History,* vol. 1, edited by David Thomas and Barbara Roggema, 83–98. Leiden: E. J. Brill, 2009.

———. "Muslims in Western Canon Law, 1000–1500." In *Christian–Muslim Relations: A Bibliographical History*, vol. 3, edited by David Thomas and Alex Mallett, 41–68. Leiden: E. J. Brill, 2011.

———. "Sharing Meals with Non-Christians in Canon Law Commentaries, 1160–1260: A Case Study in Legal Development." *Medieval Encounters* 14, no. 1 (2008): 41–77.

———. "'You Still Believe Like a Jew!': Polemical Comparisons and Other Eastern Christian Rhetoric Associating Muslims with Jews from the 7th–9th Centuries." *Entangled Religions* 11, no. 4 (2022). https://doi.org/10.46586 /er.11.2022.9643.

Freidenreich, David M., and Véronique Plesch. "What is That to Us? Eucharistic Liturgy and the Enemies of Christ in the Beam of the Passion." *Studies in Iconography* 41 (2020): 104–30.

Friedberg, Emil, ed. *Corpus iuris canonici*. 2 vols. Leipzig: Tauchnitz, 1879. Reprint, Graz: Akademische Druck- u. Verlagsanstalt, 1959.

———, ed. *Quinque compilationes antiquae*. Leipzig: Tauchnitz, 1882. Reprint, Graz: Akademische Druck- u. Verlagsanstalt, 1956.

García y García, Antonio, ed. *Constitutiones Concilii quarti Lateranensis una cum Commentariis glossatorum*. Vatican City: Biblioteca Apostolica Vaticana, 1981.

García y García, A., P. Gemeinhardt, G. Gresser, T. Izbicki, A. Larson, A. Melloni, J. Miethke, et al., eds. *Conciliorum oecumenicorum generaliumque decreta: Editio critica,* vol. 2, part 1. Turnhout: Brepols, 2013.

Géraud, H., ed. *Chronique latine de Guillaume de Nangis de 1113 à 1300 avec les continuations de cette chronique de 1300 à 1368.* Paris: Renouard, 1843.

Gero, Stephen. *Byzantine Iconoclasm during the Reign of Leo III.* Louvain: Secretariat du Corpus SCO, 1973.

Ghewond. *History of Lewond, the Eminent Vardapet of the Armenians.* Translated by Zaven Arzoumanian. Wynnewood, PA.: St. Sahag and St. Mesrob Armenian Church, 1982.

———. *Lewond Vardapet, Discours historique.* Translated by Bernadette Martin-Hisard. Paris: ACHCByz, 2015.

Gibson, Margaret Dunlop, ed. *An Arabic Version of Acts of the Apostles and the Catholic Epistles . . . with a treatise On the Triune Nature of God.* London: C. J. Clay and Sons, 1899.

Gibson, Margaret T. "The Latin Apparatus." In *The Eadwine Psalter: Text, Image, and Monastic Culture in Twelfth-Century Canterbury,* edited by Margaret T. Gibson, T. A. Heslop, and Richard W. Pfaff, 108–22. London and University Park: Modern Humanities Research Association in conjunction with the Pennsylvania State University Press, 1992.

Ginzburg, Carlo. *Ecstasies: Deciphering the Witches' Sabbath.* New York: Pantheon, 1991.

Glaber, Rodulfus. *The Five Books of the Histories.* Edited and translated by John France. Oxford: Clarendon Press, 1989.

Glazer-Eytan, Yonatan. "Conversos, Moriscos, and the Eucharist in Early Modern Spain: Some Reflections on Jewish Exceptionalism." *Jewish History* 35, nos. 3–4 (2021): 265–91.

———. "Jews Imagined and Real: Representing and Prosecuting Host Profanation in Late Medieval Aragon." In *Jews and Muslims Made Visible in Christian Iberia and Beyond, 14th to 18th Centuries: Another Image,* edited by Borja Franco Llopis and Antonio Urquízar-Herrera, 40–69. Leiden: E. J. Brill, 2019.

Grabar, Oleg. *The Dome of the Rock.* Cambridge, MA: Harvard University Press, 2006.

Graeve, Mary Ann. "The Stone of Unction in Caravaggio's Painting for the Chiesa Nuova." *Art Bulletin* 40, no. 3 (1958): 223–38.

Grafton, David D. "Martin Luther's Sources on the Turk and Islam in the Midst of the Fear of Ottoman Imperialism." *Muslim World* 107, no. 4 (2017): 665–83.

Grayzel, Solomon. *The Church and the Jews in the XIIIth Century.* Philadelphia: Dropsie College, 1933.

Gréban, Arnoul. *Le mystère de la passion d'Arnoul Greban.* Edited by Gaston Paris and Gaston Raynaud. Paris: Vieweg, 1878.

Green, Todd H. *The Fear of Islam: An Introduction to Islamophobia in the West.* Minneapolis: Fortress Press, 2015.

Greenwood, Tim. "The History of Sebeos." In *Christian–Muslim Relations: A Bibliographical History,* vol. 1, edited by David Thomas and Barbara Roggema, 139–44. Leiden: E. J. Brill, 2009.

———. "A Reassessment of the *History* of Łewond." *Le Muséon* 125, nos. 1–2 (2012): 99–167.

———. "Sasanian Echoes and Apocalyptic Expectations: A Re-evaluation of the Armenian History Attributed to Sebeos." *Le Muséon* 115 (2002): 323–97.

Gregerman, Adam. *Building on the Ruins of the Temple: Apologetics and Polemics in Early Christianity and Rabbinic Judaism*. Tübingen, Mohr Siebeck, 2016.

Griffith, Sidney H. "Chapter Ten of the *Scholion*: Theodore Bar Kônî's Apology for Christianity." *Orientalia Christiana Periodica* 47, no. 1 (1981): 158–88.

———. *The Church in the Shadow of the Mosque: Christians and Muslims in the World of Islam*. Princeton, NJ: Princeton University Press, 2008.

———. "Jews and Muslims in Christian Syriac and Arabic Texts of the Ninth Century." *Jewish History* 3, no. 1 (1988): 65–94.

———. "Muhammad and the Monk Baḥîrâ: Reflections on a Syriac and Arabic Text from Early Abbasid Times." *Oriens christianus* 79, no. 4 (1995): 146–74.

———. "The Prophet Muḥammad, His Scripture, and His Message according to the Christian Apologies in Arabic and Syriac from the First Abbasid Century." In *La vie du prophète Mahomet: Colloque de Strasbourg, octobre 1980*, 99–146. Paris: Presses universitaires de France, 1983.

———. "The Syriac Letters of Patriarch Timothy I and the Birth of Christian *Kalām* in the Mu'tazilite Milieu of Baghdad and Baṣrah in Early Islamic Times." In *Syriac Polemics: Studies in Honour of Gerrit Jan Reinink*, edited by W.J. van Bekkum, J.W. Drijvers, and A.C. Klugkist, 103–32. Louvain: Peeters, 2007.

———. "Theodore bar Kônî's *Scholion*: A Nestorian *Summa contra gentiles* from the First Abbasid Century." In *East of Byzantium: Syria and Armenia in the Formative Period*, edited by Nina G. Garsoïan, Thomas F. Mathews, and Robert W. Thomson, 53–72. Washington, DC: Dumbarton Oaks, 1982.

Gross-Diaz, Theresa. *The Psalms Commentary of Gilbert of Poitiers: From lectio divina to the Lecture Room*. Leiden: E.J. Brill, 1996.

Guibert of Nogent. *The Deeds of God through the Franks*. Translated by Robert Levine. Woodbridge: Boydell & Brewer, 1997.

Halevi, Leor. "*Lex Mahomethi*: Carnal and Spiritual Representations of Islamic Law and Ritual in a Twelfth-Century Dialogue by a Jewish Convert to Christianity." In *The Islamic Scholarly Tradition: Studies in History, Law, and Thought in Honor of Professor Michael Allan Cook*, edited by Asad Q. Ahmed, Behnam Sadeghi, and Michael Bonner, 315–42. Leiden: E.J. Brill, 2011.

Halperin, David J., and Gordon D. Newby. "Two Castrated Bulls: A Study in the Haggadah of Ka'b al-Aḥbār." *Journal of the American Orientalist Society* 102, no. 4 (1982): 631–38.

Hamelius, P., ed. *Mandeville's Travels, Translated from the French by Jean d'Outremeuse, Edited from Ms. Cotton Titus C. XVI in the British Museum*. 2 vols. 1919. Reprint, London: Oxford University Press for the Early English Text Society, 1960.

Harrak, Amir, trans. *The Chronicle of Zuqnīn Parts III and IV, A.D. 488–775*. Toronto: Pontifical Institute of Mediaeval Studies, 1999.

Harris, J. Rendel. "A Tract on the Triune Nature of God." *American Journal of Theology* 5, no. 1 (1901): 75–86.

Hartmann, Wilfried, and Kenneth Pennington, eds. *The History of Medieval Canon Law in the Classical Period, 1140–1234: From Gratian to the Decretals of Pope Gregory IX.* Washington, DC: Catholic University of America Press, 2008.

Heise, Tammy. "Marking Mormon Difference: How Western Perceptions of Islam Defined the 'Mormon Menace.'" *Journal of Religion and Popular Culture* 25, no. 1 (2013): 82–97.

Heng, Geraldine. *The Invention of Race in the European Middle Ages.* New York: Cambridge University Press, 2018.

Herde, Peter. "Christians and Saracens at the Time of the Crusades: Some Comments of Contemporary Canonists." In *Studien zur Papst- und Reichsgeschichte, zur Geschichte des Mittelmeerraumes und zum kanonischen Recht im Mittelalter,* 55–68. Stuttgart: Hiersemann, 2002.

Herman, Gerald. "A Note on Medieval Anti-Judaism, as Reflected in the *Chansons de geste.*" *Annuale mediaevale* 14 (1973): 63–73.

Hilhorst, Anthony. "Ishmaelites, Hagares, Saracens." In *Abraham, the Nations, and the Hagarites: Jewish, Christian, and Islamic Perspectives on Kinship with Abraham,* edited by Martin Goodman, George H. van Kooten, and Jacques T. A. G. M. van Ruiten, 421–34. Leiden: E. J. Brill, 2010.

The Holkham Bible Picture Book: A Facsimile. Commentary by Michelle P. Brown. London: British Library, 2007.

Howard-Johnston, James. *Witnesses to a World Crisis: Historians and Histories of the Middle East in the Seventh Century.* Oxford: Oxford University Press, 2010.

Hoyland, Robert G. *In God's Path: The Arab Conquests and the Creation of an Islamic Empire.* New York: Oxford University Press, 2015.

———. "Sebeos, the Jews, and the Rise of Islam." In *Medieval and Modern Perspectives on Muslim–Jewish Relations,* edited by Ronald L. Nettler, 89–102. Luxembourg: Harwood, 1995.

———. *Seeing Islam as Others Saw It: A Survey and Evaluation of Christian, Jewish and Zoroastrian Writings on Early Islam.* Princeton, NJ: Darwin, 1997.

———. *Theophilus of Edessa's Chronicle and the Circulation of Historical Knowledge in Late Antiquity and Early Islam.* Liverpool: Liverpool University Press, 2011.

Hughes, Kevin L. *Constructing Antichrist: Paul, Biblical Commentary, and the Development of Doctrine in the Early Middle Ages.* Washington, DC: Catholic University of America Press, 2005.

Hummel, Daniel G. *Covenant Brothers: Evangelicals, Jews, and U.S.–Israeli Relations.* Philadelphia: University of Pennsylvania Press, 2019.

Hunter, Erica C. D. "Interfaith Dialogues: The Church of the East and the Abbassids." In *Der Christliche Orient und seine Umwelt: Gesammelte Studien zu Ehren Jürgen Tubachs anlässlich seines 60. Geburtstags,* edited by Sophia G. Vashalomidze and Lutz Greisiger, 289–302. Wiesbaden: Otto Harrassowitz, 2007.

Hurst, Thomas R. "Letter 40 of the Nestorian Patriarch Timothy I (727–823): An Edition and Translation." Master's thesis, Catholic University of America, 1981.

Hyatte, Reginald. *The Prophet of Islam in Old French*. Leiden: E. J. Brill, 1997.

Ibn al-Athir, Izz al-Din. *The Chronicle of Ibn al-Athīr for the Crusading Period from al-Kāmil fī'l-ta'rīkh. Part 2, The Years 541–589/1146–1193*. Translated by D. S. Richards. Aldershot: Ashgate, 2007.

Ibn Ishaq, Muhammad. *The Life of Muhammad: A Translation of Ibn Ishaq's Sirat Rasul Allah*. Translated by Alfred Guillaume. Oxford: Oxford University Press, 1955.

al-Imam al-Qurtubi. *Al-I'lām bi-mā fī dīn al-naṣārá min al-fasād*. Edited by Ahmad Hijazi al-Saqqa. Cairo: Dār al-turāth al-'Arabī, 1980.

Iogna-Prat, Dominique. *Agni immaculati: Recherches sur les sources hagiographiques relatives à Saint Mayeul de Cluny (954–994)*. Paris: Éditions du Cerf, 1988.

———. *Order and Exclusion: Cluny and Christendom Face Heresy, Judaism, and Islam (1000–1150)*. Translated by Graham Robert Edwards. Ithaca, NY: Cornell University Press, 2002.

Iogna-Prat, Dominique, Barbara Rosenwein, Xavier Barral i Altet, and Guy Barruol. *Saint Maïeul, Cluny et la Provence: Expansion d'une abbaye à l'aube du Moyen Age*. Mane, Haute Provence: Les Alpes de Lumière, 1994.

Izbicki, Thomas M. *The Eucharist in Medieval Canon Law*. Cambridge: Cambridge University Press, 2015.

Jacobs, Andrew S. *Christ Circumcised: A Study in Early Christian History and Difference*. Philadelphia: University of Pennsylvania Press, 2012.

———. *Remains of the Jews: The Holy Land and Christian Empire in Late Antiquity*. Stanford, CA: Stanford University Press, 2004.

Jacobs, Bert. "The Rise of Islam according to Dionysius of Tell-Maḥrē." *Le Muséon* 133, nos. 1–2 (2020): 207–34.

Jakob, Joachim. *Syrisches Christentum und früher Islam: Theologische Reaktionen in syrisch-sprachigen Texten vom 7. bis 9. Jahrhundert*. Innsbruck: Tyrolia Verlag, 2021.

Jerome. *Commentary on Galatians*. Translated by Andrew Cain. Washington, DC: Catholic University of America Press, 2010.

———. *Hebrew Questions on Genesis*. Translated by C. T. R. Hayward. Oxford: Clarendon Press, 1995.

———. *The Homilies of Saint Jerome*. Translated by Marie Leguori Ewald. Washington, DC: Catholic University of America Press, 1964.

Jones, C. Meredith. "The Conventional Saracen of the Songs of Geste." *Speculum* 17, no. 2 (1942): 201–25.

Jordan, William Chester. *The French Monarchy and the Jews: From Philip Augustus to the Last Capetians*. Philadelphia: University of Pennsylvania Press, 1989.

———. "Home Again: The Jews in the Kingdom of France, 1315–1322." In *The Stranger in Medieval Society*, edited by F. R. P. Akehurst and Stephanie Cain Van D'Elden, 27–45. Minneapolis: University of Minnesota Press, 1998.

Kalmar, Ivan Davidson. "Jesus Did Not Wear a Turban: Orientalism, the Jews, and Christian Art." In *Orientalism and the Jews*. Edited by Ivan Davidson Kalmar and Derek J. Penslar, 3–31. Waltham, MA: Brandeis University Press, 2005.

Kaplan, M. Lindsay. *Figuring Racism in Medieval Christianity*. New York: Oxford University Press, 2019.

Katz, Rita. "Inside the Online Cesspool of Anti-Semitism that Housed Robert Bowers." *Politico Magazine*, October 29, 2018. https://www.politico.com/magazine/story/2018/10/29/inside-the-online-cesspool-of-anti-semitism-that-housed-robert-bowers-221949/.

Kaufmann, Thomas. *Luther's Jews: A Journey into Anti-Semitism*. Translated by Lesley Sharpe and Jeremy Noakes. Oxford: Oxford University Press, 2017.

Kedar, Benjamin Z. *Crusade and Mission: European Approaches toward the Muslims*. Princeton, NJ: Princeton University Press, 1984.

———. "*De Iudeis et Sarracenis:* On the Categorization of Muslims in Medieval Canon Law." In *Studia in honorem eminentissimi cardinalis Alphonsi M. Stickler*, edited by R. I. Castillo Lara, 207–13. Rome: Libreria Ateneo Salesiano, 1992. Reprinted in *Franks in the Levant, 11th to 14th Centuries*. Aldershot: Variorum, 1993.

———. "The Jerusalem Massacre of July 1099 in the Western Historiography of the Crusades." *Crusades* 3 (2004): 15–75.

Kedar, Benjamin Z., and Denys Pringle. "1099–1187: The Lord's Temple (*Templum Domini*) and Solomon's Palace (*Palatium Salomonis*)." In *Where Heaven and Earth Meet: Jerusalem's Sacred Esplanade*, edited by Benjamin Z. Kedar and Oleg Grabar, 132–49. Jerusalem and Austin: Yad Ben-Zvi Press and University of Texas Press, 2009.

Kendi, Ibram X. *How to Be an Antiracist*. New York: One World, 2019.

Kennedy, Hugh. *The Great Arab Conquests: How the Spread of Islam Changed the World We Live In*. London: Weidenfeld & Nicolson, 2007.

Kidd, Thomas S. *American Christians and Islam: Evangelical Culture and Muslims from the Colonial Period to the Age of Terrorism*. Princeton, NJ: Princeton University Press, 2009.

Kinoshita, Sharon. *Medieval Boundaries: Rethinking Difference in Old French Literature*. Philadelphia: University of Pennsylvania Press, 2006.

Klepper, Deanna. "Historicizing Allegory: The Jew as Hagar in Medieval Christian Text and Image." *Church History* 84, no. 2 (2015): 308–44.

Knaust, Heinrich. *Von geringem herkommen schentlichern leben schmehlichem ende des Türckischen Abgots Machomets und seiner verdamlichen und Gottslesterischen Ler*. Berlin, 1542.

Kolb, Robert. "The Influence of Luther's Galatians Commentary of 1535 on Later Sixteenth-Century Lutheran Commentaries on Galatians." *Archiv für Reformationsgeschichte* 84 (1993): 156–84.

Krautheimer, Richard. "Introduction to an 'Iconography of Mediaeval Architecture.'" *Journal of the Warburg and Courtauld Institutes* 5 (1942): 1–33.

Kritzeck, James. *Peter the Venerable and Islam*. Princeton, NJ: Princeton University Press, 1964.

Kühnel, Bianca. "Jerusalem in Aachen." In *Monuments & Memory: Christian Cult Buildings and Constructions of the Past: Essays in Honour of Sible de Blaauw*, edited by Mariëtte Verhoeven, Lex Bosman, and Hanneke van Asperen, 95–105. Turnout: Brepols, 2016.

Kühnel, Gustav. "Aachen, Byzanz und die frühislamische Architektur im Heiligen Land." In *Studien zur byzantinischen Kunstgeschichte: Festschrift für Horst Hallensieben zum 65. Geburtstag*, edited by Birgitt Borkopp, Barbara Schellewald, and Lioba Theis, 39–57. Amsterdam: Hakkert, 1995.

Laeuchli, Samuel. *Power and Sexuality: The Emergence of Canon Law at the Synod of Elvira*. Philadelphia: Temple University Press, 1972.

Lamoreaux, John C. "Early Eastern Christian Responses to Islam." In *Medieval Christian Perceptions of Islam: A Book of Essays*, edited by John V. Tolan, 3–31. New York: Garland, 1996.

Landes, Richard. "The Massacres of 1010: On the Origins of Popular Anti-Jewish Violence in Western Europe." In *From Witness to Witchcraft: Jews and Judaism in Medieval Christian Thought*, edited by Jeremy Cohen, 79–112. Wiesbaden: Otto Harrassowitz, 1996.

Langmuir, Gavin. *Toward a Definition of Antisemitism*. Berkeley: University of California Press, 1990.

Lavin, Marilyn Aronberg. "The Altar of Corpus Domini in Urbino: Paolo Uccello, Joos Van Ghent, Pierro della Francesca." *Art Bulletin* 49, no. 1 (1967): 1–24.

Leo Africanus. *A Geographical Historie of Africa*. Translated by John Pory. London, 1600.

Lepage, Yvan G., ed. *Le Roman de Mahomet du Alexandre du Pont (1258)*. Paris: Klincksieck, 1977.

Leshock, David B. "Religious Geography: Designating Jews and Muslims as Foreigners in Medieval England." In *Meeting the Foreign in the Middle Ages*, edited by Albrecht Classen, 202–25. New York: Routledge, 2002.

———. "Representations of Islam in the Wakefield Corpus Christi Plays." *Medieval Perspectives* 11 (1996): 195–208.

Levenson, David B. "The Ancient and Medieval Sources for the Emperor Julian's Attempt to Rebuild the Jerusalem Temple." *Journal for the Study of Judaism in the Persian, Hellenistic, and Roman Period* 35, no. 4 (2004): 409–60.

Linder, Amnon, ed. *The Jews in the Legal Sources of the Early Middle Ages*. Detroit: Wayne State University Press, 1997.

Lipstadt, Deborah E. *Antisemitism Here and Now*. New York: Schocken, 2019.

Lipton, Sara. *Dark Mirror: The Medieval Origins of Anti-Jewish Iconography*. New York: Metropolitan Books, 2014.

———. *Images of Intolerance: The Representation of Jews and Judaism in the Bible moralisée*. Berkeley: University of California Press, 1999.

Lloyd, G.E.R. *Polarity and Analogy: Two Types of Argumentation in Early Greek Thought*. Cambridge: Cambridge University Press, 1966.

Love, Erik. *Islamophobia and Racism in America*. New York: New York University Press, 2017.

Luther, Martin. *D. Martin Luthers Werke: kritische Gesammtausgabe*. Weimar: Böhlau, 1883–2009.

———. *Luther's Works*. St. Louis: Concordia, 1955–.

MacDonald, Gerald J. "*Hamihala*, A Hapax in the *Auto de los Reyes Magos*." *Journal of Romance Philology* 18, no. 1 (1964): 35–36.

Magnier, Grace. *Pedro de Valencia and the Catholic Apologists of the Expulsion of the Moriscos: Visions of Christianity and Kingship*. Leiden: E.J. Brill, 2010.

Mansi, Giovanni Domenico. *Sacrorum conciliorum nova et amplissima collectio*. Venice, 1782.

Map, Walter. *De nugis curialium: Courtiers' Trifles*. Edited and translated by M.R. James. Revised by C.N.L. Brooke and R.A.B. Mynors. Oxford: Clarendon Press, 1983.

Mármol Carvajal, Luis del. *Descripción general de Africa*. Granada, 1573. Reprint, Madrid: Consejo Superior de Investigaciones Científicas, 1953.

Marr, Timothy. *The Cultural Roots of American Islamicism*. Cambridge: Cambridge University Press, 2006.

Martin, Therese. *Queen as King: Politics and Architectural Propaganda in Twelfth-Century Spain*. Leiden: E.J. Brill, 2006.

Martyn, J. Louis. *Galatians*. Anchor Bible. New York: Doubleday, 1997.

Maser, Matthias. "Rodrigo Jiménez de Rada and His *Historia Arabum*: An Extraordinary Example of Inter-cultural Tolerance?" In *Languages of Love and Hate: Conflict, Communication, and Identity in the Medieval Mediterranean*, edited by Sarah Lambert and Helen Nicholson, 223–38. Turnhout: Brepols, 2012.

Mastnak, Tomaž. *Crusading Peace: Christendom, the Muslim World, and Western Political Order*. Berkeley: University of California Press, 2002.

McClure, Adrian. "In the Name of Charlemagne, Roland, and Turpin: Reading the Oxford *Roland* as a Trinitarian Text." *Speculum* 94, no. 2 (2019): 420–66.

McGinn, Bernard. *Antichrist: Two Thousand Years of the Human Fascination with Evil*. San Francisco: HarperSanFrancisco, 2005.

Memoria de don Enrique IV de Castilla. Madrid: Fortanet, 1913.

Menéndez Pidal, Ramón, ed. *Auto de los Reyes Magos*. In *Revista de archivos, bibliotecas, y museos* 4 (1900): 453–62.

Meserve, Margaret. *Empires of Islam in Renaissance Historical Thought*. Cambridge, MA: Harvard University Press, 2008.

Millar, Fergus. "Hagar, Ishmael, Josephus, and the Origins of Islam." *Journal of Jewish Studies* 44, no. 1 (1993): 23–45.

Miller, Gregory J. "Theodor Bibliander's *Machumetis saracenorum principis eiusque successorum vitae, doctrina ac ipse alcoran* (1543) as the Sixteenth-Century 'Encyclopedia' of Islam." *Islam and Christian–Muslim Relations*, 24, no. 2 (2013): 241–54.

———. *The Turks and Islam in Reformation Germany*. London: Routledge, 2018.

Mingana, Alphonse, ed. and trans. "The Apology of Timothy the Patriarch before the Caliph Mahdi." *Bulletin of the John Rylands Library* 12 (1928): 137–298. Translation reprinted in *The Early Christian–Muslim Dialogue*, edited by N. A. Newman, 167–267. Hatfield, PA: Interdisciplinary Biblical Research Institute, 1993.

Minov, Sergey. "Christians, Jews, and Muslims in the Syriac *Story of the Mystery Hidden in the Eucharistic Offering.*" *Aramaic Studies* 19, no. 2 (2021): 198–214.

Monteira Arias, Inés. "Seeking the Origins of Christian Representation of Islam: Anti-Muslim Images in Romanesque Art (Eleventh to Thirteenth Centuries)." *Islamophobia Studies Yearbook* 7 (2016): 86–112.

Monter, William. *Frontiers of Heresy: The Spanish Inquisition from the Basque Lands to Sicily.* Cambridge: Cambridge University Press, 1990.

Moore, John C. *Pope Innocent III (1160/61–1216): To Root Up and to Plant.* Leiden: E. J. Brill, 2003.

Moore, R. I. *The Formation of a Persecuting Society: Authority and Deviance in Western Europe, 950–1250.* 2nd ed. Malden, MA: Blackwell, 2007.

Moralejo Alvarez, Serafín. "Pour l'interprétation iconographique du Portail de l'Agneau a Saint-Isidore de León: Les signes du zodiaque." *Les Cahiers de Saint-Michel de Cuxa* 8 (1977): 137–73.

Muldoon, James. *Popes, Lawyers, and Infidels: The Church and the Non-Christian World, 1250–1550.* Philadelphia: University of Pennsylvania Press, 1979.

Müller, Wolfgang P. "The *Summa decretorum* of Huguccio." In *The History of Medieval Canon Law in the Classical Period, 1140–1234: From Gratian to the Decretals of Pope Gregory IX*, edited by Wilfried Hartmann and Kenneth Pennington, 142–60. Washington, DC: Catholic University of America Press, 2008.

Mundill, Robin R. *The King's Jews: Money, Massacre, and Exodus in Medieval England.* London: Continuum, 2010.

Murphy, Tim. *Representing Religion: History, Theory, Crisis.* London: Taylor & Francis, 2014.

Murray, Michele. *Playing a Jewish Game: Gentile Christian Judaizing in the First and Second Centuries CE.* Waterloo, ON: Wilfrid Laurier University Press, 2004.

Nagel, Alexander, and Christopher S. Wood. *Anachronic Renaissance.* New York: Zone Books, 2010.

Nau, François. "Un colloque du patriarche Jean avec l'emir des Agareens et faits divers des années 712 à 716." *Journal Asiatique* 11, no. 5 (1915): 225–79.

Neiwert, David. "When White Nationalists Chant Their Weird Slogans, What Do They Mean?" *Hatewatch* (blog). Southern Poverty Law Center, October 10, 2017. https://www.splcenter.org/hatewatch/2017/10/10/when-white-nationalists-chant-their-weird-slogans-what-do-they-mean.

Newman, Hillel I. "Jerome's Judaizers." *Journal of Early Christian Studies* 9, no. 4 (2000): 421–52.

Newsom, Carol A. *Daniel.* Louisville, KY: Westminster John Knox Press, 2014.

Nibley, Hugh. "Christian Envy of the Temple." *Jewish Quarterly Review* 50, no. 2–3 (1959–60): 97–123 and 229–40.

Nicholas of Lyra. *Postilla moralis.* In *Biblia sacra cum glossa interlineari, ordinaria, et Nicolai Lyrani Postilla.* Venice, 1588.

Nickel, Gordon D. *Narratives of Tampering in the Earliest Commentaries on the Qur'an*. Leiden: E. J. Brill, 2011.

Nirenberg, David. *Anti-Judaism: The Western Tradition*. New York: W. W. Norton, 2013.

———. *Communities of Violence: Persecution of Minorities in the Middle Ages*. Princeton, NJ: Princeton University Press, 1996.

———. *Neighboring Faiths: Christianity, Islam, and Judaism in the Middle Ages and Today*. Chicago: University of Chicago Press, 2014.

Oberman, Heiko A. *Luther: Man between God and Devil*. Translated by Eileen Walliser-Schwarzbart. New Haven, CT: Yale University Press, 1989.

O'Callaghan, Joseph F. *Reconquest and Crusade in Medieval Spain*. Philadelphia: University of Pennsylvania Press, 2003.

Odilo of Cluny. *Vita sancti Maioli*. In *Bibliotheca Cluniacensis*. Paris, 1614.

Ogle, Marbury B. "Petrus Comestor, Methodius, and the Saracens." *Speculum* 21, no. 3 (1946): 318–24.

Olster, David M. *Roman Defeat, Christian Response, and the Literary Construction of the Jew*. Philadelphia: University of Pennsylvania Press, 1994.

O'Meara, Carra Ferguson. *The Iconography of the Façade of Saint-Gilles-du-Gard*. New York: Garland, 1977.

O'Sullivan, Shaun. "Anti-Jewish Polemic and Early Islam." In *The Bible in Arab Christianity*, edited by David Thomas, 49–68. Leiden: E. J. Brill, 2007.

Otto of Freising. *Chronica, sive Historia de duabus civitatibus*. Edited by Adolf Hofmeister. Hannover: Hahn, 1912.

———. *The Two Cities: A Chronicle of Universal History to the Year 1146 A.D.* Translated by Charles Christopher Mierow. New York: Columbia University Press, 1928.

Pakter, Walter. *Medieval Canon Law and the Jews*. Ebelsbach: Rolf Gremer, 1988.

Papadopoulos-Kerameus, Athanasios, ed. *Analekta Hierosolymitikēs Stachyologias*. St. Petersburg: Kirschbaum, 1891–98. Reprint, Brussels: Culture et civilisation, 1963.

Paris, Matthew. *Chronica majora*. Edited by Henry Richards Luard. London: Longman, 1880.

Parker, Patricia. "Preposterous Conversions: Turning Turk, and Its 'Pauline' Rerighting." *Journal of Early Modern Cultural Studies* 2, no. 1 (2002): 1–34.

Parmentier, M. F. G. "No Stone upon Another? Reactions of the Church Fathers against the Emperor Julian's Attempt to Rebuild the Temple." In *The Centrality of Jerusalem: Historical Perspectives*, edited by Marcel Porthuis and Chana Safrai, 143–59. Kampen: Kok Pharos, 1996.

Patton, Pamela A. *Art of Estrangement: Redefining Jews in Reconquest Spain*. University Park: Pennsylvania State University Press, 2012.

———. "The Cloister as Cultural Mirror: Anti-Jewish Imagery at Santa María la Mayor in Tudela." In *Der mittelalterliche Kreuzgang: Architektur, Funktion und Programm*, edited by Peter K. Klein, 317–32. Regensburg: Schnell & Steiner, 2005.

———. "An Islamic Envelope-Flap Binding in the Cloister of Tudela: Another 'Muslim Connection' for Iberian Jews?" In *Spanish Medieval Art: Recent*

Studies, edited by Colum Hourihane, 65–88. Tempe: Arizona Center for Medieval and Renaissance Studies, 2007.

Paull, Michael. "The Figure of Mahomet in Middle English Literature." PhD diss., University of North Carolina Chapel Hill, 1969.

———. "The Figure of Mahomet in the Towneley Cycle." *Comparative Drama* 6, no. 3 (1972): 187–204.

Penn, Michael Philip. *Envisioning Islam: Syriac Christians and the Early Muslim World*. Philadelphia: University of Pennsylvania Press, 2015.

———. "*John and the Emir*: A New Introduction, Edition and Translation." *Le muséon* 121, nos. 1–2 (2008): 65–91.

———. *When Christians First Met Muslims: A Sourcebook of the Earliest Syriac Writings on Islam*. Oakland: University of California Press, 2015.

Pennington, Kenneth. "Innocent III and the Divine Authority of the Pope." Reprinted in *Popes, Canonists and Texts, 1150–1550*. Aldershot: Ashgate, 1993.

Perceval, José María. *Todos son uno: Arquetipos, xenofobia y racismo. La imagen del morisco en la Monarquía Española durante los siglos XVI y XVII*. Almería: Instituto de Estudos Almerienses, 1997.

Peter the Venerable. *Against the Inveterate Obduracy of the Jews*. Translated by Irven M. Resnick. Washington, DC: Catholic University of America Press, 2013.

———. *Peter the Venerable: Writings against the Saracens*. Translated by Irven M. Resnick. Washington, DC: Catholic University of America Press, 2016.

———. *Petrus Venerabilis: Schriften zum Islam*. Edited and translated by Reinhold Glei. Altenberge: CIS, 1985.

Peters, Edward, ed. *The First Crusade: The Chronicle of Fulcher of Chartres and Other Source Materials*. 2nd ed. Philadelphia: University of Pennsylvania Press, 1998.

Petrus Alfonsi. *Dialogue against the Jews*. Translated by Irven M. Resnick. Washington, DC: Catholic University of America Press, 2006.

———. *Petri Alfonsi Dialogus*. Edited by Carmen Cardelle de Hartmann, Darko Senekovic, and Thomas Ziegler. Florence: SISMEL, 2018.

Pettegree, Andrew. *Brand Luther: 1517, Printing, and the Making of the Reformation*. New York: Penguin, 2015.

Pick, Lucy K. *Conflict and Coexistence: Archbishop Rodrigo and the Muslims and Jews of Medieval Spain*. Ann Arbor: University of Michigan Press, 2004.

———. "What Did Rodrigo Jiménez de Rada Know About Islam?" *Anuario de historia de la Iglesia* 20 (2011): 221–35.

Pinson, Yona. "The Iconography of the Temple in Northern Renaissance Art." *Assaph: Studies in Art History* 2 (1996): section B, 147–74.

Purchas, Samuel. *Purchas His Pilgrimage*. London, 1613.

Pysiak, Jerzy. "Saint Louis as a New David and Paris as a New Jerusalem in Medieval French Hagiographic Literature." In *The Character of David in Judaism, Christianity, and Islam: Warrior, Poet, Prophet and King*, edited by Marzena Zawanowska and Mateusz Wilk, 154–87. Leiden: E.J. Brill, 2021.

Qiu, Linda. "Trump's Evidence-Free Claims About the Migrant Caravan." *New York Times*, October 22, 2018. https://www.nytimes.com/2018/10/22/us/politics/migrant-caravan-fact-check.html.

Ralph of Caen. *The Gesta Tancredi of Ralph of Caen: A History of the Normans on the First Crusade.* Translated by Bernard S. Bachrach and David S. Bachrach. Aldershot: Ashgate, 2005.

———. *Radulphi Cadomensis Tancredus.* Edited by Edoardo d'Angelo. Turnhout: Brepols, 2011.

Rawcliffe, Carole. *Leprosy in Medieval England.* Woodbridge: Boydell & Brewer, 2006.

Raymond D'Aguilers. *Historia Francorum qui ceperunt Iherusalem.* Translated by John Hugh Hill and Laurita L. Hill. Philadelphia: American Philosophical Society, 1968.

Reinink, Gerrit J. "The Beginnings of Syriac Apologetic Literature in Response to Islam." *Oriens Christianus* 77 (1993): 165–87.

———. "Early Christian Reactions to the Building of the Dome of the Rock in Jerusalem." *Xristianskij Vostok* 2 (2002): 227–41. Reprinted in *Syriac Christianity under Late Sasanian and Early Islamic Rule.* Aldershot: Ashgate, 2005.

———. "The Lamb and the Tree: Syriac Exegesis and Anti-Islamic Apologetics." In *The Sacrifice of Isaac: The Aqedah (Genesis 22) and Its Interpretations,* edited by Ed Noort and Eibert Tigchelaar, 109–24. Leiden: E.J. Brill, 2002.

———. "Political Power and Right Religion in the East Syrian Disputation Between a Monk of Bēt Ḥālē and an Arab Notable." In *The Encounter of Eastern Christianity with Early Islam,* edited by Emmanouela Grypeou, Mark Swanson, and David Thomas, 153–69. Leiden: E.J. Brill, 2006.

Renard, Jean Pierre, ed. *Trois sommes de pénitence de la première moitié du XIIIe siècle: La "Summula Magistri Conradi", les sommes "Quia non pigris" et "Decime dande sunt."* Louvain: Centre Cerfaux-Lefort, 1989.

Resnick, Irven. "The Jews' Badge." In *Jews and Muslims under the Fourth Lateran Council: Papers Commemorating the Octocentenary of the Fourth Lateran Council (1215),* edited by Marie-Thérèse Champagne and Irven M. Resnick, 65–79. Turnhout: Brepols, 2019.

———. "Peter the Venerable on the Talmud, the Jews, and Islam." *Medieval Encounters* 24, nos. 5–6 (2018): 510–29.

Retsö, Jan. *The Arabs in Antiquity: Their History from the Assyrians to the Umayyads.* London: RoutledgeCurzon, 2002.

Reynolds, Gabriel Said. "On the Qurʾān and the Theme of Jews as 'Killers of the Prophets.'" *Al-Bayān* 10, no. 2 (2012): 9–32.

Rodrigo Jiménez de Rada. *Roderici Ximenii de Rada: Historiae minores, Dialogus libri vite.* Edited by Juan Fernández Valverde and Juan Antonio Estévez Sola. Turnhout: Brepols, 1999.

Riley-Smith, Jonathan. *The Crusades: A Short History.* New Haven, CT: Yale University Press, 1987.

———. "The First Crusade and the Jews." In *Persecution and Toleration: Papers Read at the Twenty-Second Summer Meeting and the Twenty-Third Winter Meeting of the Ecclesiastical Historical Society,* edited by W.J. Sheils, 51–72. Oxford: Basil Blackwell, 1984.

Risālat al-Kindī ilá al-Hāshimī. Damascus: al-Takwīn liʾl-Ṭibāʿah waʾl-Nashr waʾl-Tawzīʿ, 2005.

Robert the Monk. *Robert the Monk's History of the First Crusade: Historia Iherosolimitana.* Translated by Carol Sweetenham. Aldershot: Ashgate, 2005.

Robinson, Neal. *Christ in Islam and Christianity.* Albany: State University of New York Press, 1991.

Rodríguez Barral, Paulino. *La imagen de judío en la España medieval: El conflicto entre cristianismo y judaísmo en las artes visuales góticas.* Barcelona: Universitat Autònoma de Barcelona, Servei de Publicacions, 2009.

Roggema, Barbara. "Biblical Exegesis and Interreligious Polemics in the Arabic *Apocalypse of Peter—The Book of the Rolls.*" In *The Bible in Arab Christianity,* edited by David Thomas, 131–50. Leiden: E. J. Brill, 2007.

———. *The Legend of Sergius Baḥīrā: Eastern Christian Apologetics and Apocalyptic in Response to Islam.* Leiden: E. J. Brill, 2009.

———. "Muslims as Crypto-Idolaters—A Theme in the Christian Portrayal of Islam in the Near East." In *Christians at the Heart of Islamic Rule: Church Life and Scholarship in ʿAbbasid Iraq,* edited by David Thomas, 1–18. Leiden: E. J. Brill, 2003.

———. "Salvaging the Saintly Sergius: Hagiographical Aspects of the Syriac Legend of Sergius Baḥīrā." In *Entangled Hagiographies of the Religious Other,* edited by Alexandra Cuffel and Nikolas Jaspert, 55–83. Newcastle upon Tyne: Cambridge Scholars, 2019.

Roig, Jaume. *The Mirror of Jaume Roig: An Edition and an English Translation of MS. Vat. Lat. 4806.* Edited by Maria Celeste Delgado-Librero. Tempe: Arizona Center for Medieval and Renaissance Studies, 2010.

Romero, Luis A., and Amina Zarrugh. "Islamophobia and the Making of Latinos/as into Terrorist Threats." *Ethnic and Racial Studies* 41, no. 12 (2018): 2235–54.

Roose, Kevin. "On Gab, an Extremist-Friendly Site, Pittsburgh Shooting Suspect Aired His Hatred in Full." *New York Times,* October 28, 2018. https://www.nytimes.com/2018/10/28/us/gab-robert-bowers-pittsburgh-synagogue-shootings.html.

Rosenblum, Jordan D. "Why Do You Refuse to Eat Pork?: Jews, Food, and Identity in Roman Palestine." *Jewish Quarterly Review* 100, no. 1 (2010): 95–110.

Rosenkranz, Simone. *Die jüdisch-christliche Auseinandersetzung unter islamischer Herrschaft, 7.–10. Jahrhundert.* Bern: Peter Lang, 2004.

Rowe, Nina. *The Jew, the Cathedral, and the Medieval City: Synagoga and Ecclesia in the Thirteenth Century.* Cambridge: Cambridge University Press, 2011.

Rubenstein, Jay. "What Is the *Gesta Francorum,* and Who Was Peter Tudebode?" *Revue Mabillon* n.s. 16 (2005), 179–204.

Rubin, Miri. *Corpus Christi: The Eucharist in Late Medieval Culture.* Cambridge: Cambridge University Press, 1991.

———. "*Ecclesia* and *Synagoga:* The Changing Meanings of a Powerful Pairing." In *Conflict and Religious Conversation in Latin Christendom: Studies in Honour of Ora Limor,* edited by Israel Jacob Yuval and Ram Ben-Shalom, 55–86. Turnhout: Brepols, 2014.

———. *Gentile Tales: The Narrative Assault on Late Medieval Jews*. Philadelphia: University of Pennsylvania Press, 1999.

Runnymede Trust. *Islamophobia: A Challenge for Us All*. 1997. https://www.runnymedetrust.org/publications/islamophobia-a-challenge-for-us-all.

———. *Islamophobia: Still a Challenge for Us All*. Edited by Farah Elahi and Omar Khan. 2017. https://www.runnymedetrust.org/publications/islamophobia-still-a-challenge-for-us-all.

Rupp, E. Gordon. *The Righteousness of God: Luther Studies*. London: Hodder and Stoughton, 1953.

Rusch, Adolf, ed. *Biblia cum glossa ordinaria Walafridi Strabonis aliorumque et interlineari Anselmi Laudunensis*. 1480/81. Reprinted as *Biblia latina cum glossa ordinaria: Facsimile Reprint of the Editio Princeps*. Turnhout: Brepols, 1992. http://gloss-e.irht.cnrs.fr/.

Sabellicus, Marcus. *Enneades*. Venice, 1504.

Sahas, Daniel J. "The Face to Face Encounter between Patriarch Sophronius of Jerusalem and the Caliph 'Umar ibn al-Khaṭṭāb: Friends or Foes?" In *The Encounter of Eastern Christianity with Early Islam*, edited by Emmanouela Grypeou, Mark Swanson, and David Thomas, 33–44. Leiden: E. J. Brill, 2006.

———. *John of Damascus on Islam: The "Heresy of the Ishmaelites."* Leiden: E. J. Brill, 1972.

Sahner, Christian C. "The First Iconoclasm in Islam: A New History of the Edict of Yazīd II (AH 104/AD 723)." *Der Islam* 94, no. 1 (2017): 5–56.

Said, Edward W. *Orientalism*. New York: Vintage, 1979.

Sanders, E. P. *Paul: A Very Short Introduction*. Oxford: Oxford University Press, 2001.

Sandys, George. *A Relation of a Journey*. London, 1615.

Sapir Abulafia, Anna. *Christians and Jews in the Twelfth-Century Renaissance*. London: Routledge, 1995.

Scarfe Beckett, Katharine. *Anglo-Saxon Perceptions of the Islamic World*. Cambridge: Cambridge University Press, 2003.

Scheil, Andrew. *Babylon under Western Eyes: A Study of Allusion and Myth*. Toronto: University of Toronto Press, 2016.

Schoenfeld, Devorah. *Isaac on Jewish and Christian Altars: Polemic and Exegesis in Rashi and the* Glossa Ordinaria. New York: Fordham University Press, 2013.

Schultz, Kevin M. *Tri-Faith America: How Catholics and Jews Held Postwar America to Its Protestant Promise*. Oxford: Oxford University Press, 2012.

Schwarz, Eduard, ed. *Kyrillos von Skythopolis*. Leipzig: J. C. Hinrichs, 1939.

Schweller, Russell. "'Mosaic Arabs': Jews and Gentlemen in Disraeli's Young England Trilogy." *Shofar* 24, no. 2 (2006): 55–69.

Scotto, Davide. "The Conflation of Judaism and Islam in Hernando de Talavera's Conversion Plan." *Jewish History* 35, nos. 3–4 (2021): 293–328.

Septimus, Bernard. "Petrus Alfonsi on the Cult at Mecca." *Speculum* 56, no. 3 (1981): 517–33.

Shahid, Irfan. *Rome and the Arabs: A Prolegomenon to the Study of Byzantium and the Arabs*. Washington, DC: Dumbarton Oaks, 1984.

Shani, Raya. "The Iconography of the Dome of the Rock." *Jerusalem Studies in Arabic and Islam* 23 (1999): 158–89.

Shepardson, Christine C. *Anti-Judaism and Christian Orthodoxy: Ephrem's Hymns in Fourth-Century Syria.* Washington, DC: Catholic University of America Press, 2008.

Shoemaker, Stephen J. *The Death of a Prophet: The End of Muhammad's Life and the Beginnings of Islam.* Philadelphia: University of Pennsylvania Press, 2012.

Siberry, Elizabeth. *Criticism of Crusading, 1095–1274.* Oxford: Clarendon Press, 1985.

Silk, Mark. "The Abrahamic Religions as a Modern Concept." In *The Oxford Handbook of the Abrahamic Religions,* edited by Adam J. Silverstein and Guy G. Stroumsa, 71–87. Oxford: Oxford University Press, 2015.

———. "Notes on the Judeo-Christian Tradition in America." *American Quarterly* 36, no. 1 (1984): 65–85.

Simonsohn, Shlomo. *The Apostolic See and the Jews.* 8 vols. Toronto: Pontifical Institute for Mediaeval Studies, 1988–91.

Smith, Jonathan Z. *Drudgery Divine: On the Comparison of Early Christianities and the Religions of Late Antiquity.* Chicago: University of Chicago Press, 1990.

Sophronius. *Fêtes chrétiennes à Jérusalem.* Translated by Jeanne de La Ferrière. Paris: Migne, 1999.

Soskice, Janet Martin. *Metaphor and Religious Language.* Oxford: Clarendon Press, 1985.

Southern, R. W. *Western Views of Islam in the Middle Ages.* Cambridge, MA: Harvard University Press, 1962.

Soyer, François. "The Recycling of an Anti-Semitic Conspiracy Theory into an Anti-Morisco One in Early Modern Spain: The Myth of *El Vengador,* the Serial-Killer Doctor." *eHumanistica/Conversos* 4 (2016): 233–55.

Spector, Stephen. *Evangelicals and Israel: The Story of American Christian Zionism.* Oxford: Oxford University Press, 2009.

Spellberg, Denise A. *Thomas Jefferson's Qur'an: Islam and the Founders.* New York: Vintage, 2013.

Stafford, Samuel Aaron. "The Creation of Arabian Jewish Tradition: The Myth and Image of Muḥammad's Jewish Companion ʿAbdallāh ibn Salām (d. 43/663) in Classical Islam." PhD diss., University of Virginia, 2019.

Stalls, William C. "Jewish Conversion to Islam: The Perspective of a *Quaestio.*" *Revista española de teología* 43, no. 2 (1983): 235–51.

Stantchev, Stefan K. "'Apply to Muslims What was Said of the Jews': Popes and Canonists between a Taxonomy of Otherness and *Infidelitas.*" *Law and History Review* 32, no. 1 (2014): 65–96.

———. *Spiritual Rationality: Papal Embargo as Cultural Practice.* Oxford: Oxford University Press, 2014.

Strickland, Debra Higgs. "Meanings of Muhammad in Later Medieval Art." In *The Image of the Prophet Between Ideal and Ideology: A Scholarly Investigation,* edited by Christiane J. Gruber and Avinoam Shalem, 147–163. Berlin: De Gruyter, 2014.

————. *Saracens, Demons, and Jews: Making Monsters in Medieval Art*. Princeton, NJ: Princeton University Press, 2003.

Stroumsa, Guy G. *Barbarian Philosophy: The Religious Revolution of Early Christianity*. Tübingen: Mohr Siebeck, 1999.

Stuczynski, Claude Bernard. "Two Minorities Facing the Iberian Inquisition: The 'Marranos' and the 'Moriscos.'" *Hispania Judaica* 3 (2000), 127–43.

Summerlin, Danica. *The Canons of the Third Lateran Council of 1179: Their Origins and Reception*. Cambridge: Cambridge University Press, 2019.

Swanson, Mark. "Beyond Prooftexting (2): The Use of the Bible in Early Arabic Christian Apologies." In *The Bible in Arab Christianity*, edited by David Thomas, 91–112. Leiden: E. J. Brill, 2007.

Szilagyi, Krisztina. "Muhammad and the Monk: The Making of the Christian Baḥīrā Legend." *Jerusalem Studies in Arabic and Islam* 34 (2008): 169–214.

Szpiech, Ryan. "Prisons and Polemics: Captivity, Confinement, and Medieval Interreligious Encounter." In *Polemical Encounters: Christians, Jews, and Muslims in Iberia and Beyond*, edited by Mercedes García-Arenal and Gerard Wiegers, 271–303. University Park: Pennsylvania State University Press, 2018.

————. "Saracens and Church Councils, from Nablus (1120) to Vienne (1313–14)." In *Jews and Muslims under the Fourth Lateran Council: Papers Commemorating the Octocentenary of the Fourth Lateran Council (1215)*, edited by Marie-Thérèse Champagne and Irven M. Resnick, 115–37. Turnhout: Brepols, 2019.

Tanner, Norman P., trans. *Decrees of the Ecumenical Councils*. Vol. 1. London and Washington, DC: Sheed & Ward and Georgetown University Press, 1990.

Tannous, Jack. *The Making of the Medieval Middle East: Religion, Society, and Simple Believers*. Princeton, NJ: Princeton University Press, 2019.

Tartakoff, Paola. *Conversion, Circumcision, and Ritual Murder in Medieval Europe*. Philadelphia: University of Pennsylvania Press, 2020.

Taylor, Charles H. "French Assemblies and Subsidy in 1321." *Speculum* 43, no. 2 (1968): 217–44.

Taylor, David G. K. "The Disputation between a Muslim and a Monk of Bēt Ḥālē: Syriac Text and Annotated English Translation." In *Christsein in der islamischen Welt: Festschrift für Martin Tamcke zum 60. Geburtstag*, edited by Sidney H. Griffith and Sven Grebenstein, 187–242. Wiesbaden: Otto Harrassowitz, 2015.

Taylor, Miriam S. *Anti-Judaism and Early Christian Identity: A Critique of the Scholarly Consensus*. Leiden: E. J. Brill, 1995.

Teipen, Alfons. "Jews in Early Biographies of Muhammad: A Case Study in Shifting Muslim Understandings of Judaism." *Journal of the American Academy of Religion* 88, no. 2 (2020): 543–68.

Temkin, Owsei. *The Falling Sickness: A History of Epilepsy from the Greeks to the Beginnings of Modern Neurology*. 2nd edition. Baltimore: Johns Hopkins University Press, 1971.

Tertullian. *Against Marcion*. Translated by Ernest Evans. Oxford: Clarendon Press, 1972.

Teter, Magda. *Blood Libel: On the Trail of an Antisemitic Myth.* Cambridge, MA: Harvard University Press, 2020.

Theodore bar Koni. *Liber scholiorum.* Edited by Addai Scher. Paris: Republica, 1912.

———. *Livre des Scolies.* Translated by Robert Hespel and René Draguet. 2 vols. Louvain: Peeters, 1982.

Theophanes. *The Chronicle of Theophanes Confessor: Byzantine and Near Eastern History, AD 284–813.* Translated by Cyril Mango and Roger Scott. Oxford: Clarendon Press, 1997.

———. *Theophanis Chronographia.* Edited by Carl de Boor. Vol. 1. Leipzig: Teubner, 1883. Reprint, Hildesheim: G. Olms, 1963.

Thiessen, Matthew. *Paul and the Gentile Problem.* Oxford: Oxford University Press, 2016.

Tien, Anton, trans. *Apology of al-Kindi.* Reprinted in *The Early Christian–Muslim Dialogue: A Collection of Documents from the First Three Islamic Centuries (632–900 A.D.), Translations with Commentary,* edited by N. A. Newman, 355–545. Hatfield, PA: Interdisciplinary Biblical Research Institute, 1993.

Timothy I, Patriarch of the Church of the East. *Die Briefe 3–29 des ostsyrischen Patriarchen Timotheos I.* Edited and translated by Martin Heimgartner. 2 vols. Louvain: Peeters, 2021.

———. *Die Briefe 40 und 41 des ostsyrischen Patriarchen Timotheos I.* Edited and translated by Martin Heimgartner. 2 vols. Louvain: Peeters, 2019.

———. *Disputation mit dem Kalifen al-Mahdī.* Edited and translated by Martin Heimgartner. 2 vols. Louvain: Peeters, 2011.

Tolan, John V. "Anti-Hagiography: Embrico of Mainz's *Vita Mahumeti.*" In *Sons of Ishmael: Muslims through European Eyes in the Middle Ages,* 1–18. Gainesville: University Press of Florida, 2008.

———. "European Accounts of Muhammad's Life." In *The Cambridge Companion to Muhammad,* edited by Jonathan E. Brockopp, 226–50. Cambridge: Cambridge University Press, 2010.

———. *Faces of Muhammad: Western Perceptions of the Prophet of Islam from the Middle Ages to Today.* Princeton, NJ: Princeton University Press, 2019.

———. "A Mangled Corpse: The Polemical Dismemberment of Muhammad." In *Sons of Ishmael: Muslims through European Eyes in the Middle Ages,* 19–34. Gainesville: University Press of Florida, 2008.

———. "Of Milk and Blood: Innocent III and the Jews, Revisited." In *Jews and Christians in Thirteenth-Century France,* edited by Elisheva Baumgarten and Judah D. Galinsky, 139–49. New York: Palgrave Macmillan, 2015.

———. "Peter the Venerable on the 'Diabolical Heresy of the Saracens.'" In *The Devil, Heresy, and Witchcraft in the Middle Ages: Essays in Honor of Jeffrey B. Russell,* edited by Alberto Ferreiro, 345–67. Leiden: E. J. Brill, 1998.

———. *Petrus Alfonsi and His Medieval Readers.* Gainesville: University Press of Florida, 1993.

———. *Saracens: Muslims in the Medieval Christian Imagination.* New York: Columbia University Press, 2002.

———. "'A Wild Man, Whose Hand Will Be against All': Saracens and Ishmaelites in Latin Ethnographical Traditions, from Jerome to Bede." In *Visions of Community in the Post-Roman World: The West, Byzantium and the Islamic World, 300–1100*, edited by Walter Pohl, Clemens Gantner, and Richard Payne, 513–30. Farnham: Ashgate, 2012.

Torquemada, Juan de. *Tractatus contra principales errores perfidi Machometi*. Rome, 1606.

Tottoli, Roberto. *Biblical Prophets in the Qurʾān and Muslim Literature*. London: Routledge, 2002.

Tudebode, Peter. *Historia de Hierosolymitano itinere*. Edited by John Hugh Hill and Laurita L. Hill. Paris: Librairie Orientaliste Paul Geuthner, 1977.

———. *Historia de Hierosolymitano itinere*. Translated by John Hugh Hill and Laurita L. Hill. Philadelphia: American Philosophical Society, 1974.

Tueller, James B. *Good and Faithful Christians: Moriscos and Catholicism in Early Modern Spain*. New Orleans: University Press of the South, 2002.

Turquet de Mayerne, Louis. *Histoire générale d'Espagne*. Paris, 1635.

Usener, Hermann. "Weihnachtspredigt des Sophronios." *Rheinisches Museum für Philologie* 41 (1886): 500–16. Reprinted in *Kleine Schriften*, 4:162–77. Leipzig: Teubner, 1913.

Valognes, Jean-Pierre. *Vie et mort des chrétiens d'orient: Des origines à nos jours*. Paris: Fayard, 1994.

van Koningsveld, P. S. "The Apology of al-Kindî." In *Religious Polemics in Context: Papers Presented to the Second International Conference of the Leiden Institute for the Study of Religion*, edited by T. L. Hettema and A. van der Kooij, 69–92. Assen: van Gorcum, 2004.

van Lent, Jos. "*The Apocalypse of Shenute*." In *Christian–Muslim Relations: A Bibliographical History*, vol. 1, edited by David Thomas and Barbara Roggema, 182–85. Leiden: E. J. Brill, 2009.

Van Zile, Matthew P. "The Sons of Noah and the Sons of Abraham: The Origins of Noahide Law." *Journal for the Study of Judaism in the Persian, Hellenistic, and Roman Period* 48, no. 3 (2017): 386–417.

Vasiliev, Alexander A. "The Iconoclastic Edict of the Caliph Yazid II, A.D. 721." *Dumbarton Oaks Papers* 9/10 (1956): 23–47.

Vicens, Belen. "Swearing by God: Muslim Oath-Taking in Late Medieval and Early Modern Christian Iberia." *Medieval Encounters* 20, no. 2 (2014): 117–51.

Vidal, Jean-Marie. "La poursuite des lépreux en 1321 d'après des documents nouveaux." *Annales de Saint-Louis des Français* 4 (1900): 419–78.

Vincent, Bernard. "The Geography of the Morisco Expulsion: A Quantitative Study." In *The Expulsion of the Moriscos from Spain: A Mediterranean Diaspora*, edited by Mercedes García-Arenal and Gerard Wiegers, translated by Consuelo López-Morillas and Martin Beagles, 19–36. Leiden: E. J. Brill, 2014.

Ward, Walter D. *The Mirage of the Saracen: Christians and Nomads in the Sinai Peninsula in Late Antiquity*. Oakland: University of California Press, 2015.

Weaver, Simon. "A Rhetorical Discourse Analysis of Online Anti-Muslim and Anti-Semitic Jokes," *Ethnic and Racial Studies* 36, no. 3 (2012): 483–99.

Weber, Loren J. "The Historical Importance of Godfrey of Viterbo." *Viator* 25 (1994): 153–95.

Weiss, Daniel H. *Art and Crusade in the Age of Saint Louis.* Cambridge: Cambridge University Press, 1998.

———. "*Hec est domus domini firmiter edificata:* The Image of the Temple in Crusader Art." In *The Real and Ideal Jerusalem in Jewish, Christian, and Islamic Art: Studies in Honor of Bezalel Narkiss on the Occasion of His Seventieth Birthday,* edited by Bianca Kühnel, 210–17. Jerusalem: Hebrew University, 1998.

William of Tyre. *A History of Deeds Done Beyond the Sea.* Translated by E. A. Babcock and A. C. Krey. New York: Columbia University Press, 1943.

———. *Willemi Tyrensis Archiepiscopi Chronicon.* Edited by R. B. C. Huygens. Turnhout: Brepols, 1986.

Williams, John W. "Generationes Abrahae: Iconografía de la Reonquista en León." In *El tímpano Románico: Imágenes, estructuras y audiencias,* edited by Rocio Sánchez Ameijeiras and José Luis Senra Gabriel y Galán, 155–80. Santiago de Compostela: Xunta de Galicia, 2003.

———. "Generationes Abrahae: Reconquest Iconography in León." *Gesta* 16, no. 2 (1977): 3–14.

Wilkinson, John. *Jerusalem Pilgrimage, 1099–1185.* London: Hakluyt Society, 1988.

———. *Jerusalem Pilgrims before the Crusades.* Warminster: Aris & Phillips, 2002.

Wolf, Kenneth B. "The Earliest Latin Lives of Muḥammad." In *Conversion and Continuity: Indigenous Christian Communities in Islamic Lands, Eighth to Eighteenth Centuries,* edited by Michael Gervers and Ramzi Jibran Bikhazi, 89–101. Toronto: Pontifical Institute of Mediaeval Studies, 1990.

Wolfensohn, Israel. *Kaʿb al-Aḫbār und seine Stellung im Ḥadīt und in der islamischen Legendenliteratur.* Gelnhausen: Kalbfleisch, 1933.

Yolles, Julian, and Jessica Weiss. *Medieval Latin Lives of Muhammad.* Cambridge, MA: Harvard University Press, 2018.

Zacour, Norman. *Jews and Saracens in the Consilia of Oldradus de Ponte.* Toronto: Pontifical Institute of Mediaeval Studies, 1990.

Zerner, Monique. "La capture de Maïeul et la guerre de liberation en Provence: Le depart des sarrasins vu a travers les cartulaires Provençaux." In *Millénaire de la mort de Saint Mayeul, 4e abbé de Cluny, 994–1994,* 199–210. Digne-les Bains: Société scientifique et littéraire des Alpes de Haute-Provence, 1997.

Index

Abd al-Malik, 66, 72
Abdallah ibn Salam, 111, 112–13, 246n17
Abraham: in Genesis, 20, 32, 49, 52, 56; in the New Testament, 22–25, 29, 219; Jews and Muslims as heirs of, 39–43, 123, 126, 211, 234n12; Muslim characters speak of, 90, 93; relationship of Christian practice to, 40, 45, 49–50, 62
Abrahamic covenant: biblical references to, 20, 23–27, 56, 59; Christian claims to, 42, 43, 72, 191; Jewish and Muslim claims to, 36, 41–43, 84; Jews and Muslims excluded from, 48, 55, 124; State of Israel as fulfillment of, 211
Abrahamic religions, 210–11
Ademar of Chabannes, 166–70, 221, 258n12
Agasse, Guillaume, 171–73, 177, 178, 225, 259n27
Albert of Aachen, 58, 222
Alexander II, 56–57, 60, 61, 63, 133, 222
Alexander III, 133–34, 251n7
Alexandre du Pont, 118, 119–23, 225
Alfonsi, Petrus, 111–16, 186, 223
Altarpiece of the Virgin, 160–62, 225
America, conceptions of, 7, 13, 209–14
Amina, 123–29, 249nn18–19
anachronism, rhetorical value of, 78, 156, 158–60, 190–91
Anidjar, Gil, 6–7, 11, 178

Animal est substantia, 136–37, 138, 224
Antichrist: early Christian conceptions of, 71, 168, 175; Jews and Muslims associated with, 70, 80, 83–84, 186–88; Muhammad as, 128–29, 181, 249n22, 250n24; Muslim caliphs as, 67, 69, 72, 168, 170
anti-Christian: Jews and Muslims as, 7, 11, 12, 30, 165, 172, 178, 179–80, 188–92, 211; pope as, 203
anti-Islam, 13, 194–95, 199–202, 206–7, 209, 211
anti-Judaism: defined, 3–6, 194, 229n6, 230n13; early Christian, 9, 30–31, 32; in Eastern Christian sources, 36–37, 39–40, 88, 92, 93, 97–98, 101; in European Christian sources, 122, 129, 148, 166, 194–99, 201–2, 206; in the present day, 5, 7, 209, 212–13, 215, 230n8; Paul and, 20, 191–92, 207
antimuslimism, 194, 211, 263n3
antisemitism: anti-Judaism and, 4–5, 7, 13, 194, 229n6; in Luther's works, 195; in the present day, 210, 213, 214–15; spelling of, 229n4, 263n3
Apocalypse of Peter—Book of Rolls, 240n12, 246n17
Apocalypse of Pseudo-Methodius, 39, 234n8, 235n21
Apocalypse of Pseudo-Shenute, 69–72, 220, 234n8, 239n6

Founded in 1893,
UNIVERSITY OF CALIFORNIA PRESS
publishes bold, progressive books and journals
on topics in the arts, humanities, social sciences,
and natural sciences—with a focus on social
justice issues—that inspire thought and action
among readers worldwide.

The UC PRESS FOUNDATION
raises funds to uphold the press's vital role
as an independent, nonprofit publisher, and
receives philanthropic support from a wide
range of individuals and institutions—and from
committed readers like you. To learn more, visit
ucpress.edu/supportus.